Magdalena

WADE DAVIS

Magdalena

River of Dreams

ALFRED A. KNOPF

NEW YORK   TORONTO   2020

THIS IS A BORZOI BOOK
PUBLISHED BY ALFRED A. KNOPF AND ALFRED A. KNOPF CANADA

Published in the United States by Alfred A. Knopf,
a division of Penguin Random House LLC, New York,
and in Canada by Alfred A. Knopf Canada,
a division of Penguin Random House Canada Limited, Toronto.

www.aaknopf.com
www.penguinrandomhouse.ca

Knopf, Borzoi Books, and the colophon are registered
trademarks of Penguin Random House LLC. Knopf Canada
and colophon are trademarks of Penguin Random House Canada Limited.

Library of Congress Cataloging-in-Publication Data
Names: Davis, Wade, author.
Title: Magdalena : river of dreams / Wade Davis.
Description: First Edition. | New York : Alfred A. Knopf, [2020] |
Includes bibliographical references and index.
Identifiers: LCCN 2019022605 | ISBN 9780375410994 (hardcover) |
ISBN 9780525657897 (ebook)
Subjects: LCSH: Magdalena River (Colombia) |
Colombia—History. | Colombia—Description and travel.
Classification: LCC F2281.M23 .D38 2020 | DDC 986.1—dc23
LC record available at https://lccn.loc.gov/2019022605

Library and Archives Canada Cataloguing in Publication
Title: Magdalena : river of dreams / Wade Davis.
Names: Davis, Wade, author.
Identifiers: Canadiana (print) 20190158980 |
Canadiana (ebook) 20190159014 |
ISBN 9780735278929 (hardcover) | ISBN 9780735278936 (HTML)
Subjects: LCSH: Magdalena River (Colombia)—History. |
LCSH: Colombia—History.
Classification: LCC F2281.M23 D38 2020 | DDC 986.1/16—dc23

Jacket photograph: *Cauca—still 01:42*. From the *Atlas of the Andes* series
2014 © Camilo Echavarría

Manufactured in the United States of America
First Edition

For Martín von Hildebrand,
friend and brother, who more than any other
allowed me to see and understand the ways of a forest
that fires the hearts of all good people of the world

And even in our sleep, pain which cannot forget falls drop by drop upon the heart, until in our own despair, against our will, comes wisdom through the awful grace of God.

—AESCHYLUS

Contents

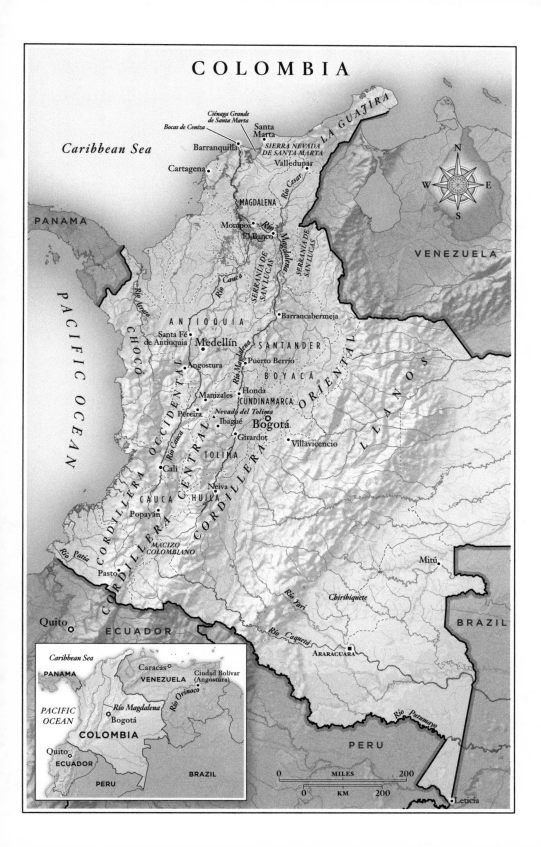

C O L O M B I A

Caribbean Sea

PANAMA

PACIFIC OCEAN

Cartagena
Barranquilla
Bocas de Ceniza
Ciénaga Grande de Santa Marta
Santa Marta
SIERRA NEVADA DE SANTA MARTA
Valledupar
Río Cesar
LA GUAJIRA

VENEZUELA

MAGDALENA
Mompox
El Banco
Río Magdalena
SERRANÍA DE SAN LUCAS
SERRANÍA DE SAN LUCAS

Río Atrato
Cauca
Río

Barrancabermeja

ANTIOQUIA
Santa Fé de Antioquia
Medellín
Angostura
SANTANDER
Puerto Berrío
BOYACÁ

CHOCÓ

CORDILLERA OCCIDENTAL
CORDILLERA CENTRAL
Río Cauca
Río Magdalena
CORDILLERA ORIENTAL

Manizales
Pereira
Honda
CUNDINAMARCA
Nevado del Tolima
Ibagué
Bogotá
Girardot
Villavicencio

Cali
TOLIMA

CAUCA
HUILA
Neiva
Popayán

L L A N O S

MACIZO COLOMBIANO

Río Patía
Pasto

Mitú

Río Vari
Chiribiquete

Río Caquetá
ARARACUARA

Río Putumayo

Quito
ECUADOR

PERU

BRAZIL

Leticia

Inset map

Caribbean Sea

PANAMA
Caracas
VENEZUELA
Ciudad Bolívar (Angostura)
Río Orinoco

PACIFIC OCEAN
Río Magdalena
Bogotá
COLOMBIA

Quito
ECUADOR

PERU

BRAZIL

0   MILES   200
0   KM   200

Preface

Travelers often become enchanted with the first country that captures their hearts and gives them license to be free. For me, it was Colombia. The mountains and forests, rivers and wetlands, the mysterious *páramos*, and the beauty and power of every tropical glen and snow-crested equatorial peak opened a doorway to a wider world that I would spend my entire life coming to know. In ways impossible fully to explain, the country allowed me, even as a boy, to imagine and dream. Coming of age in Colombia in the early 1970s, living on the open road, sleeping where my hat fell, I was never afraid. The warmth of the people enveloped a young traveler like a protective cloak, tailor-made for wonder. The land itself inspired one "to risk," as I wrote in the frontispiece of an early teenage journal, "discomfort and uncertainty for understanding." *Colombia me dio alas para volar.* Colombia, as a friend once remarked, gave me the wings to fly.

This strange affair, the love of a boy for a land and a people, began innocently enough in 1968 when my mother, a modest but determined Canadian woman, told me that Spanish was the language of the future. She worked all year as a secretary to earn enough money to allow me to join a small party of schoolboys that a language teacher proposed to take to Colombia. At a time when most Canadians and Americans had never experienced a commercial flight, the South American destination was terribly exotic, as indeed was the character of the man leading the adventure. The teacher was English by birth, dapper in appearance, with a scent of cologne that in those days gave him the fey veneer of a dandy, an impression betrayed by the scars on his face and a glass eye that marked a body blown apart in the war. A perfect foil to orthodoxy, Mr. Forrester was mischievous, slightly transgressive, and more than a little subversive, traits of character that made him a total inspiration to teenage boys on the loose.

At fourteen, I was the youngest of the group and the most fortunate, for unlike the others, who spent a sweltering season in the streets of Cali, I was billeted with a family in the mountains above the valley, at the edge of trails that reached west to the Pacific. It was a classic Colombian scene: children too numerous to keep track of, an indulgent father, a grandmother who muttered to herself on a porch overlooking flowers and fruit trees, an angelic sister who more than once carried her brother and me home half-drunk to a mother, kind beyond words, who stood by the garden gate, hands on hips, feigning anger as she tapped her foot on the stone steps. For eight weeks, I encountered the warmth and decency of a people charged with a strange intensity, a passion for life, and a quiet acceptance of the frailty of the human spirit. Several of the older Canadian students longed for home. I felt as if I had finally found it.

Six years later, in the early spring of 1974, I returned to Colombia with a one-way ticket and no plans save a promise not to return to the United States until Richard Nixon was no longer president. I had just a small backpack of clothes and two books, George Lawrence's *Taxonomy of Vascular Plants* and Walt Whitman's *Leaves of Grass*. At the time, I believed that bliss was an objective state that could be achieved simply by opening oneself unabashedly and completely to the world. Both figuratively and literally I drank from every stream, even from tire tracks in the road. Naturally I was constantly sick, but even that seemed part of the process, malaria and dysentery fevers growing through the night before breaking with the dawn. Every adventure led to another. Once on a day's notice I set out to traverse the Darién Gap. After nearly a month on the trail, I became lost in the forest for a fortnight without food or shelter. When finally I found my way to safety, I stumbled off a small plane in Panama, drenched in vomit from my fellow passengers, with only the ragged clothes on my back and three dollars to my name. I had never felt so alive.

Along the way I became an acolyte of the legendary botanical explorer Richard Evans Schultes. He, too, had found his life in Colombia. When, years later, I would write his biography, it was inevitable that the book, *One River*, would be a love letter to a nation by then scorned by the world. *El río*, the Spanish-language edition, came out in 2002, a year that marked a low point in Colombia's fortunes. At a time when the nation's very capacity to endure was being called into question, the publication of a book on botanical exploration, with a print run of just five hundred copies, hardly warranted attention. But a great strength of *El río*—its potent secret, as Colombian friends would later say—was the quality of the translation. Some 150 pages longer than the English original, *El río* in many ways belonged to the late Nicolás Suescún, an inspired and exceedingly generous Colombian writer and poet who set his own work aside to translate the text in a manner so elegant as to transform the language into something altogether new, while remaining absolutely loyal to the original narrative.

For several years, as my work straddled the globe, I lost track of *El río*. Only when I returned to Colombia in 2008 did I learn that in my absence, the book had taken on a life of its own, with word of it spreading, especially among the young. A first clue surfaced in Santa Marta when, quite by chance, I came upon a student on the beach reading a frayed copy of an edition that was completely unknown to me. Three days later, while interviewing former minister of defense Rafael Pardo in his home in Bogotá, I noticed an unblemished copy of that same edition on his desk. *El río*, it turned out, had been embraced not just by naturalists—botanists and anthropologists, as one might expect—but by a wide array of Colombians, old and young, men and women, artists, musicians, corporate executives and priests, politicians from across the political spectrum, and even notorious figures such as Fabio Ochoa, the imprisoned former leader of the Medellín Cartel, whose sister Marta called me out of the blue, just as I came out of the shower at the airport lounge in Doha, asking that I consider visiting her brother in the federal penitentiary in Georgia. The book, she said, meant a great deal to him.

By the time a third edition of *El río* appeared, in 2009, I had a better understanding of its quixotic success, if only because so many Colombians had shared their thoughts and insights and, in some instances, their gratitude. Because of cocaine, Colombia had become a pariah nation, its every citizen stained and suspect by association. Leading political figures were regularly challenged by the foreign press or humiliated as they traveled abroad as official representatives of the country. In a story known and frequently retold on the Colombian streets, in taxis and bars, among merchants and shopkeepers in the central market, Colombia's ambassador to the United States Carolina Barco, former minister of foreign affairs, daughter of a Colombian president, was strip-searched at Washington's Dulles airport simply because she was Colombian. The customs agent dismissed her claim of diplomatic privilege, waving off her protest with an obscenity, barked as if from the mouth of a dog.

Colombians, most of whom have never used or seen cocaine, have lived with the consequences of the trade for two generations. For four terrible years, from 1996 to 2000, a kidnapping occurred in Colombia every three hours of every day. Altogether thirty thousand men, women, and children were torn from their families, many never to return. By 2012 nearly five million Colombians had abandoned their country, some by choice, others desperate to escape the violence. Within Colombia, those displaced by the conflict numbered more than seven million. Imagine how differently the people of the United States would feel about their War on Drugs, not to mention their casual consumption of cocaine in bars and boardrooms across the nation, if they knew that as a consequence of both obsessions, no fewer than eighty million fellow Americans would be driven from their homes or forced into exile.

El río resonated with Colombians in part because it exposed such cruel hypocrisies, even as it presented a portrait of a land and a people completely in defiance of the dark clichés. To be sure, Colombia has been convulsed for more than fifty years by a brutal conflict that left some 220,000 dead. The missing number close to 100,000.

Every family has suffered. Yet in a nation of 48 million, the number of actual combatants at any one time, including the army, the leftist guerrillas and all paramilitary forces, never surpassed 200,000. The great majority of Colombians have been innocent victims of a war fueled almost exclusively by the unprecedented profits of the drug trade, a flood of illicit wealth that for a time had traffickers processing currency like hay, weighing bales of hundred-dollar bills just to estimate the value. Without the black money, readily taxed, stolen, or siphoned away, the struggle of the leftist guerrillas would have fizzled out decades ago, and the blood-soaked paramilitary forces might never have come into being.

Cocaine has been Colombia's curse, but the engine driving the trade has always been consumption. In the early years, as small-time Colombian hustlers joined forces with American Vietnam vets, pilots who flew the cocaine to Texas and Florida, no one knew how sordid it would become, or that the business would unleash such fratricidal violence. The cartels rose out of the barrios and country clubs of Medellín and Cali, but the ultimate responsibility for Colombia's agonies lies in good measure with every person who has ever bought street cocaine and every foreign nation that has made possible the illicit market by prohibiting the drug without curbing its use in any serious way.

After all the violence, the rivers of blood, the tens of thousands of lives lost to murder, prison, and war, there is more cocaine consumed today than at any time in history. The drug remains in play for the simple reason that in the lonely streets of New York, the office cubicles of London, the desolate bars and one-room flats of Miami and Madrid and every other glass-clad city of the world, cocaine makes people feel good, if only for a time. In the years since I first visited the Sierra Nevada de Santa Marta and sat among the Arhuaco spiritual leaders, the *mamos*, listening as they spoke of the gift that coca, the "divine leaf of immortality," implied for the world, the American government alone has spent more than $1 trillion in its War on Drugs. Today, nearly fifty years on, there are more people in more places using worse drugs in worse ways than at any time since the outbreak of this misguided crusade.

Colombia is most assuredly not a place of violence and drugs; it is a land of *colores y cariño*, where the people have endured and over-come years of conflict precisely because of their character, which is itself informed by an enduring spirit of place, a deep love of a land that is perhaps the most bountiful on earth, home to the greatest eco-logical and geographical diversity on the planet. It speaks volumes of the strength and resilience of the Colombian people that through all these difficult and impossible years, the nation has maintained its civil society and democracy, grown its economy, greened its cities, created millions of acres of national parks, and sought meaningful restitution with scores of indigenous cultures, a progressive record unmatched by any other nation-state.

Colombians today long for peace. Those of a certain age look back to a time when the country made sense, before the rivers were awash with the dead. Those born into the cauldron of war yearn simply for a chance to live in a land without fear, where violence no longer clouds the destiny of the young. Memories and longing, I suspect, drew many readers to the narrative of *El río*, which in part recounts my experience as a student in the 1970s, free to travel at will in Colombia to any place my feet took me: from Chocó to the Putumayo, Cauca to the coast of Magdalena, Nariño to the far hori-zons of the Llanos.

In the end, *El río* surely belongs neither to me as author nor to Nicolás as translator but, rather, to the young people of Colombia, an entire generation, perhaps two, that like the nation itself has not deserved the ravages of these last many years. In 2009, when the third edition was published, Colombia was still very much a nation at war, and vast reaches of the country remained off-limits for ordi-nary people. In the new foreword I expressed "my fervent hope that one day all young Colombians will be free, as I was, to travel with-out fear to every crossroads and forest stream, every mountain and *páramo*, the primordial slopes of the Macarena and into the very heart of the Amazon. That time will come. If in the meantime this book might inspire a few travel plans, let it be as a map of dreams."

Mercifully, the promise of peace has come to Colombia, and sooner than many imagined possible in 2009. The signing of the accords in Cartagena on September 26, 2016, sent a powerful mes-sage to every nation that while the world might be falling apart,

Colombia was falling together. It will be a long, slow, and uneven process of reconciliation and rebirth. Sporadic violence is certain to flare. Intense pressure will be brought to bear to exploit lands and forests long insulated from development by the conflict. The corrosive influence of cocaine will remain, unless governments everywhere have the courage to destroy the illicit trade with the cleansing stroke of legalization, a dim prospect despite being widely acknowledged as the only rational solution.

For the nation to heal, Colombians will have to find their way to forgiveness, even as they honor always the memory of loved ones so cruelly and unjustly taken from this life. War is easy. Peace will be hard. But it brings with it limitless possibilities. Today, two generations of young Colombians forced to flee the conflict are returning from New York, London, Paris, and Madrid, with highly developed skills in every conceivable field of endeavor, placing their nation on the verge of an economic, cultural, and intellectual rebirth unlike anything ever seen in Latin America. Within the country, literally millions are on the move. Some displaced by the violence are finding their way back home. Others almost as pilgrims are taking to the open road in search of work, family, and new lives. In 2016 alone, some twenty million Colombians traveled within their country, close to half of the national population.

As men and women from Valledupar to Pasto, Manizales to Mocoa, Bucaramanga and Buenaventura to Barrancabermeja, Cali, Medellín, and Bogotá are at last free to discover their own homeland, all of Colombia has awoken to the realization that because of the conflict, vast regions of the nation, long isolated by the war, have been mercifully spared the ravages of modern development. This perhaps will be the real peace dividend, the opportunity for the nation to consciously and deliberately decide the fate of its greatest asset: the land itself, along with the forests, rivers, lakes, mountains, and streams. If the lowland rain forests of Ecuador, to cite but one example, have since 1975 been utterly transformed by oil and gas exploration, colonization, and deforestation, the Colombian Amazon, though now under threat, has remained until recently an essentially roadless expanse of pristine forest nearly the size of France. Decisions made today about the future of all the wild lands of Colombia will benefit from the wisdom of indigenous elders and the insights of decades of scientific research, all informed by an awareness of the importance of biological and cultural diversity that simply did not exist when the fate of lowland Ecuador was determined fifty years ago. Rarely in history has a nation-state been given such an opportunity to envision its future, and such a reprieve from the industrial forces that have devastated so much of the world over the last half century.

As Colombians chart their way forward, everything hangs in the balance. Some months ago, outside Santa Marta on the banks of the Don Diego River, an old friend and revered Arhuaco elder, Mamo Camilo, summed up the challenge. "Peace will not matter," he said, "if it is only an excuse for the various sides of the conflict to come together to maintain a war against nature. The time has come to make peace with the entire natural world."

In a short story by Jorge Luis Borges, a European woman asks a professor from Bogotá what it means to be Colombian. The man hesitates before replying, "I don't know. It is an act of faith." Colombia is like that. Nothing is as expected. Magical realism, celebrated as Colombia's gift to Latin American literature, is within the country simply journalism. Gabriel García Márquez wrote of what he saw. He was an observer, a practicing journalist for most of his life, who just happened to live in a land where heaven and earth converge on a regular basis to reveal glimpses of the divine.

Only in Colombia can a traveler wash ashore in a coastal desert, follow waterways through wetlands as wide as the sky, ascend narrow tracks through dense tropical forests, and reach in a week Andean valleys as gently verdant as the softest temperate landscapes of the Old World. No place in Colombia is more than a day removed from every natural habitat to be found on earth. Cities as cultured as any in the Americas were for most of their history linked one to another by trails traveled only by mules. Over time, the wild and impossible geography found its perfect coefficient in the topography of the Colombian spirit: restive, potent, at times placid and calm, in moments tortured and twisted, like a mountain that shakes, crumbles, and slips to the sea. Magic becomes the antidote to fear and uncertainty. Reality comes into focus through the reassuring lens of the phantasmagoric. A god that has given so much to a nation, as Colombians never fail to acknowledge, always gets his piece on the back end.

Certainly there was some kind of magic at work in the genesis of this new book, which celebrates the Río Magdalena, Colombia's river of life. In 2014, I was invited to Bogotá by Héctor Rincón and Ana Cano, both acclaimed journalists from Medellín, to help promote the Amazon volume of their series *Savia Botánica*. With the backing of Grupo Argos, one of Colombia's most prominent corporate citizens, they had assembled teams of botanists, photographers, and journalists to survey the five major regions of Colombia with the goal of producing an elegant illustrated book on each—the Llanos, Amazonas, Chocó, the Caribbean coast, and the Andean Cordilleras. These *Savia Botánica* volumes were not to be sold, but gifted as complete sets to every library in the country, all with the goal of sending a message to a new generation of young Colombians that theirs was not a land of violence and drugs, but rather a place of unparalleled natural wealth and beauty, home to, among many wonders, more species of birds than any other country in the world.

One day, as we wrapped up a discussion of the latest *Savia Botánica* volume, I casually mentioned that, having focused on the Colombian landscape, perhaps it was time to pay attention to the rivers. I proposed, half in jest, that we do a book on the Río Magdalena, the Mississippi of Colombia, the vital artery of commerce and culture that runs a thousand miles south to north, traversing the entire length of the nation. To my surprise and delight, my new friends embraced the idea without hesitation, as indeed did Grupo Argos, which immediately offered its unconditional support for the project. That whimsical remark turned out to be a defining moment, for the research and writing of this book would in the end consume nearly five years.

Colombians think of the Magdalena as having three sections—Alto, Medio, and Bajo—divisions with overlapping and even shifting boundaries that nevertheless reflect geographical, historical, and cultural distinctions far more profound than the simple terms high, middle, and low would imply. Thanks to the generosity of Grupo Argos, I was able to explore the Magdalena in all its dimensions, from source to mouth, in all months of the year, with every shift of the seasons, from the uplands of the Macizo Colombiano to the sand and stones of the Caribbean shore. Altogether, I made five extended forays to the river: two with the *Savia* team, led by Héctor Rincón and Ana Cano, surveys that covered the entire drainage, and two subsequent explorations that concentrated on the Medio Magdalena and the musical traditions of the lower river and the Caribbean coastal plain. The fifth brought me back to the Arhuaco *mamos*, old friends from my time in the Sierra Nevada, as we returned to Bocas de Ceniza to make ritual payments at the mouth of the river, even as the streets of Barranquilla erupted all around us with the magic and joy of Carnaval.

The Río Magdalena is not just the country's main artery; it's the reason Colombia exists as a nation. It is the lifeline that allowed Colombians to settle a mountainous land that geographically may well be the most challenging place on the planet. Within the Magdalena drainage live four of every five Colombians. It is the source of 80 percent of the nation's economic wealth, the engine that drives the economy, the river that powers the lights of the great cities. Like the Mississippi, its shadow to the north, the Magdalena is both a corridor of commerce and a fountain of culture, the wellspring of Colombian music, literature, poetry, and prayer. In dark times, it has served as the graveyard of the nation, a slurry of the shapeless dead. And yet always, it returns as a river of life. Through all the years of the worst of the violence, the Magdalena never abandoned the people. It always flowed. Perhaps, as this book suggests, it may finally be time to give back to the river, allowing the Magdalena to be cleansed of all that has soiled its waters. Colombia as a nation is the gift of the river. The Magdalena is the story of Colombia.

Magdalena

Bocas de Ceniza

The mouth of the Río Magdalena is the color of the earth. To the north, beyond a sea of golden clouds, the Caribbean sky fades to lapis blue in the falling light. To the west, the sun sets upon the Atrato and the rain forests of Darién, the Gulf of Urabá, and all the lost islands of Panama. To the east, the beaches and rocky shores run away to Santa Marta and beyond, past the Ciénaga Grande, the vast wetland that shimmers as a great mirror to the heavens, to the soaring flanks of the Sierra Nevada de Santa Marta, the highest coastal mountain range on earth, reaching finally to the sands of the Guajira, the desert peninsula where Colombians reinvented grit, commerce, resilience, and passion.

To the south, upriver, the lights of Barranquilla glow as a distant halo over a city that from its inception has inexplicably turned its back on the river that gave it life. Founded between 1627 and 1637, it remained a small fishing village until the arrival of commercial steam vessels in 1824, but even then, it could never decide whether to be a port on the river or a city on the sea. The building of a railroad from Barranquilla 400 miles upriver to Salgar in 1872 opened the way for a great maritime outlet to the world, and oceangoing vessels entered the river mouth for the first time, struggling against a current that carried the weight and promise of an entire nation. Indeed, one might say that the Magdalena carried the land itself.

By 1883, its burden of sediments and silt had once again buried the estuary, rendering the river mouth impassable.

In 1893, the construction of the world's longest and most elaborate pier at Puerto Colombia, on the coast twelve miles west of Barranquilla, redirected commerce for a decade, but by 1906, attention returned to the potential of Bocas de Ceniza, the actual mouth of the river. With grand plans, both to dredge the river channel and to construct a modern port at Barranquilla, the government hired an American engineering firm in 1907, only to turn to the Germans in 1912, then a national consortium in 1919, until finally, in 1924, with little accomplished, the flow of money was directed once again to the Americans. Puerto Colombia was abandoned, its magnificent pier left to crumble into fragments of concrete and iron. In 1943, in a move tainted by the scent of politics, the use of any of the port facilities at Puerto Colombia was prohibited by law. Ultimately, all that remained was destroyed by the sea.

The river mouth, meanwhile, was reinforced with a long line of breakers, parallel to the flow, intended to direct the Magdalena into a narrow channel, concentrating its force that it might sweep all sediments to the sea. Unfortunately, the barriers, built at considerable expense over nearly a decade, achieved quite the opposite effect, trapping the sediments and clogging the estuary as never before. The global economic crisis of 1929 suspended work for several years, and it was not until 1936 that President Alfonso López Pumarejo, crossing into the mouth of the Magdalena aboard a destroyer of the Colombian navy, accompanied by an entourage of ministers, admirals, governors, and mayors, was able to officially inaugurate the new canal and the proposed Maritime and Fluvial Terminal, facilities that would not in fact be completed until 1939. "Barranquilla," he declared, "is, from now on, a port of the sea." Regrettably, this proved to be wishful thinking.

For a time, beginning in 1936, seagoing freighters, vessels of serious draft, were able to make their way into the river and reach the city. But they were fighting the power of a river born a thousand miles to the south in the Macizo Colombiano, a rugged knot of mountains that soars over the continent, giving rise not just to the Magdalena but to the Ríos Putumayo, Cauca, Caquetá, and Patía, not to mention the three great branches of the Andes, which fan out in Colombia as immense cordilleras, running northward toward the broad Caribbean coastal plain.

In the body of Colombia, the Río Magdalena is the main artery. A new river, as measured in geological time, with a drainage encompassing fully a quarter of the nation, it flows from one end of the country to the other, through an astonishingly diverse landscape of glaciers and snow-covered volcanoes, cloud forests and *páramos* saturated by rain. Fed by lakes and countless mountain streams, it falls into a great lowland depression once covered by rich tropical forests, mangroves darkened by caimans, and waterways manicured by manatees. Scattered across the entire basin of the lower river are literally thousands of shimmering wetlands, some the size of the sky. Indeed, the entire Bajo Magdalena is a world of water, which ebbs and flows with the seasons, causing the river itself to overflow its banks, reaching a width in places of as much as fifty miles, even as its estuary expands to embrace and define both the geography and hydrology, not to mention the economy and culture, of all coastal Colombia.

Attempts over the years to transform Bocas de Ceniza, focused narrowly on reconfiguring just the mouth of the river, invariably proved to be quixotic gestures that defied nature and brought to mind King Canute's famous failure to hold back the ocean waves. Every year the Río Magdalena, despite its meanderings, carries 250 million tons of silt to the sea, the equivalent of eighteen hundred large industrial truckloads of sediments being dumped at the river delta every day. The engineers, despite their best efforts, never really had a chance. The names of the enterprises charged with taming the river, building the breakwaters, and dredging the channel changed by the decade, but none managed to achieve the impossible. The river silted up in 1942 and 1945, and again in 1958 and 1963. Millions of dollars had been invested, and no doubt many additional millions will be spent in the future on new and perhaps improved plans to industrialize the river mouth, but in the end, the Río Magdalena will always roll on, carrying all things to the sea, merging, as Shakira so gracefully sings, the body of Colombia like a lover to the waters of all the world.

.   .   .

From the river settlement of Las Flores, an old fishing village today engulfed by the outskirts of Barranquilla, a narrow-gauge railway runs north along the Magdalena, past modest shipyards and repair shops, restaurants and docks, rusted barges tethered to the shore. Reaching the coast where the wide crescent beaches are covered with plastic refuse and kelp, it continues onto the original breakwater built in the 1920s, a narrow jetty of tumbled riprap that stretches for several miles into the sea. The rock foundations remain solid, but the track, twisted and dilapidated, with short sections patched with wooden poles in place of iron, has clearly seen better days.

The open-air cars, with their coughing and sputtering engines, frequently derail, prompting a frenzy of excitement as passengers unload and small crews of young men furiously lift the carriages back onto the rails. When two cars going in opposite directions meet on the single track, the passengers move from one to the other with quiet and polite efficiency—unless, of course, music is heard, coming from a radio, perhaps an old cassette player; then everything is forgotten as people mingle and invariably someone begins to dance. *Vallenatos*, stories of the soul sung with an accordion's plaintive cry, generally imply but a short delay. But if the rhythm is *cumbia*, sensuous and seductive, and the long skirts of the women begin to twirl with each tight turn of their feet, one best come up with new plans for the day.

Bocas de Ceniza is a popular tourist destination, mostly for Colombian families and students. The tracks reach half the length of the spit to a narrow roundabout where, beneath the protective gaze of a white Madonna perched on a cement pole, everyone gets off to wander. Small children, impeccably dressed, dart about like butterflies. Teenage girls, in tight jeans and tank tops sparkling with rhinestones, defy gravity as they delicately make their way on high heels further down the jetty, tiptoeing among the stones and twisted remnants of the rail tracks. Older women search in vain for shade, settling for a cold drink, perhaps a *raspado*, a cone of shaved ice drenched in syrup.

The jetty is lined on both sides by small wooden shacks, home to

the men and women who live on the rocks, fishing by night, sleeping by day. In the bright sun, their absence is felt; the place feels
lifeless and deserted. The spit of stones is in no place more than
thirty feet across. On one side is the sea, dark and brooding, with
waves pounding the rocks and surging onto the jetty itself. On the
other side flows the Magdalena, brown with silt, too toxic to drink,
contaminated by human and industrial waste, which flows into it
from every town and city in a drainage that is home to forty million
Colombians. The fishermen use the river to wash their clothes and
to bathe, but not even the hardiest among them would dare drink
the water. Some with their recollection of darker days, when bodies regularly floated by and the river served as the graveyard of the
nation, hesitate even to eat the fish.

Theirs seems a precarious existence, perched on the edge of
a narrow jetty, living in shacks tacked together from old boards
bleached grey by the sun. Exposed as they are, a single wave could
sweep away their lives. And yet, as if in conscious defiance of despair,
rejecting any overtures of pity, all of them have painted their homes
with poetry, simple declarations of faith and contentment, all signed
by the authors. "I am happy to live at Bocas de Ceniza," declares
Wilfrido de Ávila Barrios. "Thanks to the fish, I raised my sons and
sustained my family and for that reason I never want to leave this
place, that's my wish and that of my family." The shingle hanging
over the door of Gilberto Hernández's home reads, "What I like
about this place is the peace that I breathe only here, the fish and
the sounds I hear in the crashing of the waves." Written across the
entire façade of one dwelling, owned by a handsome young man of
twenty, single and with no interest in marriage, are the simple lines:
"Here lives Beethoven. Here one breathes peace, love, and tranquil-
lity."

Only as the light fades, and the happy if overheated tourists
trudge back to the carriages that carry them home to the city, does
the small community of fishermen come alive. Men and women
emerge from their homes and gather around open fires, drinking
tintos, small shots of coffee, and getting ready for the night. They
work only in the dark, making their way to the very end of the
jetty, where a strong north wind always blows. They fish with kites,

crafted of plastic and small bits of wood, that rise in the wind and carry their long lines, rigged with perhaps a dozen hooks, along with plastic bottles as floats, far out into the darkness. Illuminated by the glow of their headlamps, they clamber over the rocks, working their lines, even as the waves crash upon the rocks, sending great cascades of spindrift and salt water across the jetty. Silhouetted against the night sky, they appear truly heroic—defiant, independent, and free.

This is the entire spirit of the place, its reason to be. Among the most respected and venerable of all the fishermen is Andrés de la Ossa. He is a slight man with a soft face and the rough hands of one who has worked with fish and the sea all of his life. Born in Cartagena, Andrés arrived at Bocas de Ceniza in 1962. The jetty has been his home for more than fifty years, a span that corresponds to the duration of the conflict that has long tormented Colombia. In a wild and ragged country, the jetty has always been safe. "Nothing happens here," he explains as he pulls in his line to rebait the hooks. "Everything is normal—people come and deal with one and they see everything as it has always been. Simple and true. There are times when the fishing is good and times when it is bad. But the water is always there, and there will always be fish in the sea."

Asked about the Río Magdalena, the other side of the jetty, he speaks as if the river is a completely different world, one of darkness and strife. Nets get caught in the rocks on the river side. The water can't be drunk. Those living on the jetty have to haul potable water from the city. Just the previous Sunday, on the day of the Lord, Andrés had fished two bodies out of the river, a man and a woman wrapped together in a carpet. During the worst of the violence, he added, the flow of corpses was constant. Most were headless, but you could sometimes identify the FARC guerrillas from their rubber boots, the same as those that he had used as a child working a small patch of land owned by his uncle.

In the early hours of a new day, invited to stay, I rested on a wooden bunk in the room of a man I had just met, grateful and impressed as ever by the generosity and kindness of ordinary Colombians who have little to give. With the sound of ocean waves pounding against the rocks on one side of the shack and the slow surge of a river too tainted to drink flowing by on the other, I thought of how people everywhere take water for granted, fouling our rivers and lakes, forgetting that fresh water is among the rarest and most precious of commodities. If all the water on earth could be stored in a gallon container, what is actually available for us to drink would scarcely fill a teaspoon.

We spend billions sending probes into space to seek evidence of water on Mars or ice on the moons of Jupiter even as we squander the wealth of nations on industrial schemes that compromise the limited supply of fresh water on our own blue planet. In Christian faith, we equate water with spiritual purity, baptizing infants with holy water dripped in the form of a cross upon their brows or by immersing them completely in sacred basins, from which they emerge graced with the promise of salvation. And yet even as we bless our children with this precious essence drawn from living bodies of water, we think nothing of defiling those very rivers with raw human waste on a scale, and in a manner, that can only be described as shameful.

We live on a water planet. Two atoms of hydrogen bonded to an atom of oxygen, multiplied by the miracle of physics and chemistry, are transformed into clouds, rivers, and rain. A droplet in the palm of a hand rolls about, fortified by surface tension, a wall of oxygen atoms. Spilled to the ground, it changes shape to match whatever it touches, yet adheres and bonds to nothing save itself. The unique physical properties of water alone allow tears to roll down the skin, perspiration to bead on the nape of the neck, blood to flow. Breath condenses, soft as mist. Rainwater runs as rivulets through cracks in the clay. Streams slip away. Rivers of ice harden and flow.

Water can shift states, becoming gas, solid, or liquid, but its essence can be neither created nor destroyed. The amount of moisture on the planet does not change through time. The water that slaked the thirst of dinosaurs is the same as that which tumbles to the sea today, the same fluid that has nurtured all sentient life since the dawn of creation. The sweat from your brow, the urine from your bladder, the very blood in your body will ultimately seep into the ground to become part of the hydrological cycle, the endless and infinite process of evaporation, condensation, and precipitation that makes possible all of biological existence. Water has no beginning and no end. To slip one's hand into a river is to return to the point of origins, to connect across the eons to that primordial moment, impossibly distant in time, when celestial bodies, perhaps frozen comets, collided with the Earth and brought the elixir of life to a lonely, barren planet spinning in the velvet void of space.

In the morning, the small community on the jetty reveals yet another of its many moods. All the fishermen are also merchants, masters of their destinies, sharing the same entrepreneurial spirit that allows millions of Colombians to survive and even thrive in economic circumstances that could well cause a more despairing people to abandon hope. It's not for nothing that Colombia has been described as *la tienda de la esquina*, the shop on the corner. The fishermen of Bocas de Ceniza live always with uncertainty, their fortunes shifting each and every night. Some return with baskets of fish, silver *sábalo* and *corvina*, *róbalo*, *lisa*, and *burel*, and happily make their way to the markets of Barranquilla. Others, having worked the same waters, inexplicably come home with nothing to show for their hours of patient labor. A night or two of misfortune may slip by, but empty results over days invariably provoke talk of mystical beings, such as El Mohán, the master of fish and lover of water who, from his underground palace of gold, punishes any fisherman who violates nature.

The one person on the jetty who never fails to return with fish lives alone in what was once the home of the harbor pilots, a gutted concrete ruin decorated with graffiti of flying angels and a blond mermaid with a tail featuring all the colors of the rainbow. The man is said to be touched, and his constant success is believed by the other fishermen to be God's way of compensating for his misfortune. A young woman was explaining this when a giant freighter came into view, moving silently downriver, just the other side of the jetty, dwarfing in scale the wooden shacks, what remained of the pilots' house, and the towering cement Madonna. Here was industry and commerce writ large. An oceangoing vessel at the mouth of the Río Magdalena, flying another nation's flag, carrying the wealth of Colombia to the world, just as foreign ships have done for five hundred years, ever since the Spaniards arrived and first made their way along the mysterious Caribbean shores.

Under orders from the Spanish Crown, Rodrigo de Bastidas reached the coast of South America in 1501. Sailing westward from the Guajira, his eye drawn to the snowcapped mountains that soared higher than any in the known world, he met the Tairona, the most elaborate civilization encountered by the Spaniards up to that time. Dazzled by their gold work, which was among the most beautiful ever produced in the Americas, he called for the establishment of a series of trading posts and then pushed on, continuing his explorations of the northern shoulder of the continent. On the first of April, he came upon a river of such power, fury, and violence that it disgorged fresh water, brown and laden with silt, miles into the sea. Bastidas described its estuary as the *bocas de ceniza*, even as he christened the river Río Grande de la Magdalena, in recognition of the date of his discovery, which was the day of conversion of the saint María Magdalena. As he noted in his log, the river was "very grand indeed."

There were, of course, already many names for the river—Yuma, Guaca-Hayo, Karakalí, Kariguaña, and others—all of which spoke of the great cultures and chieftains that thrived along its length, across lands that remained for the moment beyond reach of the Spaniards. Their attention was focused on consolidating their hold on Santa Marta and pacifying the Tairona, the first act of the Spanish conquest. In a war as savage and cruel as any subsequent campaign in Mexico or distant Peru, the invaders set fire to farms and homes, destroyed temples and sanctuaries, shattered or burned all sacred objects. Captives were crucified or left to die hung from metal hooks stuck through their ribs. Priests were drawn and quartered, their severed heads placed in iron cages to rot. In obscene public spectacles, Spanish friars, known to the Tairona as "black robes," let fighting dogs loose to disembowel all those accused of having sex as the Tairona had always done, in the open, in full daylight. Children conceived in the dark, they believed, were at risk of being born blind. Those Tairona who escaped death fled the coast, retreating high into the forests and hidden valleys of the Sierra Nevada de Santa Marta, a mountain redoubt that came to be known to them as the Heart of the World. Avoiding sustained contact with outsiders for nearly three hundred years, the survivors and their descendants embraced the good fortune of their salvation, even as they transformed their civilization into a devotional culture of peace.

To this day, the peoples of the Sierra Nevada—the Kogi, Wiwa, and Arhuaco—remain true to their ancient laws, the moral ecological and divine dictates of the Great Mother, the Madre Creadora, and they are still led and inspired by a ritual priesthood known as the *mamos*. In their cosmic scheme people are vital, for it is only through the human heart and imagination that the Madre Creadora may become manifest. For the people of the Sierra Nevada, humans are not the problem but the solution. They call themselves the Elder Brothers. We who threaten the Earth through our ignorance of the sacred law are dismissed as the Younger Brothers. They believe and acknowledge explicitly that they are the guardians of the world, that their prayers and rituals literally maintain the cosmic and ecological balance of the planet. For generations, they have watched in horror as outsiders have violated the Madre Creadora, tearing down the forests that are the skin and fabric of her body and poisoning the rivers, the actual veins and arteries of her life.

Though the mouth of the Río Magdalena lies well beyond the Black Line, which marks the extent of their traditional lands, the peoples of the Sierra Nevada nevertheless take responsibility for the river, recognizing as they do that all things are connected. When it is necessary and spiritually auspicious, they embark on pilgrimages to Bocas de Ceniza to make offerings, ritual *pagamentos*, and prayers. As Jaison Pérez Villafaña, a close Arhuaco friend, explained when I once accompanied him and a party of twenty or more men and women from the mountains to the sea, "We do not call the Sierra Nevada the Heart of the World simply because it occurs to us, but because the rivers that come from the mountains join with all the different rivers to bring cold to the sea. Every animal that lives in the forest, on the mountain, on the earth also lives because of the sea. One feeds on the other, and that balance is the one we know and respect. Everything in balance. The air becomes wind, the wind condenses into clouds, the rain falls from the clouds and runs over the earth through the rivers to the sea, where it arises again, carried by the wind."

Ice is formed that it may cool the sea, which in the absence of fresh water would become too hot. Yet if the sea becomes too cold, Jaison said, it won't be able to yield its energy to give light and life to the world. When a river meets the sea, these two energies merge, just as coca, the sacred *hayo* leaves, brings together the *poporo*, a gourd from the mountains, with lime, derived from shells found in the sea. Rivers are like people. When they are small, they must be cared for. When they grow and come together with other streams, they must learn to socialize and get along; and as they increase in strength, they must give to the greater community, yielding some but not all of their water. As they age, reaching their final years as they enter the oceans of the world, they are seeking a return to the Madre Creadora, for the sea is the uterus of all origins. "We know," Jaison concluded, "so much more about life than the Younger Brothers. We never destroy a river, for to do so would be to destroy ourselves."

The Arhuaco make no distinction between the water found within the human body and what exists outside it. "Our blood that flows through our veins," a young woman once told me, "is no different from the water that flows through the arteries of life, the rivers of the land." They see a direct relationship between urine, blood, saliva, tears, and the water of a river, a lake, a wetland, a lagoon. And in this, they are undoubtedly correct. Humans are born of water, a cocoon of comfort in a mother's womb. As infants, our bodies are almost exclusively liquid. Even as adults, only a third of our being has solidity. Compress our bones, ligaments, muscles, and sinew, extract the platelets and cells from our blood, and the rest of us, nearly two-thirds of our weight, stripped clean and rinsed, would flow as easily as a river to the sea.

From Jaison, I was astonished to learn that traditionally Arhuaco *mamos* made pilgrimages not just to the mouth of the Río Magdalena but to its very source. Traveling more than a thousand miles upriver, they conducted ceremonies and made offerings, singing to the water, assessing its health and well-being at every point along its flow. It was their way not only of caring for the river but of ascertaining how other indigenous nations measured up as cosmic stewards. Rivers, the Arhuaco maintain, are a direct reflection of the spiritual state of a people, an infallible indicator of the level of consciousness a community possesses. Rivers, simply put, are the soul of any land through which they flow.

As the *mamos* made their way to the source of the Magdalena, over the many weeks and months of the journey, the first thing they did upon arrival in any settlement was to offer prayers to the river, gauging its condition, singing songs in its honor. Thus, from their perspective it follows, as the *mamos* say, that for Colombia today to free itself of violence, to cleanse and liberate its soul, it must also return life and purity to a long-suffering river that has given so much to the nation. When I shared with Jaison my own plans to visit the headwaters of the Magdalena, he said very simply, "To clean ourselves, we must clean the river; to clean the river we must clean ourselves."

When I left Bocas de Ceniza, ultimately heading south to Cauca and the first phase of an intermittent journey the length of the Magdalena, the wisdom of the *mamos* stayed with me, as it always does. Whatever weight one gives to their words, however one chooses to recognize, celebrate, or even dismiss their contributions to the patrimony of the nation, one thing is indisputably true: Imbuing water with a sense of the sacred as they do is not contrary to science but, rather, an acknowledgment of the complexity and wonder of ecological and biological systems that science alone has illuminated.

ALTO MAGDALENA

In life and death, by night and day, the Magdalena flows, destined for all eternity to fade away at Bocas de Ceniza only to be reborn in the distant heights of the Macizo.

—GERMÁN FERRO

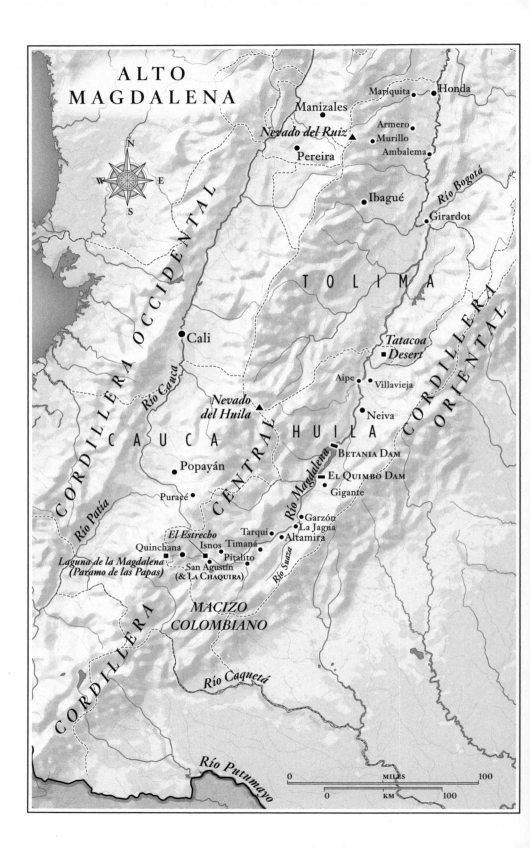

Fountain of the World

From the south, the journey to the source of the Río Magdalena begins in Popayán, a timeless university town with cobblestoned streets and old colonial buildings, white and dazzling against the soft green hillsides of the upper Cauca Valley. The route follows the highway south toward Pasto before turning east at Rosas, where the road climbs slowly through rich plantings of *maíz* and *frijoles*, *tomate de árbol*, *patata dulce*, cucurbits, *aguacate*, and guava that yield, as elevation is gained, to a patchwork of wheat and barley fields spread amidst the remnants of elfin cloud forests. It is wild, solitary land, remote and inhospitable.

The few towns along the way—Los Robles, Río Blanco, Barbillas—are lonely by Colombian standards, their streets abandoned at midmorning, hardly a soul in sight. In Río Blanco, a few boys were playing basketball, and the sound of their ball against the backboard ricocheted like a gunshot around the empty plaza. The church was shuttered. The forlorn figure of a saint stared down at the street from a crumbling niche. Right beside the church, the entire wall of a house had been freshly painted with a colorful mural celebrating the life of a political leader, recently killed. An old woman, alone on a park bench, explained that it had been a robbery, just a fortnight ago. The man had foolishly neglected to bring along security when he picked up a payroll. The quote on the mural suggested other possibilities: "For those of us searching for new ways to lead; giving a voice and value to the people is our only hope in a nation ruled by oligarchs willing to kill out of greed."

Beyond Río Blanco, as the road climbs into the Macizo Colombiano, the rugged knot of mountains that dominates much of southern Colombia, the scale of the land changes with each passing mile. Homesteads are widely scattered, simple adobe houses nestled low to the ground, their tin roofs glittering in the sun. The small farms cling to the sides of impossibly steep slopes, families connected to distant neighbors by narrow tracks that run along the ridgelines of mountain spurs and zigzag up the face of ancient landslides, all covered in verdant vegetation. Small puffs of smoke rise from the fields, signs of the constant struggle to keep the *monte*, the forest and the wild, at bay.

Gradually, the road leaves behind all signs of human life as clouds roll in and the land disappears in a veil of mist. Water seeps from every seam of the cut bank, pools in potholes in the gravel, and then runs impartially down the grade until tumbling off the side of the road; small spouts come together as rivulets, fall as cascades, become streams and raging cataracts that ultimately coalesce to give rise to rivers. Visibility drops to nil, forcing the driver to slow to a crawl, a torment for any Colombian. Then, quite unexpectedly, a gust of wind clears the mist to reveal the first signs of the *páramo*, a vast treeless expanse of vegetation that is one of Colombia's great natural wonders.

Perhaps because the country is home to over half of the world's *páramos*, many Colombians fail to appreciate the rarity of these exotic and mysterious ecological formations and, indeed, their importance to the hydrological cycle. Farther south in Peru and Bolivia, the plateaus and valleys above eleven thousand feet are arid, barren, windswept, and cold—a highland desert, or *puna*, useful only for the grazing of alpacas and vicuñas. Nearer the equator, the same elevation is equally forbidding, only it is constantly wet. The result is an otherworldly landscape that seems on first impression eerily like an English moor grafted onto the spine of the Andes. In the mist and blowing rain, there are only the espeletias, tall and whimsical relatives of the daisy, spreading in waves to remind you that you are still in South America. With bright yellow flowers that burst from a rosette crown of long, furry, silver leaves, espeletias look like plants that belong in a children's book. The common name in Spanish is *frailejón*, the friar, because seen from a distance the plants can be mistaken for the silhouette of a man, a wandering monk lost in the swirling clouds and fog.

A Colombian who surely does appreciate the wonder of the *páramos* is my good friend and companion on this leg of the journey, William Vargas, a botanist trained at the Universidad del Caldas. Born the son of a fisherman in the small community of La Jagua, on the banks of the Magdalena in the department of Huila, William is a story that has no rational explanation, despite a long history and precedent in the annals of Colombian science. Just as a young lad from Aracataca, responding only to the rhythms of his heart and his passion for a river, rose to the highest realms of literature and culture, so too have certain boys and girls, enchanted from birth by the sheer beauty of their country and the wealth of its botanical legacy, been singled out to become truly gifted naturalists. Like Gabriel García Márquez, they too succeeded in the face of impossible odds, as if summoned to science by a higher calling, a mystic force of destiny transcending class, poverty, logic, and even fate.

One such scholar was the revolutionary hero Francisco José de Caldas. A self-taught naturalist, inventor, mathematician, and geographer, Caldas rose to become an official member of the Royal Botanical Expedition to Nueva Granada, led by José Celestino Mutis. In 1801 he accompanied Alexander von Humboldt as the great German naturalist and geographer traveled the length of the nation to Quito. In the eclectic spirit of science at the time, Caldas studied plant taxonomy with Humboldt's companion Aimé Bonpland, a noted botanist, even as he taught Humboldt a method of his own invention for measuring altitude by recording the boiling point of water. He also shared his sketches of the cartography of the upper Magdalena, which allowed Humboldt to produce the first complete map of the river, later published in Paris with full credit given to Caldas. Humboldt, destined to be recognized as the most famous and learned man in Europe, was astonished that a young Colombian, born and raised in the small provincial town of Popayán, could know so much, possess a mind honed to such scientific precision.

Together, as they traversed the Andes, Humboldt and Caldas studied not just the flora and fauna but the geography, meteorology, and geology. It was a glorious age of science and knowledge. Minds were wide open, and scholars had yet to be obliged to narrow their focus and embrace specialties, unlike the academics and scientists of today, condemned always to know more and more about less and less. In a move emblematic of this broad embrace of scholarship, in 1805 the botanist Mutis appointed the naturalist Caldas to a position as astronomer, director of the Astronomic Observatory in Bogotá. These were all men of the Enlightenment whose imaginations embraced the full sweep of existence, scholars living in a land where virtually everything was new, including the quest for freedom. Alas, captured by Spanish royalists in 1816, Caldas was summarily executed by orders of Pablo Morillo, Count of Cartagena, who notoriously dismissed pleas for clemency with the infamous phrase "Spain does not need savants." Perhaps not, but Colombia did, then, and certainly today, more than ever.

As a small boy too poor to own shoes, William looked to Caldas as a hero, in part because the scholar had lived for a time in La Jagua, in a modest house on the waterfront, right next door to the Vargas family home. William did so well in school that by the time he entered grade three, he was known to his friends and teachers as "El Sabio Caldas." He was already obsessed with plants, especially orchids, which he collected and propagated, making detailed drawings before bringing new generations back to the wild to enhance the natural populations. When he discovered Darwin and *The Origin of Species*, he was warned by the town carpenter, a man of some local influence, that the blasphemous book would warp his mind, a possibility that only piqued William's interest.

Formal schooling in La Jagua ended at fifth grade, and William's family lacked the resources to send him away to study in the nearby town of Garzón. Fortunately, his mother was close to Father

Francisco Cadena, a kindly and learned mentor who saw her son as destined for the clergy. Thus, with the church fronting the costs of transport, William found himself leaving La Jagua every morning well before light, only to return each afternoon in time to gather firewood, which he sold to his neighbors in order to repay the village priest and buy food for his family. As the best source of wood was the remnant forest on the far side of the Magdalena, William's small *negocio* implied a daily adventure, one that continued for several years. With a machete hanging from his neck, he would swim across the river, eyes alert for water snakes and *jaguarundí*. On his return, he would bundle the wood, securing it with rope to make a small raft, which he rested upon while going home, floating across the river with the current, peacefully watching the nighthawks and parrots as they darted across the evening sky.

School in Garzón was an inspiration, especially the classes of Professor Rengifo, who taught history, geography, and mathematics and dazzled William with his ability to speak five languages. Graduation, however, presented a crisis, for Garzón, but thirty minutes down the road, was the farthest William had ever traveled from La Jagua. Neiva was unknown to him, Bogotá and Medellín as distant as Oz. Still, his goal, indeed his dream, was to become the first of his family to attend university.

Curious yet uncertain, feeling that he had to know something of his country and the world before pursuing further studies, William joined the army in 1985. This brought him finally to Neiva, where he was based for three months before being assigned to a remote outpost in the department of Caquetá. There, by chance, he ran into a disheveled gringo, an eccentric botanist who had been placed under the protection of the battalion by authorities in Bogotá who knew they could not keep the man away from the forest, despite the obvious dangers. The wayward scientist turned out to be Al Gentry, a highly regarded plant explorer known for both his odd personal habits and for having collected more specimens in more remote places than anyone in the history of South American botany. Gentry was one of a very small handful of scholars who could identify any Amazonian or Andean plant merely by holding a blossom to the light. Inspired by the encounter, William began to collect everything of interest he could find—plants, insects, even birds—much to the consternation of his fellow soldiers, who constantly chastised him while on patrol to keep his eyes focused straight ahead, where the enemy would be, and to stop looking at the ground or high into the trees.

For reasons that remain unclear, upon leaving the army, William immediately tried to enlist in the navy. Fortunately, on the day of his physical, he shoved his foot into a shoe and was badly bitten by a scorpion, which left him momentarily disabled, ending his naval prospects and sending him back to La Jagua to convalesce. An opportunity arose to study in Manizales. But as he traveled to the university, disaster struck. A fellow passenger offered to share some cookies. William accepted gratefully and ate three. Within thirty minutes, a strange blue veil descended over his vision. Later, the last thing he could recall were the lights of a passing truck dissolving into serpents before his eyes. This happened on a Sunday, and he did not come back to consciousness until the following Thursday. Four days had passed, and William had no memory of anything. Everything he owned had been stolen, even as the thieves had left him to stagger and drift on the side of the road in a sea of psychotic delirium.

Travelers in Colombia revel in rumors of any number of bizarre possibilities; it is part of the allure of the land. But in fifty years, I had never met anyone, local or foreigner, who had suffered William's fate. As it turned out, he had been dosed by a knockout drug derived from various species of tree daturas, all in the genus *Brugmansia*, shamanic plants known throughout the Andes as *borrachero*, the drunken one, or, more ominously, the jaguar's intoxicant. Members of the Solanaceae, the botanical family that also includes potatoes, tomatoes, tobacco, and all the hexing herbs of European witchcraft, daturas have long been a drug of choice for dark magicians throughout the world. The very name is derived from the name of bands of thugs and thieves in ancient India who used the drug to stun and disorient their victims.

All daturas contain in their seeds and flowers, leaves, stems, and roots powerful tropane alkaloids, atropine and scopolamine, drugs that in high dosages induce a state of psychotic delirium, with visions of hellfire, a sensation of flight, total amnesia, and a burning thirst. People exposed to the drugs often die, drowning as they try desperately to slake their thirst in shallow puddles of water. Curiously, all species of *Brugmansia*, the tree daturas, are always found growing near people, in hedgerows and fields, beside houses, often in graveyards, never in the wild. Shamans and *curanderos* throughout the Andes turn to *borracheros* when everything else fails, with the idea that by just touching the realm of madness unleashed by the plant they might acquire knowledge and illumination.

For William, it was not an auspicious start to a university career. Once before he had nearly died, at the age of six in La Jagua when he was run over by a tractor. But this was different, a total psychic assault on the mind and soul; an experience that would haunt him for several months, delaying the start of his studies. All of this ultimately worked to his advantage, as it led to his meeting Mélida Restrepo, a superb field botanist who would completely inspire his life as a scientist and collector. His thesis, a study of the flora of Quindío, grew into his first book, which became something of a sensation for a botanical text, attracting even the attention of the *vendedores ambulantes* of Medellín, who, with mixed results, hawked it at traffic lights to unsuspecting morning commuters not quite ready for an 814-page guide to the plants of the central Andes.

With all of his botanical wanderings, William had become an authority on the *páramos*, attracted not just by their rare flora but by an entire universe to be discovered in their ecology, their geological history as revealed by their soils, the diversity of insects and birds. In the field, he often wore a red headband, hoping to attract hummingbirds, all the winged dancers drawn to the long tubular corollas of his favorite genera: purple lobelias and red fuchsias, magenta iochromas, crimson gesneriads, the bright orange blossoms of the climbing bomareas.

All day during our ascent from the crossroads at Rosa on the Pasto highway, he had been in and out of the truck like a jackrabbit, making collections of clusias and tibouchinas, blue and red salvias, yellow calceolarias and wild mustards, passionflowers and Andean rhododendrons, delicate and rare. With his black beard and thick head of hair, intense dark eyes, and arms, legs, and torso with the strength of roots, William doesn't exactly look like a botanist. I tease him that if his life had led to the guerrillas instead of the army, his nom du guerre would surely have been Rasputin. His charm lies in his humility and humor, his passion for plants, and, above all, in the way his eyes ignite in the presence of a novel idea, be it from the realm of science, literature, philosophy, history, or politics.

As a field botanist, William is a national treasure, truly worthy of his childhood nickname El Sabio Caldas, a tropical specialist who knows the flora so well that if a plant is unknown to him, it is almost certainly new to science. I had watched only that morning as he stormed up a cut bank to retrieve the leaves and flowers of an epiphyte, which he immediately recognized as a new species of *Anthurium*, a genus that includes some of our most common houseplants. It was hard to know what was more impressive, the precision of William's taxonomic eye or the wonder of a country blessed with such botanical diversity, with so much still waiting to be discovered, that one could stumble upon a large and conspicuous plant growing along a simple roadside, only to find that it was new to science. In Europe, the discovery of a single new species would be the highlight of a botanist's career. In Colombia, for plant collectors like William, it is almost a daily occurrence. Already he has discovered more than a hundred, and his career as a plant explorer has just begun.

After six hours, close to dark, we finally reached the Finca Los Milagros, owned by a generous couple, Gulbert Papamija and Ana Lía Anacona, who also run a small *posada*, or inn, catering to the traders and tourists who travel the Camino Nacional, the remnants of the old colonial road between Cauca and Huila. A narrow track, accessible only to horses and travelers on foot, it follows ancient indigenous pathways, up and over the Macizo, passing by the Laguna de la Magdalena, the actual source of the river, before falling away over two days to the valley of the Río Quinchana and the approaches to San Agustín, the site of the most extensive and mysterious pre-Columbian remains in all of northern South America.

At ten thousand feet, the air was damp and cold. We laid out our bedrolls, then gathered on the open veranda for great steaming bowls of *sancocho* as Gulbert's brother Parménides, a park ranger, briefed us on plans for the morning. Our route would take us across Puracé, one of Colombia's oldest national parks, where the magic of the Macizo Colombiano, which covers some 13,000 square miles, is compressed into just 320 square miles. Small by the standards of Colombia's national parks, Puracé is nevertheless a place of superlatives, with 362 lakes and lagoons and more than a dozen dramatic *páramos*, all with names that could only have been coined by campesinos: El Apio, El Buey, Las Papas—celery, ox, and potatoes. Rising over the *páramos*, forming the backbone of the park, are seven snow-clad volcanoes 14,000 feet or higher, with Puracé itself reaching to 15,030 feet. Within the park, Parménides added, arise some of the great rivers of Colombia, the Caquetá and the Cauca but also the Patía and the Magdalena, born of the same body of water, La Laguna de la Magdalena. The biological bounty includes more than two hundred species of orchids, rare populations of wax palms and Andean oaks, mountain tapirs, cougars, and spectacled bears, as well as some 160 species of birds, including carunculated caracaras, sunbeam hummingbirds, and Colombia's national bird, the symbol of its patrimony, the Andean condor.

Joining Parménides on the trek would be his colleague Carlos Guerra, also a park official, along with two *arrieros*, Arnulfo Males and Jimmy Marín, who would wrangle the horses and look after the mules. I took an immediate liking to all four men and was especially impressed by the pride Parménides and Carlos had in their work. Puracé had been a major zone of conflict, the redoubt of an active FARC front, off-limits to visitors for years. Altogether, throughout the nation, some forty-five park guardians lost their lives in the violence, caught, like most rural Colombians, between the three sides: forced at gunpoint to service the guerrillas with fuel, food, or transport, only to be accused of collaboration by the army, a crime certain to provoke savage retribution from the paramilitaries. Throughout the country, small towns became mute, for the only option was silence. People turned their backs on the madness and went about their business, eyes half-shut, heads down, gaze averted, hoping only not to be noticed.

In the half-light of dawn, I could just make out the horses, teth-

ered to the fence rails, and, off to one side of the yard, the silhouette of William staring up into the branches of a dense shrub or
small tree that rose above the hedgerow. When we met for breakfast, the table was covered by his collections: the bright red blossoms of *flor de quinde*, *Iochroma fuchsioides*, the hummingbird's flower,
and the dramatic flowers of a tree datura. The creamy white lobes,
together with the distinct yellowish striations running parallel along
the length of the salmon-colored corolla, identified it as *Brugmansia
sanguinea*, perhaps the most beautiful of all these shamanic plants,
and one of the possible sources of the very drugs that had caused
William such trauma as a young aspiring student. I knew it well,
for my professor and mentor, Richard Evans Schultes, the legendary botanical explorer, had found a new and rare subspecies on the
northern slopes of Puracé, three days before the volcano blew in
1946. He had named it *vulcanicola*, in memory of the eruption that
nearly took his life.

Schultes had been drawn to the Macizo Colombiano, as it was
the one region in all of the Andes, north of Peru and south of the
Caribbean coast, where coca was still used and revered by indigenous people. Today, half a century later, the coca plant has been
demonized throughout Colombia as the source of the drug singularly responsible for the country's agonies, the fuel of the fire of war
without which the conflict would have fizzled out decades ago.

But coca is not cocaine, any more than potatoes are the equivalent of vodka. In the 1970s the Botanical Museum at Harvard,
under the leadership of Professor Schultes, secured support from
the U.S. Department of Agriculture to conduct the first compre-
hensive and modern scientific study of the botany, ethnobotany,
and nutritional value of all cultivated species and varieties of coca.
The results showed that the leaves, as consumed by indigenous people, serve as a mild and benign stimulant that is both beneficial to
their health and highly nutritious, with no evidence whatsoever of
toxicity or addiction. Nutritional assays revealed that coca leaves
contain a host of vitamins, more calcium than any other cultivated
plant—especially useful for Andean communities that traditionally
lacked dairy products—and enzymes that enhance the body's ability
to digest carbohydrates at high altitude, an ideal complement for a

potato-based diet. Indeed, three and a half ounces of the leaves, the typical daily consumption in the Andes, more than satisfies the recommended dietary allowance for calcium, phosphorus, iron, vitamins A and E, as well as riboflavin. Coca facilitates well-being, eases digestion, and demonstrably relieves the symptoms of altitude sickness, or *soroche*. As a plant stimulant, coca—or *hayo*, as it is known in Colombia—is without doubt more useful and less irritating than coffee, chocolate, or black tea.

None of this will come as a surprise to students of South American history. In the immediate wake of the conquest, the Spaniards wrote glowingly about the plant. In his *Royal Commentaries*, Garcilaso de la Vega stated that the magical leaf "satisfies the hungry, gives new strength to the weary and exhausted, and makes the unhappy forget their sorrows." Pedro Cieza de Léon, who traveled throughout the Americas between 1532 and 1550, noted that "when I asked some of these Indians why they carried these leaves in their mouths . . . they replied that it prevents them from feeling hungry, and gives them great vigor and strength. I believe that it has some such effect."

The most effusive praise came from Jesuit priest Antonio Julián, who in 1787 published *The Pearl of America*, an account of his decade in Santa Marta, and the subsequent eight years he spent at the Pontificia Universidad Javeriana in Bogotá. His formal mandate was to report on the economic potential of all the natural products of the Caribbean coast. But his heart clearly was captured by *hayo*, or coca, which he writes about in the most positive of terms, even as he tries to account for why the economic potential of the plant as a stimulant and tonic had yet to be realized, words that echo powerfully to this day:

> We Spaniards, so easily swayed by foreign ideas and so quick to embrace their fashions as we are enthusiastic in giving up our own and not attaching importance to them, we allow the Indians to eat and find sustenance in an herb that could prove to be a very profitable new commercial endeavor for Spain while providing health to Europe, serving as a cure and tonic for so many ills, a replenisher of lost strength, and

a prolonger of human life. It is the herb called Hayo, celebrated in the Province of Santa Marta, and throughout the New Kingdom. In Potosí, Kingdom of Perú, it is known as Coca.

I feel great disbelief that Europe does not make use of the Hayo, given the great consumption of tea and coffees. I attribute this to four causes. The first is ignorance about the excellent qualities of Hayo. The second is that the Spanish nation has not been ambitious in introducing new fashions to other countries, even as we are willing to accept alien ones. The third is that foreign nations have more profit and advantages in promoting the use of tea and coffee. The fourth is that news has not spread, and the time has not yet come to make taking Hayo a fashion.

It may be that Hayo like all things will arrive in due time, and with the news that I provide of its admirable virtues and effects, it would be introduced not as an idle, or useless, or destructive fashion to households and people, like others that arrive from overseas, but rather one that is healthy, useful, and beneficial to the well-being, vigor, and strength of the body, and that promotes long and prosperous maintenance of the individual.

In his enthusiasm for what he saw as the life-giving potential of *hayo*, Father Antonio Julián questioned Spanish attempts to limit its cultivation and consumption, noting that it had originally been grown throughout the interior, from the Río Fusagasugá to the Río Magdalena, along the coast from the Guajira and the Sierra Nevada de Santa Marta, in the valley of the Río Cesar, and on the flanks of the cordilleras running away to the south. He lamented that such a wondrous plant, a key commodity in the indigenous trading networks, had fallen under the wrath of the Spaniards, who had foolishly prohibited its use.

Today, efforts to eradicate coca in Colombia and block the commercialization of the leaves are being driven by pressure from the very country whose consumption of cocaine made possible the illicit trade that for fifty years has been the primary cause of Colombia's misery. The American government has long demonized the plant. In Peru, programs to eliminate the traditional fields, supported by the United States, began in the 1920s, fifty years before a black-market trade in the drug even existed. The real issue was not cocaine but, rather, the cultural identity and survival of those who traditionally revered the plant. The call for eradication came from officials and physicians, both Peruvian and American, whose concern for the well-being of the Andean peoples was matched in its intensity only by their ignorance of Andean life.

Even were the complete removal of the plant to be desirable, it's highly unlikely that Colombia could ever eliminate the cultivation of coca. The financial incentives for small family farmers are too great, and the potential growing areas too vast and inaccessible, especially in the ecological and altitudinal zones where cultivated coca thrives. Aerial eradication efforts are also doomed to failure, even as they compromise pristine forests and taint the soil and waterways with toxins. Indeed, it is not unreasonable to ask why any of Colombia's biodiversity, perhaps its greatest national asset, not to mention the health and well-being of its children, should be put at risk to satisfy the misguided policies of a foreign country whose people seek salvation and contentment in the false promises of a drug best used as a topical anesthetic to numb the senses. Having endured the consequences of the illicit trade for so many years, perhaps now is the time for Colombia to reclaim a stolen legacy by celebrating coca for what it really is, what the Inca saw it to be: "the divine leaf of immortality." Marketed as a tea or nutraceutical, coca could become Colombia's greatest gift to the world, dwarfing the commercial success of coffee. Nothing wrong with coffee, of course, but its origins do lie in distant Abyssinia. Coca was born in Colombia.

Jimmy Marín wrapped a blindfold around the head of his mule as he got ready to load our gear. Moving to the right side of the animal, he positioned a saddle pad, anchoring it with a *retranca* on the back and a *pretal* on the front to keep it from sliding. Then, with motions too effortless and quick to follow, he lifted and secured one sack and then the other, tying them off to the saddle cinch with the *sobrecargo*, a long piece of rope tied tightly with the *nudo de encomienda*, a slip knot that would allow him to easily adjust the loads once on the trail. It took Jimmy mere minutes to finish what was for him a mundane task, something he had no doubt done multiple times a day for all of his adult life. But to my eye, every time an *arriero* loads a mule, a small window opens onto the entire history of Colombia.

The Río Magdalena has always been the commercial artery of the nation; its drainage is the source of much of the country's wealth and home to its largest cities, Bogotá, Medellín, and Cali, as well as Barranquilla, Manizales, Neiva, and Pereira. And yet for more than three hundred years, the only way to move goods and people from the cities, ranches, and farms of the uplands to the Magdalena was by mule along *trochas* cut through the forests and carved into the sides of mountains. Foreign travelers who experienced this narrow traffic were both mystified that a modern nation could be dependent on such simple transport and horrified by the conditions they encountered en route: precipitous exposures, mules buried chest-deep in mud, dead oxen along the edge of the trail, often with vultures perched on top. That Colombia protected and even domesticated the fearsome *gallinazos*, precisely because they consumed carrion and kept the trails clean, did not assuage those already perplexed by the incomprehensible slang of the *arrieros*, not to mention their curious habit of rubbing their tired feet every evening with lard and melted wax scented with lemon juice.

Everything in Colombia moved on the backs of mules, driven by young men who learned their skills from their fathers, along *caminos de arriería* that fell away from the Andean heights to link every town and city to the Río Magdalena. By 1850, for example, Bogotá was an established capital, a cultured city of museums and universities soon to be known as the Athens of South America. Yet virtually everything to be found at that time in the homes of the rich, in the shops, in the laboratories and factories—from French champagne and cologne to German tools and scientific equipment, Dutch linens and English umbrellas, not to mention basic building supplies such as iron, copper, and cement—all of it had reached Bogotá from the head of river navigation at Honda, on the backs of mules along a track that predated the arrival of the Spaniards. Construction materials for the Puente de Occidente, the historic suspension bridge on the Río Cauca that links the two geographies of the department of Antioquia, were sourced on-site, all save the twelve-hundred-foot lengths of cable, essential components of the design. These had to be imported, and they could not be cut or spliced. The solution was a mule train of ten or more animals, each carrying a small spool of wire, no more than three hundred pounds in weight, with each load tethered to the following mule by the continuous strand of cable. If something was too big to carry—a piano, perhaps, or an industrial engine—it was simply disassembled and loaded in pieces. One story tells of an *arriero* who reached a small mountain town with a complete electric plant, along with everything necessary for its installation. He was greeted as a hero and toasted upon his arrival with *aguardiente* and cascades of blossoms as the entire community celebrated the arrival of light.

Just as all foreign imports arrived by mule, so too agricultural and other domestic products reached distant markets via the same *caminos de arriería*. Tobacco from the hills beyond Ambalema, coffee from Manizales, gold from the mines of Segovia, and virtually everything produced in the growing industrial center of Medellín, including the 250,000 Panama hats exported in 1915 alone— everything moved thanks to the strength, skill, and endurance of the *arrieros* and their animals. It was a unique culture of the open sky, of men and boys whose home was the ground beneath their feet, and whose moods and passions set them completely apart from ordinary cowboys, or *vaqueros*. *Arrieros*, to this day, don't just dislike horses; they disdain them. Who would want to work with horses, so often petulant, preening, and precious, when an uncomplaining mule is tougher, lives longer, is cheaper to feed, less vulnerable to disease, capable of carrying far greater loads, and, like the men themselves, as solid as the stones that mark the trails that define their lives?

People on the edge of death in the Andes are said to be getting ready to "cross a *páramo*." As we left the Finca Los Milagros, destined for the Páramo de las Papas, I happily had no disturbing premonitions, nor apparently did William, but we did notice that the sky over the mountains was black with rain. The trail climbed through the last of the fields before crossing a wooden bridge over a fast-moving stream flush with water from the night rains. Parménides identified it as the source of the Caquetá, one of Colombia's greatest rivers. I held my horse back as the others went ahead. The water was so clear, the banks verdant with dense thickets of ferns and stones luminescent with lichens. I had once spent a month on the Río Japurá, as the Caquetá is known in Brazil, and on another botanical expedition had flown over the confluence of the Río Apaporis and the Caquetá just upriver from the Colombian frontier settlement of La Pedrera. Recalling how effortlessly the Caquetá absorbs the Apaporis, as it does a host of tributaries, the Yarí, Caguán, Cahuinari, Pira Paraná, Mirití-Paraná, Orteguaza, and Purui, all mighty rivers, I found it somehow miraculous to be standing at its very source, knowing what awaited every drop of water on what would be a journey of nearly two thousand miles out of the mountains and into the basin of the world's greatest forest.

The trail came to a fork, with one track heading directly to the Laguna de la Magdalena, and the other rising toward higher ground and the Mirador de Santiago. We chose the latter, which followed the remnants of the historic Camino Nacional, passing first through a long tunnel of thick vegetation before following the ridgeline of a steep nose that rose all the way to the windswept heights. By the time we reached La Piedra del Letrero, a massive stone incised with an impressive concentration of pre-Columbian images and iconography, everything was wet and grey: the leaden sky, the dark forlorn horses, the black ponchos that did nothing to keep back the rain.

As we huddled for warmth, Parménides explained that the land had at one time been cursed. Scores of travelers had met their end here, until at this very site, upon this mysterious yet magical stone, a Catholic priest had performed an exorcism, casting away the demons and breaking the curse. As I ran my hands over the abstract designs, circles and triangles that completely covered the vertical face of the boulder, I wondered what the site was really saying. The early Spaniards did everything in their power to crush the spirit of the indigenous peoples, destroying their temples, tearing asunder their sanctuaries, quite unaware that it was never a shrine that the

Indians worshipped but the land itself: the rivers and waterfalls, the rocky outcrops and mountain peaks, the rainbows and stars. Every time a Catholic priest planted a cross on the ruins of a temple or lay claim to a shrine by spinning a new story in an attempt to co-opt its power and resonance, as clearly had been the case here at La Piedra del Letrero, he merely confirmed in the eyes of the native people the inherent sacredness of the place.

We continued on foot, resting the horses. The land opened onto a vast and seemingly limitless *páramo*, speckled with the yellow-and-silver crowns of thousands upon thousands of espeletias. On the distant horizon, waterfalls fell from the faces of mountains, which fused on the skyline into a single undulating massif, fading into nothingness in the mist. At twelve thousand feet, we could feel the altitude. Slowly, we tramped across the sodden ground and trudged up a steep slope to reach the Mirador de Santiago, with the hope of glimpsing the Laguna de Santiago, which gives rise to the Lambedulce, one of the very first affluents of the Río Magdalena. The mood of the landscape invoked a sense of the sacred. I recalled what our friend Jaison had said about the pilgrimages of his people, and tried to imagine Kogi and Arhuaco *mamos* arriving at these heights at last, having followed the river all the way from the sea. Presumably they would have encountered the Yanacona, a Quechua-speaking people transplanted by the Inca to the Macizo to pacify the region and consolidate their rule, a common practice as the empire rapidly expanded to the north and south. From them the *mamos* would have learned, in a perfect convergence of thought and belief, that all the lakes of the *páramos* were under the protection of Mama Ati, the mother of waters, a deity that must surely have evoked for the Kogi and Arhuaco memories of their own Madre Creadora. People, according to the Yanacona, could approach the lakes only as pilgrims, calling out in prayer to all the ancient mothers, "My body is the earth, my blood the water, my food the air, my spirit the fire."

Nothing quite so sublime passed our lips. At first, all we could make out was the ground at our feet and the top edge of a cliff face that fell away precipitously into the clouds. Then, as the wind whipped rain across the heights, the clouds parted for just a few moments and we saw the leaden surface of the small lake, circled by stones, espeletias, and dense tufts of grass. Almost immediately the weather closed back in, and with no chance of seeing any of the other ponds and lagoons that lie beyond Santiago, we dropped back down several hundred feet to the shelter of a field of massive boulders that looked west to the Laguna de la Magdalena. Our initial plan had been to make our way to its shore and drink from the outlet, the actual origin of the river. But in the rain and cold, this seemed an unnecessary and even silly gesture, for it was abundantly clear that the entire Macizo was in fact the source of the Magdalena. The water that soaked our feet, the clouds that burst over the valley, the veil of rain that obscured the contours of the lake and swept across the face of every mountain, the very mist before our eyes—all of it would eventually condense and coalesce in one of the many thousands of streams, brooks, and springs that burst from the Macizo and fall away to give rise to the Río Magdalena.

So instead we slogged on, following a stone path that, as it dropped from the heights, drew water from every source, becoming before long indistinguishable from any one of the surging *quebradas* that roar down the many mountains of Colombia in the wake of the rains. It made for rough going, especially as William and I were both wearing cheap rubber boots, the same as those commonly used by campesinos and long ago adopted by the FARC. The thin soles provided no protection from the rocks, forcing one to pay attention to every step, disrupting the rhythm and slowing the pace. It made you wonder how guerrilla armies managed to move as they did, with such an impediment. I remarked to no one in particular that if all that cocaine money had been used to equip the cadres with decent boots, the outcome of the war might well have been different. William's face revealed that even the thought of a FARC victory was something too terrible to joke about.

We soon left behind the gentians, heathers, and all the tenacious herbs of the *páramo* and entered the upper reaches of the cloud forest, a dense and impenetrable tangle of giant ferns and bamboo, gnarled shrubs and small trees, *mano de oso, sietecueros, encenillos,* all draped in moss, their bark dappled with liverworts and lichens, their trunks entwined by climbing vines, their branches festooned with epiphytic bromeliads, orchids, and ferns. Some two thousand feet below our highest point, we caught up at last with the Lambedulce, the stream that flows out of the Laguna de Santiago, just above its confluence with the Magdalena, which was still no more than a precocious *quebrada*, roaring out of a narrow cleft in the Macizo.

While Jimmy led the horses and mules down and across the creek bed, we passed across a wet and slippery log that spanned the banks. We were by then tired, wet, and miserable, and without much thought, we pressed on. Only later did I recall the significance of that modest confluence, hidden away in the thickets of the forest. It marked the literal divide where two of the great mountain ranges of Colombia are born. As long as we had the rushing waters of the Magdalena to our left, we were on the flank of what would become the Cordillera Oriental, which runs north, separating Andean Colombia from the vast grasslands of the eastern Llanos and the Amazon, and ultimately forming the border between Colombia and Venezuela. But as soon as we crossed over the Magdalena, which we did at the Santa Marta bridge, we were walking along the base of the Cordillera Central, the range that runs up the center of the nation, separating the Cauca from the Magdalena, rivers that don't come together until they reach the wetlands and *ciénagas* that lie beyond Serranía de San Lucas, where the last remnants of the Cordillera Central fall away to the Caribbean coastal plain. The entire rest of the day, as we stumbled out of the mountains toward San Antonio and the place where we planned to spend the night, we all felt a strange surge of energy. The mountain walls were so close, and as the sun broke through the clouds and the ancient stone path fell away like mercury through the forest, we could literally reach down and touch the geographical origins of a great nation.

The Hospedaje El Cedro is a small dairy farm carved from the forest a day from the nearest road. It was a simple yet beautiful place, with pastures running down to the Magdalena, where jacaranda trees in full bloom rose over the fields, their blue blossoms falling gently onto the backs of milk cows as they graze. Travelers stay in a wooden ranch house, with rooms aligned dormitory-style, all of them opening onto a covered porch overlooking the river. There is a separate kitchen, where Jimmy and Parménides and our crew hung out, huddled by the fire, drinking coffee, perhaps a *roncito* for warmth and strength. William moved a table to the porch and, after a short rest, began to process his collections. He took notes, and pressed each specimen between numbered sheets of newsprint, ultimately preserving them in bundles soaked with alcohol and placed into plastic bags and burlap *costales*. The radio played constantly, all *vallenatos*. It was tuned to Radio Pitalito, "La Poderosa del Huila," leaving no doubt that we had left the department of Cauca far behind.

A young girl passed around hot bowls of raw cane sugar and lemon, which in the moment was indescribably delicious and restorative, a drink of pure energy. After thirteen hours on the trail, I was totally spent. As I savored the *aguapanela*, it crossed my mind, as it had several times on the mountain, that I was clearly no longer the young man who at a moment's notice had agreed to cross the Darién Gap on foot in the distant spring of 1974. My exhaustion aside, I had no illusions that ours had been anything but a simple walk along defined trails, accompanied by cheerful and experienced guides, supported by both horses and mules, with plenty of food and even a small portable gas stove, which had miraculously delivered hot coffee at the summit as we stared down into the clouds, trying to discern the outlines of the Laguna de Santiago.

Still, the wind, rain, and cold had exacted a toll. As I recalled the extremes of the day, a glint of sunlight on the wing of a black caracara, the strange mysterious moods of the vast and otherworldly *páramos*, our awkward descent over stone tracks that had caused even the mules to stumble, I thought of what the early Spaniards had endured, not just in crossing the Macizo Colombiano but on journeys of conquest and discovery that had lasted months: men and horses dying by the day, the survivors plagued by disease, reduced to gnawing on boot leather and saddle bags for sustenance, under constant threat of attack as they moved through jungles and across mountain heights unlike anything any of them had ever experienced. To be sure, they had unleashed in the Americas untold horrors.

They were all veterans of murderous religious wars, survivors that Europe, for all its depravity, could not kill. Arriving in a New World that defied all orthodoxy, leaving them disoriented, confused, fearful, and fraught, they had clung to the few certainties that endured: power, greed, conquest, and gold. One can celebrate or lament the consequences of the Spanish conquest, but it is surely impossible to deny the courage, grit, endurance, and zeal that ultimately drove these men to madness and fame, wealth and glory, triumph, humiliation, dishonor, and death.

The first to enter Colombia from the south was Sebastián de Belalcázar, a lieutenant under Francisco Pizarro; Belalcázar had fought in Peru and then pushed north to establish the city of Quito, in Ecuador. There, he met a young man who claimed to be subject to a great ruler who possessed such wealth that each day he covered his body with gold dust and bathed in a sacred lake, washing away the precious powder as a sacrifice to the gods. The kingdom lay far to the north, in a land known as Cundinamarca, "the heights where the condors dwell." This was the beginning of the legend of El Dorado.

Sebastián de Belalcázar had every intention of being the first to find the city and exploit its riches. In 1536, accompanied by a force of two hundred Spaniards and a vast entourage of porters and servants, he marched north. In southern Colombia, he readily overwhelmed tribes that within memory had been vanquished by the Inca, who had advanced north as far as the Angasmayo River. Belalcázar founded Cali and Popayán, both in 1536, and then, after a two-year hiatus, launched a second expedition, continuing north across the cordillera into the mountainous lands of the Macizo. There he met serious resistance, not only from the Páez, Guambiano, Andaquí, and Pijao, but from scores of indigenous cultures now lost to history, known only by names scratched into parchment by the few literate priests who walked in the shadow of the soldiers, most of whom could neither read nor write: Coconuco, Puracé, Popayan, Papallata, Yalcón, Cambi, Otongo, Ohoco, Oporapa, Maya, Moscopan, Quinchana, Mulanes, and Culata. We know almost nothing about these peoples, but their names come alive as whispered messages from the past, reminding us of a time when the Macizo Colombiano was both densely populated and a vital crossroads of the Andean world.

Leaving in his wake a trail of ashes and blood, Belalcázar crossed the Macizo, then followed the Magdalena from its source, drawn like a lodestone to the lands of the Muisca, and the great chieftains of the central Andes. El Dorado was within his reach. Meanwhile, on the northern coast, another Spaniard had his own plans for the mysterious kingdoms of gold said to lie at the heart of the continent. Gonzalo Jiménez de Quesada was a lawyer by training, a highly educated man with a passion for philosophy. That he would become the model for Cervantes's *Don Quixote* suggests something of the fate that awaited him.

Even as Belalcázar fought a war of extermination in the south, Quesada, with loot and pillage the goal, set off for the interior from Santa Marta in a two-pronged advance. Two hundred men in five ships under the command of Diego Hernández Gallego were to overcome the torrent of the Bocas de Ceniza and fight their way up the Magdalena. Quesada would go overland, through jungle and swamp, leading a force of nine hundred men and eighty-five horses. It was not a good idea. All of the lower Magdalena, from Santa Marta to what is today Tamalameque, was the land of the Chimila, a people said to be as "numerous as ants, as fierce as lions." As the Spaniards advanced, they were constantly harassed by native warriors, who darkened the sky with arrows and poisoned darts. The attackers came out of nowhere, like shadows, only to thrust their *chonta* spears and slip away into the forest. Those few who stood their ground were a fearsome sight. All were naked, their bodies stained with achiote, their faces painted in red, white, and black, each man adorned with a great crown of heron feathers.

Quesada's soldiers and their horses died by the day, if not killed by the Chimila, then taken by caimans, struck by poisonous snakes, bitten by deadly insects, devoured in their sleep by jaguars, or killed after falling into hidden traps, pits lined by the Chimila with sharpened stakes soaked in venom. Having exhausted their limited supplies within weeks, and with no knowledge of the abundance of the lands through which they trudged, the Spaniards were soon reduced to eating a thin gruel of wild roots boiled with boot leather. Men, delirious for want of salt, fought each other for the flesh of those who had already perished.

The small fleet did not fare much better. All but two of the brigantines sank in the Magdalena estuary. The survivors, constantly alert to native attacks, inched their way upriver, the men tormented by caimans and clouds of mosquitoes, as they hacked their way through dense jungles, pulling the ships against the current. Unlike the ghostlike and emaciated troops serving under Quesada, those fighting the river were at least well fed. Early accounts describe back eddies so rich and abundant that fish could be caught by hand, or simply lifted out of the water with baskets. Turtles were so plentiful on the lower Magdalena that later travelers described them as obstacles to navigation. One chronicler, Fray Pedro Simón, reported that on a river journey of but thirteen days, his party, scattered in ten small vessels, gathered ninety-one thousand turtle eggs.

Still, the going was excruciatingly slow. Having left the coast in early April, they did not reach the native settlement of Tamalameque until July, and not until October did they stumble to a rendezvous with Quesada's men at La Tora, the location today of Barrancabermeja. What happened next is uncertain, but most accounts suggest that Quesada, having recruited most of Gallego's men to his cause, replacing his dead, wisely elected to dispatch the ships with skeletal crews back to Santa Marta, a journey that retraced in mere days what had taken the men weeks to achieve running against the current. Quesada then turned his attention to conquest.

La Tora turned out to be a major center of exchange that attracted indigenous traders from throughout the basin: Panche, who dominated the valley upriver as far as Honda, but also Zenú from the west, Malibú from the wetlands of the great depression, and Muisca, who came out of the highlands all the way down to the Magdalena to barter emeralds and salt blocks for cotton, gold, conch shells, and snails, *hayo* and lime, fish hooks, feathers, butterflies, and even children to sacrifice to the gods. Trade implied peace, and such was the atmosphere of goodwill at La Tora that the highland Muisca named the river the Yuma, or Río del País Amigo, the river of friendship.

When Quesada saw the Muisca finery, exquisite gold ornaments and blankets intricately woven from the purest of cotton and wool, he decided immediately to abandon the river and make his way to their kingdom in the clouds. Setting out to the east, he and his men entered the forests of the Panche, a people, he discovered, willing to trade gold for human flesh. They also encountered the Muzo, by repute cannibals who ate their own dead. All did not go well. Thirty-six Spaniards died. Had Quesada not learned of a native route, the Camino de Opón, all of them might well have perished. Instead they were able, difficult as it was for the horses, to climb slowly out of the torrid lowland forests, eventually reaching the verdant savannahs of Bogotá, which Quesada claimed in the name of his king on August 6, 1538.

After the Spaniards' passage through the swamps and jungles of the Magdalena, the lands of the Muisca greeted them with the freshness of the dawn. The valley was exceedingly beautiful, an emerald paradise floating against the backdrop of enormous mountains that scored the skyline. Cultivated fields covered the entire basin; the rich black soils supported an astonishing variety of crops, all of which were new to the Spaniards: yellow and purple potatoes, papayas, *piña*, and *plátano*, *maíz* and quinoa, *arracacha*, *achira*, *aguacate*, *granadilla*, cherimoya, *guama*, *tomate de árbol*, *patata dulce*, *oca*, *mashwa*, and *ulluco*. Even the most modest of native homes had extraordinary workmanship; wooden façades inscribed with complex designs, abstract patterns of the moon and the sun and a host of celestial bodies. Their high, conical thatched roofs were all topped with a central mast, which was stained bright red with plant dyes, achiote and madder root. The temple complexes of the rulers, with their vast patios and ceremonial sanctuaries all encircled by enormous decorated walls, could only be compared, the Spaniards would recall, to the palaces of Troy. They called the domain of the Muisca El Valle de los Alcazares, the Valley of Castles.

A deeply religious people, the Muisca believed in a single creator, Chiminigagua, the source of light and the progenitor of the sun and the moon and all the stars. The first human was a woman, who rose from a lake to the north of Tunja holding in her hand a small boy, who grew to be her husband, the father of their five children, the primordial ancestors of the Muisca. All of this was remembered in daily practice. In every home there was a shrine, and each man and woman possessed a personal idol, an intermediary to the gods that was never out of reach. Men would bring their idols to the fields, rest beside them at night, carry them into battle to fight with sword in one hand, and a conduit to the divine held aloft in the other.

The land itself was perceived as being sacred, a vast and expansive temple, with certain forests and lakes consecrated to the divine such that not a tree was allowed to be cut, nor a drop of water removed. On auspicious occasions priests would lead great processions to these natural sanctuaries and make offerings of gold at the hermitages, tossing emeralds into the sacred lakes: Guatavita, Guasca, Siecha, Teusacá, and Ubaque. When a person of prominence died, the body was wrapped in the finest of woven cloth, but only after the entrails had been removed and the body cavity filled with gold and precious stones.

Like the Arhuaco and Kogi today, whose languages are Chibchan in origin, the Muisca were guided by a powerful priesthood, the training for which was austere in the extreme. Young boys acquired priestly status through their mother's brother. The training consumed twelve years of empowerments, after which the initiate, ears and nose ceremonially pierced, would be gifted with a calabash, a *poporo* containing *cal*, powdered lime derived from precious shells gathered at the sea. The lime facilitates the release of the small amount of stimulant found in coca, or *hayo*. The priest would consume these sacred leaves every day for the rest of his life, along with tobacco, and at times datura and *yopo*, seeds of a forest tree containing the most powerful hallucinogenic agent known, a tryptamine that does not distort reality as much as dissolve it. Once ordained, the Muisca priests remained celibate, living on a modest diet with very little sleep, drawing their own blood as a sacrament, as they balanced all of the forces of the natural world and the universe beyond.

In the temples, the priests also oversaw the well-being of those destined to be fed to the sun: war captives and slaves, children of distant tribes, and even the scions of the most prominent Muisca

families. To have a child offered to the gods implied a personal loss
but also a gift of grace, an act certain to elevate the victim into the
realm of the divine, and the surviving family to the highest levels of
honor, status, and prestige within the culture. Once consecrated,
capable of speaking directly with the sun, those destined to be sacrificed were not permitted to touch the ground. Each ate only from
their own bowls, food sprinkled with gold. Their deaths as offerings marked both recognized ceremonial occasions and moments of
transition and peril: the sowing and harvesting of fields, the loss of a
ruler, the departure of an army to war. In times of drought, Muisca
priests threw ashes into the sky to generate clouds and then climbed
to the highest summits to sacrifice children to the rising sun, removing their hearts and viscera and severing their heads to anoint all
the east-facing altar stones with blood. The bodies of the sanctified
dead were left as food for the divine.

On first contact, the Muisca had little to fear from Quesada and
his soldiers. Of the more than nine hundred men who had set out
with him from the coast, a mere 166 survived. Nearly all were feverish, recovering from wounds, or, at best, severely depleted by the
long march up from the Magdalena. The Muisca were a million
strong. Their lands, the size of modern-day Belgium, were divided
into two main provinces, each led by a separate leader. The cacique
of Bogotá could field an army of at least sixty thousand men, fully
equipped with spears, arrows, wooden shields, and swords. Tunja,
the smaller but wealthier of the two chieftains, both in gold and
emeralds and the fertility of the land, had a smaller force of forty
thousand. Initially, the Muisca believed that the Spaniards were
themselves the children of the sun and the moon, sent by the creator
to punish them for their sins. Their word for the invaders was *uchies*,
from *usa*, meaning "sun," and *chía*, meaning "moon."

What unfolded over the following months was the story of the
conquest: a Spanish force of just eight score men, along with dis-
gruntled local recruits, confronting a combined Muisca army of one
hundred thousand. Andalusian steel against weapons of wood, as
native foot soldiers attacked armored horses in displays of courage
and gallantry as quixotic and hopeless as would be the sacrifices of
foot soldiers today taking on the full power of a modern tank. The

Spaniards were merciless and cruel, not just by nature but by strategic design; their tactics had been conceived to shatter morale and leave their enemies psychologically broken. Through all of 1537 and the first months of 1538, Quesada and his force laid waste to the Muisca kingdom, defiling the temples, burning homes, violating the women. In desperation, native priests climbed to the highest mountain escarpments to fling their own newborns into the void as offerings for the Spaniards to eat, with the hope that such sacrifices might appease the anger of these devils that had descended from the sky to destroy their world.

The gods did nothing, and the Spaniards marched from triumph to triumph. On August 6, 1538, Quesada established Santa Fe de Bogotá as the capital of a new kingdom, Nuevo Reino de Granada, named in honor of the city in Andalucía where he had studied law. Often described as the one intellectual among a small army of rogues and adventurers, Quesada, like so many leading Spaniards, remained obsessed with legalities, even in the midst of carnage and conquest. Thus, having taken possession of all Muisca lands in the name of his sovereign emperor, Charles V, he officially resigned his commission, formally severing his obligations to his superior, Pedro Fernández de Lugo, who remained in Santa Marta awaiting news of the expedition. He then called for an immediate election that would anoint him captain general, granting him complete and independent authority over the vanquished.

Even as Quesada consolidated his power and took measure of his loot, a pile of precious objects high enough to conceal a mounted horseman, gold and emeralds that in value would rival the riches taken by Pizarro in his conquest of Peru, disturbing news came to him from the south. From quite different ends of the known world, not one but two other Spanish expeditions had already reached the lands of the Muisca, arriving some months before Quesada; this suggested that their claims might take precedence over his. One was led by Sebastián de Belalcázar, whose quest for El Dorado, as we have seen, had begun six months before in Quito. In command of the other party was a German, Nicolás Federmann. Working for a syndicate of bankers with ties to the Spanish Crown, Federmann had marched south from Venezuela, crossing the vast and empty grasslands of the eastern Llanos. After reaching farther south than any explorer before him, Federmann had turned west toward the flank of the Andes, then thrust into the mountains, lured by the same tales of El Dorado that had fired the ambitions of Quesada and his men. The one key difference was timing. Federmann and his men, 170 altogether, all half-starved and half-mad, had reached the upland valleys of the Muisca fully three years earlier.

Quesada had no choice but to call for an official parlay. The three ragtag armies came together on what is now the savannah of Bogotá. Belalcázar's men, plump with pillage, having eaten their way north through the rich upper basin of the Magdalena, appeared almost regal in their purple tunics, all fringed in gold and bedecked with jewels. Quesada's command, fresh from their victories over the Muisca, had gone native; most wore *mantas* of cotton or wool. Those serving under the feverish Federmann appeared as savages, gaunt and skeletal, still dressed in rags and animal skins, as if after three years they had yet to discover the bounty of the lands they had so earnestly claimed.

At first there was an awkward standoff, with each party eyeing the others with suspicion and murderous contempt. All had endured impossible agonies. Each had willed El Dorado into being. All had come for gold, and only some would find it. Conquest was a zero-sum game. Then, by all accounts, the tension dissolved in an instant as Federmann broke into laughter, overwhelmed by the absurdity and irony of their situation; the three would be conquerors of the same kingdom, each having arrived at the ends of the earth by different paths, all seduced by a legend that was just a story, a myth, a fantasy conceived by the fates to test the minds and souls of men. No one was pleased, but as both Quesada and Belalcázar also began to laugh, a wave of relief came over the men, who knew that no blood would flow that day.

Quesada persuaded his rivals to return with him to the coast, to Cartagena, and thence to Spain, where each would be free to present his claims and make his case before the king. Federmann and Belalcázar agreed. Charging their men with the mission of bringing civilization to the Muisca, the three leaders departed, retracing Quesada's path to the sea. What had been a journey of eleven months from the coast to the heights of Bogotá, they managed to compress into twelve days, reaching Santa Marta well before the waning of the first moon. In July 1539, from Cartagena, they sailed together for Spain.

Meanwhile, the fury of those Spaniards left behind on the heights of Bogotá was unleashed on the Muisca. Men and women everywhere were tortured to reveal the location of mines, only to be murdered for failing to deliver impossible quotas. Resistance provoked slaughter. The ruthless suppression of a final rebellion in 1541 marked the beginning of the end, as the Muisca culture slipped away, with the language itself disappearing by the early eighteenth century.

An eyewitness to the fate of the Muisca was a humble priest, Fray Jerónimo de San Miguel, who shared his dismay in a letter written to his king, dispatched from Santa Fe de Bogotá in the early months of 1550. His hope was to influence a debate sanctioned by the pope that would have enormous consequences for Spanish policies in the New World. As Bartolomé de las Casas, the king's official "protector of the Indians," mounted a theological defense of the rights of native people, he was countered by Juan Ginés de Sepúlveda's assertion that natives were by nature less than human. Fray Jerónimo, who was clearly in the camp of Las Casas, wrote of what he had seen in the first years of Spanish domination:

> And first I wish to say that in this kingdom . . . such vast and profound cruelty has been committed that if I did not know it to be unmistakably true, I would never believe that a Christian heart could conceive of such cruel and fierce inhumanity. There is no torment or cruel treatment that has not been inflicted onto these sad and miserable natives by those who pride themselves on being your Highness's faithful subjects. They have burnt some natives alive, and cut off hands, nose and tongue and other members of others, with great cruelty. Many others they have hanged, both men and women. They have thrown natives to the dogs, cut

off breasts of women and committed cruelties such that the
very thought of these acts would make anyone who is a little
bit Christian tremble.

In the end, none of the three adventurers who came together
to decide the fate of the Muisca civilization would be rewarded
with the governorship of the lands they all so ruthlessly coveted. In
Seville, Quesada would become entangled in a web of legal assaults
that soon exhausted what wealth he had brought from the Indies.
He would return to the New World, only to die in poverty in 1579,
his body ravaged by leprosy. Belalcázar also faced legal challenges,
launched by a conspiracy of bitter rivals. He ended up in a Spanish
prison, and by the time he returned to the Americas he was broken
and humiliated, overwhelmed by suffering; he would die in Cartagena in 1551. Federmann was the first to perish, at sea in 1542,
taken by a storm that shattered his ship. None of them realized
their dreams. Each died in disgrace and misery. As warriors, they
had destroyed so much, but as men they created little.

The morning was glorious as we rode away from El Cedro. The sun
was bright, and the cool air smelled of dust and stones washed by
rain, and *manzanito*, eucalyptus, and pine, mixed with the scent of
grasses, ferns, and all the common herbs and shrubs of Colombian
mountain trails, buddleias and alders, *mortiño* and great thickets of
mora, hedgerows of eupatoriums and lantana. Having crossed the
Río Magdalena the previous afternoon to reach the farm, we had
the river on our right; the route still carried us along the flank of
the Cordillera Central. At the La Junta bridge, we crossed the Río
Ovejeras, a surging mountain stream joining the Magdalena from
the west. The elevation was seventy-four hundred feet.
    We had come down nearly a vertical mile from our highest
point on the traverse, and as the morning faded toward noon, the
sun became hot. The horses leaned into the day. Looking back, the
great cleft in the Macizo that we had followed from the heights was
wrapped in cloud, its slopes dense with vegetation. The trail ahead
ran indifferently through pastures and across streams, rising up steep

tracks deeply eroded by generations of mule and horse traffic, only to fall away into another draw to cross yet another stream. Some hours passed before we finally crossed back over the Magdalena and once again found ourselves in the Cordillera Oriental. Walking the horses, we clambered up one final brutal ascent, reaching Alto Quinchana, which seemed in the moment to be the very top of the world. From there it was a gentle ride along a forested ridge that soon opened to reveal the entire Quinchana Valley. Already the river had grown, swollen by scores of small brooks and three significant affluents: the Lambedulce, Las Barbas, and El Santuario. On foot, we had only covered perhaps twenty-five miles, but in that short distance, the Magdalena had fallen some sixty-five hundred feet.

The *trocha* stayed high until reaching and traversing a precipitous slope leading to a series of switchbacks that zigzagged down to the river. By late afternoon, we were across the Barandillas bridge, our tired horses slowly clip-clopping their way along the still and eerily quiet streets of Puerto Quinchana, the first town in Huila. While waiting for transport, we ate in a local restaurant, then rested along the roadside. Quinchana had long been a place of killings and kidnappings, with a FARC presence strong enough to ensure that most everyone had, at one time or another, been swept up in army or paramilitary reprisals. Some have called the town haunted, a landscape of ghosts where people survived only by cultivating a passion for silence. Driving out of town toward San Agustín, I saw a small girl at the door of the shuttered church, playing with a butterfly she had somehow tethered to a yellow thread.

San Agustín

Tales of the Spanish conquest invariably recall Pizarro's exploits in Peru or the adventures of Hernán Cortés and his men as they sacked the Aztec capital of Tenochtitlán in 1521. Curiously, the equally dramatic events that unfolded in Colombia in those very years tend to be overlooked, dismissed by history as if a sideshow, which is rather odd. The geography of the northwest corner of South America presented, if anything, far greater physical challenges than either Peru or Mexico. Pizarro engaged the forces of the Inca simply by walking across the beaches at Tumbes in 1532, his first landfall. Quesada and his men endured hell, long before even reaching the lands of the Muisca in 1537. And for all the wealth that came out of Peru, it was Colombia that sent the most gold to fill the coffers of the Spanish Crown, along with emeralds and precious stones by the sackful. Certainly, in the early years, as Spain consolidated its victories and tried to make sense of the peoples and lands it had vanquished, Peru got the better press. What transpired in Nueva Granada was ultimately told in important early works such as Juan Rodríguez Freyle's *El carnero,* his account of the destruction of the Muisca, published in 1638, and in the classic general histories of the conquest by Pedro Simón, *Noticias historiales de tierra firme en las Indias Occidentales* (1626), and Lucas Fernández de Piedrahíta,

Historia general de las conquistas del Nuevo Reino de Granada, which appeared in 1676.

But, in general, such chroniclers were relatively few and they came later, whereas in Peru they existed by the score and from the earliest years. In the sixteenth century alone, major works were written by Juan de Betanzos (1551), José de Acosta (1553), Francisco López de Gómara (1553), Agustín de Zárate (1555), Juan de San Pedro (1560), Juan de Matienzo (1567), Hernando de Santillán (1563), Fernando de Montesinos (1570), Juan Polo de Ondegardo (1571), Pedro Sarmiento de Gamboa (1572), Cristóbal de Molina (1575), Diego Cabeza de Vaca (1586), Diego Dávila Brizeno (1586), Niculoso de Fornee (1586), Pedro Cieza de León (1590), and Martín de Murúa (1590).

The Peruvian literature of the seventeenth century was more temperate, but no less prolific. The contributions came not only from Spanish scholars such as Francisco de Ávila (1608), Diego González Holguín (1608), José de Arriaga (1621), Vasco de Contreras y Valverde (1650), Bernabé Cobo (1653), and many others, but also from a new generation, born in the Americas and forged by the very amalgam of worlds that their books described, men like Titu Cusi Yupanqui (1570), Garcilaso de la Vega (1609), and Felipe Guamán Poma de Ayala (1613).

Garcilaso's worshipful, even mystical account, *Royal Commentaries of the Incas and General History of Peru,* had enormous influence, inspiring in particular the American historian William Prescott, author of *The History of the Conquest of Mexico* (1843) and *A History of the Conquest of Peru* (1847). Widely read in Europe and the United States, heralded as classics upon publication, Prescott's books, through their very success, helped promote, intentionally or not, a false narrative that effectively excluded Colombia from the great saga of the Spanish conquest.

Hiram Bingham, in particular, was heavily influenced by Prescott, and his meteoric rise to fame in the wake of his discovery of Machu Picchu, a site well known at the time to local farmers, offers another clue as to why the drama of Colombia's prehistory has been overshadowed. The early chroniclers in Colombia rarely if ever encountered monumental ruins certain to fire their imaginations, as they did in both Mexico and Peru. Such sites existed in Colombia but remained hidden. Ciudad Perdida, the lost city of the Tairona in the Sierra Nevada de Santa Marta, was discovered by looters, or *huaqueros*, only in 1972. Archaeologists did not begin work until 1976. Constructed fully 650 years before Machu Picchu, Teyuna, as it is known to the Arhuaco and Kogi, is as dramatic a monument as any to be found in the Americas.

Surpassing even the wonder of Ciudad Perdida, both in scale and significance, is San Agustín, the most extensive and mysterious of all archaeological sites in Colombia. It too, and again for reasons lost in the mists of memory, was never found by the early Spaniards. Not until 1758, fully 222 years after Sebastián de Belalcázar had marched his small army across the Macizo Colombiano, his attention deflected by his obsession with El Dorado, would letters reach church leaders in Bogotá describing fields of massive megalithic statues, demonic and otherworldly. Friar Juan de Santa Gertrudis, who filed the reports, had been traveling on foot from his lowland mission among the Andaquí to Bogotá, along the traditional trade route that crossed the headwaters of the Magdalena, linking the jungle to the interior of the country. As he passed through the hamlet of San Agustín, at the time just a cluster of five mud huts, the local cleric told him of the strange stones. What Santa Gertrudis discovered upon investigation shook him to the core. The statues, to his eye, clearly depicted mitered bishops in pontifical garb, and they were undoubtedly Franciscans. Yet the Order of Saint Francis had not been established until 1209, and these monuments, half-buried in the ground, covered in lichen and other plant growth, were clearly much older. What's more, it was well known that until the arrival of the Spaniards, the Indians had lacked metal tools. This left only one haunting possibility. The only one capable of carving such stones was the very demon whose essence the fearsome images so clearly invoked. Friar Juan de Santa Gertrudis realized, to his horror, that he was standing quite literally in the devil's own workshop.

If later visitors and investigators offered more reasoned explanations, all were equally speculative. In 1797 Francisco José de Caldas visited the site and, to his immense credit, made no attempt to interpret or explain anything. He simply left in awe, astonished by works of art about which, he ventured, nothing might ever be known. Others who studied the site in the early years often distorted scientific understanding, projecting onto the megaliths fanciful theories that took on the authority of orthodoxy, simply because there was no one present to challenge the underlying assumptions. More responsible scholars limited their work to the massive task of surveying the site and registering the more than five hundred figures that were scattered across the landscape.

In 1825 two noted antiquarians from Lima, Swiss-born Johann Jakob von Tschudi and his native colleague and companion, Mariano Eduardo de Rivero, explored San Agustín, and in 1851 they published the first illustrations of the megaliths in a lavish portfolio otherwise dedicated to the monuments of pre-Columbian Peru. Two years later the Italian geographer Agustín Codazzi issued a preliminary inventory of the statues. Not until 1911, however, did the megaliths finally come to the attention of the world, unveiled in a series of photographs at the International Congress of Americanists in London by the German geographer Karl Theodor Stöpel. A surge of interest resulted in a fully equipped archaeological expedition, led by Konrad Theodor Preuss, which set out for Colombia in 1913.

It was not a trivial passage. Just to reach San Agustín required a twelve-day journey by steamer up the Río Magdalena to Honda, and from there a five-day trip by mule to Neiva, through a hot and barren landscape. Though not more than a hundred miles beyond Neiva, the wooded valleys and northern flanks of the Macizo Colombiano had not been colonized until the late nineteenth century. It, too, remained remote and wild country. The march south from Neiva consumed another three days. By the time Preuss and his small team reached San Agustín, he no longer questioned why so few had beheld the wonders of the ancient site. "One feels lost here," he wrote home, "as on a dead-end street. Perhaps to this is due the oblivion in which the antiquities of this region have remained." The expedition remained in the field for three months, photographing and taking precise measurements of the monuments, making molds of some, all the time doing their best to ignore the rain, the damp cold at night, the glaring heat by day, the clouds of insects, the lack of food, the malarial fevers that rose in the night only to break deceptively with the dawn.

Whether it was the team's general state of misery or its singular focus on the megaliths, their dimensions, imagery, and distribution, Preuss came to see everything through the lens of death. Thus began a long academic tradition of interpreting the entire site of San Agustín as one vast burial ground, a monumental necropolis of an ancient civilization, the physical traces of which, aside from their burials, had been swept from the face of the earth. This perspective echoed that of the many tribal peoples who lived in the region after the collapse of the civilization responsible for the great monuments. Local people to this day know the Magdalena as it flows through the ancient hills of San Agustín as the Guaca-Hayo, *el río de la tumbas*, the river of the tombs.

None of this made a great deal of sense to the renowned Colombian anthropologist Gerardo Reichel-Dolmatoff, or to his wife, Alicia Dussán, a fine archaeologist in her own right. When they first visited San Agustín, their eyes went not to the ground, the burial tombs so dramatically aligned across the site, but to the horizon: the distant heights of the Macizo, the fertile hills and ridgelines that ran away to the north, the gorge that so quickly became a formidable canyon as the Magdalena cleaved the Cordilleras and began its run to the sea. The entire complex of San Agustín, they noted, consisted of hundreds of monumental statues, all anthropomorphic, sprawling across more than a thousand square miles, embracing both banks of the Río Magdalena. In aspect and scale, they might rival, as had been suggested, the great statues of Easter Island, but their symbolism was totally rooted in the Americas, the Amazon in particular. That the site was situated on the very forested slopes traversed by the Río Magdalena, the mother of all rivers, was for Reichel-Dolmatoff the key to understanding the genesis of the entire complex.

The notion that San Agustín was somehow isolated, he noted, both in time and space, reflected only the perception of those scholars, foreigners for the most part, who had struggled so hard to reach it. At six thousand feet, it was in fact ideally situated between fertile highlands and the abundance of the tropical lowlands, and readily

serviced by both, along trails that in mere days traversed an altitudinal range of more than ten thousand feet, a rarity in Colombia.
Low and easily accessible passes lead to the Ríos Caquetá and Putumayo to the south and east, the Cauca and Patía to the west, and to
the northeast the Guaviare, which ultimately reaches the Orinoco.
Heading south, the same trails that carried us across the Macizo,
as well as other routes leading across Puracé to the Cauca Valley,
continue all the way to the Ecuadorian frontier and beyond. In no
way isolated, San Agustín was the locus of a complex and extensive
network of trade routes that spanned all of southern Colombia.

The valley itself was highly productive. Warm, humid air rising from the lowlands and meeting the cool winds of the mountains condensed into rain, which fell throughout the year onto rich
volcanic soils, dark and fertile. The well-watered fields supported
great harvests of *hayo*, yuca and sweet potatoes, fruit trees of a dozen
varieties, and, of critical significance, not one but two maize crops
a year. Only such abundance could have generated the surplus food
upon which the entire enterprise of San Agustín was dependent.

Once again Reichel-Dolmatoff did not get lost in the details.
He saw all around him an entire landscape transformed by labor,
hills leveled for burials, massive earthworks constructed to serve as
the foundations of sacred sites, roads reaching out to distant quarries. All of it implied a highly stratified culture of immense sophistication, with a central authority powerful enough to mobilize and
support workers in the thousands, and a religious mandate sufficiently persuasive to compel men, even under duress, to sacrifice
their lives, exhausting their physical bodies, in order to drag massive stones across impossible distances that they might be erected as
spirit guardians to provide comfort in death for the privileged few,
the very exploiters of their lives and labor.

This broader vision in no way diminished the wonder and mystery of the megaliths. To the contrary, it merely suggested that envisioning the prehistory of San Agustín through the study of its burial
sites alone is as challenging as would be an attempt to reconstruct
European civilization, should only its cemeteries survive the ravages
of nuclear war. Indeed, as Reichel-Dolmatoff revealed in all of his
studies, it is only through an appreciation of the broader geographi-

cal and cultural contexts that one can even begin to understand what these enigmatic and monumental statues may be trying to say.

With Reichel-Dolmatoff's insights very much in mind, I spent several days wandering through the noted features of the archaeological park, laid out and carefully labeled for the many tourists who are finally pouring back into Colombia. Though helpful and essential, the curation errs somewhat in suggesting, or at least implying by its design, that each of these named concentrations—Las Mesitas, El Tablón, El Cerro de la Pelota, and others—stands alone, as if outdoor museums, elegantly situated in grass clearings carved from the surrounding forests. A broader view reveals that there are in fact no features on the entire landscape, nothing to be seen this side of the horizon in every direction, that does not show some sign of pre-Columbian occupation: the slight shadows in the ground of earthworks, house sites, and ancient fields, the potsherds and obsidian flakes readily found in the wake of virtually every footstep.

Across the Río Magdalena at Isnos, a large horseshoe-shaped mound, clearly of human origins, rises to reveal a dramatic vista to the northwest, toward a forked hill known as Cerro de la Horqueta. The slopes of the *cerro*, all the land skirting its base, and indeed everything that can be seen was at one time worked by whoever occupied the site. The name, El Alto de los Ídolos, suggests that the entire complex served a purely religious function, which may not be true. On the western arm are six massive tombs, enormous slabs each containing a monolithic sarcophagus. The eastern side features freestanding statues and burial mounds. But these ceremonial features, dramatic as they are, occupy but a small fraction of the surface of an enormous space that may well have supported other societal needs. Excavations in just one of several middens revealed a thick mantle of debris several feet deep. A single one-square-yard plot contained in but eight inches of stratigraphy more than fifteen thousand potsherds, each the story of a life, a memory of a distant morning when water was drawn from a well or a bowl of frothy *chicha* was passed into the hands of a warrior by a loving wife—each, in short, a window onto the full complexity of the civilization that moved heaven and earth to create this place.

Some of the most dramatic megaliths are found just two miles outside the town of San Agustín at a site known as Las Mesitas. There are actually three concentrations of monuments here, labeled A, B, and C. At each, the burial tombs have been reconstructed and the interpretive information, though well displayed, remains superficial, indicating how little we know even today. The basic architecture, however, is self-evident. At the center of each of the barrows is an underground chamber built of huge vertical slabs of stone, and within each tomb are the large and imposing statues that once served as guardians of the dead. As with all funerary traditions, the ultimate goal was to wrestle with eternity and come out on top.

In every case, the bodies at San Agustín were entombed in lateral chambers, ensuring that the remains did not come into contact with the earth. Each chamber was excavated at the bottom of a vertical shaft dug from the surface, and blocked off so that the shaft could be filled without dirt falling onto the corpse. Within the actual death vault, the walls were adorned with bright paintings, abstract designs, and human-like figures, and the floor lined with utilitarian finery and precious objects to adorn the body in the afterlife. There was room, too, for wives and slaves, who were buried alive to give comfort to the dead.

Around the tombs, other megaliths stand like sentinels. Some have fallen over; others look as if cast aside by the treasure hunter who long ago plundered the tombs. Carved sometime during the first millennium A.D., though possibly much earlier, they depict animals and demons: eagles with fangs, felines copulating with men, faces emerging from the tails of snakes. In many instances, the figures have cheeks budging with stylized quids of *hayo*. These are the oldest representations of coca and the earliest evidence of the plant's revered status in the ancient civilizations of the Andes.

Some of the megaliths are as much as twelve feet tall and weigh several tons. As for the meaning of the imagery incised into the stone, no one can really say. You can only look and report what you see, much as Reichel-Dolmatoff did in all of his pioneering work in Colombia, confronted, as he so often was, by the unknown. Imprecise and frustrating as this may be, it can also free one's imagination, often in exhilarating ways. Here are my impressions, sketched in a journal many years ago, when I first visited San Agustín, and later cited in my book *One River*:

> The images on the statues, worn and beaten into the stone by a people who had no metal tools, are lurid, monstrous, even frightening. Though captured in time and removed from the cultural context that once gave them meaning, they retain a brooding ferocity, a taut, aggressive power that seems at every moment ready to burst out of the confines of the stone. Some of the monoliths are surprisingly naturalistic: a stout eagle clasping the head of a snake by its beak, toads emerging from enormous boulders. But the majority are phantasmagoric visions of transformation, with the jaguar as the dominant iconographic symbol. There are felines overpowering women, men mutating into cats, and jaguar-toothed rodents dominating men whose genitals are bound by ropes to their waists.
>
> At Mesitas B, I came upon a massive triangular head over seven feet high with enormous bright eyes, a broad smile accentuated with fangs, and two highly stylized protuberances in the cheeks. Again, clear evidence of coca, or *hayo*. The other monolith of note was a six-foot columnar guardian statue, a warrior bearing a club across his chest in one hand and clasping a stone in the other. Above his head loomed a spirit being, protective and domineering. Again, in each of the cheeks was a prominent bulge. It, too, shared the essence of the jaguar, the nostrils flared, the eyes glaring.
>
> Clearly what we are seeing is the essence of the Amazon becoming manifest in the Macizo, a place of disease and a place of healing, brought to the highlands through the imagination of whoever carved these stones. According to any number of Amazonian peoples, the jaguar was sent to the world to test the will and integrity of the first humans. The jaguar can be good or evil; it can create or destroy. The jaguar is the force the shaman must confront. To do so, he takes *yagé*. If he can tame the jaguar, he can direct its power

for good. But if the dark aspect of the wild overcomes, then the jaguar is transformed into a devouring monster, the image of our darkest selves. Either way, human and jaguar become one and the same.

The message for the culture is clear: The jaguar spirit must be mastered if the moral and social order is to be preserved. The wildest of instincts, like the impulses of the natural world, must be curbed if any society is to survive. This may be what these stones are all about. In guarding the dead, the stones of San Agustín reveal what it means to be alive, even as they warn of the consequences of failure. Those who lived here did not have a lot of time or patience for compromise. They knew what they believed and they knew it was true because *yagé*, the sacred plant, revealed it to them.

The dominant motif in all of the megalithic monuments of San Agustín is transformation. The theme recurs throughout the Americas, from ancient civilizations that predated San Agustín, the Chavín and Olmec in particular, to the myriad of living Amazonian cultures of today. The protagonist is always the shaman, a gifted individual who invokes techniques of ecstasy to soar away to distant metaphysical realms to work deeds of supernatural rescue. Under the influence of sacred plants, the shaman can turn into a bird, a jaguar, a harpy eagle. His feline power, according to the Páez, gave birth to thunder. For the Tairona, gold had nothing to do with currency or wealth. It was the living physical manifestation of the divine, the gift of the first shape-shifter, the primordial shaman. In his hands, gold became imbued with all the numinous power and energy of the sun, the source of eternal life. The Tukano say that even should a shaman be devoured by serpents, he will always emerge whole, transformed, elevated to a higher state of insight and awareness, capable of healing the sick, giving comfort and reassurance to the dying, guiding the dead and granting them eternal life.

Perhaps this is what the people of San Agustín had in mind. Not those working like beasts in the quarries perhaps, but those in power, enjoying the luxury of idle time to contemplate their mortality. As they gave the orders for the construction of such elaborate tombs, surely their goal was to protect and preserve the bodies of the political and religious elite just long enough that they might live on, carried away upon the wings of trance and transformation, to achieve everlasting life.

After I'd spent several hours in the sun wandering from tomb to tomb, thinking only of the dead, it was a delight to finally head into the cool shade of the forest. The three concentrations of monuments at Las Mesitas are all connected by a trail that leads down to the Lavapatas, a beautiful mountain stream, broad and perfectly clear, that flows over a smooth bed of dark stone. Every surface is decorated with intricate motifs, images of snakes, lizards, and monkeys, depictions of human forms, and abstract designs that serve also as channels that lead the water into square pools carved deeply into the rock, allowing it to tumble over effigies, or cleanse the surface of stones. A lovely covered bridge crosses the stream, providing a perfect vantage over the entire site. From this elevated perspective, the many designs and patterns, shapes and troughs, curious when seen from the shore, suddenly fuse into one glorious celebration of the sacred, the living essence of life, pure water flowing over the spiritual dreams of these ancient men and women, whoever they were.

Here, carved into the bedrock of a surging stream, was the antidote to death. A place of life that gave meaning to the entire site plan of Las Mesitas, built as it was on a flat man-made plain bordered by waterways that come together to flow, as all the waters of San Agustín do, into the Magdalena. This sense of the river as creative essence, a source of joy, a living inspiration, came back to us later in the afternoon when we scrambled along the stone banks at El Estrecho, a cleft in the earth just upriver from San Agustín where the entire Magdalena, having burst out of the Macizo, is chastened by volcanic stone, forced to run for a quarter mile through a chasm not six feet across. If the river was a child, this was a form of discipline. At El Estrecho, the Río Magdalena seems, if only for that short stretch, to be under the thumb of a schoolmaster, which perhaps explains why the many young boys and girls, picnicking with their families, radiated such joy and delight as the river finally escaped the rocks and continued its rambunctious run to the sea.

After leaving El Estrecho, we made one more stop, perhaps the most revealing of all. In the dark hills and amid the ruins of San Agustín, the Río Magdalena is ever present, yet rarely seen. The forests are dense, the lay of the land is in places confusing, and all the towns and settlements are aligned with the roadways. One major site, however, speaks directly to the relationship between those who created the civilization of San Agustín and the river that made all of it possible. The trail to La Chaquira crosses meadows and pastures for a mile or more before falling away steeply to a promontory looking out across a deep chasm, through which flows the Magdalena. It is a stunning sight. Finally, here is the river, exploding out of the country, running away through a dark ravine and all the rolling hills and uplands of Huila.

Overlooking the entire valley, carved into the vertical face of a massive triangular boulder, is a large shamanic figure with saucers for eyes and thin arms elevated on either side of the torso, with wide-open palms facing outward in a gesture of grace. The aspect of the form is benign, thankful, at peace. The thighs are exaggerated, the feet turned out in rest, the lines deeply carved into the midsection accentuating a triangular space in the groin, a focal point of generative power and fertility. The stone faces east, aligned to the point where the rising sun breaks the horizon on the equinox. Another jaguar shaman looks to the north, the stone carved to display prominently an erect penis. A receptive female figure looks south. Other rocks are decorated with animals of both the lowland forests and the highest mountain walls. Far below, climbing out of the gorge, is the faint outline of the ancient trail that once linked La Chaquira to El Alto de los Ídolos. Created by the very people of San Agustín responsible for the burial tombs and all the monuments to death, La Chaquira is, by contrast, a celebration of life, effigies of procreation eternally watching over the departure of a river that was for them what it surely could be for all Colombians today, el Río Grande de la Magdalena, the river of life.

Valley of Sorrows

In Colombia, every town tells a story. William and I reached Timaná, nestled in the foothills of the Macizo not fifty miles downriver from San Agustín, late in the day as golden light fell upon the tiled roofs and whitewashed walls of a settlement that is home to thirty thousand, with a history that reaches back to 1538. San Calixto, the oldest cathedral in Huila, soars over the main square, testament to the triumph and enduring power of the Catholic faith. Shadowing its red-brick façade is the canopy of a massive ceiba, planted at the very center of the plaza to commemorate the final liberation of the slaves in 1851 by President José Hilario López, a progressive leader who also supported a free press, agrarian reform, and the separation of church and state. With limbs the width of trunks, and great spreading branches that reach like serpents to and beyond all corners of the square, the tree stands for all the liberal impulses that in Colombia have always opposed the conservative dictates of the church.

Together, sacred tree and glorious cathedral embody the political fault line that has long haunted the nation. It began as a schism between revolutionaries imbued with the secular and scientific ideals of their age and a landed gentry that joined the rebellion against Spain, motivated not by dreams of the Enlightenment but by the opportunity to displace the regal regime with themselves, a new privileged class anointed by God and destined to lead a national government faithful always to the clergy, tradition, and the past. Over time, as rivers of blood flowed, the two sides, Liberal and Conservative, red and blue, came to see each other not as political adversaries but as mortal enemies, such that regions of the country tainted with the hue of one party would live in anticipation and constant fear of retribution from the agents of the other. The weakness of the federal state, together with a tortuous mountain landscape that hindered transportation and communications, encouraged strong regional identities even as it empowered local strongmen only too willing to exploit this reciprocity of hatred.

In the wake of independence, Colombia would endure eight civil wars and fourteen regional conflicts in eighty years. Between the spasms of violence, the two sides would forge pacts, but they never fully reconciled. If the Conservatives fought alongside the army, the Liberals would form their own militias. If the army stood with the Liberals, the Conservatives fought against both. Wars began for the most spurious of reasons. In 1885, a short but bloody affair remembered as La Batalla de La Humareda started simply because the president at the time named a Conservative to serve as director of the National Library, and another as ambassador to London. La Guerra de los Supremos flared in 1839, with no meaningful results save the total destruction of the fleet of Magdalena riverboats, including the *Unión*, a steamship commissioned in Glasgow that had cost the country more than a million dollars.

Some of the wars might seem almost comic, had the consequences not been so dire. In 1899, a collapse in coffee prices in the Liberal bastion of Santander drew the attention of the *cafeteros* to the excessive expenses of a Conservative president in Bogotá too old and frail even to sign his own name. A state of emergency was declared, and the army moved on Santander, arresting all those "disaffected from the government," meaning all Liberals. A Liberal militia of eight thousand went after the Conservatives, who were aligned with the army. Their first move was to seize control of several Magdalena riverboats, two of which, the *Elena* and a dredge known as the *Cristóbal Colón*, immediately crashed, killing all on board, as none of the rebels had the slightest experience at the helm of a ship.

What became known as the War of a Thousand Days continued

for three years, with the two sides literally hacking each other to death, leaving the country in ruins; by the end there were no fewer than eighty thousand dead out of a total population of just four million. The war cost the country five times its national budget, prompting a collapse in the value of the currency that left the peso trading at twenty-two thousand to the dollar, ten thousand times higher than the exchange rate had been in 1889. The loss of Panama was just one lasting casualty of the war. Between 1886 and 1900, one out of every twenty Colombian deaths was caused by violence.

At the foot of the ceiba, in the shade of the plaza, William showed me yet another potent symbol: a solemn monument, the pride of Timaná.

"Ferocity and fury," he said, "the crucible of the nation."

The bronze sculpture portrayed a strong and beautiful woman, black and naked save for a fringe of feathers hung from a string around her waist. In one hand she holds an ax; in the other she lifts aloft the severed head of a Spanish nobleman, Pedro de Añasco, the founder of Timaná. Around the base of the statue was a ring of flowers, blossoms scattered in reverence by the local Páez, who still pay homage to the memory of La Gaitana, a martyr to freedom remembered for but a single day when she took her revenge, before disappearing into the shadows of time.

"No one really knows who she was, yet she is never forgotten. Just watch."

Sure enough, as we lingered on a park bench, an elderly native woman shuffled across the square and placed a small bouquet at the feet of La Gaitana. Facing the statue, with her back to the cathedral, she knelt and furtively made the sign of the cross. I turned to William for an explanation.

Even as Sebastián de Belalcázar in 1538 made his way toward the lands of the Muisca, he remained obsessed with the tenuous line of supply and communication that stretched behind his forces to his distant base in Quito. Approaching the savannah of Bogotá, he dispatched one of his lieutenants, Pedro de Añasco, south with orders to establish at Timaná an outpost that would protect the route through the upper Magdalena to Popayán and beyond.

Living behind a wooden palisade, close to the current site of the modern town, Añasco and his men found themselves constantly harassed by warriors of a dozen nations, all rumored to be cannibals with a preference for Spanish flesh. Masking their concerns, the Spaniards demanded tribute from all caciques and turned to terror to secure tactical advantage over tribes that they, in fact, desperately feared. From some, they accepted great and mysterious gifts of food, only to learn later that the native peoples believed that their enemies had to be fully satiated before being killed if their deaths were to bring honor to either victim or victor.

When a small group of Yalcón led by a young man and his mother delayed a payment assigned by the Crown, the Spanish commander decided to make an example of both of them, seizing the boy and ordering that he be burned alive. The mother escaped, but not before hearing the death wail of her child. Seeking revenge, she took the name Gaitana and rallied all the chiefs in rebellion, men known to history only as Inando, Pionza, Añolongo, and Meco.

In the last months of 1539 the uprising spread like wildfire, bringing into battle all the tribes of the upper Magdalena, the Yalcón, Moguex, and Apirama, from the north the Páez, from the south the Andaquí and Timaná, and from the northeast the formidable Pijao. In a whirlwind of fire and blood, La Gaitana and her army overran the Spanish garrison at Timaná, killing every Spaniard and seizing Pedro de Añasco, whom she tortured piteously. First, she gouged out his eyes. Then, having sliced his face and laced a cord through his cheeks, she dragged him blind and bleeding through the streets of the town, exposed to the scorn and wrath of all, until finally he died, his throat cut and his head severed by her blade. After this, La Gaitana simply disappeared, never to fight again.

The Spaniards unleashed a war of extermination. Aided by the treacherous Cacique Matambo, who betrayed his people for silver, they readily crushed the remnants of the revolt, then moved on to destroy every vestige of indigenous life in the entire upper Magdalena. The Páez would survive, hidden away along the high crests of the Cordillera Central, on the snow flanks of Huila, and in the valley of the river that today bears their name. The Andaquí, originally from Timaná, the hills of San Agustín, and the mountain valleys reaching to the source of the Magdalena, escaped to the east, following the Caquetá into the lowlands, where they were slowly consumed by the forest. By 1851 a mere 630 men, women, and children had survived, from a nation that had once scattered warriors by the hundreds across every flank of the Macizo Colombiano and beyond. Of all the other tribal nations mentioned in the early Spanish documents—the Chumepa, Cambi, Yacua, Otongo, and many others—we know very little, their only legacy being a few place-names appearing still on maps of the country.

The one people that did not slip silently into the darkness of history were the Pijao. Living north of the Páez, along the eastern slopes of the Cordillera Central from La Plata to Ibagué, and north to the territory of the Quimbaya, they were the most feared indigenous group in all of the upper Magdalena. Their skulls deliberately deformed in childhood, they went into battle naked, their bodies painted and adorned with feathers, with breastplates of gold, terrifying nose ornaments, and necklaces of teeth cut from the jaws of their enemies. Women went to war with the men, both armed with spear throwers and slings, wooden clubs, poison darts, and great spears honed from the wood of *chonta* palms. In battle, they always dominated the high ground and launched carefully orchestrated and staged attacks, often at dawn, with terrifying sounds of conch trumpets and drums, horns and the human voice. Prisoners were sacrificed to the gods. Enemies killed in battle were eaten, their skulls kept as trophies, their skin dried and filled with ashes, to be displayed as plunder of war. The Pijao especially valued the heads of both Spanish soldiers and their horses, which they preserved with resins, processing the skins to be stretched to cover the heads of battle drums. With the strength and ease of caimans, they saw no impediment in the Río Magdalena, readily defying its currents, swimming its width, often with a prisoner in each hand. They had nothing but contempt for the whimpering pleas of their victims. Their martial ideal as warriors was to endure without a sign of weakness or pain the torture and dismemberment by wild dogs that capture by the Spaniards invariably implied.

In 1543, the Pijao destroyed the town of Los Ángeles, in the Neiva Valley, and later attacked Ibagué. Twenty years later, they overran and slaughtered the inhabitants of San Vicente; in 1569, they destroyed Villavieja, and in 1577, San Sebastián de la Plata, again killing all of the Spaniards and burning every structure to the ground. In the end, however, they were no match for the forces of the Crown. By 1611, the Spaniards had launched no fewer than forty-eight expeditions against the Pijao, bringing the nation to the edge of extinction. One of the very last to die was a ninety-year-old man who refused to relinquish a wooden idol to the black robes, even as the dogs tore him apart.

By the first decades of the seventeenth century, all native resistance in the upper Magdalena had ended. The homeland of the Páez, it was reported in 1608, was "so desolate that the troops could not find Indians to fight, houses to plunder, or roots or grains to eat." Those indigenous people that remained "went about thin and emaciated until life was ended, for the soldiers saw corpses of people dead of hunger or sickness at every step." As the colonial period began, and the *encomienda* system reduced all natives to servitude, the fate of the surviving indigenous people was to endure a life of suffering: smallpox, massacres, floggings, debt peonage, and imprisonment, all condoned by the benevolent grace of the Christian church.

William was keen to reach La Jagua. I, too, looked forward to meeting his parents and seeing the town where he had been born. Still, as we stumbled north, dropping out of the hills toward the spreading valley, I managed to persuade him to detour off the main highway toward Tarqui, where we dallied on a bridge high over the Magdalena, watching as scores of young boys in a gaggle of laughter defied gravity, launching themselves into the river. We stopped, too, in Altamira, just long enough to visit a small artisanal factory where men fueled great clay ovens with wood while a dozen cheerful women hovered around a long table, molding biscuits made with the flour of *achira*—*Canna edulis*—a specialty of the town and a reminder of how many rare and unusual cultivated plants are to be found in the mountains of southern Colombia.

We arrived in La Jagua just as the sun settled on the far side of the Magdalena. After picking up a few gifts and supplies for the family, we made our way to William's home, a small whitewashed house on the riverfront. A neatly painted wooden door, mint green with yellow trim, opened onto a beautiful courtyard, with a long, furnished patio facing a garden densely planted with fruit trees and medicinal herbs, plantains and yuca, epiphytic ferns and bromeliads, and flowering orchids of a dozen varieties or more. Being one of five boys, with ties to just about everyone in La Jagua, William was immediately buried in the embrace of family; men, women, and children of all ages kept pouring through the door with great gasps of delight. I shook hands at least twice with everyone, and only as the first wave of excitement settled and the crowd parted was I able to identify his parents. I was just saying hello when a cousin swept us onto a sofa, and another appeared with a tray of *tinto* and *aguardiente*, coffee and shot glasses of raw sugarcane liquor. William's mother beamed like the sun. His father stood with evident pride, and I noticed for the first time that he was missing an arm. Both looked very much like the people in the old photographs that hung behind them on the patio wall, generations of the Vargas clan, captured in black and white and sepia, stiff and formal in the way of family portraits in small-town Colombia.

For reasons no one could explain, La Jagua had escaped the spasms of growth that had afflicted virtually every other urban center in the valley. Founded in 1550, upon land that belonged to the Yalcón, the nation of La Gaitana, it remains a settlement of simple houses, cobbled streets, with a small plaza graced by a modest church. The population of some fifteen thousand has since colonial times stayed almost eerily constant. To the west, a sparsely forested floodplain reaches to the river. The Magdalena flows. The clouds gather, and every afternoon the wind blows from both the central and the eastern cordilleras, spinning like a vortex. Spirits abound, and since the time of Francisco José de Caldas, who in 1770 convened a great gathering of herbalists and *curanderos* from all of the Alto Magdalena, the town has been known as a center of sorcery and white magic, famous for its *brujas* and healing arts. It is a place in balance with all the energies of existence, with fertile soils and bountiful waters, mountains and valleys, moonlight and stars.

Just below the town, the Magdalena absorbs a major affluent, the Río Suaza, the crystal river where William spent every afternoon in his youth. He once described himself as a riparian child, in contrast to the truly amphibian people living on the lower Magdalena. The people of the *ciénagas*, the great wetlands, he noted, live immersed by the Magdalena. The river influences every aspect of their lives, from their food to their music, the way they move, even the color of their dreams. The people of La Jagua and the upper Magdalena always keep one foot on the land. They fish without canoes, from the shore, walking and throwing their nets, or *atarrayas*, as they make their way upstream, one eye on the water, another turned back to the land, where spirits linger. William grew up with tales of La Patasola, the one-legged guardian of the forests, a spirit being that sometimes takes the guise of a beautiful woman to lure violators of nature deep into the forest, where she transforms into a monster with eyes of fire and a Medusa head with jaguar teeth ready to rend the flesh and suck the blood of her victims. Is it any wonder, I teased him, that he became a botanist, dedicated to conservation?

Racing the setting sun, we headed for William's favorite swimming hole on the Suaza. As we slipped away from his family, I noticed a historic plaque on the house next door identifying it as having been the home of Francisco José de Caldas. The building was the first thing William bought once he had sufficient money.

"Some say he was born in Popayán," William explained, "but we know Caldas came from here. We can't prove it, but neither can they."

I thought of young Caldas, destined to become Colombia's most illustrious naturalist and scientist, a young man so earnest and disciplined, heading to Bogotá with a mule train laden with leather trunks filled with notebooks and botanical specimens, herbarium sheets, insects and stuffed birds, a collection of minerals and rocks. A solitary scholar infused with the intellectual fire of the age, breath-

lessly seeking an audience with Mutis and then Humboldt, offering
his services to the latter, willing to do anything to join the great
expedition as it made its way south to Popayán and Quito. His wish
came true, but with it came disappointment. Caldas had time for
nothing but science and nature. Humboldt lived life and was astonished to learn that young Caldas was so lacking in personal passion
that he had hired an agent to help him find a spouse. Caldas, for his
part, was appalled that Humboldt insisted on taking time off for fun.
From Ecuador, where they parted ways, Caldas would write in horror, "This man is transforming Quito into a Sodom and Gomorrah
and leading the most dissipated life possible." Caldas returned to
Popayán and, in time, to La Jagua.

William led me along a dirt track that ran through a dry forest
of scrub and frail acacias before turning back to the banks of the
Suaza. For him, every blade of grass along the trail resonated with
a story. Shadows marked the ground where trees had fallen in his
absence. He told of an old man, Argemiro, single and without family, who had taught him all he knew about the river: how to walk
along it, throw a net, how to catch each kind of fish. Though unable
to read or write, Argemiro knew everything: the names and uses of
every plant, how to make masks, costumes, musical instruments, all
the songs and music of the river. Once, William recalled, while they
were camped out by the river, Argemiro made music with just a pig
bladder and a toothpick, sounds that had birds spinning in the trees.

Argemiro was also a healer, as William discovered at the age of
seven when, on a fishing trip, five hours on foot from home, he collapsed on the far bank of the Magdalena, dizzy with fever. Argemiro
cleared away the vegetation, made him a bed in the sand, and slipped
away to the forest; he returned some hours later with a root, which
he crushed and mixed with water. The concoction was impossibly
bitter, but William's fever broke within minutes. William would
later identify the tree as *Acacia farnesiana*, a denizen of dry tropical
forests whose leaves and roots are used throughout Colombia as a
treatment for malaria.

Above all, as William recalled, Argemiro taught him and all the
boys of his generation to have respect for themselves and for the
river. Know its moods, he would say, recognize its power, yield to

its strength, and be thankful for its bounty. For those, like William, too poor to own shoes, Argemiro offered not pity but pride. Those with feet toughened by time, he pointed out, could walk across hot desert stones, crush thorns along forest trails. Besides, he claimed, only fools fish wearing shoes. Only when barefoot, in touch with nature, feeling the way the fish move, knowing their names, *bocachico*, *patalón*, *peje*, *cucha*, *dorado*, could one properly throw the *atarraya*.

William grew especially close to Argemiro, in part because the old man lived next door to his family in the house that had belonged to Caldas. Every day Argemiro found an excuse to turn up at the Vargas table, and always there was food for him. Argemiro never had any money until he sold his house to William, just before passing away. The entire Vargas family was at his side when he died. In William's mind, there was little to distinguish between the scientific brilliance of Caldas and the folk genius of Argemiro. For him, both were mentors, scholars cut from different cloth who nevertheless came to their knowledge and wisdom through a common lens, the direct empirical observation of nature, the very essence of the scientific method.

What William most remembers from his youth was the abundance and variety of fish. When he was eight, he often worked a creek known to have plenty of a small fish, not more than six inches long, with a huge head and prominent lips. They were easy to catch and delicious to eat. For years they were a family staple. Only as William came of age as a scientist and began to travel the country did he realize that nowhere else in Colombia had he encountered such a creature. By chance, some five years ago, he stumbled upon an academic paper that led him to suspect that the species was exceedingly rare. He returned home and collected a specimen. To his astonishment, an ichthyologist, a colleague at his university, identified it as a new species, later described as *Cucha cabezona*. For more than twenty years, William's family had been dining almost every night on an endangered species, endemic to streams of La Jagua and completely unknown to science.

"Since then," he said, "I've gone looking for that fish. I've asked around. People say it's no longer here. Perhaps it is, but if so, it has become very scarce."

Like all fishermen, William looks back to a time of abundance that stands in marked contrast to the depleted river of today. Yet he does so not out of nostalgia but with the eye of a naturalist. He sees the Magdalena as a single ecological system, all driven by a hydrological cycle influenced by climate, rainfall, and the turning of the seasons. With new species of fish still being discovered—eight since 2013 alone—no one really knows how many once thrived in the river, though estimates range from 220 to 290. More than half of these are endemic, found nowhere else in nature. Among those hovering on the brink of extinction are two that not a generation ago commonly graced the dining tables of Colombians, *corocoro* and *bocachico*, the latter long known as the king of the river.

Virtually all of these species follow an annual round dictated by nature and nursed by the ebb and flow of the river. The fish swim upstream in the first half of the year, and with the onset of the rains they spawn, remaining in the river or returning downstream to feed and nurse in the *ciénagas* and wetlands of the lower Magdalena. Block this cycle of life and rebirth, and the consequences for the fishery are dire. And this, of course, is precisely what occurred, quite literally, with the building of the Betania Dam in 1981 and the subsequent construction of El Quimbo, another massive dam which came online in 2015. Located downriver from La Jagua, some thirty miles above the city of Neiva, the Betania Dam had an immediate impact on the entire Magdalena fishery. The annual spawning run, the *subienda*, the wave of life and fecundity that brought natural wealth and prosperity to every inhabitant in the entire Magdalena basin, from the *ciénagas* to the sierra, was shut down, turned off like water at a tap. La Jagua, a town that had lived on fish for all of its history, had to turn to chicken, pork, and beef, even as the people sought new ways to make a living.

The dams are only one cause of the river's agonies. The Magdalena drainage as a whole has lost close to 80 percent of its forest cover, more than half in the last thirty years alone. Erosion darkens its flow, with some 250 million tons of silt and debris each year. Few rivers in the world have been so adversely affected by sediments. Industrial pollution, agricultural runoff, and raw sewage pumped into the river by virtually every municipality in the drainage only compounds the crisis. Every day, more than thirty-two million Colombians go to the bathroom and flush their waste directly into a river that is the vital artery of their nation, the lifeblood of their land, the spiritual fiber of their being.

Fish stocks in the Magdalena have collapsed by 50 percent in thirty years. The overall harvest plunged 90 percent between 1975 and 2008. In less than a decade leading to 1997, the total weight of fish landed for local and regional markets dropped from 2,404 tons to a mere 657. At least nineteen species are facing extinction—as, in an economic sense, are forty-five thousand fishermen, all with families to support. Every day, desperate men do whatever it takes to land fish, defying laws designed to protect the fishery, always with more efficient nets and technologies, legal or not, designed to capture anything that swims, forfeiting the future for the essential needs of today.

Meanwhile, on the banks of the Río Suaza, William, like all of his neighbors, throws his *atarraya* just for the feel of it, an act of nostalgia, with no expectation of catching a fish.

"Fishing in the Alto Magdalena, above the dams," he says, "in the Valle de las Tristezas, the Valley of Sorrows, is a thing of the past."

As we drove away from La Jagua, heading north toward Garzón, William pointed out places he remembered well: the crossroads at the outskirts of town where he used to hail rides to school, fields where ghosts had been seen, the home of an old woman, a spinster all her life, who finally found love and marriage in her nineties, much to the delight of the entire community. In Garzón, he showed me all the hidden refuges of prayer and seclusion, the cathedral, temples, churches, and monasteries, all the sacred spaces of a community long known as the religious capital of Huila. Every second building seemed to be a sanctuary dedicated to God. It was no wonder that Father Cadena had so confidently offered to pay for William's education, certain that the lad would join the clergy. Beyond Garzón, the road turned back to the Magdalena and then north. Since leaving the heights of the Macizo, we had dropped nearly ten thousand feet, and the river had grown with scores of streams and tributaries—the Ríos Granates, Guarapas, Timaná, Naranjos, and Suaza.

Between La Jagua and Garzón, and for another sixty miles to Gigante and beyond, the Magdalena runs through a narrow gorge, a cleft in the landscape with the very dimensions, orientation, and geological substrata that cause dam builders to swoon. As pure works of engineering, these massive structures, such as Betania and El Quimbo, are inspiring. In 1900, there was not a single dam in the world higher than fifty feet. By 1950, there were 5,270. Thirty years later, there would be 36,562. Today, worldwide, there are more than 800,000 dams, 40,000 of which are at least fifty feet in height. Over the last fifty years, on average, every twelve hours has seen the construction of a dam on a scale unimaginable at the turn of the twentieth century.

The problem, of course, lies in the details. Construction of Betania began in 1981, long before there were any requirements for social and environmental impact assessments. Cormagdalena, the government agency charged with managing and protecting the river, was not established until the Constitution of 1991, which was adopted four years after Betania came online. El Quimbo, located twenty miles upstream, just above the mouth of the Río Páez, has had an even greater impact on the Magdalena Valley, inundating twenty thousand acres of farmland, displacing five hundred or more families, creating a thirty-four-mile-long reservoir with an average width of close to a mile. Together, El Quimbo and Betania generate nearly a quarter of Colombia's energy needs. Unfortunately, in the spasm of conception and construction, these signature public work projects neglected to incorporate the one design feature that allows hydroelectric dams to legitimately lay claim to being benign and sustainable sources of clean energy: fish ladders engineered into the structure of the dams that allow migratory species to stay true to their breeding and spawning regimes.

The real question for Colombia and the Río Magdalena is how many more dams are needed to secure the country's energy future. Colombia currently produces enough energy to meet its domestic needs; 70 percent of this power is derived from hydroelectric generation on rivers other than the Magdalena. Surplus energy is today exported to Venezuela, Panama, and Ecuador. It is not at all clear that further supplies on a massive scale will be necessary. Nevertheless, in 2009 Colombia entered into a partnership with the Chinese government to develop a master plan for the Magdalena, a blueprint for development. The cost of the study was roughly US$6.5 million, 90 percent of which was paid for by the Chinese, with the clear expectation that the Hydrochina Corporation, then China's largest hydroelectric engineering firm, would be first in line when construction contracts were awarded. It didn't work out that way, as the first contract went to the Brazilian firm Odebrecht, a controversial transaction that had the scent of scandal from its inception.

For the Magdalena, the far greater concern is the scale of the ambitions as outlined in the master plan. With no apparent rationale save for the fact that the construction could be done, the plan calls for as many as eleven, possibly fifteen, additional dams to be placed in the Alto Magdalena alone, on a section of the river that has already been severely impacted by the presence of just two, Betania and El Quimbo. The argument in favor of further growth suggests that four additional dams would allow Colombia to reduce its consumption of fossil fuels by the equivalent of a million tons of coal a year. A noble goal, but one hard to reconcile with the fact that Colombia has the largest coal deposits in South America and for years has been eagerly expanding the extraction and export of the resource, often to the detriment of the Río Magdalena. In 2013, three ships owned by the Alabama-based Drummond Company sank in the river. The American coal giant, whose Colombia holdings alone are worth an estimated US$3 billion, was obliged to pay a fine of just US$3.5 million.

After the United States, China is Colombia's largest trading partner, and the thought of the Chinese transforming the rivers and landscapes of the country, as they are in the process of doing in nations around the world, left both William and me longing for a shift in mood. We drove on for a time without speaking, even as the radio blared. William was the first to snap the gloom. There was an alternative, he explained, a legal precedent with immense promise. In 2016, the Constitutional Court of Colombia, the highest judicial authority in the land, had granted rights to a river. Not the Magdalena but the Atrato, which runs the length of the western department of Chocó, through a vast lowland rain forest cut off from the Amazon by the rise of the Andean Cordillera and today the heartland of Afro-Colombian culture. At the essence of the historic decision was a formal recognition that nature itself has legal standing, with inherent rights not dissimilar to those of human beings. A river is not merely a source of water or a channel for transportation but rather a living entity inextricably linked to the destiny of all those influenced or touched by its flow. The well-being of its river is the measure of the health of a community, and both are as one in the eyes of the law. This is precisely what the Arhuaco and Kogi *mamos*, the priests of the Elder Brothers, have been saying all along. To have such convictions embraced by a nation-state represents a shift in thinking both dazzling in its audacity and profoundly hopeful in its implications. If such constitutional protections can be granted to the Río Atrato, as William noted, they must surely in time be extended to the Magdalena and, indeed, to all the rivers of Colombia.

Though situated in a broad and fertile valley, with a strategic position commanding all the approaches to the upper Magdalena, Neiva, today the largest city and the commercial heart of Huila, nevertheless struggled to be born. In 1539, Juan de Cabrera laid down the outlines of a town on a flat stretch of ground close to what is now the municipality of Campoalegre. A decade later, the residents followed Juan de Alonso y Arias to a new site closer to the river. This turned out to be an inauspicious move, for in 1569, the entire settlement was annihilated by the Pijao in a last spasm of indigenous resistance. Finally, in 1612, Diego de Ospina y Medinilla reestablished Neiva where it was always destined to be, on the banks of the Río Magdalena, where tributaries named for gold and sacred trees washed over thickly forested islands, and the waters ran slow, dense with fish of a hundred varieties.

Land for rice, cotton, cacao, and coffee, a fluvial artery for transport, and long, hot days with the equatorial sun high overhead spurred the growth of one of the few cities that to this day has never turned its back on the river. The waterfront walk remains its most notable urban feature, a broad promenade of shops and stalls and small restaurants where families gather by morning and lovers come together at the end of day. In the open-air fish market, men process their catch, while their women, with the slightest provocation, launch into heartfelt laments recalling the mornings of their youth when fathers and brothers returned with tubs brimming with fish. In the light of such memories, today's haul, spread across a dozen tables in the shade, appears meager, a shadow of what once was. Still, to anyone unfamiliar with the fishery, it offers an amazing array of exotic and beautiful creatures with strange shapes and odd appendages, fish that to the temperate eye belong less on a plate than in the pages of a rare scientific monograph.

Along the low banks of the river is a row of wooden canoes, *piraguas*, brightly painted in red, blue, yellow, and green. In design and scale, they vary little from the original craft that the first people of the river carved with bone and shell tools, transforming trees into sleek and sturdy vessels. In time, as the growing settlements of the Alto Magdalena sought outlets to markets downstream, the great canoes were augmented with *guaduas*, bamboo rafts large enough to carry small herds of cattle or great stores of tobacco and rice, coffee, cotton, indigo, and dried fish. Much as the *arrieros* employed the simplest of methods to transport on land the merchandise of a nation, so the agricultural bounty of the Alto Magdalena was carried from Neiva downstream to Girardot and Honda on floating platforms, bound together with rope, technically no more sophisticated than the *tercio de leña*, the pile of firewood that, as a boy, William cobbled together every night as he crossed the Magdalena at La Jagua.

Transportation improved somewhat in 1561 when Hernando de Alcocer and Alonso de Olaya Herrera, having expanded the original native road from Bogotá to the Magdalena at Honda, turned their attention to the challenge of the river. With a design inspired by Chinese woodcuts, images first brought to Europe by the Portuguese, they ordered the construction of massive dugouts, carved from ceiba trunks twelve to twenty-six yards in length. To these, they added additional wooden side boards to increase capacity, and awnings woven from palm fronds to provide shelter from the elements. Capable of carrying as much as thirty tons of cargo, both passengers and freight, these *champanes*—the name was a Spanish iteration of the Chinese word *sampan*—were the main form of transport on the Magdalena for 250 years. Each required a crew of ten to eighteen, men of enormous strength who, working together with poles and paddles, could fight the current, pushing aside the river to make their way upstream, dragging the weight of elephants in their wake.

As the indigenous people faded away, devastated by disease, their place was increasingly taken by men and women dragged in shackles from Africa. But those who would work the *champanes* were not slaves or indentured laborers. By 1580, the native population had fallen by 90 percent. Africans, arriving in ever-increasing numbers, were sold to mines and plantations, dockyards and quarries. But a lucky few escaped, slipping away to establish maroon communities, *palenques*, isolated deep in the forests, where the rhythms of the ancient continent were never lost. Resisting with savage ferocity any attempt to return them to bondage, these former slaves forged a unique culture, inspired in good measure by their African antecedents. Their language was their own, Spanish words truncated to fit the meter of African speech. They served their gods, spinning into trances, handling burning embers with impunity, demonstrating the power of their faith. With senses that had been honed in Angola and Congo, Ghana and Niger, they searched the forests of the New World for food and fibers, healing herbs and poisons. Always they watched for signs of intruders, slavers, and hostile parties seeking bounties and women. Many had been warriors in the great armies of the kingdoms of Dahomey and Mali. They armed themselves as they could, with machetes and muskets, slipping into towns to barter or steal—powder and shot, iron and cloth, tools, axes, and knives. In time, some found ways to stay, wrapped in anonymity, sheltered by the color of their skin, disappearing in the shadows of a colonial society that asked nothing of the lowest of the low, save that they be prepared to work as ferociously as beasts. And so they did, becoming the engine of the entire river trade, filling every position as crew on the *champanes*. Known as *bogas*, they lived without rules, a riverfront culture of scoundrels and rogues, openly defiant, shameless in their rejection of conventions and rules, loyal only to freedom, each other, and the river.

Travel by *champán*, to say the least, was always an adventure. Schedules and timetables did not exist. One moved according to the rhythms of the river and the whims of the *bogas*, who worked only when inclined to do so. The length of stay in any port depended always on the availability of grog, whiskey, and rum. When the voyage was underway, passengers in all their finery had to endure searing heat and humidity, infestations of mosquitoes and biting flies, the threat of caimans and poisonous snakes, wretched food, and a constant haunting cacophony that left them all yearning for silence. The source of their torment were the blasphemous screams and howls of the *bogas* as they moved up and down the length of the vessel, a pounding, rotating rhythm that thrust the *champán* forward with constant pressure against the current.

As he traveled up the Magdalena in 1801, Alexander von Humboldt described the complex choreography. With the depth and volume of water, it was rarely possible for the *bogas* to make contact with the actual bed of the river. Thus, the massive *champanes*, some capable of carrying 120 bales of cargo, each with a weight of 250 pounds, had to cling to the shores, allowing the men purchase and leverage for their poles: roots and tree trunks, gravel banks and mudflats. As a helmsman steered the flat-bottomed vessel from the stern, the pilot orchestrated the movement of the men. In the bow, beyond the protective awning, the six *bogas*, all naked save for loincloths, each wielded a two-pronged pole three times the height of a man. As three of them moved toward the awning, pressing their poles against their chests, the other three walked toward the front of the vessel, with arms uplifted, holding their poles horizontally above the heads of those engaged. Three of the *bogas* reached the bow precisely as the other half of the team came to the awning. At that instant, be it day or night, those at the bow dropped their poles into the water, while those at the awning swung theirs up in the air. The result was a continuous motion, a constant momentum such that the *champán* never had a chance to slip back downstream. The work demanded what Humboldt called "Herculean strength," but muscle power alone was not enough. The bodies of the men, callused and scarred across the nipples and chest from the constant friction of the poles, had to move in rhythm, with the precision of a well-drilled military unit. Humboldt saw it as a form of dance, a perfect balance of power and grace.

For all of this, *bogas* received meager compensation. But, critically, they were always paid in advance, a point of pride for men who had once been slaves. Food was constant and plentiful, and the money always came three days before the work, allowing time for the purchase of a new shirt, a gift for a lover, liquor for the brothers. And always there was the reward of the downstream journey, when the only hazards were shifting sands and spinning eddies, snags and deadwood along the shore. As the vessel floated with the current, the *bogas* would lie awake at night, caressed by the innumerable silences of the stars, free and unfettered, while the passengers below quivered in discomfort, so afraid of the Magdalena that they habitually went to confession and often modified their personal wills before embarking on a river journey. Still, for even the most pampered and uncertain of travelers, the *champanes* were a triumph, reducing the time from Cartagena to Honda from two months in a *piragua* to a mere thirty-five days.

Neiva represented one more thing that for me was quite personal. When I first traveled in Colombia as a young student, I came to know a kind and generous old man, Noel Prince, father of daughters and a Liberal to the core. Some might even have described him as a Communist, which he never was. He simply believed in the Colombian people, convinced until his last breath that the country was destined for greatness, and that its greatness would come once all Colombians were free to transcend the limits of their birth and realize their hopes and dreams. Social and economic justice was the very air he breathed. Señor Prince was a great patriot, but his definition of patriotism was Christian charity, the love and assistance one granted without thought to those in greater need. His hero in his youth had been the Liberal Party leader and presidential hopeful Jorge Eliécer Gaitán, the one politician, he claimed, who actually cared about those living in misery. It was said that the poor cried out through Gaitán's mouth. His words could silence the wind, and his oratory shook the very foundations of the established order. For this he was killed in 1948, cut down by three bullets, fired at close range as he stood in front of the Agustín Nieto Building in Bogotá, just across the street from the Black Cat Café.

Much as Señor Prince lamented the loss of such a leader, he abhorred the bloodshed and madness that swept the nation in the wake of Gaitán's assassination. From his home in La Candelaria, he once walked me through the streets, pausing at every corner to tell yet another tale of the Bogotazo, the three terrible days after the murder of Gaitán when the nation's capital burned, and the death of six thousand marked the beginning of the spasm of violence that would haunt Colombia for decades.

At the end of that long day, as we stood among the tibouchina trees in the courtyard of his home in Bogotá, Señor Prince handed me a thin paperback and said very simply but in earnest that if I wanted to understand Colombia, it was the one book that I had to read. The novel was *La vorágine* (*The Vortex*), José Eustasio Rivera's classic story of love, betrayal, and death, set against the backdrop of the jungle and the ravages of the rubber era. Opening the book, my old friend read aloud the most astonishing passage. "I have been a rubber worker," the hero says. "I have lived in the muddy swamps in the solitude of jungles with my crew of malaria-ridden men cutting the bark of trees that have white blood like that of the gods. I am a rubber worker. And what my hand has done to trees, it can also do to men."

Those transgressive words stayed with me for years, even as I came myself to investigate the horrors of the rubber era, a time when, as one Capuchin priest who was there would recall, the best thing that could be said about white men in the forest was that they didn't kill Indians merely out of boredom. For every ton of rubber produced in the northwest Amazon at the turn of the twentieth century, ten native people would die and scores would be left scarred for life, with welts and wounds, missing fingers, hands, and ears. In time, news of the atrocities slipped out, published in travel accounts and later in the formal reports of Sir Roger Casement, the British consul who in 1910 exposed the horrors unfolding along the Río Putumayo, known at the time as the River of Death. No one, however, revealed the depths of the barbarism, the utter erosion of morality, the severing of every tether to decency and civilized behavior with the language, passion, and insight of José Eustasio Rivera. From his own travels, he knew what the suffocating walls of the lowland forest could do to a man. As Gabriel García Márquez makes of the Magdalena not a setting but a character in his novels, so Rivera introduces the jungle as a living being capable of all that is good and evil in the world, a force that strips human beings to the raw, taking full measure of their character, seeing through them as surely as the yellow eyes of a jaguar unveil the heart of a hunter, with the precision of an X-ray.

José Eustasio Rivera was born in Neiva in 1888, another of these astonishing Colombians who seem to come out of nowhere and against all odds achieve singular greatness. Rivera did so with his one novel, *La vorágine*, an early and tragic death, a collection of poetry, and a remarkable journey that took him literally to the far reaches of his land. None of this could possibly have been anticipated, given his background. He came from solid Conservative stock: the son of a government official, nephew of two generals, and one of eleven children in a family that looked to God for order, certainty, and faith. Tradition and social convention led him to study law in Bogotá and, later, to accept a political post in Neiva. But the bourgeois life had little appeal for him. In his heart, he was not a functionary but a poet, one who wrote with the exuberance and passion of the American poet Walt Whitman, who famously made a muse of his own sensual body. "I carry the sky in me," Rivera proclaims in "Gloria," one of his most admired poems. "I carry the waterfall that breaks in the dark jungle, and I have molded the plain to my skull and the mountain range has been enclosed in it."

Escaping the constraints of family and faith, Rivera found freedom in the Llanos, the vast eastern plains, where he lived intermittently from 1916 through the first months of 1920. In 1918, he met Luis Franco Zapata, a wild and explosive man who six years before had eloped with his young lover, fleeing Bogotá to settle in the most remote reaches of the Amazon. Even as Rivera felt the first flush of the tropical fevers that would ultimately kill him, he sat enchanted by Zapata's stories of love and betrayal, death and decay, magic and lust in a forest that consumes men as readily as an ocean swallows a diver. Virtually every character in *La vorágine* was inspired by men and women Zapata had known, and the adventures they had endured.

In late 1921, and through the first months of 1922, Rivera joined a party of Swiss survey engineers, hired by the Colombian government to delineate the frontier with Venezuela. With no maps and no equipment more elaborate than a hand compass, they plunged into the unknown, crossing swamps and savannahs, trudging through jungles, walking for days with not the slightest sense that even a mile had been gained. By night, taken by fever, lying alone in his hammock, Rivera wrote much of what became his only novel. The story was informed by how he felt, as well as by what he saw and heard about the rubber trade.

Rivera described the jungle as if it were a creature. In this, he shared the sentiments of many of his generation, and of some Colombians today, who see the lowland rain forest as a place of danger, a green hell. The Capuchin priest Gaspar de Pinell, reaching the lower Putumayo from Sibundoy in the late 1920s, described a sojourn in a land where "tall trees covered in growths and funereal mosses create a crypt so saddening to the traveler it appears like walking through a tunnel of ghosts and witches. There, far from civilization and surrounded by Indians who could at any moment kill and serve us up as tender morsels in one of their macabre feasts, we spent spiritually blissful days." An American evangelical missionary in the Darién once told me that in the jungle he felt as if a crystal of sugar on the tongue of a beast, impatiently awaiting dissolution.

Perhaps in the end, the forest really did consume José Eustasio Rivera. Like Sir Roger Casement before him, he desperately tried to bring public attention to the atrocities he had witnessed: human trafficking, feudal exploitation of the Bora and Witoto peoples, bloodstained torture chambers. In a flurry of righteous zeal, he traveled to New York in April 1928, hoping to secure an English translation of *La vorágine* that would amplify his voice. He also believed that distancing himself from Colombia would allow him to focus on a new book that would reveal the corruption at the heart of a recent and widely publicized pipeline deal that had allowed Standard Oil to lay claim to much of Colombia's petroleum wealth.

For a time, Rivera was the toast of the city. There was talk of movie deals, and perhaps a diplomatic position as Colombian consul. He was honored by Columbia University, where he lectured throughout the fall, even as his health began to fail. At first the illness was diagnosed as the flu, ominous in that era but not necessarily life-threatening. But then the fevers grew both in frequency and intensity. On November 27, he slipped into a coma, never to recover. Four days later, the man heralded as Colombia's greatest living writer died at twelve-fifty p.m. even as a deep blanket of snow silenced the city.

Ironically, the body of the man who had stood up for justice and against the corruption that allowed foreign companies to lay claim to the natural wealth of the nation was carried home to Colombia on a ship belonging to the United Fruit Company, which only days before had been responsible, by its own official account, for the slaughter of a thousand banana workers at Ciénaga. Arriving in Barranquilla, his body went in procession to the Iglesia de San Nicolás de Tolentino for a requiem Mass. After lying for a day in the *chapelle ardente*, the casket traveled up the Magdalena on a steamship, the *Carbonell González*, and continued from Girardot by train, arriving in Bogotá on January 7, 1929. As José Eustasio Rivera lay in state, his coffin veiled by the Colombian flag, more than fifteen thousand men, women, and children passed by his body in prayer. Two days later, he was buried in the Central Cemetery of Bogotá.

Leaving Neiva, we finally had a chance to ride the river. Our transport, an old speedboat with red vinyl seats and velvet dice dangling from a cracked windshield, was a far cry from the simple and efficient *piraguas* still used by the fishing families whose homes we passed on our run downriver to the old colonial town of Villavieja. There wasn't a lot to see. The odd kingfisher, egret, and heron. Every so often, signs of modern Colombia: a new highway bridge, sleek and elegant in design, or, at one place, industrial power lines crossing the river, strung between giant towers that marched to the horizon. The sun was high and hot, and there was little movement along the shore. Most of the homesteads were simple thatched huts planted on the riverbanks higher than the flood line, yet as close to the water as prudence would allow, along with railed enclosures for livestock and small gardens of papayas, edible palms, and mango trees. Zebu cattle clustered in the shade of the few trees that still stood along the shore. At every landing on both sides of the river, small children slipped in and out of the water with the ease of river otters.

The sun cast its glare upon a world of simplicity and struggle, where the eyes of the young strain to see the lights of the city, and old men and women resign themselves to twilight nights of silence and solitude. Here, I thought, was the face of rural Colombia, and one of the great challenges for the nation. As the cities swell, with waves of immigration from the countryside, a full quarter of the rural population lives in poverty. Despite years of progress in the arts, education, technology, conservation, urban planning, health, and security, this land blessed with natural resources and national wealth is still haunted by a fundamental distortion that must surely be addressed if the nation is to honor its democratic ideals and realize its full economic potential. Bolivia embraced agrarian reform in 1952. Peru did so in 1965, albeit with decidedly mixed results. In Colombia, by contrast, some estimates suggest that as much as 90 percent of the arable land, aside from that owned by the state, remains in the hands of just 5 percent of the people. Given the tangle of claims in the wake of the conflict, such figures are difficult to confirm. According to INCORA, the Colombian Institute for Agrarian Reform, drug traffickers, paramilitaries, and other armed groups either bought or appropriated, often by force, as much as 11 million acres. Whatever the final statistics, there is little doubt that years of instability and war have left a small minority of individuals and private entities in control of most of the good land in the country, a concentration of ownership that is the greatest single indicator of the social inequality that used to drive my old friend in La Candelaria to distraction. As little as he sympathized with the political agenda or the sordid tactics of the FARC, it was hard to argue, he would say, that their original focus on land did not shine a light on an essential issue afflicting the country. Land reform, he added, does not imply expropriation. It simply addresses issues of fairness, opportunity, and economic justice, providing the basic potential for a truly democratic and equitable society in which the disenfranchised and dispossessed will find a place, and no men or women will ever again feel compelled to turn to violence and war in order to have their voices heard.

Villavieja was blinding in the midday sun, a warren of white-washed colonial houses that drew us to an unexpected world. A first sign lay in the Capilla Santa Bárbara, today a paleontological museum stuffed with fossils, including that of a primate said to be twenty-five million years old. Not exactly what the Jesuits had in mind when they consecrated the chapel in 1748. The collections, many of which date to the Cretaceous, sixty-five million years ago, all come from the Tatacoa Desert, the driest and most formidable landscape in all of the Valle de las Tristezas. Since before the town of Gigante, we had been passing through an increasingly parched land, with William pointing out remnants of the dry tropical forest that is one of Colombia's most unique and endangered ecosystems. But as we approached the Tatacoa, the scattered shrubs and small trees, *pelá, payandé, chaparro, iguá, guásimo*, and *guayabo cimarrón*, fell away to reveal a landscape unlike anything to be found in the rest of the Magdalena, or indeed in all of Colombia. With deeply eroded gullies and draws, red crumbling soils, a pronounced stratigraphy along the dry remnants of riverbeds, it evokes less South America than the American Southwest. Though a geographic island of just 130 square miles, the Tatacoa has the feel of a totally different world. It's as if God, having decided to give Colombia one of everything, decided on a whim to place in the rain shadow of the Cordillera Oriental a small patch of ground sliced directly from the surface of Mars.

Plants alone keep the Tatacoa tethered to the earth, with dozens of rare and unusual species of cacti, *arepo* and *melcocha, cabecinegro, candelabro* and *cardón*, along with scores of desert shrubs and small trees, *jatrophas* as well as *tatamacos, crucetos, retamos, mosqueros, naranjuelos*, and *totumos*. There are strange birds as well, no fewer than seventy species, including many endemics, feathered beauties that with all of Colombia to choose from, elect to live out their evolutionary destinies in the confines of an ecological island almost never dampened by rain. So clear and constant are the skies over the Tatacoa that it has long been the site of an astronomical observatory, a lens to the heavens. In the evening, as the sun goes down, warm winds blow off the distant mountains. The entire landscape is bathed in soft lavender light, and the Tatacoa becomes, according to local lore, a gathering place of ghosts.

As night came on, I stumbled upon a solitary grave in the corner of a field bordered by barbed wire. The ground was so desolate and unyielding, it made me wonder why anyone would bother to put up a fence. The grave was marked by a simple wooden cross, upon which was written "José Ricardo Córdoba, February 23, 2009." It seemed odd that a man would be laid to rest alone and far from the hallowed ground of a cemetery. Perhaps the cross represented not where the man was buried but the place where he disappeared, one of the many thousands who during the worst of the violence simply became lost to memory, phantoms to families and friends, a mere notation in a great national registry of the dead.

Girardot and Honda

Girardot, located on the far bank of the Magdalena a hundred miles north of the Tatacoa, is a rarity in Colombia, a city of immense commercial importance with virtually no past. As late as 1840, when towns like Timaná and La Jagua looked back three centuries to their origins, the closest thing to a settlement near the site of Girardot was a hamlet called La Chivatera, "The Goat Farm." Some knew the place as the Paso de Flandes, a reference to the dramatic turn to the west that the Magdalena takes as it runs away from the foothills of the Cordillera Oriental. A parish was not established until 1866, and as late as 1886 the population remained a mere two thousand. Girardot's transformation into Cundinamarca's second city, the most important transportation hub in all the Alto Magdalena, was a consequence of timing, geography, and a wave of entrepreneurial energy unleashed by peace.

In the last years of the nineteenth century, Cundinamarca experienced an economic bonanza, fueled by coffee exports and only partially dampened by the fiscal crisis that followed the War of a Thousand Days. Girardot actually benefited from the conflict, as scores of refugees fleeing the carnage, Liberals for the most part, sought refuge in a place with a shallow history where the agony of defeat might be forgotten and those who had lost everything could reinvent their lives. The war had been ignited as coffee farmers who shared the Liberal commitment to free trade and open markets rebelled against a Conservative government that stifled growth with punitive tariffs and custom duties that left coffee growers operating at a loss. With the peace agreement came the promise of fiscal reforms, along with a general political amnesty that provided the citizens of Girardot all the cover they needed as they built their city as a beacon for everything modern. With no past to constrain them, they made a fetish of the future.

For some time, Girardot had been an important stop for the *vapores*, the paddle wheelers, that worked the Alto Magdalena, from Honda to Neiva. In 1907 the railroad arrived, linking the town and its port to Bogotá and providing an outlet to the river for the coffee farms of Cundinamarca. In 1923, the government hired a British firm, W. G. Armstrong Whitworth & Company, to design an iron bridge—unprecedented in scale—that would span the Magdalena at Girardot, connecting, for the first time, east and west, the two sides of the nation. Then, as Bogotá grew, the *cachacos*, those born and raised in the capital, realized that even with marginal roads and tires smooth as river stones, they could escape the damp and cold of the savannah and within three hours tumble down the mountains and find heat and sunshine on any day of the year. Girardot happily became Bogotá's tropical bedroom. The first major hotel, the Cisneros, opened for business in 1884; in time, there would be more than 150, along with dozens of private clubs, water parks, and other resorts.

As a new century unfolded, the city became a magnet for every possible form of transport, including some that remained untested, just dreams in the heads of dreamers. Gonzalo Mejía was a wealthy *paisa* who spent much of his youth as a student in France, where he became good friends with Louis Blériot, the aviator and inventor who achieved global fame in 1909 by becoming the first to fly across the English Channel. Returning to Colombia, and in the midst of a particularly miserable passage up the Magdalena, Mejía had a moment of revelation. The solution to all the woes of river travel would be a new kind of vessel, a *deslizador*, as he called it, that would use the power and efficiency of modern airplane engines to propel a basic river barge, little more than a steel slab. After long and frustrating months raising funds and working out design flaws, he was finally ready to test the prototype in early 1915. The inaugural trials in New York on the Hudson River were a triumph, and Mejía immediately ordered a second craft, which he named the *Yolanda II*. Shipped south to Colombia, the *deslizador* made its maiden voyage in the last months of the year, traveling from Barranquilla to Girardot by water in a mere four days. Within four years, various modifications and improvements allowed a second-generation vessel, the *Luz I*, to dash from Honda to Barranquilla in just twenty-four hours.

Astonishing as this record appeared to veterans of the Magdalena trade, Mejía's invention was too little and too late. By 1919, it had already been eclipsed by a rival transportation scheme that sought to eliminate the Magdalena altogether by establishing an aerial service, as it was described, that would link every city in the *cuenca*, the heartland of the nation. The company was called SCADTA, the Sociedad Colombo-Alemana de Transportes Aéreos. In charge were two German pilots, both veterans of the Great War, Herbert Boy and Hellmuth von Krohn. Initially they faced multiple challenges. Their one Junkers hydroplane, the *Colombia*, reacted badly to the only kind of gasoline that was then available in the country. The tropical heat played havoc with the plane's radiator and cooling system. There was also resistance from various authorities. As a local governor remarked, "Everyone in Huila has their little mule. It's safe transport, cheaper than your plane. It doesn't consume gasoline and it can carry anything." In response, the Germans reminded the man of the dangers of river travel, with passengers exposed to infestations and malaria, and such impossible delays and distances that schoolchildren were never able to spend the December holidays at home with their families. For any Colombian, this last concern was a dagger to the heart. The governor withdrew his objections, and the adventure was underway.

On October 19, 1920, the *Colombia* took off from Barranquilla, heading for Girardot. Waiting anxiously for the plane to touch down safely was a delegation from Bogotá headed by President Marco Fidel Suárez, along with representatives of the Vatican and various national authorities. The local clergy joined a large crowd of ordinary citizens: fishermen, riverboat men, railroad workers, washerwomen and maids, schoolchildren and teachers, shopkeepers and soldiers. Journalists from all the national and local papers were present to record the historic event, even as they discreetly placed bets on whether or not those on the *Colombia* would survive the flight. When the *Colombia* landed safely, skimming the surface of the river, both pilots were embraced as heroes, and later celebrated in the press as if mythological beings.

Colombia as a nation embraced aviation early and with singular passion. President Pedro Nel Ospina became the first head of state in the world to take office by taking an airplane, flying from Puerto Berrío to Girardot. In 1926, he toured the entire drainage of the Magdalena by air, inspecting the many development projects initiated by his government. Four years later, Enrique Olaya Herrera, the first duly elected Liberal president in forty years, supported the fledging airline industry wholeheartedly, seeing it as the obvious solution for a country tormented by its geography. Recognizing that major roads and railways, despite their formidable costs, could link only the urban centers, he ordered airfields to be built throughout the country, a network that reached the most remote and isolated outposts. He then contracted SCADTA to provide service throughout the nation. For the first time, Amazonas and the Llanos were connected to Bogotá. Students from Nariño, Caquetá, and Norte de Santander could reach their universities in hours, as opposed to days or weeks. Those living in the forests of the Chocó could be airborne in an instant, lifted off the Río Atrato on the wings of a Catalina. As one politician remarked, even the thirsty Guajira began to receive a few drops of the nation's attention.

Throughout Colombia, air travel was infused with prestige, even as Colombians became confident fliers, arguably the first citizens of the world to embrace, as a nation, the miracle of flight, not to mention its commercial potential. Colombian politicians initiated the practice of using airplanes for campaigning and conducting long-distance diplomacy, visiting leaders in neighboring lands. Airmail delivery of letters and parcels began in Colombia, with an enterprising pilot who charged a peso apiece for each of the sixty cards he stashed in his personal satchel on a flight from Barranquilla to Puerto Colombia. SCADTA would go on to become one of the first financially successful air services in the world, eventually taking the name Avianca; today it is the national airline of Colombia.

The success of SCADTA by no means implied the end of Gonzalo Mejía, who only found inspiration in failure. After the collapse of the *deslizador* scheme, he formed a partnership in 1919 with Alejandro Echavarría, founder of the textile giant Coltejer, and created his own airline, the Colombian Air Navigation Company. Unfortunately, their planes, French Farman F.40s, were made of canvas and wood and tended to splinter in the Andean extremes, often in flight. After one too many accidents, they dissolved the enterprise in 1920. Humbled yet still obsessed with mobility, Mejía tried a more conventional venture, establishing Tax Imperial, the first taxi business in Medellín. The initial step was to import a vehicle, which arrived in thirty-one boxes on the backs of mules, only the second car ever to reach the city. As business grew, Mejía needed routes for his fleet to operate, and thus began his push for a road from Medellín to the coast at Turbo, a dream that would take twenty-five years to be realized. In the meanwhile, since he had lost to SCADTA in the air, he elected to focus on the ground, and the money to be made from the certain knowledge that airplanes that flew had to have a place to land. Thus, after fifteen years of struggle, and having donated much of the land himself, Mejía supervised the opening of the Aeropuerto Olaya Herrera, Medellín's first airport.

Known by this time throughout the country as "El Fabricante de Sueños," the Dream Maker, this visionary entrepreneur had one more gift for the country. In 1919, he had imported Colombia's first movie projector, screening in Puerto Berrío a silent film that dazzled the audience. In 1924, he cast himself and his wife, along with friends from Medellín's high society, as actors in what would become the first feature film ever made in Colombia, *Bajo el cielo antioqueño*. Proper films, of course, required a proper setting, so the next step was to build the Teatro Junín, at the time the fourth-biggest movie theater in the world. If Medellín was to have such a temple to the new art of filmmaking, surely Colombia would have to develop the capacity to produce movies, and thus his final act was the creation of Cine Colombia, to this day the nation's most important theater company. Gonzalo Mejía would die the rarest of business leaders, a civic entrepreneur who accumulated not wealth but goodwill, with projects conceived in dreams, and realized for the well-being of all Colombians.

Well away from the downtown core of Girardot, where polished and orderly taxis once lined up in front of the Teatro Olympia, and streetlights today flare over a nightly carnival of chaos, a muddy track littered with debris leads to a confluence where the fate of the Río Magdalena will ultimately be decided, and with it, perhaps, the destiny of Colombia. From the left flows the main river, slow and steady, laden with silt, light brown in color, a blend of all the fertile soils and desert sands of a great valley that in geologic time remains a newborn. Coming in from the right is the Río Bogotá, bubbling with white foam, black with the color of the night.

Born in the north of Cundinamarca, at eleven thousand feet in the Páramo de Guacheneque, on land sacred to the Muisca, the Río Bogotá falls to the savannah as a small mountain stream, clear and unblemished. Passing through extensive wetlands once wild with birds, ecological formations that filter and purify like a natural sponge, it merges with a number of affluents, all of which also originate in *páramos*—Guerrero, Sumapaz, and Chingaza. It would be hard to imagine a more auspicious start for a river, a genesis as innocent and pure. Unfortunately, it soon runs into and through a capital city of more than eight million people, where nearly a third of the nation's economy is generated, and where every tributary, the Fucha, Tunjuelo, Soacha, Salitre, and many more, lie buried beneath pavement or cement, each more toxic than the last. Falling out of the mountains that form the backdrop of the city to the east, these precious streams are all poisoned within miles of their birth. Tannery and slaughterhouse waste, industrial toxins, silt and dust from cement and brickworks, partially treated sewage, plastic and garbage—everything ends up in the river. By the time the Río Bogotá escapes the city to plunge over the Tequendama Falls, it is biologically dead, utterly devoid of oxygen and with no signs of macrobiotic life. Falling ten thousand feet in a mere thirty miles, it reaches the Magdalena at Girardot slightly reinvigorated, a sign only of the extraordinary resilience of nature. Still, it remains less a river than a slurry of waste, as it pumps into the main channel of the Magdalena vast concentrations of cadmium, chromium, mercury, zinc, arsenic, and lead, not to mention volumes of human waste certain to give pause to the millions of Colombians living downstream.

The very scale and concentration of pollution that enters the Río Magdalena at Girardot is discouraging but also, in a certain sense, inspiring, for it suggests an extraordinary opportunity. If some means could be found to stanch the flow of pollutants into this one tributary, Colombia could go a long way toward cleaning up the entire Magdalena, especially if other cities and municipalities in the drainage come forward to mimic Bogotá's example. If this appears a purely quixotic notion, a naïve dream, consider the history of just two other rivers, both in far worse shape than the Magdalena but a generation ago: the Hudson, which enters the Atlantic just below New York City, and the river Thames, which traverses London on its short run to the sea.

As recently as the 1960s, the Hudson and virtually all of its tributaries were industrial arteries, tainted with sewage and waste and poisoned with heavy metals, pesticides, and toxic chemicals. It was not safe to swim in the river, let alone eat the fish or drink the water. Major corporations with vast industrial infrastructure dominated the politics and economy of the basin and, without the slightest reservation, used the river as a dumping ground. For a hundred years General Motors operated an assembly plant that consumed a million gallons of water a day, returning it untreated to the river. All of that massive facility's waste was emptied directly into the Hudson. It was said at the time that you could tell by the color of the river what pigment of paint was being used that day on the cars on the assembly line.

All this began to turn around in the 1970s with the passage of the Clean Water Act and the growth of a small citizens' army that stood up for the river and, through a combination of legal and political actions, faced down the corporations and ultimately won the day. The major polluters were obliged to modify their practices and pay for the cost of dredging and rehabilitating the river. To the astonishment of ecologists, fishermen, local farmers, and the corporate leaders themselves, the Hudson began to heal within months and at a rate that had even the worst of the polluters unexpectedly joining the crusade, thrilled to stand alongside their former antagonists as witnesses to the rebirth of a river that had become a symbol of national pride. Today, children swim and fish along the length of the Hudson. Families gather on beaches once tainted with tar and industrial waste. Wild creatures appear along the shores. In 2016, a tourist standing at the end of Sixty-third Street in Manhattan spotted something no one had seen in more than a century: a humpback whale frolicking in the waters of the Hudson River.

The story of the river Thames is equally dramatic. For years, Londoners treated the river as one great public latrine, flushing into its shallows raw sewage and industrial waste in equal measure. By the 1950s, the river that had carried the weight of all of British history, the symbol of the nation, the lifeblood of its people, was little more than an open-air sewer, utterly devoid of fish, incapable of supporting any form of life, lacking even a trace of oxygen in all the waters that reached for miles above and below the London Bridge. In 1957, London's Natural History Museum formally declared the river biologically dead. Today, by contrast, the Thames supports no fewer than 125 species of fish. Herons and cormorants line the riverbanks. Sightings of seals and dolphins occur every day, and even whales are sometimes seen in the river, skimming beneath the bridges of the city.

Such stories of rebirth and redemption have become commonplace as people throughout the world have embraced their rivers as symbols of patrimony and pride. The French, against all odds, have over the last three decades cleaned up the Seine. In Ohio, children now swim in the notorious Cuyahoga, a river once so polluted with solvents and industrial waste that it famously caught on fire in 1952 and again in 1969. As cities and governments note the ease and speed with which rivers can recover, politicians see the benefits of public investments actually being realized by those who are asked to cover the costs, which only encourages further action. What's more, the ecological rebirth of a river does not necessarily require huge expenditures. The first step is simply to curtail the activities responsible for the pollution. Colombian law states unequivocally that people and enterprises have no inherent right to contaminate the fresh water of the nation. The laws, many lament, are never enforced. Surely this is no excuse. Since when have Colombians needed the cover of the law to do what everyone knows to be right?

If industry is responsible for roughly a third of the pollution that enters the Magdalena, the people of Colombia account for the rest. Access to clean potable water is a human right. But if we are to demand from the state a constant supply of fresh water, do we not also have an obligation to demand that what leaves our homes, flushed through our toilets, be properly treated before being discharged into the rivers that are the basis of our prosperity?

Colombia is today at a crossroads, a country emerging from fifty years of conflict eager to tell all who will listen that it is not a place of violence and war but a land with a vast and rich natural heritage unrivaled in all the Americas. Were Colombians to devote even a small quota of their limitless energy and capital to the revitalization of the Magdalena, imagine the message they would send. A river reborn at a time when the world may be falling apart, but Colombia is falling together.

In all my travels, few people spoke more passionately about the Magdalena than Germán Ferro, director and curator of the Museo del Río Magdalena, the one institution in Colombia dedicated exclusively to the wonder of the river. We met for the first time in his museum office in Honda, an old colonial town that Germán describes as Colombia's last coastal city, an inland Caribbean port that just happens to be located five hundred miles upriver from the sea. Listening to him speak about his beloved Magdalena was like drinking from a fire hydrant, overwhelmed by a torrent of words, each more meaningful than the last. He began with what sounded like a Japanese koan.

"In Colombia, south is up, and north is down. The Magdalena comes out of the Andes only to perish in coastal sands, swallowed by the sea. It crosses the entire nation, one of the very few tropical rivers in the world that flows south to north."

Germán paused for a moment as a young woman arrived with a tray of *tintos*.

"In so many ways it's the mirror image of the Mississippi, the only other great river to flow into the Caribbean. Each drains the heartland of a continent. And just as the Mississippi contains the entire American experience, the Magdalena carries the whole of the Colombian reality. It, too, is a fountain of music, the source of our culture and civilization. Yet for too long Colombians have turned their backs on the river, indulging a strange national amnesia, as if running away from the essence of who we are as a people."

For Germán, this deep association with the Magdalena was not a matter of sentiment or nostalgia, and he certainly did not intend his reflections to be taken by his *paisanos* as flattery. He saw the Río Magdalena as having a deeply ambivalent nature, as if a sentient being capable of embodying duality and living with contradictions, much as the nation itself does. It creates its own universe of extremes. For half the year, it runs in flood, feeding the wetlands. In the dry season it shrivels, as sandbars become exposed, riverboats run aground, and only water flowing in from the *ciénagas* keeps the river moving to the sea. For much of Colombia's history, the Magdalena has served as the nation's graveyard, carrying the unknown dead, faceless corpses floating downstream, with vultures perched aloft feeding on the decaying flesh. But it has also been a river of hope, a source of food and fresh water, a muse of poets, the inspiration for song.

"In life and death, by night and day," Germán said, "the Magdalena flows, destined for all eternity to fade away at Bocas de Ceniza, only to be reborn in the distant heights of the Macizo."

As we stepped out of his office and moved along a short open hallway toward the exhibits, I asked Germán what led him and his colleagues to establish the museum in Honda just above the river in a renovated building that had once served as a horse stable.

"My task as a teacher," he replied, "is to excite people. It's an exercise of contagion, to spread an emotion that will ignite the souls of young people, in particular, and bring them back to the Magdalena. This building was perfect, long and narrow like the river itself.

The exhibits were conceived from the start to invoke an actual journey, be it by *piraguas, champanes,* or *vapores.*"

"And why Honda," I asked, "as opposed to a larger city likely to attract more visitors?"

"Our entire mission at the museum—and, I suppose, my purpose in life—is to reconnect Colombia to the river that gave it birth. Honda marks the divide between the Magdalena's two realities, the Macizo Colombiano and all the high country running away to the south, and to the north the vast Caribbean coastal plain, all the wetlands, *ciénagas,* and endless ocean shores. The museum had to be here. Honda is the linchpin."

All of this made perfect sense, given the history and geographical setting of the city. Founded in 1539 by Gonzalo Jiménez de Quesada, perched above the formidable rapids that mark the traditional head of navigation on the river, Honda grew in the commercial shadow of Cartagena, serving for three centuries as the sole conduit to Bogotá. Virtually all imported goods and domestic manufactures coming up the Magdalena from the coast had to be offloaded at Honda to begin the long and perilous journey overland to the capital, or to be hauled around the cataracts to vessels operating in the upper reaches of the drainage. Merchants feeding on the trade poured their wealth into their city. Honda's former glory can still be sensed in what remains of the old quarter, the Alto del Rosario, a warren of narrow cobblestoned streets overhung with balconies draped in bougainvillea, with ornate stone walls decorated with orchids and bromeliads, and brightly colored house façades with great carved doors that still open to reveal private worlds of wealth and leisure, cool interior patios shaded by elegant palms and the spreading branches of plumerias and a host of flowering trees.

On a hidden promontory are the remnants of a military battery that once dominated the heights overlooking the streams that meet the Magdalena at Honda, Quebrada Seca, Gualí, and Guarinó. Crossing these are some thirty bridges, each a window onto Honda's past and its historic role as Colombia's transportation nexus. The most famous is the Puente Navarro, widely reported to have been designed and manufactured by the same firm responsible for the Golden Gate Bridge in San Francisco. This, unfortunately, may not be true. In a deal facilitated by an American engineer then living in Honda, Norman Nichols, the Puente Navarro was in fact designed and manufactured by the San Francisco Bridge Company of New York, a firm that played no role in the later construction of the Golden Gate, which was completed only in 1937, nearly forty years after Bernardo Navarro Bohórquez opened his toll bridge over the Magdalena.

Still, the Puente Navarro, the first iron bridge to be built in all of South America, remains impressive, a potent symbol of Honda's last period of true commercial prosperity, a golden age between 1850 and 1910. Tobacco exports from Ambalema were at a peak. Gold and silver flowed from the mines of Mariquita. Coffee came from Manizales. Foreign architects and engineers laid plans for a modern central market that would boast no fewer than 148 iron columns. By night, diplomats made their way down the Calle de las Trampas to opulent consulates built without reference to cost or the logistical challenges of sourcing marble and stone in the quarries of Europe. And on the river, all was well. During the annual spawning run, or *subienda*, people from all over the country descended on Honda, trebling the population, as they harvested a hundred tons of fish in a matter of weeks, all of it dried and shipped out of the valley to Medellín and Bogotá, Barrancabermeja, Manizales, and Ibagué. As parents worked and fish nestled in the riverbanks to hatch their young, children splashed in the shallows, catching *bocachico* with their bare hands.

Honda's slow decline began as Girardot came into being a hundred miles upriver, with modern infrastructure that allowed it to displace the colonial port as the transportation hub of the region. Germán's father was an engineer, one of many sent to transform Girardot into the city it became. The family would visit him on weekends, dropping down from Bogotá to *tierra caliente*, as it was known, where Germán and his friends would hang out around swimming pools, flirt with girls, and drink lemonade and *gaseosa* in the shade. He would later recall in astonishment how little sense any of them had of the presence of the Río Magdalena. No adult ever bothered to mention that in coming to Girardot they had dropped into a river valley that had defined their nation. Germán came to

understand and embrace the Magdalena as he did only when an
academic obsession drew him to its shores. His doctoral research
focused on the culture of the *arrieros*, the muleteers so essential
to transportation and trade. As he mapped their tracks, it became
graphically clear that every trail and all roads ultimately reached the
Magdalena. Major routes such as the ancient path from Bogotá to
Honda, or the Camino de Nare, the Islitas road linking Antioquia
to Puerto Nare, served literally as the umbilical cords of the nation,
vital arteries without which commerce would collapse. Colombia as
a country was a gift of the Magdalena.

"Let me share two moments that moved me a great deal," said
Germán. The first story recalled an experience he had with the
Yucuna at Araracuara on the banks of the Río Caquetá, deep in the
Colombian Amazon. He had been there for the ceremonial inaugu-
ration of a beautiful *maloca*, a community longhouse, a celebration
of great significance that ought to have fully absorbed the energy of
the indigenous leaders. Yet in the midst of all the ritual, the dances
and songs, the elaborate exchanges of gifts, food, and offerings, the
capitán of the Yucuna turned to Germán and asked, out of the blue,
"My friend, how is the Magdalena?"

"I was so astonished," Germán recalled. "He didn't ask about
the Yarí or the Apaporis or any of the rivers of his homeland. He
had heard that the Magdalena was something special, unlike any
other river in Colombia. Perhaps not as large as the rivers that flow
east into the Amazon. The Putumayo, Guaviare, Isana, Caquetá—
all of these dwarf the Magdalena in size, and he knew it. But he was
not thinking about physical dimensions. His concern was the living
essence of the river, and the way it was being treated by the people.
Here was a Yucuna elder living in relative isolation in the forest,
whose life would never be impacted by the fate of the Magdalena,
and yet he felt a certain responsibility for its plight. If only more of
us shared such generosity of spirit! If only more of us cared."

His story reminded me of what I had learned from the Arhuaco
and Kogi, and I told Germán about their pilgrimages up the Magdalena to the Macizo and the source. He noted that we, by contrast, can barely conceive of rivers as living entities. On maps, he
remarked, we depict them always in blue, when all the great rivers

are brown, fertile and thick with silt and sand carried away as they carve valleys and move mountains. I asked whether he thought it might ever be possible to galvanize public support and actually clean up the Magdalena.

"To clean up the river," he replied, "would be to wash the soul of the nation. If we are ever to reconcile, we need to come to terms with the past, with violence, death, and a time when rivers ran red with blood. But to have true peace, we must reestablish a link to the Magdalena. That is the key. If a people do not understand their roots, they cannot trust their future."

"So you see peace as being connected to the fate of the river?" I asked.

"Of course," he replied. "And not just in terms of metaphor. That's the other story I wanted to share with you. I'll never forget the moment when I first heard that the peace agreement had been signed in Havana. By chance I was at the very confluence of the Río Cauca and the Magdalena. I was completely overwhelmed by what I can only call geographical emotion, a sense of space, as if the spirits were emerging from the earth. I stripped off my clothes and placed my head in the river. As I stood in the sun, the water dripping down my naked body, I began to weep. Rivers of tears flowed as I realized that my son could grow up in a country at peace. A river that has known every tragedy, that has carried the dead and all the misery of the nation, that has suffered along with all Colombians, a river that I love so much, and there we were by its waters as peace came over the land."

The Miracle of Murillo

As we toured the museum, Germán encouraged me to think of the Magdalena not just as a river but as a *cuenca*, a broad valley where all life from the river's edge to the highest summits falls under its spell. One map in particular, a long artist's rendering focusing on the topography of the basin, revealed in dramatic fashion that as we had been traveling down the river, the mountain flanks on both sides of the ever-widening valley had soared into the very heavens. Rising above Honda to the south and west, crowning the Cordillera Central, were no fewer than five volcanic peaks, each higher than any mountain in the European Alps, with the tallest, Nevado del Ruiz, reaching to nearly eighteen thousand feet. At one time, all were covered in ice and snow. Quindío and Cisne are today barren, two of the eight major peaks in Colombia to have thawed completely over the last century. As recently as 1900, the summit ice cap of Nevado del Ruiz covered forty square miles; in 1959 its extent was roughly thirteen square miles. Today only four square miles of ice remain, and this is destined to disappear within our lifetimes, along with the remaining icefields on Nevado del Tolima and Nevado de Santa Isabel. Runoff from the glaciers of these peaks is the primary source of fresh water for more than forty small towns nestled along the upper flanks of the Cordillera Central. One struggles to imagine what will become of these communities, not to mention historic settlements such as Guamo, Espinal, and Ambalema, when the Nevado del Ruiz no longer shines over the deep valley of the Magdalena.

I left the museum with the strongest sense that before dropping any further toward the coast, we had to go high, which is how William and I ended up two days later on the farm of Héctor Botero, drinking rum and watching as the clouds slipped over the sun and radiant light illuminated the silhouettes of wax palms along the crest of the mountain slopes that fell away at our feet. Héctor was a gracious host, a *paisa* and a perfect Colombian, the son of a Liberal father and a mother born Catholic and Conservative, the granddaughter of a general from the War of a Thousand Days. In his sixty-five years, Héctor had known only war, and he had developed a healthy disregard for politics, polemics, and anything that would distract him from his singular devotion to the land. He lives alone, and would have it no other way. In a simple home kitchen, with milk from Jersey cows, he makes the finest cheese, which he carries to market three times a week. It earns all that is needed, which is just enough to allow him to dream up new schemes to improve the farm. His ultimate goal is to turn much of the pasture into a forest of native trees, a project he began as a boy with his brother, sourcing saplings in the valley and transporting them to the farm in wooden crates strapped to the sides of mules.

Héctor's father, a prosperous businessman in Medellín, bought their remote family farm in 1958 largely to escape La Violencia, the conflict then tearing apart the nation. At the time there was no road access and no power. It took four hours by horse to reach Murillo, the nearest town. In splendid isolation, on land as beautiful as any in Tolima, the family sat out the war, with chickens and pigs and sufficient dairy cows to produce two hundred and fifty gallons of milk a day, all of which was processed into cheese, much as Héctor does today, only on a far grander scale.

Hidden away in the shadow of the great volcanoes, the Botero family managed to dodge the worst of the violence, but ultimately they could not avoid death, which came unexpectedly to his father when Héctor was just twelve, on the same day his mother gave birth to her last child, Héctor's youngest brother. A pall fell over the farm: birth and death, joy and sorrow, with each emotion balancing and muting the other, leaving the family numb with grief and uncertainty. It was then that the war reached into even the deepest recesses of the land, spreading across Héctor's life like a wind-borne pestilence.

Some say La Violencia began in 1946. Others point to the assassination two years later of the great hope of the people, Jorge Eliécer Gaitán. In truth, it was only a matter of time before Liberals and Conservatives faced off in fratricidal conflict. By 1953, tens of thousands of Colombians had been killed. That year General Gustavo Rojas Pinilla overthrew the Conservative president, Laureano Gómez, establishing military rule for the first and only time in Colombia's history. A truce imposed by the army lasted until 1955, when the military dictator himself shattered the peace by going after Liberal strongholds in the east and south of Tolima. War raged intermittently through 1957, when Rojas Pinilla was overthrown. Conservatives and Liberals, united for the moment by their common desire for power, declared a National Front, promising to share the presidency, with one party presenting a candidate who would rule for four years, to be followed by a leader from the other side selected by his party. The Liberals were up first, and placed in office Alberto Lleras Camargo, who immediately offered a general amnesty. Driven by fear and mistrust, few responded and the conflict continued, resulting in another forty-four thousand dead by the early 1960s. By then, the reasons for the war, the classic clash between red and blue, Liberal and Conservative, had been largely forgotten. A new generation of guerrilla fighters was emerging, inspired by events in Cuba and for a time, at least on paper, motivated by political ideals. But killing does something to a man, and many of the veterans of La Violencia, surviving combatants on both sides, had become little more than thugs, dedicated to robbery, kidnapping, extortion, and murder.

As far as Héctor was concerned, one killer is as bad as the next. The worst, as he recalled, was a Liberal, Jacinto Cruz Usma, who went by the alias Sangrenegra, or "Black Blood." A man without actual politics, let alone convictions, he lived simply to rob, rape, and kill, murdering anyone he considered to be even remotely aligned with the Conservative Party. In February 1962, he assaulted a mili-

tary convoy, prompting the army to launch a campaign of extermination across the Liberal stronghold in northern Tolima. A year
later, Sangrenegra killed and beheaded eight innocent campesinos
in Totaré, throwing their heads into the river. Later that same day,
he stopped a bus on the road from Alvarado to Anzoátegui and for
no particular reason killed thirteen passengers, including a police
lieutenant. Such random and pointless atrocities continued until the
spring of 1964 when, wounded in a firefight, Sangrenegra took his
own life rather than fall alive into the hands of the authorities.

Conservatives, for their part, had the Chulavitas, the "Black
Birds," militias dressed always in black who swept into towns to
massacre any Liberals they could find. *Pájaros* referred to those who
killed and disappeared as quickly as birds. Both sides sired sinis-
ter methods of murder, devised as markings on the dead, signatures
conceived to sow terror. The Necktie Cut left the tongue dangling
from a slit in the throat; the decapitation known as the Monkey
posed the headless victim cradling his head in his lap. In the Vase,
the four limbs were severed and inserted into what remained of the
body like flowers in a jar.

The clergy, aligned for the most part with the Conservatives, did
little to quell the conflict, save for placing two entrances in the sides
of every church, a red door for Liberals and a blue one for Conservatives. Some parts of the country, including the Caribbean coast
and certain inland cities such as Honda, largely escaped the conflict.
But in the regions particularly afflicted by the violence—the west
of Antioquia, the north of Tolima, all the Cordillera Occidental of
Valle del Cauca, the south of Santander, Boyacá, Cundinamarca,
and much of the Medio Magdalena—the only person in any town
immune and relatively safe was the village priest, though even this
was not always the case.

Pedro María Ramírez was a staunchly Conservative cleric
assigned to the Magdalena town of Armero, at the time a Liberal
bastion. In the wake of the assassination of Gaitán and the Bogotazo, the priest was seized by a mob and killed, ultimately buried
naked, his clothes having been torn from his body. Those responsible were taken by the law and jailed, only to be visited every night by
the dead man's ghost, which hovered over their cells. The bishop of

Ibagué declared that no priest would be assigned to the community, and thus no family would be able to celebrate the baptism of a child or hear last rites performed for the dead. All would be condemned to purgatory. For nearly forty years, Héctor maintained, the people of Armero lived in a state of limbo, haunted always by the last words uttered by Father Ramírez before he was killed: *"No quedará piedra sobre piedra de Armero."* In Armero, not a stone will remain. Never in his wildest imaginings had Héctor expected to see the day when this terrible curse would be realized. But he did.

Héctor told many such stories, each more disturbing than the last. Through all these years he lived on the edge of uncertainty, never knowing his fate, with periods of relative calm inevitably broken by spasms of violence. In 1985, the FARC kidnapped his uncle, his mother's brother, Eduardo Alzate García, then governor of Tolima. Eduardo was held naked and barefoot in the jungle for a month, threatened with death every day, then finally released, only to die days later a broken man, a victim of physical and psychological torture. Then came the ELN (National Liberation Army), a rival guerrilla force heavily influenced by Cuba and liberation theology, and by reputation much more doctrinaire and rigidly Marxist than the FARC. As far as Héctor was concerned, one Communist bandit was the same as the next, though he knew it was the ELN that established camps on the ridge above the farm. For several months the guerrillas sowed the forest with defensive rings of antipersonnel mines, which were simply abandoned when, harassed by the Colombian air force, the outlaw army eventually moved on.

Some years later, a FARC cadre appeared out of nowhere to demand that Héctor give up his small dairy business and establish an agricultural cooperative. They gave him the choice of doing their bidding or abandoning the farm. Héctor chose to walk away, quite literally, without pausing to look back on the land where his father lay buried. For nearly a decade he lived in exile, mostly in the foothills of the Andes in Meta, where he rented a small farm and set up another dairy. For several years, the guerrillas there let him be. But then one day they appeared, an entire FARC front, with a warning that the war would soon be upon him. Héctor had but two weeks to sell his cows. The guerrillas took everything they could use. Then came the bombs, destroying much of Héctor's house. The army came through, followed by paramilitaries, who stole what little was left. Once again, Héctor had lost everything: home, equipment, possessions, not to mention his personal investment of a decade building up the dairy.

With no choice but to start over, Héctor returned to the family land in Tolima, defying anyone who would deny him his heritage. Reaching the farm after a series of misadventures, he went immediately to the spring. The water still ran, as it had for his father. The land was as he remembered, and yet, at the same time, everything had changed.

"One never bathes in the same creek," he explained, "for the water is always new, and so too is the man."

Like so many Colombians I met along the Magdalena, Héctor found his peace by letting go of the past and looking only to the future. The entire focus of his life today is the forest of native trees that long ago flowered in his dreams.

Murillo is one of those small and picturesque Colombian mountain towns that force you out of bed in the middle of the night, simply for the joy of watching the streetlights fade as the sun breaks the horizon and soft morning light glows over the promise of a new day. William and I had scurried away from our lodgings in the dark, following a road that petered out within a few blocks to a dirt track that climbed higher into the hills. We scrambled to the top of a grassy knoll just as a chorus of songbirds heralded the dawn. William identified every species by sound, red tanagers and warblers, flycatchers and wrens. My attention was on the light and the layout of the town, the rooftops and the streets slowly coming alive with the clip-clopping of mules and the shouts of *arrieros*. The massive church, with its spire and vaulted roof, yellow walls with green trim running along and over every feature, was impressive but oddly out of proportion with its surroundings, as if plunked into the community by a child playing with toys. The people lived in modest wooden homes, all with brightly painted façades of blue and pink and orange, each a unique design and clearly a mark of distinction and pride for the families. Behind this public display, entire streets awash in color, the low houses opened in the back to outdoor kitchens, clotheslines, and cages for guinea pigs and rabbits. Gardens and fields spread between every city block. There was no separation between urban and rural space; in every home the countryside slipped effortlessly into the family parlor. From the heights, we could look down and see the lives of the people as they stirred. An old woman left her washing to milk a cow tethered to a roof pole of her house. A young girl readied herself for school. Children chased chickens. Dogs wandered between kitchens and fields, as if guarding the entire community.

The day before, in a local restaurant, I had met Adelfa Pineda Ibáñez, the mother of nine and, at eighty-eight, a woman of deep memory with nothing to fear and no reason to shy away from the truth. Elegant and refined, yet clearly of the people, she was heavyset but strong, with long white hair pulled back in a tight bun. Her face was deeply lined and bronzed by the sun. Her eyes sparkled. One of twelve children, she had been born in 1928, when Murillo was just a cluster of palm and thatched houses. The town grew in the 1940s as men and women from both sides sought refuge from La Violencia. One main street running past the church was settled by Liberals from Santander. Conservatives from Boyacá built their homes along the street running parallel to it, one block over. The façades on all the houses are today bright and joyous, but after four generations, some families still refuse to speak to one another.

"There has been violence here," Adelfa told me, "since before I knew myself. Every boy is born with a gun on his shoulder."

For Adelfa the world shifted, falling off its axis, with the death of Jorge Eliécer Gaitán. "I remember when they killed him. April ninth. We all went to the top of the mountain and wept. It was very sad. Gaitán died for his greatness. He was rock hard, a fighter like a lion. For us, he's not really dead. His name is written in red letters across our hearts."

For the longest time, Adelfa resigned herself to war, with little confidence that she or the country would ever again know peace. As she saw it, once Gaitán was gone, even God gave up hope. "God became bored," she said, "and he left, never to return."

But then something remarkable occurred, and it was this story that had drawn me to Murillo and, that morning, to the hilltop promontory overlooking the town. Murillo sits in a basin surrounded by hills to the south and, to the north, a long, gently descending ridge covered with pasture and remnants of Andean forest. It was there, Adelfa had told me, that God returned to work his miracle.

Soaring over Murillo, not twenty miles to the west, is the Nevado del Ruiz, a volcano that has been active for two million years. What makes it especially dangerous is the impact that hot gases and lava can have on summit glaciers. When the mountain erupts, icefields melt, generating massive flows of water, ice, pumice, and other rocks, which mix with clay to form lahars, massive rivers of mud that race down the flanks, achieving speeds of up to sixty miles per hour. The laws of physics dictate that the size of the stones and the amount of debris that such a flood can move is directly proportional to the square of the velocity of the water. Thus if the flow's velocity quadruples due to the rush of meltwater from the summit icefields, the amount of debris that it can carry multiplies sixteen-fold. The upper slopes of the Nevado del Ruiz, with an incline of twenty to thirty degrees, serve as a virtual launchpad. As a lahar descends, eroding soil, dislodging rocks, swallowing vegetation, it becomes ever larger and more powerful, its destructive force only increasing with distance from the eruption.

When the Nevado del Ruiz erupted in 1595, the explosion was heard sixty miles away, and a river of mud swept the length of the valleys of the Gualí and Lagunilla Rivers, killing more than six hundred people. In 1845, a mudflow from the mountain sparked by an earthquake reached more than forty miles down the Lagunillas before dividing into two, one branch continuing down the valley, and the other turning ninety degrees to the north, flowing into the Río Sabandija, before ultimately rejoining the first branch as it entered the Río Magdalena. In mere hours, these mudflows covered more than sixty miles, killing roughly a thousand people.

In November 1984, geologists monitoring the Nevado del Ruiz noticed an increase in seismic activity near the volcano. In September 1985, a massive ejection of ash raised concerns. A month later, an Italian team of volcanologists determined that magma had reached the surface, increasing both the likelihood of an eruption and the risk of lahars. In early November, volcanic activity once again spiked, with any number of ominous signs. Finally, at 3:06 p.m. on November 13, 1985, the Nevado del Ruiz erupted, sending some thirty-five million tons of magma and volcanic dust into the atmosphere. After decades of dormancy, Kumanday, as the mountain was known to the indigenous Pijao, had come alive.

The people of Murillo noticed the black columns of ash only minutes before the mountain exploded, giving the community just enough time to abandon their homes. Some, led by the mayor, tried to escape to high ground. Most raced to the plaza by the church. There they gathered, clinging to family members and neighbors, embracing children, faces turned to the priest, who led them in prayers and gently eased them toward the terrible realization that they were all about to die. The sky was illuminated with a strange yellow light. Ash began to fall like snow. Then, as the power went out, everything became dark. Black rain fell as a thunderstorm swept up from the valley. Nothing and no one could be seen. Mothers ran their hands over the faces of their children, reading their features like braille. Even as Adelfa's children and their children huddled around the family matriarch, a massive debris flow was gathering speed and strength, roaring down the mountain. Everyone knew that Murillo lay directly below the summit, on the logical gravitational line that any lahar was almost certain to follow. As men wept and nuns shook with fear, Adelfa remained stoic, standing tall, her face without emotion, her eyes staring at the ridge that ran past the town to the north. She knew that God had returned when half the face of the Nevado del Ruiz roared by, deflected to the other side of that ridge such that not a single man, woman, or child lost their life that day in Murillo.

Adelfa's salvation seemed all the more miraculous as we continued our journey along the high flanks of the Cordillera Central, across the canyons of the Ríos Lagunillas, Azufrado, and Gualí, and to the shattered face of the great volcano. The sheer volume of material cut loose from the frozen heights defies measurement. The entire landscape was transformed. Massive headwalls reveal where the mountain once stood, until carried away as a river of mud capable of dislodging anything in its path, sweeping boulders the size of houses into its flow. As William and I gazed over the vast chasm carved from the mountain, neither of us spoke, though we shared the same thought. This was not the slow march of geological time. It was evidence of a force capable of reconfiguring a mountain and rewriting the history of the earth in an afternoon. We both shuddered to imagine what we would see when we reached the valley floor at Armero, a town that, unlike Murillo, had absorbed the full force of the mountain's wrath.

On the eve of the tragedy, Armero was the third-largest town in Tolima, home to nearly thirty thousand. It was the commercial center of an immensely prosperous agricultural region that produced 30 percent of the nation's rice, along with vast stores of cotton, sorghum, and coffee, all made possible by the rich volcanic soils deposited over the centuries by successive eruptions of the Nevado del Ruiz. Everyone in Armero knew that the volcano, located but thirty miles away, remained active, but as there had not been a serious eruption in 140 years, they dulled their senses by dismissing the volcano as the "Sleeping Lion." They also overlooked the awkward and uncomfortable fact that their modern town had been built on the very site where in 1845 a river of mud from the Nevado del Ruiz had buried alive a thousand innocent victims.

What transpired in Armero would shake Colombia to its core. Already the nation was in mourning, spiritually shattered after M-19 guerrillas, acting at the behest of Pablo Escobar, had only the week before seized the Palace of Justice in Bogotá, taking hundreds of hostages, scores of whom would die, along with twelve supreme court justices, in the final confrontation with the army. It was a dagger into the heart of democracy, leaving many to wonder if the very idea of Colombia as a nation would endure. Then came the news of Armero.

As they had in Murillo, scientists had warned both local authorities and the national government. Seismic activity had been increasing for a year. Other indicators were equally ominous. As Swiss volcanologist Bernard Chouet later recalled, "The volcano was screaming, 'I'm about to explode.'"

Civil defense agencies, responding to these warnings, had printed hazard maps indicating the key danger zones, which included the entire geographical footprint of the town of Armero. A month before the eruption, these maps appeared in national newspapers, but the news did not trickle down to the people. Politicians in Bogotá, citing the fact that the volcano had been dormant for 140 years, accused the volcanologists and civil defense workers of fearmongering. No scientist, they pointed out, could predict with precision if or when an eruption would occur. Preventative measures would be both costly and likely to cause panic, and could not be taken in the absence of certain signs of clear and imminent danger. As a result, no one alerted the local people as to the seriousness of the threat.

On the fateful evening of November 13, even as ash fell upon the town, both the mayor and the priest spoke on local radio, reassuring the people that there was nothing to fear, encouraging them to remain in their homes, secure and calm. Meanwhile, as authorities from Murillo and Líbano and other communities closer to the mountain tried desperately to warn Armero of what was coming, the power failed. Telephones and radios fell silent. All that could be heard was the thunder and wind of a growing storm that loosed a black rain on the town, masking the sound of the mudslide roaring down the mountain, toward the valley. The mayor of Armero, broadcasting on a battery-powered ham radio, was in the midst of telling the people that he did not believe "there was much danger" when the initial wave obliterated his home, burying him and his family alive.

First came a wall of water, a flood that upended cars and swept clean every street. Then, shortly before midnight, the first lahar hit, a river of mud and debris a hundred feet deep, moving at close to thirty miles per hour, rolling over the town for nearly twenty minutes. The second wave moved at half the speed, taking twice as long to run through what was left of Armero. Yet a third surge left in its wake complete devastation. Altogether the destruction went on for two hours, as survivors clung to debris, desperately trying to float above the mud, even as massive boulders crushed everything in their path and sharp stones lacerated the air. Those swallowed by the flow mercifully died of asphyxiation within a minute.

The lahars that formed on the Nevado de Ruiz that terrible day would course through six different river valleys as they fell toward the Magdalena, growing fourfold in size, achieving depths of more than 100 feet, with widths of up to 160 feet. The gravitational force and sheer mass of the flow caused the lahars to spread out as they reached flat terrain, blanketing the ground with mud and debris fields fifteen to twenty feet deep. The mudslide that surged down the Chinchiná Valley destroyed four hundred homes and buried alive eighteen hundred people in the town of Chinchiná. The lahars that followed the valley of the Lagunilla struck Armero, killing three out of every four residents, virtually erasing the town. Some twenty-three thousand men, women, and children would perish. Five thousand houses would be lost. Altogether, thirteen villages would be destroyed, leaving thousands dead, and more than twenty thousand traumatized survivors homeless and without means of support. The financial losses totaled US$6 billion, fully a fifth of Colombia's GNP. It was the worst natural disaster in the history of South America.

Today Armero is a shadowland, a ghostly landscape of memory and loss. Trees grow where dollhouses once stood in the bedrooms of little girls, and the names of the dead are etched above buried doorways that once welcomed home fathers from distant fields, mothers from church, children from the first day of school. There is one image that Colombians will never forget: a photograph of Omayra Sánchez, a young girl of thirteen who lay trapped in the rubble for three days as rescue workers struggled to free her from the mud and debris and the tangle of disfigured bodies that had set like concrete around her innocent being. She remained strong until the end, patient and hopeful, without a word of despair, not a trace of self-pity.

As I wandered through the ruins, along streets empty and silent, in the lee of crumbling churches, temples long abandoned by priests, past walls where lianas covered windows that once opened to the world, I found myself glimpsing Omayra's face at every turn, the image of her near death that had flashed around the world. What the world did not see was the spirit with which that brave young child lived, and the faith that carried her, ever hopeful, into a better world. Should she have died? No. Ought those responsible for all the failures that led to such loss of life at Armero be held responsible? Perhaps yes, though blame is always easy. Omayra Sánchez, in all her innocence and youth, displayed in her most perilous moments a strength and resilience that is found in all good Colombians, and it is surely this quality of character that will carry the country forward if it is to shed the shadows of the past and emerge into the light.

There was one more place to visit before William would return to his family and I'd begin the long journey to the coast. Founded in 1541, nestled in the foothills of the cordillera just west of Honda, Mariquita is perhaps best remembered as the tropical town where Spanish viceroys set up their court every season to escape the cold and damp of Bogotá. It was also the place where Gonzalo Jiménez de Quesada went to die in 1574. Impoverished and alone, his body swollen with leprosy, the conqueror of the Muisca passed away in disgrace, quite unaware that in time his body would be interred in the Cathedral in Bogotá and that he would be honored, in memory, as the founder of Colombia's capital city. In Mariquita, he is remembered today by a rather forlorn statue, recumbent in a cloister protected with chicken wire in the corner of a church, a bearded and armored soldier staring into the heavens with eyes the color of robin's eggs.

What drew William to Mariquita was not the ghost of Quesada but, rather, a small private garden that for him is a place of pilgrimage. Located in the backyard of an old colonial home, it is neither elegant nor well maintained, and it is certainly no match for the formal botanical gardens to be found in all the great cities of Colombia. What sanctifies the site for scholars is the identity of the man who once owned the house. As William pointed out, every tree and shrub in the garden can be traced to a seed or cutting that passed through the hands of the Spanish friar José Celestino Mutis, patriarch of American botany and the inspiration of every plant explorer who has ever stood alone in the forests of Colombia, as if prostrate before the gates of awe.

Among the first to fall under Mutis's spell was Alexander von Humboldt, whose fame in Europe rivaled that of Napoleon. Humboldt originally intended to explore Africa, but the sight of a simple flower, the purple blossoms of bougainvillea, a plant native to the Americas, caused him to shift his sights to the New World. Having explored the forests and plains of Venezuela, he sailed to Cartagena in the last days of 1801, intent on reaching Ecuador and the great volcanoes that soar farther from the center of the earth than any other mountains in the world. The easiest route would have taken him across Panama, and then south by sea to Guayaquil. Instead, he chose to travel forty days up the Río Magdalena to Honda. From there he walked another four days over bare rock and through dense forests, until finally the sky cleared and the horizon unveiled the verdant savannah of Bogotá. Every step took him farther away from Ecuador. Every day on the trail risked the well-being of his party. By the time they reached Bogotá, Humboldt's close companion, the botanist Aimé Bonpland, was shaking with malaria, incapable of further movement. They would be stuck in the city for a month as Bonpland recovered, a delay that delighted Humboldt, allowing him that much more time to pay homage to the man he had gone out of his way to meet, José Celestino Mutis.

Their visit in the end stretched to two months. Mutis regaled Humboldt with stories of Guatavita and the legend of El Dorado; the technical challenges of extracting salt from the mines of Zipaquirá; the curative powers of quinine; the mystery of curare, the flying death; the influence of the gravitational pull of the moon on barometric measurements; the manner by which flowers unfurl to greet the rising sun. Humboldt spoke of biogeography, the anatomy of manatees, the phosphorescent fireflies of Honda, the character of stones. When he showed Mutis his preliminary map of the Magdalena, the older man suggested a few changes and improvements, which Humboldt immediately incorporated. Together they walked the hills and grasslands, as Mutis fed his visitor mangoes imported from the coast, a fruit then unknown in Europe, and oranges from his own garden. Humboldt marveled at the plantings of greens and other vegetables, all from seeds brought to the Americas by Mutis: asparagus, lettuce and chard, cauliflower, eggplant, celery, beets, spinach, basil, garlic, squash and lentils, mustard and mint.

Humboldt trusted Mutis, sharing his private concerns about the treatment of the *silleteros*, those who hoisted the wealthy onto their backs, in chairs, and carried them up and down the mountain trails of the nation. Or the inhumane and cruel abuse endured by the *cargueros*, porters who transported merchandise, which he had witnessed on the road from Honda to Bogotá. He told Mutis of natives he had met who complained of gold miners disturbing the tranquility of the dead. For indigenous people, gold had no monetary value. It was the essence of the sun, positioned beneath the ground to illuminate the paths of shamans as they traveled to the realm of the animal masters. "The pursuit of gold," Humboldt would later write of the mines of Mariquita, "is a European affliction verging on delirium."

That Mutis and Humboldt connected as they did speaks to the kind of man Mutis had become, despite his role as a cleric. Humboldt embodied the values and aspirations of the Enlightenment. He published monographs on biogeography and natural history, but also powerful critiques of slavery and broadsheets advocating social reform. He openly loved men and never married. He spent his fortune freely on intellectual and scientific passions, having arranged that all assets that remained at the time of his death be given away. Perhaps some of Humboldt's convictions and proclivities unsettled Mutis, a man who came of age long before the romantic age of revolution. But like Humboldt, Mutis studied the world and all that was in it. Science brought them together. Both moved readily between disciplines, with Mutis in particular achieving excellence as a botanist, mathematician, astronomer, physicist, linguist, and physician. For his part, Humboldt was deeply impressed that an elderly priest who had achieved so much, with but a few years to live, could embrace new ways of thinking as if an intellectual child of the enlightened age that he and his generation were bringing into being.

José Celestino Mutis had never been a conventional scholar. Born in Cádiz in 1732, he studied medicine, graduating from the University of Seville in 1755, at a time when all physicians were also botanists. After some months at the Real Jardín Botánico in Madrid, he accepted a post as the personal physician for the viceroy of Nueva Granada, embarking for the Americas in September 1760, arriving in Bogotá in late February of the following year. Almost immediately, his presence swept over the staid and conservative city. Though ordained and devout in every way, he understood that church and scholarship need not be at odds. He found comfort in the fact that science addresses the question "How?," whereas only religion can answer the ultimate question "Why?" Though isolated in the New World, he effectively anticipated the intellectual liberation of the Enlightenment a full generation before European thinkers freed their minds of the tyranny of absolute faith.

As a botanist, he began his studies by investigating cinchona, the Andean shrub that yields quinine, at the time the only effective treatment for malaria. As an astronomer, he determined the longitude of Bogotá by measuring with care the extent of an eclipse on one of the satellite orbs of Jupiter. As a linguist, he responded to Catherine the Great's prescient call for the documentation of all languages of the world by compiling dictionaries and grammars of any number of indigenous languages in the Andes and along the Magdalena. In 1762, he inaugurated a chair in mathematics at the Colegio del Rosario, an academic position that allowed him to celebrate the revelations of Copernicus and teach the principles of Newtonian physics. For this transgression, he was brought before the Inquisition in 1774. He was quickly exonerated, quite possibly because the authorities so deeply valued his more practical scientific contributions to the challenges of mining silver and distilling rum.

All of this was but a preamble to Mutis's greatest achievement, the Royal Botanical Expedition, formally endorsed and inaugurated by the king of Spain in 1783. For the next twenty-five years, until his death in 1808, Mutis would be free to wander, licensed to explore the most remote reaches of an unknown land. His conduit to the interior was the Río Magdalena. From late 1783 until 1791, among the most productive years of the survey, Mutis based the expedition in Mariquita, in the very house we had come to see. There is a restaurant now in the great hall where Mutis received his guests, and the tranquility of the garden is disturbed by the raucous laughter of young children dragged to the place by parents with only a tourist's sense of who and what the great man represents in the history of Colombian science. Still, it was a joy to see the children there, running about, playing among the trees, having fun.

Over lunch, William grew almost wistful, thinking of the Colombia Mutis had known. In 1761, the Spanish friar made the first inventory of fish in the river, reporting that a two-pound *dorado* had simply leapt into his boat, followed by an equally plump *bocachico*. Turtles were so abundant that Mutis managed to collect 390 eggs in fifteen minutes. As for caimans, they lined the shores in such numbers that the sun barely reached the sand. What impressed William the most was Mutis's botanical legacy: twenty-four thousand voucher specimens collected, six thousand precise and elegant drawings, along with vast collections of wood, seeds, resins, and fruits. Despite the time it took for letters to reach Europe, Mutis throughout his life maintained contact with Carolus Linnaeus, the Swedish botanist who invented binomial nomenclature, the use of genus and species, which is the foundation of modern systematic classification. He and Linnaeus originated techniques and methods of preserving specimens that botanists use to this day. Mutis's plant collections can still be found in the herbaria of the Real Jardín Botánico in Madrid. The botanical plates drawn by his artists can still be seen and studied. And seeds he'd sown had grown into the trees that shaded us in his garden, as William and I drank the last of our beer and made ready to say good-bye, easing our way into the slow rhythms of a *despedida*, a Colombian farewell.

MEDIO MAGDALENA

The river speaks to all of its terrible burden, all the bodies.
To clean the river is to clean the national soul.

—JUAN MANUEL ECHAVARRÍA

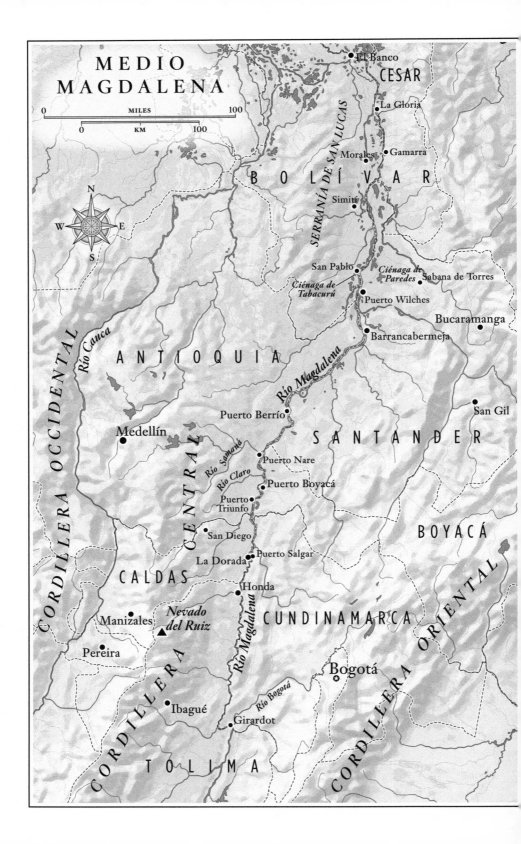

MEDIO
MAGDALENA

0 ——————— MILES ——————— 100

0 ——————— KM ——————— 100

N
W — E
S

El Banco

CESAR

La Gloria

SERRANÍA DE SAN LUCAS

Morales
Gamarra

B O L Í V A R

Simití

San Pablo
Ciénaga de
Paredes
Sabana de Torres

Ciénaga de
Tabacurú

Puerto Wilches

Bucaramanga

Barrancabermeja

Río Cauca

A N T I O Q U I A

Río Magdalena

San Gil

Puerto Berrío

S A N T A N D E R

Medellín

CORDILLERA OCCIDENTAL

Río Samaná

Puerto Nare

Río Claro

Puerto Boyacá

Puerto
Triunfo

CORDILLERA CENTRAL

San Diego

B O Y A C Á

La Dorada
Puerto Salgar

C A L D A S

Honda

Nevado
del Ruiz

C U N D I N A M A R C A

Manizales

Río Magdalena

CORDILLERA ORIENTAL

Pereira

Bogotá

Río Bogotá

Ibagué

Girardot

T O L I M A

CORDILLERA

The Forgotten Land

A Colombian friend once described the Medio Magdalena, the long stretch of river between Honda and El Banco, as the backyard of the nation. In 340 miles, even as the valley expands as the cordilleras fade away on distant horizons, the Magdalena grows, absorbing the Ríos Negro and La Miel, Cimitarra and Opón, the Lebrija, Nare, Carare, Sogamoso, and a host of other smaller affluents. By the time it reaches Puerto Berrío, some ninety miles from Honda on a direct bearing, the width has more than doubled, to eighteen hundred feet. Nearing the wetlands and *ciénaga* of Simití, another 120 miles downstream, the Magdalena divides into two great arms that envelop for more than thirty miles a succession of great islands, the largest of which, Morales, extends the breadth of the river to more than twenty miles.

As it runs unimpeded to the sea, falling some 650 feet in elevation before reaching El Banco, the Río Magdalena defines the boundaries of no fewer than nine Colombian departments: Tolima, Cundinamarca, Caldas, Boyacá, Antioquia, Santander, Bolívar, Cesar, and Magdalena. The river is claimed by all, and yet all are dominated by distant urban centers that have historically remained tethered to the river by only the most tenuous lines of communication, the tracks of the *arrieros*. The various river settlements grew to serve the needs of their departments: Puerto Salgar for Cundina-

marca; La Dorada for Caldas; Puerto Boyacá for Boyacá; Puerto
Berrío, Puerto Nare, and Puerto Triunfo for Antioquia; Puerto
Wilches for Santander; La Gloria for Cesar; and El Banco for Magdalena. Commerce dominated each port, and for those who worked
the trade, the river became a single community, each town a familiar
stop.

But many who lived along the Magdalena seldom went beyond
the limits defined by their own sense of place, and that often implied
no farther than the next bend in the river. Surrounded by dense
forests that reached to the distant mountains, in a hot, tropical basin
with notorious rates of malaria that ravaged children and discour-
aged settlement, the towns along the river were kept alive by the
economies of the hinterland. From the perspective of their department capitals, they were distant and isolated frontier outposts where
the people lived unto themselves and national authorities had at
best a muted presence. Over time, the Medio Magdalena earned
a reputation for independence and lawlessness, one that was only
confirmed as the region became both a refuge for the innocent and
a place of exile and opportunity for all the drifters, smugglers, and
petty *bandidos* that color the pages of Colombia's past.

From the beginning, the river running through the Medio Magdalena was all about the movement of goods and people. Tobacco
from Ambalema passed through the hands of German merchants in
Barranquilla to reach markets in New York and Hamburg, where it
was paid for in gold and celebrated as the finest product of its kind.
Vegetable ivory, derived from the seeds of the *tagua* palm, emerged
in the 1880s as one of Colombia's leading exports, earning literally
its weight in gold. Before the age of plastics, *tagua* was the basis for
every button on every garment worn in the industrialized world,
and Colombia was the main source. Cotton from Neiva kept alive
the textile mills of England, especially as exports from the American
South dwindled with the outbreak of the Civil War in 1861. From
these same cotton fields of the Alto Magdalena came the raw product that two generations later made possible the textile industry of
Medellín, with the founding of Coltejer in 1907 and Fabricato, a
decade later, in 1920. Cotton for the mills of Medellín, cacao from
Cúcuta, coffee from Manizales, leather and hides from Cundina-

marca, livestock from Bolívar destined for Jamaica—everything traveled by river, including the engineers and priests, artists and academics, physicians, politicians, common laborers and ranch hands, and all the many thousands of immigrants who washed ashore in Barranquilla throughout the nineteenth century: Italians, Germans, Syrians, and Lebanese, all destined to find new lives in the interior of the country. In a mountainous land where geography alone impeded and defied the growth of a modern state, the Río Magdalena literally made commerce—and, thus, Colombia—possible. Thanks to the river, in 1950 a merchant could ship a bushel of coffee from Medellín to London for less than it cost to send it to Bogotá.

The commercialization of the Magdalena in the early years of the nineteenth century began with one man's obsession. During the revolutionary war with Spain, Simón Bolívar experienced firsthand the overwhelming strategic and geographical significance of the river. "Whoever dominates the Magdalena," he famously proclaimed, "controls the fate of men." Arriving in Cartagena from Caracas in 1813, he had immediately set out to seize control of all settlements along the lower reaches of the river—Salamina, Heredia, El Piñón, Tenerife, Guamal, Tamalameque, El Banco, Mompox, Ocaña, and Cúcuta—in a military campaign that would earn him the name for which he would be known around the world, and through all history: "El Libertador." In the wake of independence, Bolívar, the father of "La Gran Colombia," recognized that dependable and affordable river transportation would be essential for the prosperity of the new nation.

In 1823, in exchange for an investment of $500,000, Bolívar's government granted exclusive navigational rights to the entire Magdalena drainage to Juan Bernardo Elbers, a naturalized Colombian of German birth who, in support of the revolution, had provided the ships that allowed the insurgents to capture Cartagena in 1819. In accepting the commercial monopoly, Elbers agreed to the impossible. He was expected to import and operate the steamships, build shelters and warehouses up and down the Magdalena for passengers and freight, and, above all, maintain the river, clearing its banks, dredging the shallows, doing whatever was necessary to guarantee the commercial viability of the enterprise. Taking on this quixotic challenge, Elbers was immediately caught up in the rivalry between Bolívar and his political nemesis, Francisco de Paula Santander. In an attempt to mollify both revolutionary heroes, he named the first two imported steamships *El Gran Bolívar* and *El General Santander.* Unfortunately, both vessels were plagued with problems, and Elbers was soon obliged to import a third, *El Libertador;* he deliberately chose that name to send a message to Bolívar as to where his true loyalties lay.

From their first day on the river, the *vapores*, all steam-driven paddle wheelers, set in motion the slow transformation of the Medio Magdalena. Each vessel consumed as much as two hundred pounds of wood an hour. To fire the great furnaces that generated the steam, men worked furiously whenever the ships were underway, burning through reserves of wood that often made up more than half of a vessel's cargo. To ensure constant sources of supply, Elbers established depots along the river, leaving behind men or contracting those already living in the area to cut and pile wood. Those who did the work, reaching each day ever farther into the forest, became known as *leñateros.* The riverside outposts where they lived, carved from the *monte* but visited regularly by the *vapores*, attracted others eager to benefit from the trade: men selling their labor, women peddling flowers or fruit, fresh eggs or *totumas*, the small calabashes used by passengers to pour water over their bodies as they showered and bathed. In time, many of these stations, initially established simply to provide a dependable supply of fuel, grew into small settlements that ultimately became towns and small cities: Puerto Triunfo and La Dorada, Calamar, Puerto Nare, Tenerife, Pinillos, Zambrano, Caracolí, and La Humareda, to name a few.

Early accounts of river travelers invariably describe the regular stops for firewood as among the highlights of the day. As *leñateros* at every station cut their way farther away from the riverbanks, they used donkeys, or *burros*, to transport the wood. The amount each animal could carry—roughly seventy three-foot logs—became the standard of the trade, with each ship's efficiency being measured by the number of loads, or *burros de leña*, consumed. The *vapores* acquired reputations, with some consuming fifty *burros* a day, while others, such as the notorious *Vapor Antioquia*, required twice as much wood to cover the same distance on the water. For passengers, these rates of consumption made all the difference. Even the most efficient ships had to resupply three or four times a day, with each stop taking at least an hour as the entire crew, including waiters and kitchen staff, scrambled ashore to hoist the logs on board, having first carefully screened the wood piles for toxic toads, scorpions, and poisonous snakes.

Most vessels burned roughly three *burros* an hour heading upriver, and two going down. In the 1880s, a journey by paddle wheeler from Barranquilla to Honda took ninety hours, and the return to the coast just forty-eight, implying a total consumption of some four hundred *burros de leña* for a single round trip. By 1890, there were no fewer than seventy large commercial steamships on the Magdalena, each in constant service, all slowly consuming one of the rarest tropical rain forests on earth. A broad river valley that appeared to the *leñateros* as just another impenetrable expanse of *monte* was, in fact, the setting of an epic botanical drama, a struggle worthy of the Titans, as Amazon, Pacific, and Caribbean floras converged to resist the ambitions of all the plants slowly making their way south from Central America.

The severe impact of deforestation along the shores of the Magdalena was evident as early as 1880, when the German geographer Friedrich von Schenck reported both his concern for the fate of the forests and a far greater worry. Colombians were not just oblivious to the situation; they viewed the forest as a limitless resource that only stood in the way of development. By the early years of a new century, the steamships of the Magdalena had burned some forty million cubic yards of invaluable hardwoods: *caimito* and *comino*, *cedro*, *sangretoro*, *abarco*, and *suán*. The wrath of the passengers also fell upon the wildlife. Vessels became platforms for the hunting of manatees, blue turtles, ocelots, and jaguars. Men shot herons from the upper deck for sport. Children cut open the bellies of iguanas, replaced their eggs with manure, and tossed them back into the river. Women sported hats festooned with feathers, a fashion statement that drove flamingos and egrets to near extinction. This slaughter continued well into the twentieth century. In 1949, the Colombian priest and botanist Enrique Pérez Arbeláez, traveling down the Magdalena, observed his fellow passengers, with nothing to entertain or divert them, killing caimans with machine guns.

Alonso Restrepo, today a gentle old man retired in Cali, witnessed the first spasms of settlement in the Medio Magdalena when he went to work for the Naviera Colombiana in 1942. With a fleet of forty vessels, La Naviera, as it was commonly known, was then the largest of all the shipping companies on the Magdalena. Hired as the company's secretary, Alonso was tasked with taking the minutes at board meetings and, more importantly, reporting to management and the board about the condition of the river and the general state of affairs of all their Magdalena commercial operations. Initially he was based at the head office in Medellín, a wondrous building in the shape of a riverboat that still stands at the corner of Palacé and Avenida Primero de Mayo. In his first days on the job, Alonso naturally sought the advice of his new colleagues, some of whom had worked for the company for years.

"I never managed to find anyone who really knew the river," Alonso recalled, still astonished and saddened after more than seventy years, "not a single person who could tell me stories about the Magdalena. The board of directors had no interest at all. After three years serving the company in Medellín, not one of them had even been to the river, not once in their entire lives. All it meant to them was money. I've never met a *paisa* or a *bogotano* interested in the river. We have always turned our backs on the Magdalena. We have done so forever."

Alonso set out on his own to discover the river, traveling first by car along a route he had walked as a child, from Medellín to Rionegro and La Ceja, Abejorral to La Dorada. In time, he came to know every port from Puerto Berrío to La Gloria.

At first, Alonso recalled, the forests were mostly intact. Along the river there were known and established depots that supplied wood, but the captains were free to cut their own deals, bringing their *vapores* to shore at their discretion, contracting *leñateros* to have so many loads of wood ready by the time the vessel returned. The woodsmen, for the most part, were a brutal lot: fugitives from the law, army deserters, ex-*bogas* forced from their trade by the arrival of the steamships. They were part of a long tradition that since the time of the Spanish viceroys had seen the Medio Magdalena populated, sometimes forcibly, by the least desired people of the nation, prostitutes and the destitute, criminals and thieves, outcasts shadowed by shame, all the unwanted souls sent to the middle of nowhere, and left alone to live or to die.

It was from this place of desperation, strength, and resilience, with loyalty to nothing beyond survival, that the character of the people of the Medio Magdalena was forged. Alonso recognized this aggressive spirit in the way the *leñateros* went after the forest, as if the felling of trees were a sacramental gesture. To meet demand, they lived as nomads, constantly moving in search of new sources of supply, even as the impact of their labors extended from the forests within immediate reach of the river to the entire basin of the Medio Magdalena. Over time, the pursuit of firewood for the steamships morphed into a mission that had a particular resonance for those who saw the clearing of any forest as an act of civilization and conquest, the triumph of human will over the chaos and dangerous unpredictability of the natural world, people for whom the phrase *tumbar el monte* took on patriotic if not religious significance.

"We'd come back to pick up an order of wood," Alonso sighed as if in disbelief, "perhaps three hundred burros, a tiny patch of woodland, only to find that the entire forest was gone. You could not find a stick anywhere, not even a trace of grass where once the forest had been. And it wasn't then about cattle. None of these men had the money to buy a single cow. It was all about the act of destruction, which for them was a source of pride. Just listen to the words of Antioquia's anthem, something children grow up singing all the time: 'The ax my ancestors left me, how I love it for the sound of freedom it makes with each blow.'"

Alonso recalled the anger of some of the riverboat captains as they came upon vast openings in the forest, a thousand or even two thousand acres of burning slash, a forest destroyed not for wood but simply because it could be done, the land cleared and cleansed as if in an act of grace, the civilization of the wild: "To a man, these captains loved the Magdalena and its forests and all the wild animals and birds that gave meaning to their lives. As they stood on the bridge of their vessel, proud and alert, you could see them staring at these great scenes of destruction, even as they muttered obscenities beneath their breath."

Alonso grew wistful as he shared a final thought, "How fortunate we all are that these early pioneers in the Medio Magdalena had only axes, and not chain saws."

Today, of course, they do.

There is a tributary in the Medio Magdalena, a small river in Antioquia, that runs over a bed of green marble, passing beneath tall limestone bluffs with caves that come alive at dusk as thousands of *guácharos* emerge into the night. Spinning in the darkness, etching patterns against the stars, the birds quickly disappear beyond the highest reaches of the canopy. At dawn, they return, satiated and weary. As mist rises from the river, and the *guácharos* fall silent as they roost, there is a brief moment of calm, a sense of stillness, soon broken by a cacophony of hoots, whistles, and screams as scores of forest creatures awaken to herald the sun. Some mornings one can hear the distant sound of jungle cats, a reminder of a time, within the memory of men, when jaguars came to this secret forest to mate, seeking refuge in a river valley known only to them. It was here, within the hidden canyon of the Río Claro, that Juan Guillermo Garcés rediscovered his spiritual essence, the pure purpose that had fired his heart since childhood, a natural force that not even fifty years of violence and war could quell. His story, in many ways, is the story of the Medio Magdalena.

Like so many Colombians, Juan Guillermo's father, as a boy, dreamed of owning a cattle ranch. In the late 1940s, at a time when land in the Medio Magdalena could be claimed by anyone with the will and capacity to work, the family abandoned a comfortable life in Medellín and set out into the unknown. In the face of impossible physical challenges, with undaunted courage and tenacity, the Garcés family took on the herculean task of clearing the jungle. They shared an audacity common to every settler in every forest opening across the Magdalena basin. Their goal was not just to create a home and a source of income; it was to liberate the sky, allowing sunlight to fall upon a blanket of lush grass, open ground running to the horizon, supporting great herds of cattle, allowing men to be independent and free.

Juan Guillermo's earliest memories are of traveling from Medellín to the family ranch, passing by train to Puerto Berrío, and from there sailing up the Magdalena to La Dorada aboard the legendary *vapor* the *David Arango*. Invariably a trip that ought to have taken but a day consumed three, for in summer the river was always low, and sandbars made for a slow and patient passage. What Juan Guillermo remembers is a collage of images, furtive flashes that illuminated the mind of a child: the trumpets and drums of an orchestra swinging to the rhythms of the Caribbean, clouds of mosquitoes by night, and, by day, shores covered with caimans. One sight remained forever imprinted in his heart, mind, and spirit. It was 1952, at the height of La Violencia, and the river once again had become the graveyard of the nation. Slightly older by then, of an age that secured and froze memories, he watched as several corpses floated by facedown in the water, with vultures perched on top, feeding on the flesh of the dead.

Death came to the family in 1961, when Juan Guillermo was twelve. The worst of La Violencia was over, and a peace agreement had been signed, creating the National Front. The Garcés ranch was near Puerto Triunfo, a Conservative town. Men from the Liberal bastion of Puerto Boyacá, who had been running a protection racket for some years, continued to demand money from the family. Juan Guillermo's father refused. A day later they returned, armed with shotguns and a revolver, and left him dead. Juan Guillermo was away, attending university in Medellín. It took two days for his father's body to reach the city, and by the time the corpse was placed on display in the family home, it was already in a state of decomposition, just like the corpses that, as a boy, Juan Guillermo had seen floating on the river.

As his older brother, Jorge Tulio, took over the ranch, Juan Guillermo continued his studies. About a year after the murder of his father, he was exposed at school to both Darwin's theory of evolution and the Christian account of God's creation of the world, all on the same day. The juxtaposition intrigued him, and, though just thirteen, he confronted both his teachers and his classmates with the obvious contradiction. That very afternoon he was taken before the rector of the school and expelled.

Returning to the ranch, he went to work for his brother, clearing land. Altogether, the family had some seventy-five hundred acres, of which only a couple hundred had been reclaimed from the forest at the time of their father's death. The brothers set out to honor his dream and, with a crew of 150 workers, cleared fifteen hundred acres in just one summer. Once dry, the tangle of deadfall had to be reduced to ash. Hoping for a clean burn, they set fire to the brush on all sides, only to watch in horror as a great conflagration flared, leaving them blinded by smoke and trapped within a whirlwind of flames. Both would have perished had it not been for a ranch hand who risked his life to lead them out of the fire. As they escaped, Juan Guillermo saw scores of wild creatures—deer, foxes, ocelots—succumb to the flames. It was a sight that would change his life forever.

If his father's dream had been a ranch carved from the forest, Juan Guillermo's secret goal was to buy an encyclopedia and build a library. Despite having dropped out of school, he remained obsessed with books. With the help of a friend, he managed to buy, on credit, a collection of a hundred classics, promising to make monthly payments for two years. Knowing almost nothing about the world beyond the ranch, Juan Guillermo had no idea where to begin. So he set about devouring every book, as if in personal conversation with Alfred Russel Wallace, Marcel Proust, Émile Zola, and so many others. Hesitant lest the ranch hands think less of him, he read mostly on the sly, in quiet moments, often in the middle of the night, his book illuminated by candlelight. During the day, he sometimes hid away in the upper branches of a mango tree that grew close to his father's grave. Perched twenty feet off the ground, with the scent of ripe mangoes all around him, Juan Guillermo read Charles Darwin's *The Origin of Species*, cover to cover, from morning to dusk, in three days.

"I could not stop," he later recalled, "because I was discovering the world, an entire new universe of thought."

Inspired by Darwin, Pierre Teilhard de Chardin, and philosophers such as Arthur Schopenhauer, Juan Guillermo became every day more and more enchanted by the origins and nature of life. Science became his guiding light. On one of his rare visits to Medellín, he bought a microscope. Completely self-taught, he studied everything that struck his fancy: the spinning organisms found within a drop of water, plant cells beneath the surface of leaves, the semen of animals. On the ranch he created his own biological laboratory, conducting experiments of his own design: comparing the weight of dung in the nest of oropendola birds, measuring the relative efficacy of various biodegradable fish toxins, capturing caterpillars purely for the joy of watching them transform into butterflies through the miracle of metamorphosis.

By this point, even the most humble of the ranch hands, not to mention his mother and all his family, knew Juan Guillermo was destined for a life of knowledge. University beckoned, but having left school at thirteen, he faced entrance exams that demanded competence in chemistry, physics, algebra, trigonometry, and calculus. Fortunately, Juan Guillermo's wife—he had married at nineteen—had a brilliant cousin just out of high school, a young lad named Gustavo Echeverri, who offered to help. Every day for a year, the two met for six hours, from late afternoon to midnight. Gustavo shared with Juan Guillermo everything he knew, which, as it turned out, was more than enough for him to secure a place at the Universidad de Antioquia. Juan Guillermo returned to the city of his birth fully intent on becoming a scientist. His mother was convinced he would come back to the ranch a veterinarian, ready to help with the cattle.

Perhaps inevitably, given his character, Juan Guillermo was almost immediately swept up by the spirit of the times, the wave of protest that in the late 1960s convulsed virtually every campus and city in the Western world. Juan Guillermo, who had always rejected violence, joined MOIR, a leftist movement, and set out to organize the campesinos of the Medio Magdalena, all with the naïve yet sincere goal of transforming his country. For eight years, he built a political organization, eventually taking on the role of regional secretary, responsible for twenty-six municipalities on both sides of the Río Magdalena, from Armero to Barrancabermeja. His brother

Jorge Tulio, who anticipated the rise of the paramilitary and the wave of violent reaction that would convulse the entire basin, feared for Juan Guillermo's life, even as he assured any fellow rancher who would listen that MOIR was committed to nonviolence and that his young brother Juancho had nothing to do with the FARC, the ELN, or any of the self-professed militant revolutionaries.

Juan Guillermo knew it was only a matter of time before he would become a marked man. In the summer of 1977, he retreated to the family ranch. One night in August, with his brother away in Medellín, he found himself alone as a violent thunderstorm swept over the valley. Gustavo, the lad who had tutored him for all those many months, had been staying on the ranch but had gone to town for the evening and was not expected back until the following day. As a precaution, Juan Guillermo decided to spend the night in the room Gustavo had been using. Asleep at midnight, he was startled awake by a strange sound at the front door, followed moments later by a noise at his window. Someone was trying to pry open the shutters. Taking a revolver from beneath his pillow, he waited silently in the darkness. A crashing sound filled the room. Without hesitation, he fired into the shadows, certain that the intruder had come to murder him. Then he heard the words that would haunt him for the rest of his life:

"Juancho, you've killed me."

The voice was Gustavo's. Juan Guillermo raced to his side, reaching for his body as it fell. The bullet had pierced the chest. They spoke softly for a time, with Gustavo explaining that he had decided to come back to the ranch on a whim. With his last words, he forgave Juan Guillermo, saying that it was not his fault, that it was just the madness of the times. Juan Guillermo held his friend closely in his arms as both men wept; their tears ran together and pooled on Gustavo's cheek as he passed away. In that instant, Juan Guillermo, horrified by the violence that had overtaken his dreams, turned his back on politics forever. Renouncing his position in the movement, he became a dedicated pacifist, so committed to the sanctity of life that he would not, from that moment forward, so much as step on a passing ant or slap a bothersome mosquito.

For twenty-five years, Juan Guillermo worked as a journalist and filmmaker, even as Colombia and the Medio Magdalena descended into darkness. His response was to turn to nature. As a boy, he had first heard of the Río Claro from Eduardo Betancur, an old campesino who worked on the ranch. Some years earlier, not long after his father's death, this man had set out to hunt a jaguar that had been killing their cattle. For two months he tracked the elusive creature, which led him deeper and deeper into the forest. By the time they reached the Río Claro, the hunter had lost all desire to kill. The creature had become his ally, and he the shadow of the cat. Emerging from the forest, like a deer at the edge of a clearing, he stood dazzled by all that he saw: a riverbed of green marble, limestone cliffs covered in rare bromeliads, aroids, and ferns, and, along the shore, strange palms and flowering trees with blossoms unlike anything he had ever known. Only slowly did he realize this was the river long sacred to native peoples, a hidden valley of spirits and witches that many spoke about but few had ever seen.

As he listened to the old man's tale, Juan Guillermo knew his destiny would be somehow touched by the Río Claro. But it was not until 1968, aided by a report from a helicopter pilot, that he and his brother Jorge finally stumbled out of the forest and beheld the river's wonder. By then, the new highway from Medellín to Bogotá was under construction. Juan Guillermo realized to his horror that its right-of-way ran through the very forests that gave life to the Río Claro. He and Jorge first secured fifty acres in the heart of the canyon and then began to buy all the land in the valley, with the goal of ultimately creating a nature preserve and scientific research station, along with educational facilities that would celebrate biodiversity, clean water, and conservation.

Nothing came easily. Jorge died in a tragic plane crash. Juan Guillermo's daughter, María Isabel, an ardent conservationist tormented by the unraveling of the natural world, took her own life at eighteen. The Río Claro itself came under siege. The course of the river as it falls out of the forested hills toward the Magdalena runs near to where Pablo Escobar built his luxurious retreat, Hacienda Nápoles. In the 1980s, the region became ground zero as war flared between the Medellín and Cali Cartels, and rivers of blood flowed as paramilitaries of the United Self-Defense Forces of the Magdalena

Medio, often in collusion with the *narcotraficantes*, swept the valley clean of all subversives: petty thieves desperate to feed their families, teachers and union organizers, university students still under the spell of dreams.

For more than a decade, Juan Guillermo shied away from the violence, devoting his time to filmmaking and journalism, with only brief and furtive visits to the Río Claro. With the death of Pablo Escobar in 1993, he was able to return, but only for a time. In early 1997, guerrillas of the ELN (National Liberation Army) found Juan Guillermo sitting quietly on the banks of the river. Slipping a hood over his head, they marched him deep into the forest. After two months in captivity, Juan Guillermo overheard a radio broadcast announcing that several ELN cadres had been killed in a foiled attempt to assassinate Álvaro Uribe, then governor of Antioquia. He realized from the location and description of the attack that the guerrillas had originated from the very band that held him prisoner. Knowing that most of his captors would be away for at least two days, he plotted his escape, slipping into the forest that very night. Months later, he was kidnapped yet again. By this point, he had lost his daughter and was as close to despair as he would ever be. When they reached the ELN encampment, he dared the guerrillas to kill him. Death, he told them, meant nothing to him. He then turned his back on their guns and walked home.

Once again he was forced away from the Río Claro. Five years went by, until finally, with the demobilization of the paramilitaries and the fading fortunes of the guerrillas, he could return. With him came a beautiful new wife and partner, Ximena Arosemena, a woman of radiant grace and compassion. Together, they would realize all of Juan Guillermo's original dreams. Working closely with local people, they built an ecotourism resort widely heralded as both a biological and spiritual marvel, the Río Claro Natural Reserve. With the acquisition of five thousand acres of additional land, they created a wildlife sanctuary for jaguars and ocelots, pumas and all the creatures that had once thrived in the forests of the Medio Magdalena. Educational programs continue to bring children and youths from the barrios of Medellín into the wonder of the forest, where they learn about nature from direct experience and from professional scientists. Among the most generous supporters of the program is Álvaro Cogollo, the head of Medellín's Jardín Botánico and one of Colombia's leading botanical explorers. To date, Álvaro and his team, just while working with the young kids from the city, have discovered no fewer than a hundred new species of plants, all within reach of the crystal waters of the Río Claro.

As Juan Guillermo continues to acquire land and expand the reach of his programs, he never thinks of himself as the owner of anything. To him, Río Claro is a sacred place, a temple of nature, destined to be protected and enjoyed by all people for all time. Among its guardians will be a beautiful young woman, Oriana, his daughter with Ximena. One morning as I followed the two of them along the river, each tiptoeing along the trail, no doubt dodging ants, I overheard Juan Guillermo explaining to Oriana why he would never cut down a tree or knowingly cause harm to any creature in the forest. Her name, I later learned, was inspired by Greek mythology, a story of divine resilience, a new dawning, a child rising in the sky.

Every evening Juan Guillermo and I made our way upriver to witness the flight of the *guácharos*, for him a daily devotion. He finds inspiration in their habits, what he calls the poetry of survival. Feeding on laurels and palms, they are the only nocturnal fruit-eating birds in the world. While their eyesight allows for night vision, they navigate like bats, using echolocation, producing a high-pitched clicking noise audible to the human ear. The cry of a single *guácharo* has been likened to that of a man enduring torture—hence the common name throughout the Antilles, *diablotin*, French for "little devil." The ever-practical English called them oilbirds; they boiled down the chicks by the thousands to produce fuel for their lamps. The call of a single bird is, indeed, loud and unpleasant, but as clouds of *guácharos* emerge from the shadows, the cacophony cascades into a single harmonic tone that Juan Guillermo compares to the sound of ten thousand discordant hearts coming together as one.

As we sat together in the sand, I asked him about the prospects of peace. Like most Colombians, he anticipated a long and slow process of reconciliation, a national reckoning fraught with the possibility of failure. For too many years, he said, Colombians lived in fear, huddled behind walls, the wealthy and powerful hidden away within cordons of private security that invariably proved insufficient. Kidnappings were as common as birthdays. A new language was born. *La milagrosa*, the miracle catch, referred to roadblocks set up by armed groups on public highways, allowing them to randomly search vehicles with the hope of finding anyone worth taking. *El paseo de los millonarios* was the fate of those forced at gunpoint to go from ATM to ATM, draining their bank accounts with each transaction. *Dar papaya* was a term of ridicule for those foolish enough to leave themselves vulnerable in public. But even the most cautious, those who would never "give anyone a papaya," remained targets.

In 2000, the FARC Central Committee passed the infamous Law 002, creating a "revolutionary tax" obliging every Colombian with a net worth of more than $1 million to pay up or face retribution. The FARC's goal was to match the billion-dollar military and development aid package known as Plan Colombia, America's contribution to the conflict. In 2000 alone, the number of kidnap victims soared to 3,706. People of wealth or influence became prisoners in their own homes. Those with the means sent their children and other dependents abroad. Many simply fled. The country's capacity to function was challenged by an exodus that, by the very nature of the threat, included many of its most talented and successful citizens: scientists and scholars, business leaders, medical experts, engineers and bankers, athletes and artists, writers, musicians, journalists, politicians, and poets. Families across Colombia endured the agony of separation as their children left the country; two generations of young men and women, the hope and future of the nation, sent into voluntary exile, with no certain date of return.

Later that night, as Juan Guillermo and I returned to the main lodge for a drink, I met, quite by chance, a lovely woman, today a close friend, whose life had been defined by the very forces he had identified. Loss and exile, redemption and return. Xandra Uribe and her father, Jaime, had come to Río Claro with a large party that had just spent two days rafting the Río Samaná, another small but beautiful tributary of the Magdalena. The two of them lit up the bar, each aglow with the wonder of a river that cascades through one dramatic rapid after another, each capable of flipping a raft, as apparently had happened, leaving both Xandra and her father drifting downstream, even as the kayak guides raced to the rescue. Jaime was, as he acknowledged, completely shaken by the experience. Xandra, too, had been frightened, convinced that she was about to drown, as the current dragged her into the darkness before spitting her back to the surface, where she floated, eyes wide open, through an enchanted forest she could only compare to Eden.

On the map but a scratch, a few dots of blue indicating a river crossing two hours by road from Medellín, the Samaná is, in truth, one of Colombia's secret gardens, an oasis of biodiversity in a vast mountain landscape long compromised by settlement and deforestation. With dense forests rising steeply to the skylines and a broken, virtually impassable shoreline of massive boulders, stones the size of great monuments, the hidden valley supports more than 200 species of birds, a third as many as are found in all of Canada, and no fewer than 398 species of plants, with more endemics than occur in Scotland. There are howler and spider monkeys, jaguars and tapirs, no fewer than sixteen species of iridescent frogs, and, in the river, the rarest of migratory fish. A young botanist who had been with Xandra and Jaime could not contain his joy as he recalled coming upon a new species of palm on a previous trip down the river. Raising his glass, he heralded the Samaná as the embodiment of Colombia's true national wealth, biological riches without equal in the world.

As those at the bar slowly dispersed, with many heading off to bed, exhausted after their time on the Samaná, I followed Xandra and her father to the edge of the terrace. They took such delight in each other's company that I had initially taken them to be husband and wife. Only later, as we became friends, did I understand their unique connection. Jaime is, above all, an artist. Sensitive, inspired, generous to a fault, he makes a living as a commercial designer, an ad man, when all he really wants, or so it seems, is to be a boy again, with a life devoted to fun and play. Most of the time, it's not possible. In Medellín he and his beloved wife, Margarita, are responsible for a staff of eighty and the output of one of Latin America's most creative and influential advertising agencies, not to mention the management of one of the most beautiful and productive coffee farms in Antioquia, their pride and joy. Jaime's release comes when he travels with Xandra, be it to Cocos Island to swim with sharks or to a small and unknown river as close to home as the Samaná. When they're together, he becomes as young as his vibrant spirit and still rakish body permits, which brings them both great joy.

Xandra is the kind of daughter a good and decent man like Jaime deserves. Tall, thin, and dangerously pretty, she too is an artist, with dark eyes that light up in the presence of a new idea, a new possibility, anything curious and inspiring. Her closely cropped hair recalled London in the early 1960s: dark, elegant, and hip, like everything about her. Only much later would I learn that she normally wears her hair long, and that it was brown, not black, and that she had just recently overcome a life-threatening bout of cancer. Having faced death, she embraces life with effervescent joy. She has no time for compromise and little patience with anything that might divert her from her singular passion to learn everything she possibly can about her country, all that she missed in her many years living abroad.

Strange as it may sound, her love of Colombia finds its most perfect expression in her passion for edible beans. Her collection includes hundreds of varieties, from all regions of the country, many of which she cultivates on her farm in the hills above Medellín. Xandra loves beans the way birds love the wind and fish treasure the sea. She savors them as food, serving up astonishing meals, adding new recipes to her repertoire by the day. And she admires their beauty, equating them to precious stones, with language women normally use when swooning over trays of diamonds. Xandra employs beans as talismans and charms, and as the basis of jewelry and works of art. She decorates her home with bowls of her rarest specimens, in all colors of the rainbow. With great delight she cites ethnobotanists and archaeologists who acknowledge that of all our common foods, only beans were originally domesticated as ornaments. Among her many unusual points of pilgrimage in Colombia is CIAT, the International Center for Tropical Agriculture, the global seed bank at Palmira in the upper Cauca Valley, which stores and preserves 37,987 distinct varieties of beans, collected in 110 countries around the world. Xandra considers CIAT a sacred repository far more significant than Lourdes or the Vatican or any other stone temple built by the hands of men. Beans, she says, are the work of the divine, a gift of the gods, the source of life itself.

What she really loves about beans, I suspect, is their vitality, their strength and resilience, the speed and tenacity with which they grow, skirting and enveloping obstacles with leaves that unfold before your eyes, blossoms turning to the light as tendrils reach for the sky. Beans mean something to Xandra that only a Colombian, perhaps only a *paisa*, a child of the verdant hills of Antioquia, can understand. When she plants her seeds, she doesn't just cultivate a garden; she lays claim to the soil, as if recovering a stolen legacy. Like so many of her generation, she was driven into exile as a young girl, only to return as a woman, a stranger in her own land. Every day in her garden, she makes up for all the lost time.

City of Eternal Spring

Xandra Uribe was a child of Medellín in the 1980s. As Pablo Escobar unleashed his war against the state, random violence terrorized her city, laying waste to her teenage years. Bombs were a constant: in her neighborhood, near her school, in restaurants and bars, in the lobby of the Intercontinental Hotel just two blocks away from her home, a blast that blew in the front door and shattered the windows of her house. Only by a fluke of good fortune, a touch of pure serendipity, had her parents one night escaped death. Heading out for a simple dinner, they were about to back into a parking place in front of the restaurant when an aggressive driver behind them stole the slot. They drove on and parked up the street. By chance, as they strolled back to the restaurant, they ran into some friends and joined them for a quick drink. As they were getting ready to move on to dinner, the entire city block was rocked by a massive explosion that completely destroyed the restaurant they had originally chosen, leaving its outdoor tables mere splinters of metal and wood, reducing cars along the street to twisted and burning wreckage.

The late 1980s were a low point in Medellín's fortunes. Escobar was at the height of his power and influence. The cartel controlled 80 percent of the global market for illicit cocaine. Defying the strongest and most technologically sophisticated military force in the world, the pride of an avenging nation spending $60 billion a year fighting a war on drugs largely focused on crushing his operations, Escobar still managed to ship eighty tons of cocaine into the United States every month, generating as much as $70 million a day, so much money that his operation had to budget a thousand dollars a week just for the purchase of rubber bands to wrap the stacks of contraband cash. The sheer volume of currency coming back into Colombia, the profits of the trade, made finding secure storage a constant challenge. Each year the cartel had to write off fully 10 percent of its revenues, literally tens of millions of paper dollars gnawed, nibbled, and soiled by rats too numerous to control in warehouses and decrepit hangouts hidden beneath the radar of the law. By the age of thirty-three, Pablo Escobar personally controlled revenues exceeding $20 billion a year. His net worth was $55 billion, making him the richest criminal in history. And the bloodiest. In the seven years that Al Capone ruled Chicago, the notorious gangster was said to have personally killed thirty-three victims. In the decade of terror unleashed by Escobar, in Medellín alone, more than forty-six thousand would die.

By the end of the 1980s, Pablo Escobar owned no fewer than eight hundred properties, dispersed strategically in the barrios of Medellín, and scattered throughout rural Antioquia. Protected by rings of corruption, payoffs that bought him effective control of the city, Pablo became a law unto himself, with rivers of cash to reward the faithful and armies of assassins to punish anyone who stood in his way. *Plata o plomo,* "silver or lead," was the binary option in what became a universe of death. Escobar made a fetish of revenge, placing bounties on the lives of politicians and policemen, journalists and priests, rivals in the drug trade and anyone related to anyone he deemed to be a threat or an enemy. The wave of fear unleashed by his terror had courtroom judges quivering beneath black hoods as they tried in vain to mask their identities, young mothers in city parks nervously scanning the contents of passing prams, ordinary citizens scattering at the sight of police cars, for each was a moving target, just as every cop not on the take was a marked man. Pablo Escobar's gift to Colombia was to make life cheap and murder lucrative.

Pablo's rage grew through time, reaching crescendos of homicidal fury, but it was born in the simple resentments of a streetwise youth unwilling to have his life defined and his ambitions thwarted by a society transparently structured, as he saw it, in favor of those born to privilege and wealth. He spoke derisively, often with dripping contempt, of *la gente bien*, the "good people," those who shared the family names and lineages that allowed them to control access to the finest schools and universities, the government ministries, and all the private clubs where they drank whiskey and traded gossip and power with their cousins. And yet, much as he professed hatred for the Medellín elite, Pablo, in all his vanity, passionately desired to become a part of their world, to be accepted by the ruling families of the city on his own terms, if only to disrupt and expose their petty conceits. His great strategic error—in the end, his fatal mistake—was the miscalculation that money alone, whatever its provenance, would propel him and his family to the heights of Colombian society.

Born in Rionegro, in the hills above the city, the son of a father he hardly knew, Pablo was raised in the barrios of Medellín, nursed on the conviction that nothing would come his way, save what he seized for himself, a lesson learned directly from his mother, a fiercely proud and independent woman who would proclaim her son's innocence to the very end. When Pablo, as a little boy, returned from his first day of school having been teased for the condition of his shoes, his mother abruptly left the house; she returned that evening having stolen from a shop the finest pair she could find. Perhaps inspired by such audacity, Pablo was drawn to crime at a young age. He began with graveyards, building a small business based on the theft and bartering of stolen tombstones. As a teen, he peddled counterfeit graduation certificates, scamming the best schools of the city. He later dabbled in kidnapping and extortion, before moving on to the surging trade in imported and stolen goods, the televisions, cameras, and household appliances then flooding into Colombia from abroad, all excessively taxed by the state, which created lucrative openings for the black market. Then came a new opportunity. In the late 1960s the Mexican government, acting under pressure from the United States, blanketed the country's marijuana plantations with toxic herbicides, ruining the market and sending enterprising smugglers to Colombia, which for several years became the dope capital of the world.

Marijuana was Pablo's first foray into drugs. The challenges and opportunities were precisely those he would confront and overcome throughout his criminal career: an illicit substance easy to produce at the source, much in demand at the point of exchange, with a massive markup in value, provided one could move it across borders, negotiate a gauntlet of restrictive controls and impediments designed to block every shipment, and land it in the hands of enthusiastic consumers quite prepared to ignore the underbelly of the business, the murderous consequences of their consumption. The only problem with marijuana was its bulk, which limited the scale of the shipments and, thus, the profits.

In the early 1970s, at a time when most Americans and Colombians had never heard of cocaine, Escobar stumbled upon an informal trade that still lay in the hands of the independent drifter; young travelers who rotated through Colombia from El Salvador and Peru, drawn to a good life, which they financed by smuggling into the United States small packets of coke, hidden in their luggage or crammed unpleasantly into various body orifices. For Pablo, cocaine was the perfect solution, the answer to a smuggler's dreams. A powder far easier to transport than pot, with the promise of infinitely greater returns, it was a drug that by its very nature, the way it worked on the brain, was certain to generate ravenous demand. Much as Steve Jobs rolled the dice on smartphones, confident that markets would emerge for a product no one at the time could imagine, Pablo saw from the start the potential of cocaine, envisioning a global empire before anyone could have guessed that a drug not far removed from what a dentist employs to numb the nerves before extracting teeth would become the most coveted substance of a decade dedicated to lust, desire, and the gratification of self.

While some in the trade crammed cocaine into dolls and children's toys, or mucked about with clever modifications to suitcases and handbags, Pablo cultivated contacts that in time would allow him to export it by the ton. He began by going directly to the source, establishing networks in coca-growing regions of Peru and Bolivia, where the leaves could be readily rendered with kerosene and acid into a paste that could be transported in the wheel hubs of trucks that were already bringing contraband north from Santiago and Lima. While his drivers dispensed petty bribes at the borders, just enough to cover expectations for a load of televisions or washing machines, Pablo was in fact importing paste by the kilo to be processed into crystal cocaine in clandestine laboratories scattered throughout the barrios of Medellín. The only challenges were masking the consumption of electricity and finding ways to get the product to the consumer.

In the early years, with American authorities only vaguely aware of the tsunami about to sweep over their shores, Pablo smuggled cocaine, if not yet by the ton, most certainly by the shovelful, with each illicit gram increasing in value by a factor of fifty the moment it made landfall in Miami. At first, and for a time, Pablo and his colleagues made vague attempts to hide their money behind a maze of legal businesses, if only to indulge an illusion of legitimacy for those among the business elite of the city scrambling to invest in the wildly profitable enterprise. Xandra's father, Jaime, recalls a surreal moment in those early years when a helicopter carrying Pablo Escobar landed unexpectedly on the lawn of Medellín's exclusive Club Llanogrande and a host of silver-haired members rushed out to receive him warmly.

By no means did all of Medellín race to get in on the action. But there was certainly a time, before explosions shook the city and the streets became damp with blood, when few questions were asked, and the list of investors included any number of notable names from the elite families of the city. The flash of wealth unleashed a frenzy that encouraged even the innocent to remain blind to the circumstances of the trade. The traffickers were known simply as Los Mágicos, a reference to their ability to generate such astonishing returns, as if conjuring gold out of lead, allowing them to purchase hotels, beauty pageants, and even professional soccer teams with, in the case of Pablo Escobar, the profits of a transport company with a fleet of just three cabs. Even as he cracked *Fortune* magazine's list of global billionaires, those taxis were the sole assets of his only legally registered business.

. . .

Although inevitably the truth would emerge, and the extent of his criminal empire be revealed, Escobar could have delayed the day of reckoning had he only been prepared to operate beneath the radar of the state, as his peers in both the Medellín and Cali Cartels urged him to do. But Pablo saw himself not as a criminal but as one of the great figures in Colombian history: a latter-day liberator destined to transform the nation. Had cocaine been legal, he often mused, he would have been heralded as one of the greatest names in the history of capitalism. As an entrepreneur, he had managed to overcome determined opposition to place an illicit product within easy reach of consumers throughout the world, at a price point that brought his investors unprecedented profits. In less than a decade, he built a multibillion-dollar business, all of it based on three key components: supply chains for the raw materials, clandestine factories producing a steady and ever-increasing supply of the product, and a distribution network that spanned the globe.

Tranquilandia, just one of his hidden processing complexes, was carved from the Amazon jungle in the remote reaches of Caquetá. It featured nineteen laboratories, serviced by eight airstrips, with flights coordinated to allow a constant two-way flow of supplies and product. When Colombian police and American DEA agents raided Tranquilandia in 1984, they seized or destroyed $1.2 billion in assets, including seven airplanes, 15.2 tons of cocaine, and 11,800 drums of processing chemicals, not to mention a sophisticated electrical plant and pumping station supplying power and water to the posh dormitories that housed the hundreds of workers employed by the operation. Given the logistical challenges of the trade, the array of forces that stood in his way, the financial and military assets of those who opposed his every move, Pablo's achievement, judged purely as a commercial enterprise, was indeed nothing short of extraordinary.

Before yielding to the political ambitions that would ultimately be his downfall, Pablo tried to buy his way into legitimacy, scattering gifts to the poor, building soccer fields and schools, providing housing and health care in mountainside barrios and urban settlements untouched by the state. With an eye to his future, he paid journalists and public relations firms to promote his image as a latter-day Robin Hood, the one man in all of Colombia with the means and will to give voice and succor to the poor. Nothing pleased him more than the rumor flying around Colombia that he had offered to pay off the entire national debt. He first ran for Congress in 1982, successfully securing—some would say buying—a seat in the House of Representatives as an alternate member from the Liberal Party. His ultimate goal was the presidency, and for the briefest of moments, he may actually have believed that the highest office in the land was within his reach.

For Colombia's political and legal establishment in Bogotá, it was one thing to have suspected and known traffickers—the "kings of cocaine," as they were then described in the Medellín press—flaunting their wealth and operating criminal networks with impunity, untouched by the law. It was quite another to welcome one of them, by reputation the most powerful and wealthy of them all, into the hallowed halls of the national Congress. In a move that would cost him his life, Rodrigo Lara Bonilla, then minister of justice, aggressively opposed Escobar, publicly accusing him of being a trafficker and refusing to allow him to take his seat in the chamber. Lara Bonilla then upped the ante in a very public way by revealing to the Colombian people that several of their most popular football teams, in Cali, Medellín, Pereira, and Bogotá, were owned by drug lords. In a nation obsessed with the sport, the news was shocking. For many, it felt like a personal violation. If drug money had bought the Millonarios de Bogotá, the América de Cali, the Atlético Nacional de Medellín, teams that represented to their cities what the Red Sox and Yankees meant to Boston and New York, could there be anything, anywhere in Colombia, untainted by the cocaine business?

Even as the public absorbed the disturbing news, Lara Bonilla produced evidence of Pablo's only known and confirmed brush with the law, an arrest record from 1976 when he had been caught near the Ecuadorian border in possession of thirty-nine pounds of cocaine paste. He had not been convicted of any crime, but it was enough legally to deny him a place in Congress. The actual story was darker than even Lara Bonilla had imagined. Soon after his arrest,

Escobar had tried to buy off the judges in Medellín, where the case was scheduled to be heard. When that failed, and after months of further legal maneuvering, he simply ordered the murder of the two arresting officers, an easy solution that left the prosecution with no choice but to drop the case. The lesson was not lost on Pablo. From that moment on, his sole legal strategy consisted of bribery, intimidation, and murder. His response to any threat was to kill the messenger, which is precisely what he did to Rodrigo Lara Bonilla, who was cut down in Bogotá on April 30, 1984.

The assassination of the minister of justice provoked then-president Belisario Betancur to move forward with the one initiative that Escobar truly feared: the implementation of an existing treaty of extradition that would legally allow Colombia to release its citizens into the custody of the United States, where they might be judged and sentenced for their crimes. With Escobar's tentacles reaching through Colombia's federal judiciary, the police and the army, the security forces, and virtually every office of government, even those Colombians who objected to extradition as a violation of national sovereignty recognized that it might be the only way to remove his stain from the body and soul of the nation. In response, Escobar formed Los Extraditables, a loose association of those targeted by Betancur, kingpins with the most to lose, who shared Pablo's conviction that it was better to lie in a grave in Colombia than to live in a prison cell in the United States. Portraying themselves as victims of a weak and corrupt government under the thumb of Washington, they mounted a national media campaign to discredit the president and challenge the legitimacy of the initiative. When such dubious claims, coming but a year after the death of Lara Bonilla, failed to move public opinion, Escobar essentially declared war on the Colombian state, targeting, in short order, judges, politicians, journalists, ministers, and all and any officers of the law. No one in the country was immune.

In late 1985, even as Colombia's supreme court was considering the constitutionality of extradition, M-19 guerrillas assaulted the Palace of Justice in Bogotá, taking more than three hundred people hostage, including twenty-four supreme court justices and twenty other judges. Their stated purpose was to hold a mock trial of President Betancur; their actual goal, in an operation almost certainly financed by Pablo Escobar, was the destruction of legal records implicating M-19 cadres, as well as the criminal evidence, carefully compiled over many months, that supported the government's case against those targeted for extradition. For Escobar alone, paper files filled an entire room. In two days, six thousand documents went up in smoke, tinder for fires that raged until the siege was finally lifted by the army. The television footage of a tank crashing through the doors of the Palace of Justice, while explosions and flames gutted the upper floors, flashed around the world, like a dagger to the heart of Colombian democracy. The final skirmish left ninety-eight dead: hostages, guerrillas, soldiers, and no fewer than eleven justices, close to half the members of the nation's supreme court.

The killings did not stop. In December 1986, gunmen hired by Escobar assassinated a highly respected journalist, Guillermo Cano, then director of *El Espectador*, after the newspaper ran a series of articles critical of the cartel. The headline the following day read simply, "*¡Seguimos adelante!*"—"We Continue Onward!" But it was hard to go on when all that was decent and good was under assault by criminals who made a mockery of the state, as Pablo Escobar did when he brazenly dispatched a helicopter into a federal prison, liberating a member of the Medellín Cartel, who was filmed making his way to freedom as casually as an elderly gentleman drifting off on a midnight stroll.

By the end of the 1980s, the most dangerous job in the world was running for president in Colombia. In October 1987, Jaime Pardo Leal, head of the Unión Patriótica, was killed as he returned by road to Bogotá. By the time of his death, more than five hundred members of his party had been assassinated, a tally that would soar to more than three thousand and include another presidential candidate, José Antequera, killed in March 1989 in an attack at El Dorado airport that also injured a future president, Ernesto Samper. The most devastating loss was Luis Carlos Galán, whose vision of a new Colombia had electrified the nation, inspiring the young and leaving even those embittered by the years of violence indulging quiet dreams of a country at peace. A vocal opponent of Escobar and the cartels, Galán was ahead in the polls, almost certain to lead the

Liberal Party to victory, when he was cut down by a spray of bullets as he addressed a campaign rally on August 18, 1989.

César Gaviria came forward, anointed by Galán's son at his father's funeral. Escobar set out to kill him as well, planting a bomb on a commercial flight that Gaviria was scheduled to take on November 27. The candidate changed his plans at the last minute. Escobar did not. The bomb detonated, killing all 107 passengers and crew on Avianca Flight 203. Then, in the first months of 1990, two more presidential candidates would die, both politicians from the left: Bernardo Jaramillo Ossa on March 22, and Carlos Pizarro a month later, on April 26. Neither man had the slightest chance of winning. For Escobar they were mere afterthoughts, loose ends to wrap up before the war entered a new phase.

For the other members of the Medellín Cartel, not to mention the drug lords of Cali, the violence unleashed by Escobar was irrational and counterproductive—not just bad for business but a sign of desperation, which implied weakness, suggesting a vulnerability that drew their attention. Increasingly, in the midst of all the mayhem, the targeted assassinations, the bombs and the bravado, Pablo Escobar could sense the world closing in. In 1986, then-president Virgilio Barco had created Search Bloc, a special police unit independent of local authorities and free to do whatever was necessary to bring down Escobar and the cartels. Each member of the bloc had been hand-selected and deemed to be incorruptible; many had themselves lost relatives, friends, and colleagues, fellow cops targeted in Pablo's vendetta against the police. In December 1989, acting on an informant's tip, Search Bloc caught up with Escobar's longtime partner Gonzalo Rodríguez Gacha, one of the founders of the Medellín Cartel, and left him and his son dead in a field on the Caribbean coast. Escobar now understood that if they could find El Mexicano, as Gacha was known, they could find him. The death of Galán, the subsequent bombing of the offices of *El Espectador* in Medellín, and the terrible fate of Avianca 203 had galvanized public outrage, giving Gaviria, elected president in May 1990, the political cover he needed to pursue extradition with all the powers of his office.

Escobar would again lash out with a wave of violence, random bombings intended to force the government to negotiate on his terms. For a time this strategy worked, and he was able to regroup for several months at La Catedral, a prison palace of his own design in the hills overlooking Medellín. But the country had had enough. Escobar's list of enemies included not only rivals in the drug trade, the men of Cali and all the others, but also a Colombian government united under Gaviria with the singular mission of bringing him to justice. Even those fighting to overthrow the government, the FARC and the ELN, wanted Escobar gone, as indeed did their enemies on the right, the AUC and the other paramilitary militias. The Cali Cartel alone, working with the Castaño brothers, among the most powerful and ruthless of paramilitary leaders, spent $50 million to destroy him. Pablo had been personally responsible for the death of perhaps a thousand policemen, along with scores of journalists, judges, politicians, and any number of ordinary citizens, innocent victims all. As the tally grew, the number of people who wished him dead increased by orders of magnitude, until the world finally closed in and he found himself alone, barefoot and bleeding, his bloated body stretched across a tin roof in the sun, with a bullet in his ear. He died on December 2, 1993.

By then, Xandra Uribe was long gone from Colombia. For her family, as for many Colombians, 1989 was the tipping point. Travel within the country had become impossible. No corner of Medellín was safe. Every night the Uribe family gathered around the radio simply to verify the location of the explosions that had shattered the day. They lived in a series of bubbles, dashing from home to office to school to club, never daring to walk the streets of the city. Uncertainty consumed every moment. When Xandra realized that she could no longer distinguish the sound of thunder from that of bombs exploding in the distance, she decided to leave home, live with her grandmother, and finish her last year of high school in Miami. Reluctantly her parents agreed to let her go. Medellín at the time was no place for a seventeen-year-old girl.

It made for an awkward and lonely transition. Though safe in Florida, she lived in growing fear for her family left behind in

Medellín. With each passing week, she felt more guilty for having fled. At school she was constantly teased for being from Colombia, the land of Pablo Escobar, by American teenagers whose social lives revolved around their quest for illicit substances, with cocaine being their drug of choice. In Medellín, she had never seen, let alone used, the drug. After a difficult year, she left for university, attending Boston College and majoring in communications. After graduation, she returned to Miami, where she worked in advertising for several years, returning to Medellín whenever possible for brief visits with her family.

Her life in Miami took a turn when she met and married a Colombian musician from Montería, Jorge Villamizar, whose career was about to explode. Like Xandra, Jorge had gone abroad, while always remaining connected to his Latin roots. For a time he lived in London, working as a street performer, a busker playing for tips, honing his craft on the most unforgiving of musical stages, the cobblestones of Chelsea and Piccadilly. He then moved to Miami, where he formed Bacilos, a band that burst onto the scene in the late 1990s, known not only for a string of Grammy-winning hits—"Tabaco y Chanel," "Caraluna," "Mi primer millón"—but for creating a new sound, an inspired fusion of rock and pop with traditional music from the Caribbean coast of Colombia and the classic rhythms of salsa and merengue. With Jorge almost constantly on the road with the band, and Xandra mostly staying home, building a small greeting-card company, they remained together for eight years, until it became clear that their marriage had run its course. After an amicable divorce, Xandra went to work as a creative producer at Discovery, overseeing television productions and writing songs for Discovery Kids. A romance brought her to New York, where she became obsessed with Broadway musicals. The love affair faded, but not her passion for the theatrical genre.

For two years, she went to every musical that opened in the city, until finally a revival of *West Side Story* spun her into action. In 2009 she returned to Colombia, determined to write and produce a musical based on a children's book, *Barro de Medellín*, written by Spanish author Alfredo Gómez Cerdá. The story takes place in a barrio high above the urban core of the city. The setting, and one of the main characters, is an architectural jewel, a shining and beautiful library that brings together the neighborhood, inspiring everyone, old and young, to dream. Xandra saw in this simple tale a powerful metaphor for the rebirth of her city. She reached out to the author, who, to her surprise, immediately offered to collaborate on the project. She then went door to door, as first the mayor and then many of the top corporate figures in Medellín bought into her quixotic dream: a hip-hop musical that would bring together the finest young talent from across the city, irrespective of race or class, family, school, or neighborhood. Her goal was to use music, theater, and dance, as others had used fashion, architecture, literature, urban planning, and even horticulture, as a catalyst of change. After living much of her life abroad, she wanted not just to come home but to be part of the small miracle unfolding in her city.

The year Xandra fled to Miami, Medellín was known as the most violent and dangerous city in the world, the murder capital of the Americas, with homicide rates three times that of Beirut. The death of Pablo Escobar, four years later, brought little respite, as rival gangs scrambled to lay claim to the spoils. At this, perhaps the lowest point in Medellín's fortunes, a remarkable group of civic leaders came together with the explicit goal of saving their city. Among them was a young mathematician and scholar, Sergio Fajardo, who, a decade later as mayor, would oversee the slow transformation of the city. The cradle of change was the Medellín Academy. In a whirlwind of intellectual foment and provocation that can come about only when all bets are off and things can only get better, in the mid-1990s a small group of young planners and architects began to think in new ways, with new strategies that would become a movement known as *urbanismo social*. Rather than embellishing the urban core, as municipal governments had always done, they would focus on the most vulnerable barrios, intent on reintegrating the many parts of the city that had been lost to the violence. At the core of their philosophy was the then-radical notion that all citizens of the city deserved not only basic services—health, education, sanitation—but also places of beauty, architectural masterpieces in their neighborhoods that might become symbols of hope and pride. The goal was to close the doors on crime while opening all doors to opportunity.

Working closely with his friend and colleague Alejandro Eche-verri, a Harvard-trained architect and urban planner, the mayor and his team created vast and irresistible public spaces at a time when many *paisas* were afraid to leave their homes. They liberated muse-ums, flung open the gates of gardens long the exclusive preserve of the wealthy, built elegant and aesthetically impactful libraries in the most vulnerable neighborhoods, like the one that had inspired Alfredo Gómez, with books free to all. The message was clear: Education and knowledge were the birthright of every Colombian. They went on to complete a citywide subway system that became the pride of Medellín, as well as a network of gondolas that lift work-ing people, exhausted at the end of the day, from the valley floor to their homes in the barrios perched high on the mountains over-looking the city. Where geography promoted separation, and rival gangs eyed one another across precipitous *quebradas* and ravines, the proponents of this new urban vision literally spanned the divide, constructing beautiful footbridges, wide enough for children to play on, anchored at both ends by new public housing, elegant in design and human in scale.

Among the many institutions transformed by the *urbanismo social* was a place I knew well, the Jardín Botánico Joaquín Antonio Uribe, Medellín's famed botanical garden. In the 1970s, when I lived in Colombia as a student and aspiring plant explorer, it had been my base, as close to a home as I had for well over a year. Thanks to the generosity of the director at the time, the late Mariano Ospina, I had a small second-floor room with a balcony that looked out over a pond that came alive at night with the sounds of the forest, frogs and cicadas, screech owls and *potoos*. The grounds covered nearly thirty acres, an oasis of life and biodiversity in the heart of the city. Vari-ous habitats had been re-created, and altogether there were more than a thousand distinct species of rare tropical plants—trees, lianas, epiphytes, and shrubs. The living collection of orchids, the pride of the garden and, indeed, the city, had no equal in Latin America. On evenings when the air was still, the scent of blossoms was so strong that to walk along any of the many paths was to pass through one pocket of perfume after another, each more alluring than the last.

Beautiful as it was, and as much as I enjoyed the long nights of solitude, I was never quite comfortable living in a lavish complex sequestered from the surrounding barrio by enormous white stucco walls crowned with barbed wire and shards of glass.

So, while I kept the room at the garden, I often stayed with friends on a farm just outside the city. I was, at any rate, rarely in Medellín. As travels and botanical expeditions led me farther afield with each passing month, my time at the garden slipped away into memory. Only years later, as the city descended into darkness, did I learn that the Jardín Botánico had shared its fate and for a time had been forced to close. Tourists had abandoned Colombia. Attendance at the annual orchid fair, once a highlight of Medellín's social calendar, had plummeted. No one in the local neighborhoods could afford the cost of admission, and those from the rest of the city who could were not about to travel to the north, where Escobar's *sicarios* ruled the streets, and crime and violence had spun out of control.

When I finally returned to Medellín in 2010, after an absence of many years, it was to give a talk at the Parque Explora, a new, state-of-the-art science museum located, as it turned out, just across from the old entrance to the Jardín Botánico. To say that everything had changed would not begin to express my bewilderment. With an hour to kill before the evening event, I walked back and forth between museum and garden, trying to conjure from memory images of a place that had vanished, as if swept away into the dustbin of history. I had no sense of nostalgia. My only thought was "Good riddance." The air in the streets no longer smelled of dust, grease, and lube oil. The repair shop where boys black with soot forged parts and pounded tires; the corner bar lit up at all hours and through all seasons with Christmas decorations and tinsel; the hot-panted girls nestled in the dark doorways; the young toughs shadowed by the streetlamp, huddled around a billiard table moldy from the rain, stranded in the street; the dingy restaurant where every night I ate with the truckers, paying a dollar for the same simple meal, a plate of *fríjoles con arroz y plátano* with a bit of meat, a fried egg, or chicken feet on top—all of this was gone, replaced by a wide plaza that skirted the science museum, an open space of fountains, shade trees, seating areas with whimsical benches, and even a water park for the young. Spread along one axis of the plaza was a row of interactive exhibits, where everyone was welcome to take part and play. The price of admission to the museum was on a sliding scale, such that no one could be turned away, even the penniless. The botanical garden across the way is free to all.

The two institutions have no formal affiliation, and yet, judging from the foot traffic flowing so effortlessly across the broad pedestrian promenade running between them, visitors see garden and museum as elements of a single civic space, an indoor-outdoor experience that is the actual destination of their family or weekend outings. This is the genius of inspired urban design. From my time in Medellín in the 1970s, for example, I remembered the University of Antioquia, where I often worked, as having been located a great distance from the botanical garden. Imagine my surprise when, as I came to the far end of the new plaza and passed beneath the elevated subway line, pausing to admire the Parque Explora station, itself an architectural jewel as elegant as every other stop in the system, I saw that the university is, in fact, virtually adjacent to the garden. What I had recalled was an illusion of separation caused not by actual distance but by the miserable experience that reaching the university from the garden in those years implied: dust, fumes, bumper-to-bumper congestion, the constant noise as drivers rested their brakes and leaned on their horns. The university wasn't far. It just seemed to be, for it was such trouble to get there, especially on foot.

Today, by contrast, the Metro glides across Medellín, literally and metaphorically lifting passengers above the fray, a symbol of all that is new, promising, streamlined, and clean. Some *paisas* liken it to a beautiful ribbon that ties together the once-shattered fragments of a city, its impact psychological as much as functional. The Metro transports people, but it also collapses distance, allowing the University of Antioquia, for example, to become spatially as well as scientifically the third side of a research triangle, anchored at two other points by the Parque Explora and the Jardín Botánico. These three world-class institutions flourish today on land that only a generation ago was a dystopic roadside attraction in a neighborhood discarded by the state, as if inhabited by the unworthy. Today, the people of the same barrio inhabit the center, the heart of the reinvented urban space.

Men and women of all ages stroll along the walkway that encircles the botanical garden. A fence still rings the grounds, but it is new: tall and secure, while also being transparent and welcoming. Children peer through it, calling out to their friends. One can hear the shouts and laughter of families on the other side, picnicking on the grass. The place is alive with hundreds of visitors, school groups and cadets, birdwatchers and amateur botanists, shrouded nuns and coy young lovers. There are people everywhere, and yet in no place is the grass trampled. No blossom has been plucked, no tree blemished by a knife. Paper trash and plastic bottles cram the recycling bins. The public restrooms are as clean as the Metro, which in Medellín is saying something. The worst nightmare of the dowagers of old, the society ladies and orchid lovers who counted on the price of admission to limit access to the garden, has come true. The Jardín Botánico has, indeed, been overrun by families from the neighborhoods and all parts of the city. They all seem supremely grateful for the opportunity, and would no more damage the garden than their own homes. At the end of the day, they leave behind nothing but the echoes of their laughter and joy, and perhaps a few prayers of reflection and grace.

That the Jardín Botánico had been totally transformed was inspiring. But how this had occurred, given how notoriously conservative the management and board had always been, remained a mystery to me until some years later, when I had a chance to meet both Sergio Fajardo and Alejandro Echeverri, the very champions of the movement that had reimagined and reconfigured the city. Alejandro had just returned from a sabbatical year as a Loeb fellow at Harvard's Graduate School of Design. Sergio, having served as both mayor of Medellín and governor of Antioquia, was in the midst of a presidential campaign. He had proposed lunch at, of all places, the Jardín Botánico.

On a busy Saturday afternoon, I found them on the terrace of the small garden café, graciously posing for selfies and snapshots with *paisas* of all ages. Sergio welcomed me warmly, introducing Alejandro and then his lovely daughter, Mariana, a biologist and an ardent environmentalist. There was a wonderful synergy between the two men. Alejandro was gracious, thoughtful, personally humble, and yet ferociously proud of all that had been accomplished. A strong sense of irony and whimsy was the key to his charm. Sergio, by contrast, struck me as a natural leader with a strong personality; he was confident, charismatic, and bold, with none of the traits normally associated with politicians. He listened more than he spoke, and he asked questions in a manner that suggested he really did believe that everyone had something to say, and each person deserved to be heard. What completely won me over was his connection to Mariana, the way he looked at her, listened to what she had to say, how he softly challenged her views. There is no better measure of a man than the love and respect he has for a daughter.

At first we spoke of the campaign, with Sergio anticipating a rebound in the polls. I asked Mariana about her research. Alejandro shared his own passion for rivers, comparing their tributaries to the major transport arteries of a city; both are energetic lifelines that allow something infinitely complex to exist. No one in their right mind, he noted, would shut down, damage, or compromise the highways and boulevards that feed a major metropolitan center, for without a constant flow of supplies, places like New York would shrivel within days. Natural systems, he suggested, are equally dependent on the free exchange of nutrients and fuel, carried along waterways that must remain open and pure.

As the conversation turned back to Medellín, Alejandro gleefully recalled the early days when they had all been flying by the seat of their pants, improvising as they went along, hoping, as he put it, that the adults wouldn't notice. Sergio laughed in a way that confirmed that everything Alejandro was saying was true, that it really had been that spontaneous and experimental. Sergio had unexpectedly won the municipal election, assuming responsibility for a city in total crisis. They had plenty of ideas, none of which had ever been implemented. The desperate state of the city gave them license to try anything. So they just started doing what needed to be done, without asking whether it was possible or permissible.

"So tell me about the Jardín Botánico," I asked. "What happened here?"

"It was at first very difficult," Sergio replied. "Those who ran the garden were very resistant. They represented the most conservative elements in the city."

"Money was the key," said Alejandro. "We found out that they didn't have any."

"The Jardín Botánico was broke, with a large debt. So we made a deal. The city bought a strip of land around the entire circumference of the garden. This gave them the funds to retire their debt, and the city had the land to build the walkway that now surrounds the garden. But the deal came with conditions that we knew would transform the place."

"Free admission for all. Changing the culture so that people could actually use and enjoy the space. And then there was the wall," added Alejandro.

"For me, that was always the ultimate symbol of the old garden," I said. "It was not just a barrier; it was a billboard. Like the walls around the houses of the rich. They're there to protect the families living within, but also to send a message to everyone on the outside that they will never be allowed to cross that social divide, never be permitted to rise above their God-given station in life. I remember how much people in the barrio hated that wall."

"All of the land that became the garden was once a farm," Sergio explained, "and people still living can remember when it was a public park, enjoyed by everyone."

"So what did you do?" I asked.

"We tore it down," said Sergio. "That was one of the conditions. We would build a new wall that would secure the garden but would be transparent. A wall but not a wall."

"Actually, we didn't tear it down." Alejandro interjected.

"True," said Sergio, turning to me. "We invited the people of the barrio to do the work, with tools we provided. It became a fantastic fiesta, a mini–Berlin Wall, as the people themselves liberated the garden."

At this point I would have done anything for either man. How extraordinary that two such unlikely heroes came together at the most critical moment in the history of a great city. As urban visionaries, they saved Medellín not by imposing rules, regulations, or infrastructure from on high but by listening to the rhythm of its broken heart, and to the voices of those living in the streets, the only place where the true pulse of a city can be felt. Like healers ministering to a patient whose sickness had defied every treatment, they took risks that in normal circumstances would have been unimaginable. With their training in architecture, mathematics, design, and urban planning, they were also artists who understood that creativity is a consequence of action, not its motivation. On a mission to save their city, they embraced and remained loyal to three articles of faith: Pessimism is an indulgence, orthodoxy the enemy of invention, despair an insult to the imagination.

If politicians think of the next election, and statesmen the next generation, Sergio Fajardo envisions the archaeology of tomorrow. Not by chance did he come of age in the very decade when our species became truly urban, when for the first time in history the majority of people are living in cities, insulated from the vicissitudes of nature by structures designed and brought into being by the human imagination. With foresight rarely encountered in a politician, Sergio both anticipates and celebrates this urban future.

"Cities are living beings," he said, "organisms that expand and contract, consuming energy and ejecting waste. Collective entities that are far more than the sum of their parts. Cities reflect the aspirations and ambitions of the people living within their grasp, even as they lie in wait to mold the dreams and character of generations still waiting to be born."

With that, my time with him was over. The hour I had been promised had already stretched to two, and he was overdue at an event. In a final flurry of snapshots and parting gifts, we made ready to say good-bye. I signed books for both Sergio and Mariana, and another for Alejandro. Over our objections, Sergio insisted on paying for lunch, a gentleman to the end. Then with kisses for his daughter and warm embraces all around, he was gone, back to the campaign trail.

Alejandro stayed behind, generously offering to lead an afternoon outing, an informal tour of some of the projects that had both catalyzed the city's transformation and become emblematic of its rebirth.

"You really must experience the Metrocable," he said, with evident pride. He was referring to Medellín's innovative system of aerial tramways that operate as extensions of the Metro. Only in place of trains, they feature cabins hung from cables, gondolas of a scale and elegance one might expect to see at a Swiss ski resort, not soaring over the neighborhoods of a metropolis six degrees north of the equator. It was, in fact, the obvious solution for a city in which a large proportion of the population, the most vulnerable, live in barrios that reach farther up the surrounding mountains with each passing year. Other cities—Caracas, La Paz, Rio de Janeiro—have built individual tramways, but Medellín was the first to envision an entire network, seamlessly integrated with a citywide subway system.

From the Jardín Botánico, we walked to the Metro and caught a train heading north. Though both the station and the cars were packed, there was a civility not always experienced in crowded public spaces, in Colombia or anywhere else. And despite the heavy traffic—over half a million people ride the Metro every day—the entire system remains notably clean, unblemished by graffiti, with not a sign of trash. What seems like a small miracle, Alejandro explained, is just an expression of what *paisas* describe as "Metro culture," a public attitude born of civic pride. What might be acceptable in the streets—casually discarding a wad of gum, a cigarette butt, a plastic bottle or wrapper—simply cannot, and will not, be tolerated in a subway seen by many as the emblem of the city.

"It wasn't something we anticipated," Alejandro remarked, "but at the same time, looking back, it didn't happen purely by chance. There are certainly rules—some say too many—but regulations alone can never really determine or dictate behavior. Telling a kid that graffiti is vandalism is just an invitation for him to get out the spray paints. What happened with the subway was very different."

Metro culture, as Alejandro saw it, was fundamentally an expression of social harmony, solidarity, and self-respect. Certain standards and expectations took hold because in some mysterious way they expressed the collective will of the people. This consensus became manifest in the way *paisas* behaved: not just respectful of the Metro but protective of the totality of the physical and social space, as if the property were not public but personal, the open-air platforms the foyers of private homes.

It all began—again, according to Alejandro—with the management model by which the subway was designed, built, and delivered to the city. From the project's inception, the mayor's mantra was "respect": for the small businesses and families disrupted by the construction, for the workers toiling by day and night, for the neighborhoods destined to be transformed. The city did not impose a subway; it engaged the people, who became invested in success. What excited Alejandro was the possibility that what transpired in Medellín could be adopted as a model for other cities seeking to reinvigorate or transform their civic culture.

"If there's a formula for true and lasting social change," he noted, "it surely has something to do with motivating the ordinary person to work for the common good, knowing that the well-being of the community almost always implies a better life for the individual. That's the energy that must be found and harnessed if we're to build a better city, not to mention a new Colombia."

At the Acevedo station, we left the train and transferred effortlessly to the K line, the oldest of the five aerial lifts built to date. Completed in 2004, the year Sergio Fajardo became mayor, it climbs thirteen hundred feet in just over a mile, with stops at Andalucía, Popular, and Santo Domingo Savio, barrios that overlap and spread as a single urban blanket across the flank of the mountains to the north and east of the city. From the highest point, another line begins, which for a fare of two dollars, carries tourists and middle-class families right out of the city, across an elfin cloud forest to Parque Arví, a wild and windswept regional park that attracts nearly a million visitors a year.

But for Alejandro the real story lies on the urban slope overlooking the city and the broad expanse of the Aburrá Valley. Today, more than thirty thousand men, women, and children from the immediate neighborhoods ride the K line every day. For just twenty-five hundred pesos (about seventy-five cents), they float to the valley floor, taking in a vista that can only inspire, and connect to buses or trains that service every district of Medellín. Before the aerial tram, those living on the heights had to walk an average of five hours a day simply to reach their places of employment and return home in the evening. Communities naturally became isolated, cut off from the economic pulse of the city. High rates of unemployment and truancy sired crime and gang violence. Those who did work, commuting on foot, often to menial jobs of hard physical labor, lived in a state of chronic exhaustion, with only so much energy to spare for their families. The fast life and easy money of the drug trade had obvious appeal, especially for young men with few prospects and nothing to lose save their lives.

As we rode the gondola, skirting the rooftops, Alejandro pointed out places where people had been killed, explosions had shattered lives, car bombs had shaken awake entire neighborhoods. Not a generation ago, Pablo Escobar had controlled everything within sight. No one had been safe. People huddled in their homes. No child would be seen on the streets after dusk. Today the streets are not just crowded, they are truly congested, dense with foot traffic; families hang out on every stoop, shoppers pick through the produce at corner grocers, lovers stroll in the shadows, kids play ball. Storefronts, bright and clearly prosperous, run the entire length of the K line, from Andalucía up the slope to Santo Domingo Savio—a consequence, Alejandro explained, of innovative policies that encouraged families to open small businesses in their homes. Even the nooks and crannies, all the back alleys of the neighborhood, are lit up, with people on the move.

Reaching the crest of the mountain, we passed above the shacks and shanties that mark the end of the city, the *asentamientos informales*, a zone occupied by the most recent arrivals, families displaced from their homes or simply drawn to Medellín by the promise of work and a better life. Uncertain of their status, the newcomers hedge their bets and replicate their rural life, planting gardens and raising pigs and chickens. Old women forage for wild herbs, even as their grandchildren, in bright and perfect uniforms, tumble down the hill to the gondola station that will carry them to school.

I asked Alejandro if he could sum up, or somehow distill in a few words, the essence of their strategy, the key to their success, if indeed there was one.

"Every civic project," he replied, "large and small, neighborhood-based or citywide, implied a new beginning. Each proclaimed that Medellín belonged to everyone, and that every citizen deserved to be treated with dignity and respect. As much as the actual public works, the Metro and the bridges and all the libraries and museums and plazas, it was this conviction that drove the transformation of the city. People in neighborhoods historically marginalized began to feel they were somebody. Gang violence in the barrios plummeted. The murder rate dropped by ninety-five percent. The streets came alive as ordinary people, good and decent Colombians, set out to reclaim their city."

Challenges remain, Alejandro readily acknowledged, as might be expected in any modern city of 2.5 million. But today, Medellín ranks with Barcelona and Lisbon as among the most desirable and livable of all cities. In 2013, the *Wall Street Journal* and the Urban Land Institute, the oldest and most respected global voice when it comes to urban planning and sustainable development, celebrated the city as the most innovative and imaginative in the world. In 2012, the Institute for Transportation and Development Policy (ITDP), a global consortium focused on sustainable transportation, recognized Medellín's system of public transportation as being without equal both in terms of social equity and environmental sustainability. And in 2011, thirty-six dancers and musicians, aged ten to fifty, took to the stage in *Barro de Medellín*, a musical extravaganza that fused artistic genres, sounds, and people from neighborhoods throughout the city. It was unity in diversity, precisely what Xandra Uribe had in mind when she wrote the lyrics of one of the musical's signature songs: "*Somos del mismo barro, pisamos el mismo barro, nacimos aquí*, made in Medellín": "We are from the same soil, we walk on the same soil, we were born here, we were 'made in Medellín.'"

Cauldron of War

Not a week after returning to Medellín from Río Claro, I heard from Xandra. Her voice on the phone left little doubt that my destiny, at least for the time being, lay in her hands.

"I've found the perfect companion for you," she said, "Juan Gonzalo Betancur. He's a university professor at EAFIT, but as a journalist he covered the Medio Magdalena for more than a decade, through all the most difficult years. He has this thing about the Magdalena. He's obsessed with it. His goal in life since he was a boy was to travel the river from source to mouth, and he did."

Xandra paused to take a breath. Apparently she had, quite by chance, attended a lecture organized by one of her friends, in a series that normally features talks from travelers returning from exotic places like Tibet or Antarctica. But the speaker she had heard was Juan, who'd told of his travels down the Magdalena, a pilgrimage of a lifetime than had resulted in a book, *Los olvidados: resistencia cultural en Colombia*. As the title suggests, it's a story of resistance and survival, an attempt by Juan as a journalist to give voice to the forgotten rhythms and songs, promises and prayers of those he encountered on the river.

"He's willing to go with you," she told me. "Spring break is coming up. He has at least two weeks off."

"And what about you?" I asked.

"Of course I'm coming. It's the Medio Magdalena. I've never been there."

With that, the adventure was on.

We set out from Medellín on a Saturday, just before noon, with Juan at the wheel, doing his best to persuade Xandra that he actually knew how to drive. The rental vehicle, registered in her name, lunged and lurched for several blocks, until finally, after leaving the first busy intersection, Juan had us gliding effortlessly through the traffic. I heard a sigh of relief from Xandra in the back, as a great grin lit up Juan's face. There were small beads of sweat on his brow. He seemed nervous, like someone on a first date. I soon realized that he was simply giddy with anticipation, over the moon at the thought of returning after so many months to a river that for all his childhood had been the embodiment of his dreams. When finally as a grown man, after a passage of many years, including a hero's journey through the horrors of war—eyewitness, as he put it, to the black heart of humanity—Juan had reached the Magdalena's source and followed the river to the sea, he had not been disappointed.

"As I splashed my head and drank from the stream," he said, "I knew right away the river was alive. I could feel it. It spoke to me, and I replied. I tell you, all of Colombia is concentrated in that river. It's so obvious. The river is everything."

Juan's life, I discovered, had been bookended by stories of the Magdalena, those told to him as a child by his father and those recorded during the three-month odyssey that had taken him the length of the river in 2014. Juan's father had portrayed the river in almost mythical terms, as if a sentient being, with recollections of hot tropical nights when the stars seemed to slip in the sky to catch a better view of the *David Arango*, aglow with deck lights, silently steaming downstream. Such images, Juan recognized, came from a place of deep memory, a well of nostalgia and romance completely removed from the staid middle-class life he had actually known growing up with his father in Medellín. This had only made the Magdalena that much more enchanting.

The river that Juan came to know did not disappoint, and it remains the wellspring of his life. He still speaks of it, as both Xandra and I had experienced that morning, with the innocence and enthusiasm of a child. Mere mention of the Magdalena can bring tears to his eyes. But the intensity of Juan's devotion is also a source of melancholy, for it only deepens his dismay that his passion for the river is not more widely shared by his fellow Colombians.

Juan's goal as he set out on his journey was just to listen to the people and hear what the Magdalena had to say. As a scholar on sabbatical, he had plenty of time, and his methods, though deliberate, were wonderfully simple: He would arrive in a river settlement and hang around for as long as it took to connect with a character whose story, to his satisfaction, distilled the essence of the place. Juan had no preconceived criteria, and no way to describe in words what he was looking for. He could neither anticipate nor fail to recognize those beguiling moments when a person came forward with something to say that the world needed to hear, which Juan recognized as the essence of storytelling. So, at every stop along the Magdalena, he simply waited, sometimes for days, until such a magical encounter released him once again to the river. It was sociology, if you will, informed and inspired by serendipity.

Just as individual stories contain multitudes, Juan discovered that distinct narratives, though collected from men, women, and children at ninety different locations, found a way of coming together in a single theme, not unlike the infinite branches of a river flowing into one. What Juan ultimately observed on his journey was a nation that had largely turned its back on the Magdalena; individuals, families, and entire communities were preoccupied with survival and moving on, focused less on forgiving than simply forgetting, a sentiment he came to understand and embrace.

"*Yo defiendo el olvido*," he said, turning to me as he drove. His tone was defiant, as if laying claim to a heresy. "I defend the right to forget."

At the highest levels of society, he continued, in the media and universities, in the halls of government and the back rooms of Havana where former enemies negotiated the peace accords, all talk is of forgiveness and reconciliation.

"We build museums of remembrance, offer legal incentives for killers to come forward with the truth, all with the hope that we can build a new nation on a foundation of raw memories, a cult of transparency. I agree that not forgetting is important. But forgetting is also important. Not to deny what happened. But to allow ourselves to go on. In the cities, the violence was random, anonymous. In the small towns, and certainly in places like Puerto Triunfo and Puerto Berrío and all the riverside settlements in the Medio Magdalena, it was intimate and personal. Everyone knew everyone. An old man once told me that if he didn't forget, he wouldn't be able to get up in the morning and go to work. We were walking together down a side street in his town, and he kept pointing left and right, indicating where people had been killed. Naming names. So-and-so was shot here. This happened there. Suddenly he stopped, looked me right in the eye, and said, 'I need to forget to continue living.'"

As the road rose into the hills of Rionegro, and we then began the long, slow descent toward the Magdalena, this theme of reconciliation and recollection, guilt and grace, dominated a conversation that had both Xandra and Juan wrestling with what it implied for the future of the country. Colombians are as spontaneous and partial to laughter and joy as anyone, but they live as they love, at full throttle, with an intensity that can be all-consuming. The five-hour drive to Honda, our destination for the night, promised to be both exhausting and exhilarating. Xandra's passion was infectious. Juan was simply dazzling. A natural storyteller, and clearly a gifted teacher, he knew the story of Colombia and the Medio Magdalena as both a social historian and a journalist who had witnessed history unfolding, even as he and his colleagues risked their lives to write its first draft. The depth and extent of his knowledge was astonishing, as were the chilling tales he recounted from his years on the front lines of the conflict.

Like Xandra, Juan had come of age in Medellín in the era of Pablo Escobar. After graduating from high school in 1984, he went on to college, working in radio for four years, all with the goal of becoming a sports journalist. He especially loved cycling, and the 1980s, despite the bombs, were glory years for Colombian road racers—and for Juan, who wrote about them. Everything changed with the death of Luis Carlos Galán, in 1989. The publisher of *El Colombiano*, the newspaper where Juan was working at the time, pulled him off the sports beat and sent him to Bogotá, with orders to find out all he could about the assassination. For the next decade, Juan would cover only violence and the war. He went north to Urabá to investigate the link between guerrillas and the labor unions, and later unveiled a series of killings by paramilitaries believed to be operating under the protection of the army. Then came Escobar's bombing campaign in Medellín and the dreary task of trudging each day to yet another scene of death and devastation, duties that provoked in some of his colleagues a gallows humor, a cynicism born of helplessness.

As Escobar's terror spread, his enemies, Los Pepes—the name was an acronym for *Perseguidos por Pablo Escobar*, those persecuted by Pablo, which included the entire Cali Cartel—went after his family, his business, and his properties, famously burning his prized collection of antique cars at Hacienda Nápoles, his ranch in the Medio Magdalena. Juan was there the following morning, before the metal had cooled. When, some years later, as part of his deal with César Gaviria, Escobar revealed the location of his clandestine labs, Juan was one of twenty journalists invited to report on the druglord's operations at the Río Perancho in Chocó. He recalls a surreal moment as they all arrived, damp with sweat, and had to turn on the heaters normally used for processing cocaine to dry their clothes. They toured three immense laboratories, each assembled in the jungle at a cost of $1 million. The drugs had been dispatched by boat down the Río Atrato or by floatplane from bases hidden away in the wetlands.

Soon after returning to Medellín, Juan learned that a close friend, a police photographer, had been murdered. Every day, the war became more personal. Perhaps it was fitting that when Pablo Escobar finally met his end in 1993, shot down on a rooftop in Medellín, Juan was one of the first journalists to see the body and report the death. He still has souvenirs of the day, a hundred-peso coin picked up beside Escobar's bed and a letter that was never sent, perhaps the last Pablo ever wrote.

As the complexity and intensity of the violence increased through the 1990s, so too did the opportunities and challenges for a young journalist on the rise. Juan soon found himself covering not one but several wars, all being fought simultaneously, with fluid alliances. Leftist guerrillas of the FARC and the ELN eyed one another suspiciously as they both fought the army and the state. The paramilitaries went after the guerrillas, savaging anyone deemed to be a supporter, meaning anyone who spoke out for the poor or challenged the rich. The lords of cocaine, with their mercenaries and militias, took on anyone who got in the way of their business, even as they supported the paramilitaries, until the paramilitaries turned on them. As a journalist, it was Juan's job to make sense of an ever-changing scenario, seeking sources in a netherworld where secrecy ruled and those who asked questions, including the press, both invited scrutiny and courted death.

At the age of just twenty-two, Juan scored his first scoop, one that would secure his post at the newspaper. Sent to Puerto Berrío, on the Magdalena, notorious as a center of paramilitary activity, he interviewed Colonel Rodolfo Herrera Luna, who acknowledged on record that the army had armed, supported, and in some instances created paramilitary groups. This confirmed what many had suspected: that the army cooperated with irregular forces who operated outside of the law, using tactics denied to the army by common decency and the conventions of war. That the army had equipped local militias was not especially newsworthy; it was not illegal and had been done in the past. What was scandalous was Colonel Herrera's casual remark that in supporting the paramilitaries, the army had unleashed terror.

"Ese niño que creamos se convirtió en un monstruo," he confided to Juan. "The child we created became a monster."

At the time, Colombia was just coming to terms with the savagery of the paramilitary forces, right-wing militias that, lacking the manpower and resources to dominate the countryside, settled instead on intimidation and torture as a strategy. Though they were conventionally armed, equipped, and financed by drug money, one of their preferred weapons was the chain saw. They employed it against teachers, union organizers, human rights activists, and anyone suspected of collaboration with the guerrillas. Victims, bound by rope to a tree, remained alive as one by one their limbs were cut from their bodies; the technique, it was said, made it all the more easy to dispose of the remains. If the army had created such a monster, as Colonel Herrera admitted, then surely the army and the state bore responsibility for the monstrous acts perpetrated by the beast. This was the essence of Juan's journalist scoop, a revelation that shook the nation.

Juan covered the war as a reporter for seven years. I asked him if there was any one incident that stood out, something that for him summed up the whole sordid mess. He recalled two quite different stories, which he saw as being closely related. One year, the FARC kidnapped three policemen during Holy Week. Three months later, they were to be exchanged, and Juan was one of several journalists invited to witness the event. The reporters reached the foot of a mountain in remote northeast Antioquia just after dawn and began the long slog through the jungle to the guerrilla base, which was perched high on a ridge, directly across from an army battalion entrenched on the opposite hillside. As they entered the FARC camp, Juan noticed a blond woman with movie-star looks that literally took his breath away. Her name was Marisol, and she came from a small place in Huila. When, some weeks later, Juan happened to pass through her hometown, he sought out the mayor, who remembered Marisol as the most beautiful girl the town had ever known. But she had always wanted to get away and see the world. A FARC front came through and she fell in love with the commander, who became her ticket out of one life and into another.

"It's like that," Juan remarked. "I've spoken with dozens of kidnap victims who have been held, sometimes for months, by the FARC. They all say that not once did they hear anyone talk about politics, class struggle, and all the other rhetoric of the Left. When they'd ask their captors why they ran with the guerrillas, the answers were always the same: the pay, four meals a day, the uniforms, the sense of family, the adventure. Half of them are just kids, kids that know how to kill."

Marisol haunted Juan for some time, passing through his thoughts by day and his dreams by night. Her fate consumed him. A year went by, and one day at work, a notice came over the wires of a firefight that had left a dozen guerrillas dead. The location was close to where they had met, in the mountains in northeast Antioquia. Among the dead was a blond woman, said to be Dutch, possibly Danish. Her name, her nom de guerre, was Marisol.

"It was so pointless," he said, "such a waste. Like the entire war, a war that should never have happened. It has turned so many into monsters."

I asked Juan about his other story: "You said there were two that came to mind."

"Yes. It was in Puerto Boyacá," he replied, glancing my way. "The birthplace of the paramilitaries. The only one immune to the violence was the priest. He could be trusted, and we became friends. He lived right beside the church, and one night he heard a knock at his door. It was a local man he knew well, who was completely covered in blood. Unbeknownst to the father, the man worked as a killer, charged with dismembering victims, cutting them up alive and throwing the bits into the river. Something within him had cracked, and he just couldn't do it anymore. His bosses wouldn't allow him to stop, and now they were out to kill him. He wanted protection. Imagine. A man who cuts up bodies with a chain saw still thinks he can be forgiven and sheltered by the church. What was the priest to do, give him confession?"

Juan fell silent for the first time since driving out of Medellín. I glanced at Xandra. Her eyes had welled with tears.

"When thirty thousand people disappeared in Argentina," Juan said, "the entire world was shaken. Pinochet in Chile killed three thousand and was forever condemned as a criminal. In Colombia, the disappeared numbered as many as one hundred thousand."

The following morning as we left Honda and drove north along the Magdalena to Puerto Triunfo, Juan tracked the history that had transformed the Medio Magdalena from a backwater in the 1960s to the cauldron of violence he had known too well. His account began, as all such stories do, with the assassination of Jorge Gaitán in 1948. In the bloodlust that followed, virtually every place in Colombia, apart from the coast, became indelibly stained red or blue, Liberal or Conservative, leaving every settlement the enemy and target of one side or the other. The first *fuerzas de autodefensa*, as the right-wing paramilitaries would later be known, in fact arose from the political left, as liberal militias came together to protect land, workers, and rural farmers. When, after a decade, the conflict waned, and the nation embraced an uneasy truce with the formal end of La Violencia in 1958, significant areas of the country remained under the control of guerrilla forces. These were for the most part ragtag bands, made up of Liberals, Communists, simple campesinos, and, at the core, hardened cadres, among them dedicated revolutionaries who had refused to demobilize during the general amnesty declared by General Rojas Pinilla when he took power in 1953. Although poorly equipped, these militias transformed the marginal regions they occupied into militarized enclaves, the most notorious of which surrounded Marquetalia, a small town in Tolima.

When the guerrillas declared Marquetalia an independent republic, the announcement went largely unnoticed. What did catch the attention of Bogotá, not to mention all of Latin America, was Fidel Castro's victory in Cuba, which transformed Marquetalia overnight into a nest of subversion that had to be eliminated. With the support of the American government, fiercely anti-Communist and keen to conduct a field test of napalm, soon to be a weapon of choice in Vietnam, Colombian armed forces attacked Marquetalia from the ground and air in May 1964. The siege went on for two months. Among those who lost everything, including his family, was Pedro Antonio Marín, who subsequently adopted the name of the murdered union leader Manuel Marulanda Vélez. It was his way of sending a message that while his personal life was dead, the revolutionary struggle was only beginning.

With the army pressing from all sides, Marulanda slipped through the cordon, escaping under the cover of darkness into the forest. Those who went with him, eluding the army patrols, and not for the last time, were the nucleus of what in 1966 became the FARC, the Fuerzas Armadas Revolucionarias de Colombia, the Revolutionary Armed Forces of Colombia. Known in time as Tirofijo, or "Sureshot," Marulanda, the head of FARC's Southern Bloc, would remain on the run for forty-four years. When he finally succumbed to a fatal heart attack in 2008, he was still living in the jungle, still plotting vengeance, still driven by an abiding hatred of Conservatives and the state, a worn-out veteran of La Violencia with a $5 million price on his head and a legacy of little beyond extortion, murder, bloodshed, and misery.

In the beginning, perhaps, there had been a dream: a desire to transform society, to liberate workers, to provide land for peasant farmers, to feed and shelter the poor. Certainly the Cuban Revolution inspired a wave of hope that swept over many lives, especially the young. In 1965, a year before the founding of the FARC, seven university students, all in their twenties and trained in Cuba, slipped into the forests of Santander with their own goal of mobilizing campesinos, fomenting revolution, and ultimately overthrowing the state. Their leader was Fabio Vásquez Castaño, a young man driven to revolution by political ideals but also eager to avenge the death of his father, murdered by *pájaros*, Conservative assassins. Perhaps as a sign of their ambitions, they adopted the rather grandiose name Ejército de Liberación Nacional, the National Liberation Army. Inspired by Castro, and finding moral ground in liberation theology and revolutionary priests such as Camilo Torres, the ELN embraced a fierce nationalism, targeting foreign corporations, oil companies in particular, as exploiters and thieves, robbers of Colombia's natural wealth and violators of its patrimony.

The ELN's position was extreme, and the consequences of its actions, the destruction of pipelines in particular, proved disastrous for workers and the environment. Still, the history of the United Fruit Company alone, with the massacre of the innocents at Ciénaga in 1928, not to mention the record of the Tropical Oil Company's land grab at Barrancabermeja, or that of Standard Oil with all the corruption the writer José Eustasio Rivera was struggling to unveil at the time of his death, suggests that their assessment of foreign corporations was not completely wide of the mark.

By the same token, when those allied with the FARC, which identified from the start with the rural poor, spoke of land redistribution, they did so in a country where campesinos, fully 70 percent of actual landowners, struggled to feed their families with but 5 percent of the nation's arable land. This concentration of ownership in the hands of the few, unbecoming and unsustainable in a democracy, would only become worse as drug money flooded the market. Revolutionary uprisings are not about the twiddling of thumbs. What unfolded in Colombia in the 1960s was less the outcome of a global Communist conspiracy than the consequence of a nation's failure to address fundamental economic disparities, hardwired into the structure of its society, that no modern democratic people can be expected to tolerate or endure.

For a time, insurgent armies sprouted up all over Colombia. In 1967, from the plantations of Urabá, arose the Ejército Popular de Liberación, the Popular Army of Liberation, or EPL. In time, the Caribbean coast would produce the Partido Revolucionario de los Trabajadores, the Revolutionary Workers' Party. In the early 1980s, from the hidden valleys of the Macizo Colombiano emerged the Quintín Lame, a native force fighting to secure an independent state, an indigenous homeland to be carved from the mountains of Cauca, Tolima, Valle, and Huila. Finally, from the streets and college campuses of Bogotá, Cali, and Medellín, came the Movimiento 19 de Abril, better known as the M-19, named for the date of the national election in 1970 that many believed had been rigged in favor of the Conservative candidate, Misael Pastrana Borrero, and stolen from Gustavo Rojas Pinilla.

The trajectory of the M-19 was not dissimilar to that of radical groups on the far left in the United States and Europe at the time, fringe factions that grew out of the student anti-war movement, only to turn in frustration and anger to violence, sabotage, kidnapping, and murder. In the beginning, it was "revolution as a party," as Jaime Bateman Cayón, one of the M-19 founders, quipped. Political inspiration came as much from Bob Dylan and Che Guevara, as from the dour and puritanical figures of the Communist firmament, Marx, Engels, and Lenin. Only educated scions of the urban elite could possibly have suggested, as M-19 did, that "the revolution is not just about having enough to eat; it's about being able to eat what we like to eat." For hardened and humorless Communists like Marulanda, the members of El Eme, as M-19 was also known, were little more than pranksters; this harsh assessment was seemingly confirmed in January 1974 when they launched their most audacious mission to date, the successful theft from a museum of Simón Bolívar's sword.

The M-19 cadres were, in fact, committed urban guerrillas, not unlike the Tupamaros in Uruguay or the Montoneros in Argentina. On New Year's Eve 1979, having tunneled beneath a military arsenal, they stole more than five thousand weapons from the Colombian army. A year later, they stormed the embassy of the Dominican Republic, taking fourteen ambassadors hostage, and ultimately escaping to Cuba, richer by several million dollars. Within ten years, revolution as mischief and fun would fully morph into the bloody siege of the Palace of Justice, and the death of almost half the justices of Colombia's supreme court. By then, political ideals had long gone the way of revolutionary fantasies, obliterated by the reality of war. In 1990, a severely depleted M-19 negotiated amnesty with the government, promising to return the coveted sword and renounce violence. Once the second-largest revolutionary force in Colombia, the cadres numbered at the time of their surrender well under a thousand. Yielding to the judgment of history, these remnants, as per the terms of the agreement, formed a legitimate party that was soon absorbed into the greater body of political life in Colombia, the tangle of alliances and compromises and deals that is the imperfect basis of governance in any democracy.

For a time, such high-level negotiations held great promise. In short order, President Barco secured agreements that led to the demobilization of four guerrilla groups: M-19, as well as the EPL, the Quintín Lame, and the Partido Revolucionario de los Trabajadores. Unfortunately, several factors still stood in the way of peace. First was the question of trust. In 1982, the government of Belisario Betancur had declared a general amnesty, leading to a cease-fire that brought the FARC to the negotiating table two years later. From these talks emerged the Unión Patriótica, the Patriotic Union, a party conceived as the legitimate political arm of the FARC, a first step toward bringing the entire revolutionary movement out of the hills and potentially into the halls of Congress, as legally elected representatives of their constituents.

In a moment of great hope, any number of FARC cadres and

urban supporters emerged from the shadows. In doing so, they effectively targeted themselves for slaughter. In a betrayal that would never be forgotten or forgiven, as many as three thousand men and women would be murdered in less than a decade, including two presidential candidates, eight members of Congress, and scores of union representatives, community activists, university students, small-town mayors, and peasant leaders—in short, anyone on the left even vaguely sympathetic with the revolutionary cause. Hired assassins, drug lords, and paramilitaries were directly responsible for the killings, but elements of the security forces and the Colombian army were implicated. Not surprisingly, the FARC returned to armed struggle with a vengeance.

Sustaining what now promised to be a long and bitter war required a constant and dependable flow of arms, munitions, and medical supplies, all of which came at great cost. Cuba, its own lifeline having been severed by the collapse of the Soviet Union in 1991, offered little beyond vitriol and rhetoric. Ecuador and Venezuela provided sanctuaries, but material support was nominal. Both the FARC and the ELN had to pay for every bullet, aside from what could be stolen from the army. This implied an annual war budget of tens of millions of dollars. The way they ultimately met the financial challenge virtually guaranteed a prolonged conflict that, with each passing day, would descend into ever deeper levels of depravity.

In the beginning, small guerrilla bands kept alive by robbing banks, the local Caja Agraria for the most part, the agricultural lending institution found in virtually every rural Colombian town. But as the cadres came together into larger units, with operations spreading to all parts of the country, new streams of revenue had to be found. For the FARC's Fourth Front, which operated throughout the Medio Magdalena, the answer was extortion, kidnapping, and assassination, criminal acts readily rationalized with the neat and convenient rhetoric of revolution and class warfare. Their targets were the wealthy landowners, ranchers like the father of my friend Juan Guillermo at Río Claro, the pioneers who had cleared the forests and, in their eyes, brought civilization to the Medio Magdalena.

Such men were not about to be intimidated by armed bands of mostly teenage soldiers on a mission to redistribute both land and wealth at the point of a gun. Nor, with their long tradition of frontier justice, would they allow extortion, vandalism, cattle rustling, murder, or kidnapping to go unpunished. The army, even if mobilized in force, could not be expected to protect every remote and isolated ranch from guerrilla bands that could materialize anywhere at any time. No man of honor would, at any rate, leave the fate of his family in the hands of strangers. The only solution for the landowners, all of whom felt threatened by the FARC, was to take control of their own security, pooling their resources to create their own militias, a movement that would ultimately grow into the AUC, the Autodefensas Unidas de Colombia, a national paramilitary force that would become the third leg of Colombia's civil war.

Precisely because the FARC had the tactical advantage, able to strike at its discretion, the paramilitaries had to find a way to be psychologically if not physically present in all places and at all times. Their goal above all was to deny the guerrillas material support. Lacking the manpower to control the vast geography through which the FARC moved at will, they had to reach the rural population with an intimidating message so compelling that no campesino would dare rent his mules, carry loads, or provide the guerrillas with food, gas, or any other essential supplies. The solution was terror. If their military patrols could not be in all places at all times, fear could be. Bind a man to a tree, hack off his penis, toss it in the river, and word spreads. Lay waste to a village and kill half the men as punishment for a single transaction—the exchange by one hungry mother of a few gallons of fuel, some cassava, a box of bandages— and people will surely hesitate before offering support to the FARC. This, at least, was the idea that rationalized barbarism.

Unfortunately, the guerrillas acted with similar brutality, and made similar threats. This left villagers without a choice, condemned if they failed to deliver what was needed by the cadres and certain to invite brutal reprisals from the paramilitaries if they did. Thus, over time, the entire rural population, men and women who wanted nothing to do with the conflict, became caught in the vise of war. Innocent people were killed for being a Liberal or killed for being a Conservative; killed for being for Pablo Escobar or killed for being against him; killed for being supporters of the FARC or killed for being in favor of the AUC; killed for being rich or killed for being poor; killed for being a journalist, a human rights activist, a union leader, or even a priest ministering to the poor.

As atrocities became the norm, and reports verified the existence of schools of torture such as the one the AUC maintained in Belén de los Andaquíes in Caquetá, the fight grew personal, with any lingering political motivations on both sides overwhelmed by the passions of vengeance. In the north of Antioquia, Carlos Castaño and his brothers Fidel and Vicente established the ACCU, Autodefensas Campesinas de Córdoba y Urabá, after their father had been kidnapped and killed by the FARC. Santiago Uribe, brother of future president Álvaro Uribe, reputedly formed a death squad known as the Twelve Apostles; he, too, was driven by revenge after the FARC murdered their father. Ramón Isaza Arango, whose name would come up again and again over the coming days as we interviewed victims of the conflict, led the paramilitary militias in all the Medio Magdalena during the worst years of the violence. He first took up arms against leftist guerrillas in 1978. When, some years later, the FARC's Ninth Front tried to overrun his farm, he and eight workers fought them off. But in the end, he lost everything: farm, family, and all his livestock, leaving him with deep wells of hatred that he would draw on for much of the rest of his life.

As the violence spread, and the scale of the fighting grew, so did the costs of the war. Although many assumed that Fidel Castro and Hugo Chávez were financing the guerrillas, evidence to the contrary was the very ease with which these self-professed revolutionaries, desperate for money, slipped into the drug business. By the late 1980s, the Medellín Cartel was well entrenched in the Medio Magdalena. Like so many Colombians, the drug lords saw land as the measure of a man. Pablo Escobar's place at Hacienda Nápoles, near Puerto Triunfo, encompassed eight square miles that he had turned into a fantasy retreat, complete with man-made lakes, a private bullring, a racetrack, and a zoo stocked with elephants, antelopes, giraffes, and ostriches. From Africa, like Noah, he imported two of everything, including a hippopotamus couple, the progenitors of the large feral population that to this day plays havoc with local fishermen and small boat traffic on the Magdalena. Over the entrance gate to the ranch, he brazenly mounted a replica of the small airplane, a Super Cub, that carried his first shipment of cocaine to the United States.

Cocaine has a way of soiling everyone it touches, and in Colombia in the 1980s, it touched everyone, including the FARC and the ELN, neither of which ever denounced Pablo Escobar. As field commanders considered the money to be made, and their apologists anticipated and crafted the ideological contortions to rationalize involvement in the trade, the last shreds of legitimacy fell away from a revolutionary cause that already lay in tatters. Drug trafficking was not exactly what Jorge Gaitán had in mind when he spoke of the needs and aspirations of the poor. But for the FARC leadership, the cocaine business offered the irresistible promise of long-term financial stability, a revenue stream to complement what they already had going with extortion and kidnapping.

At first, the FARC cadres essentially ran a protection racket. They would tax production in the fields, guard the processing facilities, and offer security for shipments, all for a price. For a time, they kept away from the actual production and distribution of the drug. But this did not last. The money was too good, and over time it allowed the FARC to grow into a serious military force capable of mounting complex operations conceived not just to harass the army but to take and hold ground. In 1998, in the far reaches of the Amazon, more than a thousand FARC soldiers took on an entire battalion of the Colombian army in a coordinated attack on Mitú, a department capital, which the guerrillas held for several days. Such an action, shocking as it was for the nation and the world, could never have happened without the black money from the drug trade.

By the time the government of Juan Manuel Santos initiated peace talks in Havana in 2012, FARC's annual budget was roughly $600 million. No guerrilla army in history, operating on its own, had managed to generate such support, and none, in doing so, had become more alienated from the very people targeted as the supposed beneficiaries of the revolutionary struggle. Politically, the FARC had no standing. Widely condemned, in many quarters despised, the FARC saw its approval ratings in national polls drop so low they could scarcely be measured, registering well below 1 percent. In 2008 a social media campaign started by two young students with a single slogan, *No más FARC* ("No more FARC"), within weeks brought more than two million supporters onto the streets of Bogotá in one of the largest demonstrations in the history of the city.

On the front lines of the conflict, FARC commanders, those who remained alive after years of targeted attacks, faced growing challenges of recruitment and retention, as cadres responded to government incentives and offers of amnesty. From its 2001 peak as a military force of sixteen thousand, by 2009 the FARC was down to eighty-five hundred, mostly teenagers under the age of nineteen. The FARC's reputation and military strength aside, the problem for those seeking an end to the conflict remained the money. As long as the FARC's position in the cocaine trade was generating tens of millions of dollars a year, a small guerrilla force hidden away in the mountains of Colombia could conceivably go on fighting indefinitely. This inconvenient truth was never far from the thoughts of those in Havana arguing in favor of the government concessions that led ultimately to a negotiated peace. The alternative was the haunting possibility of endless war.

In the 1980s, Pablo Escobar had little sympathy for the guerrillas, unless they could serve his needs, as had been the case with the M-19 and the takeover of the Palace of Justice in 1985. Once settled at Hacienda Nápoles—as settled as a man on the run could be—Escobar threw his support to the paramilitaries, financing their operations, encouraging them to get into the cocaine business, even providing Israeli and British mercenaries as trainers. As early as 1982, members of the Medellín Cartel had come together in Puerto Boyacá with wealthy cattle ranchers, conservative politicians, small business owners, and, quite possibly, elements of the army and the U.S.-based corporation Texas Petroleum to form MAS, Muerte a Secuestradores, or Death to Kidnappers. The association's formal mandate was to defend land and private property and to free the landowners and their families from the threat of extortion and kidnapping. To do so, they would take the fight to the enemy. If FARC cadres could not be found, they would kill simply to make a point.

Within a year, death squads associated with MAS had been implicated in 240 political murders: of community leaders, elected officials, peasant farmers. To provide legal cover, those who financed MAS—Pablo Escobar, Carlos Lehder, Gonzalo Rodríguez Gacha, and others in the business—created ACDEGAM, the Asociación Campesina de Ganaderos y Agricultores del Magdalena Medio, or the Association of Middle Magdalena Ranchers and Farmers. While MAS assassins killed anyone deemed to be subversive, ACDEGAM built schools, bridges, and health clinics, all under the banner of patriotism. Although most of the cartel funding flowed to MAS, the various initiatives of ACDEGAM, together with the usual threats, bribes, and disappearances, ultimately resulted in the paramilitaries becoming firmly entrenched as the de facto political authorities in towns throughout the Medio Magdalena.

"They were like shadow governments unto themselves," Juan recalled. "Completely in control. The FARC had no presence at all. Which meant that the wrath of the paramilitaries fell on the innocent. Criminals who thought nothing of burying people alive, or watching as their men played soccer with a decapitated head, ruled their towns with iron fists of moral rectitude, ready to punish anyone engaged in any activity that strayed from conservative orthodoxy: tradition, patriotism, family, and faith—the Christian norm, as they defined it to be. As for the dead, they just tossed the bodies into the Magdalena."

Juan had a way of saying things that brought silence to a conversation. We drove on, catching glimpses of the river: fishermen on the shore, children playing on the bridges, families picnicking by the water. As Juan sped through one small town after another, all vibrant and alive, with shops along the roadside and fruit stands buried beneath great mounds of watermelons, mangoes, and pineapples, I found it difficult to reconcile the dystopic world Juan had known with the Colombia of today, though the events he described had occurred well within memory. I asked him if the media and the Colombian people had been aware at the time of what was going on in the Medio Magdalena.

"Of course, rumors were everywhere," he acknowledged, "but so was the violence. People turned away from knowing. It was how you survived. But as a journalist, it was my job to know. In 1990 I jumped at the chance of covering a meeting between the government and the paramilitaries in Puerto Boyacá. I remember really wanting to go. I wanted to see the end of the world. That's how we all thought of the Medio Magdalena. The end of the world. As bad as anything can get."

At the time, Juan explained, the entire region was designated a *zona roja*, a red zone of war, where the army had free rein to pursue and engage the guerrillas and to question and detain, under military law, anyone suspected of providing them with support. Puerto Boyacá was then controlled by Ramón Isaza Arango: the godfather, according to Juan, of the entire paramilitary cause. In 1977, having lost his own farm and livestock to the guerrillas, he and other vigilantes had formed El Escopetero, a mercenary militia based in Puerto Triunfo that, for a fee, offered protection to local ranchers. Isaza soon expanded his services to include social cleansing, and for six years El Escopetero sought out and selectively killed thieves, rapists, drug dealers, and kidnappers. With such credentials, Isaza and his men were a natural fit for the United Self-Defense Forces of Puerto Boyacá, which they joined in 1984. Isaza also served for two years as the head of the Peasant Self-Defense Forces of Antioquia.

"But here is where it gets interesting," Juan remarked. "In 1991, Pablo Escobar seeks an alliance with the Puerto Boyacá self-defense force and Isaza refuses. He hates everything about the drug business. So Escobar has the military commander of the Boyacá mob, Henry Pérez, killed. Isaza ends up moving on to another paramilitary group, the Peasant Self-Defense Forces of Magdalena Medio. The point is, some of these *paras* wanted nothing to do with drugs. Isaza went on to join the national group under Carlos Castaño, but he quit as soon as he realized that the AUC was also involved in trafficking. For a time, all the money allowed even the most Conservative of the ranchers and old-time landowners to divert their eyes, as if they didn't know the source of Pablo's wealth. But in the end, even his neighbors turned on him, along with the rest of Colombia."

. . .

Pablo Escobar's death, as Juan remembers, was a profoundly cathartic moment. But it made little difference in the Medio Magdalena, and Colombia as a nation only continued its downward spiral. In 1994, running as a Liberal, Ernesto Samper, scion of one of the most illustrious families in Colombia, was elected president by the narrowest of margins. Within weeks, accusations surfaced that his campaign had accepted a $6 million contribution from the Cali Cartel. Ultimately, he would be acquitted by Congress, but not before Colombia, desperately in need of strong leadership, endured the humiliation of being ruled for four years by a president unable even to travel to the United States, where his visa had been revoked.

With the nation's duly elected leader accused of collaborating with the cartel, and international institutions threatening to decertify the country for human rights abuses, Colombia was in danger of becoming a pariah nation. Internally, things were only getting worse. By the end of the 1990s, more than six hundred innocent men and women were being held captive by the FARC, hostages of war, snatched from their homes and families, their lives in the balance, condemned to trudge through fetid jungles by night, sleeping in cages by day, tormented by flies, mocked by child soldiers scarcely taller than their guns. Cruelty was a trait of character carefully nurtured by those in control of the fourteen thousand children recruited to fight and die by illegal armed groups on both sides of the conflict.

Oddly enough, what historians may remember as a turning point in Colombia's fortunes was the moment U.S. ambassador Lewis Tambs coined the term "narco-guerrilla," bringing together in neat and cogent alignment two of America's three great demons: communism and drugs. The devil would have to wait, forgotten for a time as lightbulbs went off in the heads of every American politician. For years, the U.S. embassy had been divided—with the CIA targeting leftist insurgencies and the DEA in charge of the war on drugs. The CIA and the U.S. military, hopped up after half a century of fighting Communists, had long dismissed the efforts of the DEA as police work. The DEA agents, marked men who put their lives on the line every time they left the embassy, could not believe that the CIA was chasing Cold War ghosts when boatloads of drugs unleashing waves of violence were reaching American shores every day. Missing from this in-house squabble was the obvious fact that what allowed the FARC and every other dissident group to fight was cocaine.

Once this connection was made and diplomats began to speak of narco-terrorists—a term that resonated in the halls of power in Washington—the floodgates of American military and development aid opened. The $54 million offered by President Bill Clinton in 1996 would within four years increase to $765 million. In the six years beginning in 1999, Colombia would receive well over $4 billion, making it the third-largest recipient of U.S. aid, behind only Egypt and Israel. Colombia did not squander the support. The fighting capacity and strength of its armed forces was, by all accounts, transformed.

With the army ascendant, President Álvaro Uribe, elected as a hard-liner in 2002, found himself in a position of strength when, a year later, he entered the negotiations that ultimately led to the formal demobilization of the AUC and other paramilitary forces in 2006. It was, as Juan explained, an imperfect compromise. Few on the left trusted Uribe, himself a prominent landowner who had been among the first to promote and support the paramilitary movement. As talks got underway in 2003, it was unclear whether Uribe truly wanted to neutralize the AUC or simply hoped to lower its profile. The government's terms were generous. Many paramilitaries kept their arms, refusing to disband. Those who confessed received moderate sentences that promised to return them to the streets within a decade. Though 70 percent of the paramilitaries' revenues came from cocaine, none had to reveal the sources of their funding or expose anything of their network of contacts within the Colombian army or the political elite. Despite a litany of documented atrocities, only forty-seven of the thirty-one thousand paramilitary troops who came forward in the process, with confessions acknowledging no fewer than thirty-seven thousand homicides, would be convicted of war crimes. Still, at the end of the day, with the settlement in 2006, the AUC as an open marauding force ceased to exist.

"I'm no supporter of Uribe," Juan said. "But you have to admire what he did. It was like Nixon going to China. No politician from the left could have done it."

Álvaro Uribe did not silence the voices of the extreme Right, Juan explained. They were, after all, his constituency. But in exerting his control over the paramilitaries, with the full backing of the army, he effectively neutered what had become the third leg of the conflict, independent militias that had been responsible, according to the United Nations, for fully 80 percent of the deaths during the prolonged war. Uribe showed the world that the Colombian government was prepared to acknowledge and be accountable for the actions of the murderous *autodefensa* forces, formally recognized as terrorist organizations by the United States and the European Union, that had brought to the nation both shame and international condemnation.

With the paramilitaries neutralized at least for the moment, and the army growing in strength by the day, the way was paved for the military efforts that, under the leadership of both Uribe and his defense minister, Juan Manuel Santos, in the end broke the will of the FARC and brought its representatives to the peace table in Havana. In eight years, beginning in 2002, the FARC lost well over half its cadre; by 2010, as Santos assumed the presidency, it was a much reduced force of but eight thousand fighters.

"For any number of reasons, the two men remain bitter rivals," Juan remarked. "Mostly because Santos didn't toe the Uribe line when he became president in 2010. Uribe felt betrayed, as did many Colombians on the right who voted for Santos, thinking he'd just be more of the same. But Santos surprised everyone."

Juan has been around too long and has seen too much to be impressed by politicians of any persuasion; skepticism is part of his DNA as a journalist. But as he spoke of the two presidents, Álvaro Uribe and Juan Manuel Santos, he seemed less the reporter who had covered both leaders throughout their political careers than a storyteller already looking to the past, as Uribe and Santos slipped away into history. He recalled not the enmity between them that had dominated Colombian politics for a decade but, rather, what each had brought to the table during the greatest existential crisis in the history of the country. For the first critical years, Juan noted, they had worked hand in hand, with Santos supporting Uribe and implementing the hard-line policies that let the FARC and the ELN know that the entire field of play had changed. Both men, in and out of office, came under relentless attack in the press, accused of tolerating or promoting human rights abuses, of causing unnecessary suffering, of violating the conventions of war. And no doubt, as Juan had himself reported, egregious deeds had taken place: political killings disguised as acts of war, innocent lives lost in the miasma of battle, caused by mistakes that ought never to have occurred. But all of this, Juan maintained, had to be judged not in isolation but within the context of a bloody conflict that had consumed the nation for fifty years, a war without rules from which no one emerged ethically or morally unscathed. It wasn't right. It just was.

Uribe had brought to the war an iron fist, *una mano dura*—literally, a hard hand. Santos, though forged in war, as a leader found his way to peace, putting his entire legacy on the line in a single-minded quest to return stability and prosperity to Colombia. Both men had been obliged to compromise: Uribe during the demobilization of the paramilitaries, Santos in the Havana negotiations with the FARC. Each was criticized and, in some quarters, condemned for having done so. Though neither man will ever again serve as president, each remains a magnet for the ire and resentments of those on the opposing side of the political divide that cuts deeply through the country.

In time, all of this may be forgotten. As the nation heals, if indeed it does, perceptions will change. Whatever bitterness and ill will stand between Álvaro Uribe and Juan Manuel Santos today may well dissipate as their names enter history, perhaps to be remembered as the national leaders who together made possible an end to the war.

Whether Colombia's fragile peace will endure remains uncertain, though it is Juan Gonzalo's fervent hope that it does.

"Posterity will be a ruthless judge," he said, "should anyone, in a moment of such longing, deny the people the promise of peace."

Sisters of Mercy

Puerto Triunfo is a small town built on a great bend of the Río Magdalena, on ground so low that river water regularly sweeps the plaza clean, lapping at the base of the small white church on the corner, spreading at times as far as the sports fields where today children mimic the moves of their favorite players on the very ground where twenty years ago the priest celebrated Mass in the sunlight as the community gathered in defiance of the paramilitaries to bury a martyr, the mother of Jenny Castañeda, the woman we had come to see.

Arriving late, well after dark, we found rooms at the Santa María, a modest hotel on the corner of the plaza directly across from the church and just inland from the waterfront. Juan went off to find Jenny, preferring to do so on his own. While we waited, Xandra and I took in the scene from the second-floor balcony of our hotel. Most of the town was asleep. A few couples huddled in doorways, speaking softly. It was close to ten, and the air was still hot. The only activity was along the river, where thatch-roofed restaurants, open to the air and brimming with people, ran half the length of the waterfront. There was an ice cream shop just below us, and a coffee bar, but the rest was under construction: a new boardwalk and promenade, and the rising outlines of yet another hotel, what would be the fifteenth in a community of just twenty thousand.

Puerto Triunfo, a town once synonymous with murder and violence, today sees tourism as the key to prosperity, banking on its proximity to one of the more popular attractions in the country, Hacienda Nápoles. Despite a hefty admission price of fifty thousand pesos, roughly fifteen dollars—not insignificant for a Colombian family—the theme park created from Pablo Escobar's former estate and playground attracts one hundred thousand visitors each year, and the number is growing.

Not that there is a lot to see or do. People gather for snapshots beneath the main gate, still surmounted by the small Piper airplane that reputedly carried Escobar's first shipment of cocaine to the United States. There has been a weak attempt to create a zoo from the remnants of the African wildlife he imported, though most of the animals have died, and some, like the hippos, have run wild, creating feral populations that menace local fishermen. The burnt wreckage of his antique car collection, famously torched by rivals, Los Pepes and the Cali Cartel, is on display, an odd combination of sculpture garden and junkyard. Pablo's family home is a ruin, long ago torn apart brick by brick by looters searching for hidden caches of money. The land itself is not especially beautiful: rolling hills, brown and tired pastures, worn-out ground, eroded gullies. There is a fine exhibit tracking Escobar's rise and fall, but it tells a story most Colombians either already know or would like to forget.

What draws the crowds and fills the rooms of the half dozen hotels within walking distance of the entrance gate is less the place than the aura of the man himself. Nearly thirty years after his death, Colombians approach Pablo Escobar's legacy with a host of conflicting emotions. There is, of course, horror, shame, anger, and hate. But there is also morbid curiosity, cloaked admiration, skepticism, and wonder, an almost pornographic attraction for a common man who rose to such heights, a simple *bandido* who defied the United States for over a decade, even while fighting his way to a fortune unlike anything that had been known in the annals of crime. With each passing year, as the crowds at Hacienda Nápoles attest, the greatest killer in the history of Colombia comes closer to slipping from history into the realm of myth.

Juan returned just after midnight, having made arrangements for us to interview Jenny Castañeda in the morning. He seemed visibly shaken. Apparently Jenny had told him of her latest encounter with one of the godfathers of the paramilitaries, Ramón Isaza Arango. Old and close to death, Isaza had welcomed her in his prison cell, fully aware that Jenny knew, as all had long suspected, that he had been responsible for the murder of her mother. Her mother's name, Damaris Mejía, had been number 576 on a list of victims submitted by Isaza under the *Ley de Justicia y Paz*, the agreement worked out by Álvaro Uribe that pardoned paramilitary cadres, allowing them to secure reduced prison time, provided they confessed their crimes.

"There were six hundred names on that document." Juan said. "And it was just one of several such lists of his victims. Isaza was given the maximum sentence. Eight years. If he lives, he'll be out any day, just like the rest of them."

Tears streaked Juan's face. It was late, and there was nothing to say.

The next morning, we met Jenny for coffee on the waterfront, taking a table in the open sun, well away from the visitors and locals finishing up the last of their breakfasts. Jenny was cautious but confident. It wasn't the first time she had told her story, and she had nothing more to fear. Besides, as she noted with a grin, she had cancer, and though it was in remission, she might not be long for this world. That God would afflict a young mother of just thirty-five with such an illness after all she had gone through was hardly just, she agreed, but it had, if anything, made her stronger.

Jenny Castañeda had lived in Puerto Triunfo all her life. Born in 1981, she had first known Pablo Escobar through the eyes of a little girl. Her fondest childhood memories were of Christmas, when Santa Claus arrived in Puerto Triunfo, not in a sled but in an enormous truck stacked high with presents. Dressed in their finest clothes, hundreds of children would patiently line up, aligned according to age in long queues that snaked around the plaza. Mothers carried infants. Toddlers teetered, hands clinging to the legs of older siblings. The oldest were twelve, the last year of childhood. Each knew the drill and happily played to the cameras recording the event. To ensure that no one snuck back into line to score a second gift, the children had their hands stamped with an indelible mark that, as Jenny recalled, nothing could erase.

"They were the most amazing presents, always perfect for every age, toys and games no one could afford, things no one in town even knew about. It was like magic. No one ever saw Pablo, just as no one ever sees Santa Claus, but we all knew it was him."

Jenny received a gift from Pablo Escobar every Christmas until she turned twelve, the year he was killed. By then, the paramilitary movement, which began in Puerto Boyacá, had crossed the Magdalena and taken firm control of Puerto Triunfo. The police had a token presence, but did nothing. Paramilitary rules were simple: You behaved, or you died. Anyone caught stealing, selling sex, taking drugs, or violating conservative traditions as defined by moral authorities such as Ramón Isaza Arango was killed. Jenny's entire upbringing, through all her teenage years, was tainted by massacres, kidnappings, and murder. Friends and neighbors would disappear in the blink of an eye, slipping away, as her grandmother always said, from earth to heaven, without anyone in the community saying a thing.

There was a truck, Jenny recalled, that everyone knew. It would roll into town and stop in front of a shop, a private home, even the church. If it was not dropping off a body, it was carrying off a victim. Those kidnapped seldom returned. Most were taken by powerboat to an island in the Magdalena, where they were tortured and killed, their bodies dismembered and tossed into the river. As a young girl, Jenny knew what was going on. So did her grandfather, as did the entire town. But no one ever spoke about it. They just adapted, as if the truck in question were making ordinary deliveries, as if murder were merely another business. To this day, she can vividly recall her grandfather's words, repeated verbatim every time the truck drove past their house on the plaza: "Let's get in the house. Here we have not seen anything."

But of course they had. Jenny was thirteen when she saw masked men drag a court official, a prosecutor, from his home. He resisted, and they knocked him senseless. He came to and screamed for help. No one did a thing. Dozens knew him well, and just stood nearby. The man ran. The local priest flung Jenny to the ground and covered her body as the murderers opened fire. The victim stumbled into the local bakery before falling over dead. The killers fled, leaving the body to be buried by the family, a small mercy. When Jenny told her grandfather what had happened, he quoted what had effectively become the town's unofficial motto: "The less you ask, the more you live."

Such passivity insulated the Castañeda family for a time, and it may well have kept the violence at bay indefinitely, had it not been for the spirit of Jenny's mother, Damaris Mejía, a fiery social activist. Land is at the root of all conflict in Colombia, and the concentration of ownership in Puerto Triunfo and throughout the Medio Magdalena by definition implied that there would be a large and vulnerable population of impoverished workers and landless campesinos. As if channeling the spirit, energy, and oratory of Jorge Gaitán, Damaris became their voice, their heroine, and, in time, their martyr. That she stayed alive as long as she did, Jenny now believes, was a testament to the love and respect she commanded in the community, the town of her birth. For if her words were incendiary, her deeds were essentially acts of insurrection. If the poor had no money and the government no interest in meaningful land reform, the only option, as Damaris saw it, was to invade the lands of the rich with peasant armies of squatters.

The target of the first land invasion was, to my surprise, the ranch of my good friend from Río Claro, Juan Guillermo Garcés. Apparently he and Damaris initially had some issues, but being, as Jenny recalled, "a noble man with a good heart," he was soon won over by her mother. Juan agreed to sell small lots at a fraction of market value so that no one on either side could claim that the land had been usurped at no cost. Moved by her success, Damaris launched another invasion some months later, again on Juan Guillermo's land. For a second time, he yielded. Lulled by the reaction of perhaps the only major landowner in all the Medio Magdalena who actually supported land reform, a progressive visionary who had himself worked in the region as an activist and organizer for a decade, Damaris made a fatal mistake. For her next major action, she decided to target Hacienda Nápoles, which, after the death of Pablo Escobar, had been expropriated by the state and was at the time of the third invasion being managed by the municipality of Puerto Triunfo. At this point events became tinged with a hint of the supernatural.

The mayor, already jealous of Damaris's popularity in the community, went with some thugs to the squatters' encampment and told Jenny's mother she had but two hours to leave. Damaris responded that only in death would she abandon her people. That night, visiting Jenny and her husband, Damaris had a premonition, and she mentioned out of the blue that on the next day, late in the evening, they would be the first to find out. Jenny had no idea what she meant until the following night when, well after midnight, her younger brother Andrés appeared, bearing the news that their mother had been killed. It was, as Jenny recalled, "the first time that violence had knocked at her door."

According to Andrés, three strangers had turned up and gone hut to hut until they found Damaris, who was fast asleep. They shot her six times in the head, then warned everyone within earshot not to touch the body, that it was to be abandoned to the ants. As the killers escaped, their car literally bumped into Andrés, who had heard the gunshots and was racing to his mother's side. They told him not to worry; it had just been some fireworks. Not until he reached his mother's campsite did he realize that he had come face-to-face with the murderers. The people huddled around the corpse were paralyzed by fear. Only reluctantly did one man offer to help the sixteen-year-old boy carry his mother's body home. Two years later, that Good Samaritan was found dead, murdered for defying the murderers.

For a day, a shroud of silence fell upon Puerto Triunfo, a state of shock tempered by fear. But on the second day, something truly miraculous occurred. Shy and withdrawn for all of her life, Jenny woke up as if possessed, taken over by her mother's spirit. With a stride she had never known and a voice that had never been heard, she marched into the police station and filed a formal complaint against not just the three murderers, whom her brother had readily identified, but the entire paramilitary apparatus that had held her town hostage for so long. Before the death of Damaris, such audacity would have been suicidal. A day later, it was a declaration of war, the first parry by an avenging daughter rendered fearless by grief, and embarking at the age of twenty on a lifelong mission to ensure that her mother had not died in vain.

As Damaris had wished, the religious service took place on the town's soccer field, with everyone drinking *aguardiente*. The priest broke protocol and celebrated Mass outside the church. Standing before a casket piled high with roses, he summed up her life, in words both simple and brave, certain to arouse the killers and the authorities, which everyone knew to be one and the same:

"She died like Jesus Christ. She died for our sins, and in the name of the poor."

After the ceremony, Jenny's grandfather took his daughter's body home. When they awoke the following day, the entire town was silent, bedecked with white flags and banners. Virtually every man, woman, and child in Puerto Triunfo joined the procession to the cemetery. It was a collective act of resistance, remembered years later as the moment when the people took their first steps along a path of redemption that in time would allow them to reclaim their dignity, and take hold of their destiny.

For Jenny, the struggle was only beginning. For six years, she tried to have the assassins brought to justice: killers whose identities were known to all, men she might encounter any day on the streets of her town. Only in the wake of the *Ley de Justicia y Paz* were she and her brother able to confirm what both had long suspected: that the man who had ordered their mother's death was indeed Ramón Isaza, the paramilitary leader. His confession allowed them to apply for compensation, and each received from the government seven million pesos, just over $2,000. A small token for a life.

Jenny, at any rate, was not interested in the money. She wanted Isaza and the killers, and everyone else who had lied and deceived and violated the trust of the people, to acknowledge that her mother had been a good woman, decent and true, a leader who had lived to defend those most in need, and who had died for a just cause. In court, Ramón Isaza had publicly asked for Jenny's forgiveness, acknowledging that ordering the death of Damaris Mejía was the biggest mistake his organization had made. But for Jenny, this wasn't enough. After so many years of denials and lies, of dealing with a legal system Kafkaesque in its corruption, she had become consumed with resentment and bitterness, and she was not about to forgive and reconcile. Then she fell ill, diagnosed at just age twenty-six with cancer of the lungs and thyroid.

One night in the hospital, in a rare moment of clarity between medications, she saw in her dreams an apparition, an angel who morphed from pure light into a perfect image of her mother. As the ghostly figure began to speak, Jenny realized that it really was Damaris, returned from the dead. As always, her mother was very clear. She told Jenny that she would be released in twenty days and that Jenny would leave the hospital with an important mission. Ramón Isaza would reach out to her, asking for forgiveness. This time, the spirit said, you must accept and embrace him as you would your grandfather, with a kiss, making sure that he knows that your mother forgave him long ago, and that she thanks him for all of his prayers for your well-being and recovery.

Twenty days later, the dream became a reality. Jenny was released, her cancer in remission. A phone call came in that night from one of Isaza's men, inviting her to visit him in prison. When they met, Isaza said just what her mother's spirit had predicted in the dream: He asked for forgiveness. He spoke of his many prayers for Jenny's recovery and well-being. Jenny then did just what her mother had asked. She reached out and kissed him on both cheeks, then spoke words of forgiveness and grace. As she made ready to leave, Isaza encouraged her to complete the circle of healing. Travel to Bogotá, he told her, go to La Picota, the jail that was holding "El Enfermero," the former assassin once known as "The Nurse," the one who had actually pulled the trigger on the gun that had killed her mother. And so Jenny did.

After that, it was time for her to focus on her family, her husband and little boy, as well as every Colombian who had suffered. All were part of a greater community, what her mother had always described as the family of the nation. Jenny's new mission in life is to give voice to all who had been victims of the violence, knowing as she does, as few can know, that grief can become grace, and forgiveness the antidote to despair.

As our conversation came to an end, Jenny walked toward the deck overlooking the Magdalena.

"If this river could speak," she said, "it would have the answers that countless victims are seeking. In flood, it grows, both creating and destroying, carrying death and giving life. Peace, like the river, is an unfolding process. All I know is that my son will not live in hate."

Juan Gonzalo had another friend he was keen to introduce, another young woman who embodied the story of the Medio Magdalena. Her name was Diana Ocampo, and she came from San Diego, a small town of a thousand perched in the mountains on the border of Caldas and Antioquia. She was thirty-five, the same age more or less as Jenny, and very beautiful, with long brown hair and the dark eyes of a doe. We met in a café in La Dorada, right across from the city park where Diana and her family, at the lowest point in their fortunes, had slept on the grass for two weeks, with only the clothes on their backs. A kind woman then offered them a room, which they shared for three months with nine other families. In San Diego, they had not been rich, but with their farm they had lived well, not wanting for anything. Forced to flee, they had left home with nothing, arriving on the banks of the Magdalena without "a single centavo," as Diana recalled. They were among the more than five thousand displaced people who ended up on the streets of La Dorada, itself a city of just seventy thousand.

Their nightmare began on Christmas Eve 2001. Diana's mother; her stepfather, José; and her four siblings were attending Mass when the service was disrupted by a woman nobody knew. The stranger walked up to the padre and whispered into his ear. The priest, his face the color of ash, turned to the congregation and urged everyone not to be afraid, to remain calm, and to proceed with caution. He then announced that they all had thirty minutes to evacuate the town. As Diana's mother huddled with friends and family in the church, José hurried home to get the horses and some supplies. He was back within the half hour, but it was too late. The guerrillas had taken San Diego, closing the road and prohibiting anyone from leaving. Fewer than half the residents managed to escape.

At the time, Diana was half a continent away, living in Chile and ministering to the terminally ill, having taken her vows as a nun, a Sister of Mercy. She first sensed that something was wrong during a phone call home. She could hear it in her mother's voice. After arranging for a leave from the convent, Diana returned to Colombia, landing at the small airport in La Dorada, where her mother met her with the terrible news that her brother, just seventeen, had been kidnapped by the paramilitaries. Nothing in San Diego, her mother warned, was the same. The guerrillas had arrived with lists and gone door to door grabbing anyone accused of collaborating with the paramilitaries. They shot them in the plaza and dumped the bodies at the edge of town. The *paras*, as the paramilitaries were known, did the same thing, killing anyone who so much as offered a glass of lemonade to a member of the FARC.

"You have to watch your every word," her mother cautioned. "It's best to know nothing and see nothing."

They took public transport home, local buses and *colectivos*, four hours across a war zone. The paramilitaries controlled La Dorada, but the FARC held the hills around and beyond San Diego. The hydroelectric station at Norcasia had been damaged, as had many of the bridges. In places they had to ford rivers to reach taxis or trucks lined up on the far side.

No sooner was Diana home than she was encouraged to leave, first by the army commander, and then by her stepfather, José, who had heard that the guerrillas, short a cook, intended to kidnap his daughter and force her to work in a field kitchen. Having lost one child to the paramilitary, he was not about to lose another to the FARC. As it was, their family farm had been occupied by both, with the paramilitaries holding the main house and the guerrillas camped out in the fields of maize, coffee, and sugarcane.

The two combatants, in fact, shared the same strategic goal, which accounted for the intensity of the fighting at San Diego. They both wanted land for coca production, and control of the local market and distribution of the leaves. The fertile soils and soft rains of Caldas offered an ideal habitat for the plant. The guerrillas and paramilitaries operated what amounted to rival agricultural extension services, providing seeds, fertilizers, insecticides, and even advice on how best to grow and manage the fields. Rural farmers were only too happy to oblige, for the return on coca at the time was literally a thousand times that of other crops. A kilogram of *panela*, for example, blocks of raw sugar laboriously processed from cane, sold for 600, perhaps 800 pesos, roughly 27 cents. The same weight in leaves could earn a farmer 400,000 pesos, and if processed to paste, the first stage of extracting pure cocaine, as much as 800,000 pesos. But the easy money only immersed the campesinos deeper in the conflict, and it came at a price. Selling coca to one side inevitably invited savage retribution from the other. Diana's stepfather, José, was the only farmer in San Diego to resist the temptation to enter the trade, and that is the reason, he maintains, that fifteen years on, their immediate family remains intact, having never suffered a violent death. Even her brother managed to escape the paramilitaries; he now serves as a high-ranking nurse in the army medical corps.

"Once in one of the wards," Diana said, "he came upon his kidnapper, in military uniform, but with a much lower rank. The soldier was terrified that my brother would turn him in. But he didn't do anything. Revenge is for the weak."

Like many young Colombians, Diana neither dwells on the past nor tolerates anything that will deny the promise of the future. For her, the years of war are today best remembered as a crucible out of which was born a new life. Though raised with little formal education, Diana today is the head of ASMUDGEC, Asociación de Mujeres Generando Cambios (Association of Women Igniting Change), a foundation that has become a symbol of resilience in Colombia. Focused on women affected by the violence, it operates with the foundational principle that no one is to be seen as a victim, no woman reduced to an object of pity, as if helpless and in need of rescue.

"Everything that happened, however terrible, helped us grow and made us stronger," Diana explained. "Instead of wallowing in remorse, looking around with eyes filled with hatred, it gave us the strength to see in a more mindful, compassionate way. For some reason, we have a second chance, an opportunity to rewrite history."

ASMUDGEC is one of scores of organizations to have emerged out of the ashes of the Colombian conflict, points of light in every region of the country, often led by women awakened to their destiny by the very violence they refuse to condone. As Diana recognized, there is no blueprint for a nation seeking to reclaim its soul, no training ground to teach what has never before needed to be learned. When all bets are off, the most impossible and unlikely of ideas become viable. Every Colombian today, she believes, has an equal claim to leadership. Every innovative initiative, however modest, becomes a gesture of resistance and reclamation; each inspired project, a prayer for the well-being of the entire local community.

Some months before we met, Diana had reached out to a group of campesinas in Florencia, asking them to think of an object, something that best represented who they are. Without hesitation, the farm women all mentioned their rubber boots, which some say the FARC had appropriated as a sign of its connection to the rural poor, a solidarity that most campesinos had long ago rejected. Indeed, as Diana learned, many felt a sense of violation and were keen to reclaim the symbol, so that Colombians in general would once again associate these simple rubber boots with the people of the soil, not with those who had done so much to bring misery to the land. So Diana and her team started Botas por la Paz, "Boots for Peace," hiring an artist to teach local women how to paint, allowing them to transform drab pairs of black boots into colorful works of art, inscribed with images of life and hope. The boots were a financial success, generating considerable revenue for the cooperative, but more importantly, each whimsical pair carried a political message: Botas por la Paz sounded very much like *votas por la paz*, "vote for peace."

Diana and her friends also began a theater group, El Teatro del Oprimido, "The Theater of the Oppressed," which encourages women who have suffered domestic abuse or violence due to the war to play themselves onstage. In an interactive, cathartic setting, the audience offers advice on how they might best overcome their trauma. Its success and popularity led ASMUDGEC to participate in other public events, including a week celebrating gender equality and the rights of women, which coincided with the national *Día de*

la No Violencia, "Day of No Violence." During a memorable performance in the plaza of San Miguel, a small town in Antioquia,
a group of former paramilitaries disrupted the event, hurling foul
language at the stage. The rest of the audience responded by throwing bottles at the men, forcing them to scuttle out of the venue, no
longer free to prey on the weak, like bullies broken in the face of
true character and actual strength.

"With all of this work," Xandra asked, "how do you find time to
do anything with the farm?"

"I don't," Diana replied. "I haven't been back."

Without a hint of bitterness, Diana explained that while she had
once visited San Diego, she had not actually stepped on the family
land since fleeing years ago.

"You said it's just a four-hour drive?" I asked.

"Yes. Just over seventy kilometers."

"Would you like to go?"

Diana promised to let us know, but she couldn't confirm until
she had a chance to ask her family, especially her stepfather, Don
José, who had raised her. Juan suggested that she invite him to come
along. A note reached us that night saying that he would welcome
the opportunity. Like Diana, he had not been back to their land
since being forced off by the conflict. Diana referred to her stepfather as Don José, a sign of respect, affection, and gratitude that
spoke of the deep current that ran between them. His full name was
José Aguirre Ríos.

Two days later, Diana met us at our hotel, and we were off, pausing only on the outskirts of La Dorada to pick up Don José, who
had a burlap *costal* full of plant cuttings. Diana's grace and delicate
beauty gave her an ethereal air, like a woman in constant prayer,
slightly untethered to this reality. Her stepfather, by contrast, was
a man of the soil, a true campesino, short, thin, and tough—a stick
of beef jerky adorned with whiskers and hair. He was quiet at first,
with the hesitant look of someone who had spent his life shying
away from people. But as we climbed higher into the mountains,
he became more comfortable, entering fully into the conversation.

The road rose through a beautiful landscape of green hills and
rich volcanic fields, with vistas seemingly too soft and picturesque

to have ever been the setting for the violence that has long defined Colombia to the world. The plazas of Norcasia, Berlín, and the other small towns were peaceful and gay, with church doors wide open and cafés filled with families. And yet, as José revealed more than once, in a voice inflected with caution, each place had a story, every corner and crossroads a stain, with dark memories lingering on every mountain slope like shadows in the sun.

José had seen too much to expect miracles to emerge in the wake of the government's declaration of peace. Still, he remained hopeful.

"Peace is a process," he said at one point. "It's not something you achieve or obtain from one day to the next. Forgiveness is needed; it's the only way."

José leaned on his faith, as did Diana. Her time in spiritual retreat, she maintains, the humility with which the sisters embraced their devotion to God, prepared her for the trials that awaited in Colombia. Her angelic quality, something we had all noticed, became truly luminous as we lingered on a bridge over the very river that she and her mother had forded on her return from Chile. Soaked by rain, Diana held a dark cotton shirt over her head, which fell on both sides of her face like the veil of a nun. She wore a silver cross around her neck, and as she brought her hands together as if in prayer, even the colors painted on her fingernails, each a distinct pattern, seemed radiant.

When we reached San Diego, José slipped away to do some business and visit relatives, while Diana led us to Alto de la Cruz, a high, grassy ridge with a Calvary of crosses overlooking the town. The entire community is nestled in a tight basin, with ground rising on three sides. Given time, a young boy with a slingshot making his way along the heights could drop a stone on every street corner. It would be difficult to design a more vulnerable setting for a toylike town in time of war.

"The paramilitaries were here, in the shadow of the crosses," Diana explained. She then pointed to a farmstead across the way, where the army had been based. On the far side of San Diego, a tower dominated the ridge that had been controlled by the FARC. At the height of the most terrible battle, the paramilitaries swept the rooftops with machine-gun fire, while the FARC cadres, having poisoned the water supply, pulverized the barrio at the base of their ridge with bombs they'd made from gas tanks filled with nails, glass, and human feces.

Juan was visibly shaken. In all his years as a war correspondent, he had never encountered such a perfect metaphor for the tragic reality of the Colombian conflict, all laid out before him in topography and landscape. On one side, the paramilitary. On another, the FARC. In between, but also occupying the heights, the army. All shooting at one another, unleashing a torrent of fire over the heads of innocent people forced to cower beneath their beds for days. Good and decent Colombians, unable even to leave their homes to retrieve the bodies of the dead. An entire town abandoned to suffer the horrific consequences of a bloody war that was not of its making.

In the late afternoon, we caught up with José in the ruins of what had been the family homestead. The farm was just outside San Diego, on a series of hills that rose above the main horse trail connecting the town to the hinterland. Both the main house and the immediate gardens and plantings were as one might expect in the wake of war: crumbling walls, broken windows, a shattered roof, fruit trees hacked down for firewood, irrigation pipes clogged with debris, the sour scent of decomposing vermin in what had been the family bath. José did his best to conjure the past, explaining where the barn had been for the cows, the location of pigsty and chicken coops, tracing the outline of the water tanks where he had raised fish, his main source of cash. Broken fences traced the borders of overgrown fields that had once produced plantains, yuca, sugarcane, and beans. Copses of *guadua*, a native bamboo used in construction, clogged the creek bed. They had not been wealthy, he said, but the land had supported five children, provided work for twenty men, and yielded sufficient income to buy what little was needed: rice, cooking oil, fuel, school supplies and uniforms for the children.

José has every intention to rebuild, but his immediate challenge is reclaiming the site. In Colombia, land ownership can be formal with *escrituras*, deeds and documents prepared and notarized by legal authorities, or informal with *carta ventas*, letters and oral covenants between neighbors, grounded not in bureaucratic paperwork but in trust and truth as recognized by rural communities fully cognizant of their origins. Much of Colombia, including the hills around San Diego, was settled by men and women who still live in the memories of those working the land today: grandparents or great-grandparents who staked the land, their rights secured by occupancy, sacrifice, and force of will. Forests cleared, fields sown, women and children lost to hunger and disease.

The challenge comes when the two systems—formal and informal—overlap and clash. As millions of rural Colombians were displaced by the conflict, corrupt local officials made a fortune selling off abandoned or unoccupied lands. Many buyers, notably those in the drug trade, were as unscrupulous and mercenary as the politicians profiting from the transactions. Some were simply opportunistic, others perhaps innocent and naïve. But the result was a confusion of overlapping claims and tenures, with those holding paper deeds often having the upper hand. José faced precisely this challenge, with an added complication. In his absence, another campesino, displaced from his lands in another part of the country, had been granted by the government, as part of his resettlement package, the right to plant crops on a part of José's farm said to have been abandoned. José had no desire to keep another man from feeding his family. But a deal would have to be struck.

As José spoke, Diana drifted across the broken farm with the motion of a night cloud. As much as her stepfather's fate was tied to the land, his remaining years certain to be dedicated to its renewal, Diana's life was already far away. It made sense that in fourteen years she had never come back. With the sun fading, she sat down on a large stone, surrounded by small trees on a slight rise only a few paces from the ruins of the farmhouse.

"We used to come here every evening," she said, "the whole family, and drink chocolate with bread and cheese. And always someone would ask about growing coca. It was our one chance to be able to buy anything we might ever need. We would go back and forth like an assembly. But then Don José would simply ask which of us wanted to go missing. People got rich, but then, from one day to the next, they'd end up dead."

For a few minutes, Xandra, Juan, and I just listened as Diana spoke, her face aglow in the light of dusk: "For my stepfather, the

Crossing the Macizo Colombiano

Páramo de las Papas, Macizo Colombiano

A shamanic figure carved into stone, overlooking the Magdalena gorge at La Chaquira, San Agustín

Mamo Camilo at Katanzama, an Arhuaco settlement east of Santa Marta on the Río Don Diego

Making offerings to the river, at Bocas de Ceniza

Harvesting *hayo*, or coca, the divine leaf of immortality

Making *panela*, blocks of raw cane sugar, in the mountains of Cauca

Serving *lechona*, the specialty of Tolima, a whole pig stuffed with rice, peas, and spices and cooked in a brick oven for ten to twelve hours

Adelfa Pineda Ibáñez, Murillo

Diana Ocampo returning after fifteen years to her home in San
Diego, on the border of Caldas and Antioquia

"Here lives Beethoven. Here one breathes peace,
love and tranquility," a fisherman's home, Bocas de Ceniza.

The final resting place of José Ricardo Córdoba, Tatacoa Desert

Hugo Hernán Montoya, an *animero*, stands before the tombs of the
NNs in the cemetery of Puerto Berrío.

The *animero* works with the souls of the dead as they drift in the
uncertainty of purgatory; he prays for their well-being as they atone for
their sins.

Lovers at dusk on the Puente Guillermo Gaviria Correa, above the Magdalena at Barrancabermeja

Saturday night in Nueva Venecia

Maestro Ángel María Villafañe at the entry to his personal
museum and school of music

Dancing to the rhythms of *tambora*, Barranco de Loba

Gumercindo Palencia, Hatillo de Loba

Aurelio "Yeyo" Fernández, Botón de Leiva

One of the Sons of Chandé (Los Hijos de Chandé), the musical school founded by Gilberto Márquez in the town of Tierra Firme

Maestro Ángel María Villafañe, Barranco de Loba

Schoolgirls, Nueva Venecia

Inside a *tienda*, Nueva Venecia

Ciénaga Grande de Santa Marta

The floating village of Nueva Venecia, Ciénaga Grande de Santa Marta

The end of the day on the Magdalena, just upriver of La Gloria

Xandra Uribe, on the Magdalena

Dancing in the streets, three in the morning in Cartagena

A fisherman on the Ciénaga de Tabacurú, one of many hundreds of wetlands in the lower reaches of the Río Magdalena

Author on the Ciénaga de Tabacurú,
just upriver from the town of San Pablo,
Río Magdalena, Bolívar

William Vargas, botanizing in the
mountains of Antioquia

The view from the farm of Héctor Botero, light and shadows, and along the
mountain ridge the silhouettes of wax palms, Colombia's national tree

hardest thing was being forced to leave. You can't imagine the humiliation. For an honest man, land and work is everything. For him to be displaced, an outcast, dependent on others for food, with nothing to do with his hands, unable even to visit the farm. It's one thing to be hungry and abandoned, but the worst was the shame. There isn't a word for that kind of humiliation."

Diana's thoughts tumbled one into another, in a seemingly random manner, inspired by whatever she felt in the moment. Her return to the land, she later confided, evoked emotions that could never be described—waves of light, healing, and compassion that gave her the strength to move on.

"People are in such a hurry," she said. "They want results, but we need to allow for peace to evolve. Like happiness, peace is a process, probably a lifetime process, a way of living and being, of being happy, and of being at peace."

As night approached, we made our way off the hill, with Diana in the lead, never once looking back. José had decided not to return with us to La Dorada. This was his land. He had been away for fourteen years. Now that he was back, he was going to stay. In town he had bought a bag of beans the color of rubies as a gift for Xandra. She walked away with a generous sample for her collection, a rare local variety, having first secured from José a promise that he would plant the rest in his garden the following day.

Our passage through the Medio Magdalena was taking on a strange, almost feverish quality. The land had its own beauty: a broad, meandering river the color of silt, shade trees left standing above brown and beaten fields scattered with cattle, remnant patches of forest on the hillsides, and, to the north and west, the distant heights of the Serranía de San Lucas rising in the haze, a great and final exclamation point to the Cordillera Central. But it wasn't the landscape so much as the people that had this intoxicating effect. Everyone we met seemed to be living suspended in the moment, as if coming down from a long and violent hallucination, grateful to be back and yet eager to share what they had experienced in the depths of their visions. The stories they told, though no doubt true, came across almost as allegories, fables tinged with a hint of the mystical. The unlikely rapprochement between Jenny Castañeda and Ramón Isaza, who launched the paramilitary movement from his base at Puerto Boyacá, at eighty-six the oldest surviving leader, a reformed killer whose name alone still causes a hardened journalist like Juan to shudder. The curious fact that the land invaded by Jenny's mother, Damaris, was owned by our good friend Juan Guillermo Garcés, whose very decency and kindness might have encouraged her to overplay her hand. The strange outcome in San Diego, with the FARC and paramilitary forces simultaneously occupying and destroying the farm of the one family that had refused to enter the coca trade.

On our last night in La Dorada, Diana took us to the river, to a landing at the end of a city street where a ramp goes down to the shore. It was late, and we were alone, and in the quiet we could hear the Magdalena, its relentless flow, the soft whisper of silt flowing over sand. A half-moon hung in the clouds, illuminating the spreading branches of a ceiba tree that rose over the landing. Shadows flickered on the water. The roots spread like serpents along the shore, pale in the moonlight. Xandra sat quietly on the bank. Juan photographed her silhouette. As Diana and I took a short walk along the water's edge, bats darted in and out of the shadows, sweeping insects from the air just above our heads.

"Even when we had nothing," Diana said, "before receiving anything from the Red Cross, we were afraid to eat the fish. Imagine. They had turned this beautiful river into a slurry of death. There were so many bodies. You just never knew. Sometimes a head or a leg or a decapitated corpse. Faces riddled with bullets. Bodies so bloated and decayed they fell apart to the touch."

Diana described how, as a young woman, not long after returning to La Dorada, she would sometimes sit by the river and watch, thinking of the dead, praying for their spiritual redemption and salvation. Who were they? What had they left behind? And what of their mothers and fathers, their children, crying in grief, searching in vain, condemned never to know that their loved ones had found a grave in the river that had given birth to their nation. Every act of homicide became a double murder, death by torture followed by condemnation to purgatory, leaving families cursed to live in uncertainty and shame, and victims denied the mercy of the final rites that alone allow a good Catholic to enter the gates of heaven.

"It was unspeakable cruelty."

At the height of the violence, during all the dark years leading up to 2006, the paramilitary authorities in La Dorada let it be known that anyone who brought the floating dead to shore would themselves be targeted for death. The bodies were to be left to the fish.

"When people spoke of eating the dead in the *bocachico*," Diana remarked, "it's because they really did."

The Nameless Dead

The following morning, as we left La Dorada, beginning the hundred-mile drive north to Puerto Berrío, Juan spoke of the Río Magdalena much as Diana had done the night before, describing it, as so many do, as the graveyard of the nation. It was a dark story with a long history: an artery of life becoming an avenue of death, emerging from the light like the shadow side of a great spirit.

"The river is the symbol of the country," he said, "precisely because it contains multitudes, including all that is transgressive and tragic in the Colombian experience."

Accounts from the Spanish conquest, Juan noted, tell of soldiers taken in death by the Magdalena, swallowed by its currents, consumed by caimans. During the War of Independence, as General Hermógenes Maza moved on the vital commercial center of Mompox, he was told by his superiors to limit the bloodshed. On his way downriver, the general took sixty prisoners at Gamarra. Following his orders to the letter, he sewed them alive, three at a time, into large leather bags and dumped them into the river to drown, allowing him to write his commander that the deed had been done without a single drop of blood. When Maza took Mompox by surprise, in a predawn attack from the river, he summoned all prisoners to an efficient if brutal tribunal. As he sat in a deck chair on his riverboat, *La Comandancia*, he ordered every man to introduce himself by the name Francisco. If the captive pronounced the word with a soft lisping accent on the letter *c*, a certain sign of Spanish birth, he called out, "*¡Al baño!*" or "Bath time!" With that, the prisoner's head would fall into the river, followed by his corpse. General Hermógenes Maza was perhaps the first to refer to the Río Magdalena as a "comfortable common grave." Of the two hundred prisoners taken before him that day in Mompox, only one survived. To this day, fishermen along the length of the river speak of La Llorona, a beautiful woman reduced by her son's death to a wandering cadaver, the embodiment of misery, condemned for all eternity to water the river with her tears, a symbol of all mothers who have lost sons to violence.

Death and the river was the theme that drew us downstream to Puerto Berrío, a small city best described as a place where important things happened, but a very long time ago. Along the waterfront, the headquarters and warehouses of the trading companies that once serviced the entire commercial and industrial core of Medellín lie in ruins, like a film set, frozen in time, with bits and pieces dating to the three decades beginning in 1925, when a thriving economy allowed every merchant to bounce back overnight from a devastating fire that torched the entire town, save the railway yards. The Hotel Magdalena, where men in white tuxedos and women in lace danced to the music of Matilde Díaz, the Lucho Bermúdez Orchestra, perhaps the Black Stars, in a palm-studded courtyard overlooking a broad meandering river, is today a lifeless officers' club surrounded by chain-link fences and barbed wire, accessible only to high-ranking members of the army.

Founded in 1875 as Medellín's port on the Magdalena, Puerto Berrío came of age once it was linked to the hinterland of Antioquia by rail in 1929. The connection came late. Railways were always an expensive and complicated proposition in Colombia. Mountains are the enemies of trains, which cannot negotiate any incline greater than 7 percent. That short line to Medellín, a distance of just 120 miles, took fifty-five years to complete. In the late nineteenth century, as the United States was laying track across wide-open prairies at a rate of ten miles a day, Colombia's railway construction was limited to four miles a year. Of the twelve major lines ultimately

built, nine simply connected urban centers to the Magdalena, little
more than iron mules descending along the same routes pioneered
centuries before by the *arrieros*. The only railway built not to the
river but alongside it was the Ferrocarril del Atlántico, constructed
in 1960 from Puerto Salgar to Barranquilla and the Caribbean coast.
But that, too, came late, for the country by then was enchanted with
cars and trucks, not to mention airplanes. In 1961, the Antioquia
Railway, no longer viable as a private business, sold its assets to the
National Railway Company, a state enterprise that soldiered on,
absorbing losses for years. Colombia today has twenty-three hundred miles of rail track, almost all abandoned.

As railways struggled, and an expanding network of roads and
airports laced together the nation, river traffic on the Magdalena,
the lifeblood of Puerto Berrío, began to fade. In 1925, *vapores* and
other commercial craft carried 100,000 passengers and 388,000 tons
of freight, figures that by 1956 had increased to 363,000 passengers
and 2.2 million tons of cargo. But then, even as the Antioquia Railway faced insolvency, came a second blow, the loss in 1961 of the
David Arango, the legendary vessel that stood for all that was glorious and sublime in the life of the river. With this symbol in ashes,
hearts broke and dreams died all over Colombia. Seven commercial
vapores remained in service, but the magic was gone. By 1969, the
total passenger count had declined to 22,688 and the era of river
travel was essentially over.

Arriving in Puerto Berrío late in the evening, we stayed downtown
at the Arcos del Coral, a simple workingman's hotel with one miraculous feature. The second-floor corner room, with its barracks-like
array of six single iron beds, overlooks a busy intersection criss-
crossed at window height by a tangle of electrical wires. By day the
wires are bare, but at night they support many hundreds of *golondri-
nas*, swallows that roost throughout the night until flying off to feed
in the *madrugada*, the early light of dawn. They come and go every
day, always returning to the same intersection. Though a small miracle of biology, this display of birds goes unnoticed by the people

scuttling about in the streets below: families dipping into the fried chicken shack across the way, teenagers racing by on motorcycles, old fruit vendors slowly clip-clopping along the pavement in horse carts. Perhaps no one has been told that what happens above them every night is a sign of an ancient memory, a homing signal that once brought ancestral flocks to the branches of some glorious tree, perhaps a jacaranda ablaze in blue blossoms or the yellow flush of a tabebuia that grew rooted in this place long before this broken city came into being on the banks of the Río Magdalena.

As I watched from my window both the swallows and the people below, it was hard to believe that at the height of the violence, there was, on average, a murder a day in Puerto Berrío, a figure that in the month of October, in the run-up to All Souls' Day, would triple. Three killings a day in a town with a population at the time of but twenty-seven thousand. What would become of New York City if murder took the lives of 300 people a day, year in and year out, with the death toll rising to close to a thousand in October? How would the survivors, the innocent, react? How could any people cope with the agony and stress, the uncertainty, the collapse of moral order and ethical law that such levels of homicide would imply? What would they do? What had the people of Puerto Berrío done? Had they simply averted their eyes, pretending not to know, living in shame but at least staying alive? This was the path of caution urged upon Diana Ocampo by her mother in San Diego and demanded of Jenny Castañeda by her grandfather, even as that notorious truck rolled by their home in Puerto Triunfo to deliver yet another victim to the slaughter.

In the end, both Diana and Jenny refused to give in to fear. In standing against violence, in resisting the madness, they retained both their dignity and their honor, even as they transformed their lives, each becoming a messenger of hope, a living embodiment of what Abraham Lincoln had in mind when he asked Americans in their darkest hour to look to the better angels of their nature. What Diana Ocampo and Jenny Castañeda did on their own, the people of Puerto Berrío did as a community, sending out a message of redemption and renewal that has echoed in every church, back alley, and riverside settlement along the entire length of the Río Magdalena. Like so many movements arising from the human heart and spirit, what transpired in Puerto Berrío had small beginnings.

The following morning, we set out to track down the story, seeking first a contact provided to Juan by a fellow journalist in Medellín. After some confusion, we found our man holding court in a pleasant café just off the main plaza. Heavyset yet still handsome, with a full head of hair as white as his freshly laundered shirt, Francisco "Pacho" Luis Mesa did not fit the image of an undertaker, a vocation he had apparently stumbled upon purely by circumstance. A bus driver for thirty years, Pacho was working for Rápido Ochoa on the Medellín-to-Maicao run when he and his bus were caught in an ambush, a cross fire that left one of his passengers dead. Uncertain what to do with the corpse, and with no funerary services nearby, he improvised a coffin, borrowed a car, and returned immediately to Medellín, driving twenty-three hours without stopping for food or water. When he delivered the body to the victim's mother, he felt a tremendous sense of pride and relief, overwhelmed that such a simple deed could mean so much to a family. After that, he felt only warm affection for the dead, and pity for their suffering families.

By chance, his nephew owned a funeral home. One night in 1996, he hired Pacho to pick up eight bodies on the streets of Medellín, a number that by dawn had risen to fifteen, all victims of gang violence. Enjoying the work, Pacho became a regular, known to all the young thugs and *sicarios* in the neighborhoods of Santo Domingo, 12 de Octubre, Caicedo, 20 de Julio, and Villatina as *El cucho de la funeraria*, the "dude of the dead." As he drove through the barrios, immune to fear and insulated from violence out of respect for the services he provided, mothers stood warily in doorways even as their sons brashly waved Pacho down to demand, "*¡Quiubo parcero! ¿Trajo el parce?*" "Hey, man! Did you bring our man?" Frequently, he had.

Purely as a career move, Pacho opened his own funeral home in Puerto Berrío, where business promised to be good. Serving the dead throughout the Media Magdalena, from La Dorada all the way to Sabana de Torres, two hundred miles away, he operated with extreme caution, retrieving cadavers from pastures and back alleys, often risking his life in the process. Medellín was civilized, with even the lowest of gangsters acknowledging that someone had to remove the bodies from the streets, if only to rid the neighborhoods of the smell of decay. But in the Medio Magdalena, assassins lived by another code, and when they insisted on no reprieve for the dead, and threatened with death anyone who challenged that fiat, most people listened. At least at first.

But Pacho was fearless. He was convinced he was protected by the *ánimas*, the souls of the dead that, according to ancient Catholic beliefs, remain on earth, expiating their sins before ascending to heaven. The *ánimas*, he claims, were with him when he brought that body to Medellín, even as the blood trickled out through the car door. Another time, with two dead soldiers in his trunk, he was stopped at a FARC roadblock. He faced certain death, but the sentries let him through with a warning that his life had been saved by the nuns in the backseat of his car. There were no sisters traveling with him—only the two corpses.

"What the guerrillas saw were the *ánimas*, my protective guardians," Pacho said, without a hint of doubt.

The most glorious intervention occurred on another occasion when he was again cornered by the FARC; at the last minute, a *comandante* remembered him for having found and retrieved for burial the body of one of his cadre four years before. Pacho escaped not only with his life but also a gift from the FARC of a million pesos. Divine intervention has been a constant in his life.

"It's the reason I'm still alive," he says.

According to Pacho, no one really knows the total number of dead in the Medio Magdalena. He claims to have salvaged for burial roughly 3,500 corpses, of which perhaps 2,000 were found on the water, figures almost impossible to believe. Alone, Pacho has lifted 150 bodies or parts of cadavers from the Magdalena, a more plausible if still haunting number. The horror, he added, was difficult to convey: corpses floating by with vultures aloft, their featherless heads buried in the rot, decomposing bodies falling apart when touched, skin slipping off, adhering to your skin, leaving a foul smell impossible to wash away. A stench of putrescence that lingered for days.

"The Magdalena is Colombia's biggest coffin," Pacho said,

unprompted, echoing both Diana and Juan. "The greatest cemetery in the country, given the thousands of bodies that have ended up in the river, never to be recovered."

Xandra asked the obvious question: If Pacho had retrieved from the river even half the number of bodies he claimed, how had he avoided retribution from the paramilitaries or, for that matter, the guerrillas? His answer was simple: He was not by any means the only one focused on the fate of the anonymous dead. He then encouraged us to visit the cemetery and speak with Hugo Hernán Montoya, the *animero*, the one empowered to work with the souls of the dead as they drift in the uncertainty of purgatory; he prays for their well-being as they atone for their sins and seeks salvation for those already condemned to the fires of hell.

In the heat of midday, the iron gates of the cemetery were closed, bolted with a thick chain and a lock that opened to the touch. The main processional path rising to the chapel was flanked by a garden of traditional graves, each marked and decorated with memorials: baroque angels, iron crosses, stone slabs inscribed with the names of the deceased, dates of birth and death, the bookends of mortal life. Along with simple phrases, messages of love and longing, most featured the Polaroid faces of the dead, old family snapshots sealed in plastic, protected from the elements, attached permanently to the stone.

Cemeteries exist to sanctify memory. They offer comfort to those left behind in sorrow and grief, a place for the living to gather in reflection and prayer, the illusion that a family plot is something more than an incidental concentration of corpses. A graveyard reassures even the nonbeliever of the promise of eternal life, if only in a material sense, in the form of a granite tomb, a marble statue, a simple headstone. No one wants to be laid to rest in a coffin of cardboard, their grave marked with a wooden cross. No one wants to be forgotten.

But the cemetery in Puerto Berrío was all about the forgotten. Most of the dead were interred not in private plots but in the funerary recesses of a long wall that runs the length of the cemetery. Each crypt was a square, roughly three feet to a side. These were stacked five to a column, with each individual façade decorated as if with a personal statement of loss; the overall effect was that of a checkerboard. Some squares remained plain and white, but most were painted in rich colors: mauve, yellow, purple, and sky blue. Many had offerings perched on the lower ledge of the niche, small bouquets of flowers, a glass of water, perhaps a message scrawled in pencil, a handful of coins. The lettering on all of the crypts was simple and unpolished, like that of children for whom writing remains a new discovery. Some featured just a name or a cryptic word—*Marlon Estiben, Juan de Dios, Milagros*. Others conveyed a message—"Thank you for the favors received." Many read *Escogido*, or "Chosen," followed by a personal name and the initials *N.N.* These two letters tell the same story in three different languages. In Latin, *Nomen Nescio*; in Spanish, *No Nombrado*; in English, "No Name." The wall of crypts that dominates the Puerto Berrío cemetery is a mausoleum of the unknown and newly named, sheltering thousands of the faceless dead. Each contains the remains of a victim of violence who, condemned by their killers to drift through eternity in the fog of purgatory, was brought back to spiritual life by the courage and grace of the people of Puerto Berrío, ordinary men and women, Colombians all, who fought back against evil, proclaiming their humanity one salvaged body at a time.

No one seems to be sure when or how the practice began, or why it flourished in this city, as opposed to any other town in the Medio Magdalena. Certainly, Puerto Berrío had suffered. Scores of families had lost loved ones. Any number of mothers and fathers had been left wondering about the fate of children swept away by the conflict, kidnapped and pressed into service by both the FARC or the paramilitaries, trapped in the cross fire, seduced by the allure of drug money and a life of crime. Geography also played a role, as it always does in Colombia. At Puerto Berrío, the alignment of the Magdalena generates currents, eddies, and back channels where debris floating downriver often becomes trapped, cut off from the main flow of the river, hung up for weeks. In the late 1980s and early 1990s, corpses were as common as driftwood. The paramilitaries, as they did in La Dorada, threatened anyone who interfered with the dead. Every corpse on the water was a snapshot of what awaited those who resisted: bodies decomposed beyond recognition, identities lost for all time, with no place of burial to comfort families, no final words of grace from a priest, no hope of ever reaching the kingdom of heaven. This message was intended not just for those who might oppose the actual killers—whose identity was, at any rate, seldom known—but for anyone who might dare resist the miasma of fear that was the ultimate weapon of both Pablo Escobar and, later, the paramilitaries, the only hold they had on the people.

Whether it was the sheer number of corpses spinning slowly in the eddies, or some reservoir of decency in the community that could not be denied, or even the curious Colombian belief that those who suffer torture or violent deaths can work miracles in the afterlife, the people of Puerto Berrío reached a point where they simply could not ignore what fate and the Río Magdalena had brought them. Fishermen grew tired of pretending to ignore the body parts caught in their nets, stranded on the islands, hung up in the branches of fallen trees, or tossed about by the currents. For a time, some would quietly dispose of the dead, burying the remains in the sand on the far side of islands, out of sight of town, as quickly and discreetly as possible. But scuttling in the shadows, as if in shame, had little appeal for those of Christian charity and decency. First one, and then another, and finally fishermen by the score began to retrieve the corpses from the river, bringing them to shore, where others from the town appeared with wheelbarrows to cart the cadavers to the cemetery, where women awaited to lay claim to the dead. Initially, the church resisted, but in time even priests became involved, breaking precedent to deliver last rites to the unknown dead: remnants of human life that were often little more than small heaps of putrescence held together by rags, unrecognizable rings of bone, shreds of clothing, a leg bone and a boot.

What gradually unfolded was a reciprocity of grace and longing that brought comfort to the living, offered eternal life to the dead. As each cadaver reached the cemetery, it was granted a full Christian burial, paid for by those who made the adoption. Individuals and families took on not just the costs of the funeral—roughly four hundred thousand pesos, a significant sum—but also the obligation to care for the tomb, with offerings of flowers, fresh water, and prayers for the soul of the departed. Some of the dead were given imaginary names. More commonly, families baptized the unknown victims with the names of their own loved ones also lost to the violence, a father or son, a daughter. Sharing the first name of a loved one— Pedro, Luis, Germán, or Jacinto—is a private gesture of nostalgia and memory, a means of focusing emotional loss, allowing a long-suffering mother or father to address the haunting uncertainty that any unresolved disappearance implies. But of even greater significance is the granting to the dead—collectively known as the NNs— of family surnames, which implies a complete adoption, linking the *escogido*, the chosen or selected one, to the living and, as well, to the blood lineage of all past and future generations. In Colombia, in particular, where family is a sacred trust, such sublime and self-less generosity will never go unrewarded, attracting, as it does, the attention of angels.

Naturally, those providing such services have the right to expect something in return: spiritual favors, some of which may play out in the material world. People may ask their adopted NN for help securing the funds to educate their children, build a new home, or pay the medical costs of a long-overdue procedure. And it would not be Colombia if some did not study the numbers, the dates of adoption, the placement and mathematical alignment of the crypt in the mausoleum wall and see mystical clues as to the best bets to place in the lotteries—La Nueve Millonaria, Cruz Roja, Chance, Atlántico, and many others. Fully 45 percent of all men and women aged twelve to sixty-four in Colombia lose money on these legal rackets at least once a year. One can hardly begrudge those playing the lottery in Puerto Berrío for hedging their bets with a little help from the spirits. But in general, those seen standing alone in front of the graves, silently praying for miracles, beseeching the *ánimas*, or souls of their newly adopted kin for help, are men and women in serious need, seeking outcomes that are completely deserved, earned with months of anguish and rivers of tears. Often they ask merely for the strength to endure their loss—the death of a husband, the disappearance of a daughter, or perhaps both.

In a shaded corner of the cemetery, a hidden niche beyond the common grave, I came upon a young woman who reminded me of Diana, both in age and by her gentle presence. Wearing flip-flops and a short purple dress, with an embroidered shawl draped over her head and shoulders, she was sitting on a bench, her hands clasped in prayer, when she saw me coming around the corner. I excused myself and then, for several minutes, stood quietly at her side, without speaking. The burning candles and the fresh bouquet of flowers in the niche suggested that she, like so many in Puerto Berrío, had adopted one of the NNs. When it felt right, and she was still there, I introduced myself and learned her name, Blanca Nury Bustamante.

Blanca was willing, even keen, to share a personal story that would surely have broken the spirit of most anyone born in a land less accustomed to tragedy and loss. She spoke openly, in part because she was still actively spreading the word and seeking information about the fate of her lost daughter, but also because she was on her own private mission for peace. From her purse, she pulled out a small black-and-white photograph of her little girl, taken before she disappeared at the age of nine. Blanca had been searching for nearly four years, with this blurry snapshot her only hope. Earnestly, she pointed to a small scar on the child's face, barely visible in the image, that would, she assured me, be the perfect way to identify her daughter when found. I said nothing, but I could not help but recall what Diana had said about the faceless dead, their features consumed by exposure in the river.

"I have nights," Blanca said, "that are like the day. I wake wondering when I will find my daughter. I ask the *ánimas* for strength to continue the search. I pray to God for her but also for the husband He once gave me, who was murdered. And I ask Him to help me forgive. My heart has healed and is joyful in spite of the absence of my loved ones. Sometimes my children speak of vengeance. I say no. Don't spill blood over blood. I don't want blood on my children. If God sees fit to return their missing sister, I will receive her without staining my hands."

When I asked Blanca what she hoped would come from her devotion and service to the NN who now bore her dead husband's name, she said nothing about money or winning lottery numbers or profiting personally in any way. What she longed for were the simple answers due any grieving mother.

"We don't want war," she said. "We want peace. But all the women just want to know, want to ask those who killed our loved ones: What became of them? Why did you do such terrible things? It is so unjust. They killed my husband. That hurt me greatly, but my greatest pain is not knowing where my daughter is at this moment. Is she hungry? Does she have a place to live? Is she healthy or sick? Is there anyone to help her? There are so many families in this country who feel as I do. Because for so long we had nothing but war, day and night, and now we only long for peace."

I thanked Blanca and wished her well, promising to light a candle for her daughter. Coming around the corner and back into the sunlight, I noticed Xandra and Juan speaking with a short, wiry man whose back was to the mausoleum wall. I guessed correctly that they had found Hugo Hernán, the *animero*. Dressed informally in a white T-shirt and jeans, with arms that gesticulated like wings as he spoke, Hugo didn't appear to be one capable of entering the dark realm of death to work deeds of spiritual rescue. He may have been, as Pacho had promised, a practitioner of an ancient magical art long lost to most Catholics, but in the flesh, he looked and acted just like Diana's stepfather, José, an ordinary man of firm convictions and simple resolve.

According to Juan, the fundamental role of the *animero* is to pray for the souls of those expiating their sins in purgatory, a prerequisite for any Catholic seeking to cross over into the kingdom of heaven, the ultimate quest of the faithful. The tradition originated in Tenerife, long before Christianity reached the Canary Islands, at a time when priest and physician were one, and healers both cured the sick and communicated with the dead. Brought to the New World by the early Spaniards, the idea of an ambivalent being that existed outside of the church and moved between realms like a trickster readily found a place in the syncretic fusion of Catholic and pre-Columbian beliefs that became the foundation of faith in Latin America, a Christianity guided by the written word but informed and infused by the phantasmagoric. More difficult to explain is why the tradition has been lost in almost all of Colombia. Common throughout the colonial era and well into the twentieth century, the *animero* survives as a vital fixture of the graveyard in only a small handful of towns in Antioquia, Puerto Berrío among them. As Hugo today selflessly works his spiritual magic, praying for the souls of those for whom no one prays, he does so as one of the last practitioners in an occult and esoteric lineage dating back more than two thousand years.

Hugo has served the dead of Puerto Berrío as an *animero* for eleven years, originally drawn to the calling as a way to express his gratitude and repay all the favors granted to him and his family by the souls in purgatory. But his mission began even as a child, as he started a diary that has for more than forty years faithfully chronicled the violence in Puerto Berrío and other parts of the Medio Magdalena. Among his most vivid and haunting memories are of the screams at night as people alerted the town of yet another floating corpse on the river. Just as the melody or lyric of a popular song takes over the mind of an American teenager, the short phrase "*¡Por el río va un pepe!*" became the soundtrack of Hugo's youth. "One more Pepe down the river!," yet another cadaver passing by.

As an *animero*, Hugo is neither caretaker nor guardian of the cemetery. He translates the term as "soul keeper." His work involves the physical maintenance of the dead, the processing of remains, the storage of the many hundreds of bodies that have yet to be adopted or claimed. All of these are neatly bagged and stacked like cordwood in a large, windowless room that left all of us breathless and completely in awe of Hugo's devotion. At the height of the violence, from the late 1980s all through 2006, the sheer number of dead overwhelmed the town. Hugo told of a man, Jesús Enrique Valencia, who did his bit with a tricycle and a cart, focused on the task of transporting the corpses from river to morgue. He processed at least forty bodies, carrying them like loads of dirt, dumping them in heaps upon a growing pile of the unknown dead. He never stopped, virtually living beside his cart, even while ignoring death threats and the bullets that whizzed by his head from time to time as he napped. His mother became hysterical, certain that her son would end up dead, if not by a gun then certainly from some foul disease contracted from a corpse. Jesús, Hugo remembered, worked always without gloves and never wore a mask. He wanted nothing to get between him and the dead. Eventually, his eyes burned, his clothes stank of formaldehyde, and he could not distinguish the flavors of his food. Even the simplest soup tasted only of blood.

Hugo's busiest months are November and December, the weeks following the Day of the Dead, a time when people throughout the Christian world honor loved ones who have passed away. Every night for a month, dressed in a dark, hooded robe inscribed with messages of redemption, with bell and rosary in hand, he leads a candlelit procession that grows with each passing doorway as it snakes through the neighborhoods of the city. Throughout the passage, the *animero* prays for the salvation of all souls seeking redemption and forgiveness, beseeching an all-powerful God to spare them all from the fires of hell, the infernal abyss.

"Hail Mary, full of grace. Our Lord is with thee. Blessed art thou among women, and blessed is the fruit of thy womb, Jesus. Holy Mary, Mother of God, pray for us sinners now and at the hour of our death. Amen. *Requiem aeternam.*"

Hugo claimed no formal connection to the church, and he did not pretend that his work was anything more than it appeared to be. But he did truly believe that the souls of the dead could be saved, liberated from a realm of the spirit every bit as real as the tortured recesses of this material world. He was also certain that heaven awaited the good, just as the fires of hell flickered at the feet of all those condemned by their deeds to eternal damnation. Such biblical certainties had to be true, Hugo maintained, for it was the only way to account for Colombia's agonies and all the small miracles he had witnessed. Like the story of Gloria, a young girl, an NN, unknown and adopted by a local merchant, Jair Humberto Urrego, who gave her the name. She stayed by him for six years, protecting him from danger, helping his business. Jair Humberto never asked for trivial favors, only what he needed to live a good life. When finally the time came to move her remains from the crypt to the ossuary, the desired and ultimate goal of all the unknown dead, they found that her young body had been mutilated, torn to pieces as she died. Among those attending the service, some saw drops on her tomb that appeared to be tears. And then, as they lifted the remains, actual tears fell from the bones like rain. Hugo to this day believes

that Gloria in that moment had a vision of her original family, leading her spirit to weep even as the prayers of those who had given her
eternal life washed over her soul.

True spiritual authority is always subtle, often imperceptible,
resting, as it does, in the hearts of once ordinary men. With Hugo,
it was only when he generously agreed to don his ritual regalia that
this humblest of public servants became the *animero*, the keeper of
souls. As Hugo scurried to a nearby house to retrieve his garments,
we waited in the sun, just outside the main gate. The high stucco
walls surrounding the cemetery had been transformed into a single
mural de recuerdos, a "wall of memories." Scrolls painted in a medi-
eval style ran the length of the façade. Some recorded the names of
the disappeared, in no particular order, just the names and the dates
when they were lost. Others listed not the merely dead but the *asesi-
nados*, the murdered ones, thirty names to a column, dating from the
early 1980s through 2008. Hugo returned, enshrouded in a black
rubber cape with a hood that hid his eyes. Painted on the back was a
white skull and crossbones, along with an ominous warning to anyone unprepared to walk the path to eternal light. Turning away from
the street, he faced the wall, the litany of the dead. With a rosary
in one hand, a ritual bell in the other, the *animero* slowly lifted his
arms, as the cape spread into the wings of an avenging angel.

Some dismiss what transpired in Puerto Berrío as but a sign of
Colombia's notorious embrace of the phantasmagoric, a dark
enchantment with the macabre, understandable after so many years
of violence and war. Others maintain that to rename the dead is to
appropriate their lives, a process that compounds the violation of
their dignity and further deepens the disappearance of those already
disappeared. Still others regard the professed concern for the dead
as just an angle being worked by opportunists, urban poor for the
most part, superstitious men and women concerned only with personal gain and desperate enough to believe that the spirit world
can be scammed. Both Xandra and Juan had too much faith in the
Colombian people to indulge such cynicism. We left Puerto Berrío

uncertain about many things but convinced that something mysterious and meaningful had been at play.

The most insightful explanation came some weeks later in Bogotá when Xandra and I met with one of Colombia's most renowned visual artists, Juan Manuel Echavarría. The scion of a great corporate dynasty in Medellín, Juan Manuel had long ago defied family expectations by choosing the creative path. His most recent exhibit, one that had shaken the conscience of the nation, grew out of the seven years he devoted to documenting some eight hundred tombs in the Medio Magdalena, all holding the remains of those without names, the NNs. The exhibit had replicated the feel of the cemetery at Puerto Berrío. Mounted across a dark museum space were the illuminated photographs of the tombs, and running parallel to it were a list of names of all those who had been lost, the dead and the disappeared. In this spatial juxtaposition lay the answer we had hoped to find.

Juan Manuel welcomed us kindly one evening at his home in La Candelaria, the old colonial quarter of Bogotá. The house was ancient and elegant, a warren of narrow wooden hallways and staircases that led deeper into the recesses until finally reaching the inner sanctum, a small room of carpets and books and a glowing hearth, beside which sat our host, sunk back in a chair so welcoming he could scarcely reach his drink on the side table. The dark woodwork dated to the earliest days of Bogotá, as did the glass in the interior windows. The lamps cast a pale glow, as if products of the first experiments with electricity. The amber light, the candles, and a functioning fireplace, so unexpected in Bogotá, lent a timeless air to a room that no doubt had hosted some of the great figures in Colombian history.

Juan Manuel is an ageless man at seventy-one, slight, with grey hair and a gentle face, pensive and charming, comfortable in his skin and happy to share his thoughts. He began his artistic life as a poet, a student of mythology, a novelist. But over time he realized that he had less interest in words than in imagery, and so turned to photography, hoping to write with light. Like so many born to privilege, he initially found ways to insulate himself from the violence, keeping an apartment in New York, escaping to Europe, hiding away at home in La Candelaria. In the early years, he confessed, the violence was almost an abstraction, a few notes in the papers, television reports from the distant reaches of the country—Putumayo, Chocó, Caquetá. But by 1995, at least for him, everything had changed. The conflict had become an existential threat. Violence had indelibly stained the nation. The agonies of ordinary Colombians, as Juan Manuel saw it, demanded the attention of the artist. Armed only with his camera, he set out to create a portrait of a country and a people who were becoming, with each passing day, more and more accustomed to brutality.

Juan Manuel's work in the Medio Magdalena began in 2006. His first interview was with the paramilitary chief at La Picota, a shadowy figure known by the alias Julián Bolívar. Naïveté alone led Juan Manuel to pose the first question as directly as he did:

"What do you think of those who rescue the bodies from the water?"

Bolívar, a known killer who had himself dispatched victims into the Magdalena, stunned Juan Manuel with an answer that was equally forthright:

"*Un acto heróico.*" A heroic act.

"Exactly what do you mean?" asked Juan Manuel.

"We cast the bodies into the river to obliterate them, to erase all memory. Those who rescue the dead recover evidence of our crimes, and they do so knowing that it's against our wishes. It is surely heroic for a person to defy us. For an entire community to do it, well, that becomes something very powerful, more powerful than fear."

From that moment, Juan Manuel came to see the retrieval of the dead not as a curiosity but as a powerful act of resistance, an article of faith, a collective spasm of hope. Those who had the least to give offered support and comfort to those most in need. As victims of violence themselves, the people of Puerto Berrío refused to let violence erase the memory of the nameless dead. To every faceless corpse, they offered a home, a family, a second chance to ascend to the heights of heaven.

"If Colombians turned their backs on the river," Juan Manuel said, "and, indeed, on the violence of the last many years, the people of Puerto Berrío did the opposite."

In one great cry of humanity, as Juan Manuel saw it, a community that was itself deeply wounded, with its own dead and disappeared, the many murdered in the endless nights, refused to turn its back on the violence. By defying darkness and turning instead to what Juan Manuel describes as the "undeniable beauty that lies buried like a jewel in the breast of every human being," the people honored the promise of their children, even while setting out on their own healing journey—one of forgiveness, reconciliation, redemption, and hope. Every soul salvaged from the Magdalena heard the same message that the people of Puerto Berrío will be able to convey with pride to generations as yet unborn:

"Our river brought you to us, and here we are and we will not forget."

Morita of the Manatees

We reached Barrancabermeja at dusk, just as the lights of the city laid claim to the night sky. Warm rain fell. The air was hot and humid, with the heavy scent of the tropics. The slow flow of the river worked its way around the trestles of the old railway bridge, carrying pieces of the forest to the sea. Along the waterfront, a small fleet of riverboats and ferries lit up like carnival tents. To the north, dark clouds swept across what remained of the moon, even as silent explosions of lightning revealed the huge crowns of ceiba trees, standing alone on both banks of the Magdalena.

Juan pulled over on the Puente Guillermo Gaviria Correa, a modern and imposing bridge where lovers gather to watch the lights of the oil refineries, colorful and dazzling from a distance, and the road becomes a highway running away from Barrancabermeja, down the Magdalena toward El Banco, the gateway to the Caribbean shores.

"For the longest time," he said, "the only serious commerce on the river, aside from dead bodies, has been crude oil and refined petroleum products, all of it moving to the coast in long trains of massive barges strung together and dragged by tugs. A far cry from the glory days of the *David Arango*."

Refineries dominated the skyline. Pipelines reached to all horizons. In the open country on the approaches to the city, active wellheads seemed to outnumber the cattle. When finally, hot and exhausted, we checked in to an upscale hotel right across from the entrance to the largest refinery, the bathtub in my room ran black with oil for several minutes before clear water flushed from the tap.

If there was a seed that birthed the modern saga of the Medio Magdalena, it was the discovery of oil in 1904 and the construction of the first refinery at Barrancabermeja in 1922. Until then, settlement had been largely limited to the outposts that supplied fuel for the *vapores* and a few seasonal plantations carved from the flood forests. Beyond the riverbanks, desperate men in scattered clearings still struggled to match a breed of cattle with a country that had less land than water, a torrid wilderness where parasites and pestilence afflicted humans and livestock in equal measure. Holsteins, first brought to Antioquia in 1894, proved hopeless. The Blanco Orejinegro, bred on the Caribbean coast, was tough but too small, half the size of most cattle, and useless as a source of milk. Other Colombian breeds, such as the Romosinuano, also from the coast, and the Sanmartinero, developed in the Llanos, proved adequate, but the cattle industry in the Magdalena would not take off until 1930 with the arrival of the zebu, a breed originally from India. Domesticated from a progenitor that in time would sire more than thirty distinct breeds, the zebu was ideally adapted to the tropics, a veritable fountain of milk, resistant to disease, and immune to heat and humidity. Long protected in a land where the killing of cattle is forbidden by the Hindu religion, the zebu had been used strictly as a dairy cow. The only uncertainty was the quality of the meat, an issue soon put to rest by Colombian ranchers with a passion for *carne asada* and no interest in lentils, vaqueros who, in time, would develop a Brahman breed of zebu that is today widely recognized as the finest in the world.

But first there was oil. Barrancabermeja is today a city of two hundred thousand, the largest and most important port on the upper reaches of the river, an industrial center widely known as the petroleum capital of Colombia. The name actually means "vermillion riverbank," a reference to the reddish bluffs and ravines that mark a bend in the river originally known as La Tora, a name itself derived from Latocca, "the fortress that dominates the river." It was here, according to the Chronicles, that indigenous traders from the heights of the Andes and every watershed of the Magdalena converged each year to barter. Trade implied peace, or at least the momentary suspension of war, as Gonzalo Jiménez de Quesada learned to his relief when he and his men passed through the settlement in 1538 en route to their conquest of the Muisca. They went in search of gold, even as their boots trudged through the traces of the black gold upon which the wealth of Barrancabermeja and modern Colombia would ultimately be based. "Among other strange things," one of Quesada's men reported in a letter to Don Gonzalo Fernández de Oviedo in Santo Domingo in 1541, "there is, just a day outside of the town of La Tora, a source of bitumen, a black well that boils and runs out of the earth in great quantities which the natives rub over their bodies to relieve fatigue and strengthen their legs."

A curious application, and not exactly what the Tropical Oil Company had in mind in 1920 when it beat off other multinational suitors and, through a series of shady deals and transactions, secured from the Colombian government a land grant of over a million acres in the immediate environs of Barrancabermeja. Naturally, growth came quickly. Exploration and extraction implied roads and infrastructure: pipelines, docks, airports, river barges, and satellite towns. Wealth and easy money fomented vice—prostitution, gambling, and drinking—as surely as the concentration and exploitation of labor spun into being a whirlwind of political activism. From its inception, Barrancabermeja has been a cauldron where the forces of the Left and the Right have clashed not simply as a matter of principle, as occurs in so many places in Colombia, but over actual issues that are meaningful and true: wages, benefits, social justice, and security. The stakes could not be higher. With the discovery in 1983 of the Caño Limón field, a proven reserve of more than a billion barrels of crude, Colombia became a major player; today oil accounts for fully 50 percent of the country's export earnings. Barrancabermeja is both a fountain of national wealth and a potent symbol of the country's dependence on natural resources and foreign capital and, thus, an irresistible target for those who desire to cripple or destroy the nation-state.

During the worst of the violence, according to Juan, the only men secure and safe in Barrancabermeja were the Catholic priests. At night, as the young and beautiful flocked to dance clubs dedicated to salsa and merengue, all in the spirit of the Caribbean coast, paramilitaries stalked union leaders and human rights activists in the back alleys of the city, while in distant fields and forests, cadres of the ELN, utterly unconcerned about the implications for the environment and the land, sought ways to damage or destroy the pipelines, which have always been the focus of their revolutionary zeal. The only traffic on the river were the barges that carried the refined petroleum products to the sea, and the bodies of the dead.

After so many wrenching stories of human loss and survival, it came as a relief to find ourselves in the cool of the forest, passing a gentle morning in the company of scarlet macaws, green iguanas, brown pelicans, red-footed tortoises, grey-legged night monkeys, rare and endangered parakeets and tinamous, Magdalena River turtles and otters. All are part of a wild menagerie rescued from death and returned to life by Cabildo Verde, a small and highly effective environmental organization led by James Murillo Osorio, another of Juan's extraordinary friends and contacts in the Medio Magdalena.

We first met and interviewed James at his office in the small city of Sabana de Torres, but only came to know him as we walked together through the grounds of his research station, located just outside of town. Dirt roads and a modest entrance belie the scientific significance of the place. The wildlife refuge, an island of but fifteen hundred acres in a spreading sea of oil palm plantations, contains multitudes: all the complex ecological interfaces of a broad and expanding tropical valley where upland forests encircle wetlands that feed into streams and sloughs. The result is an astonishing world of plants, water, and life that defines the amphibian realm that is the essence of the lower reaches of the Río Magdalena.

Every animal arrives at the refuge unwanted, each a victim of violence or neglect with a story to tell. Many are rare or endangered. For more than an hour we stood quietly just beyond the mesh of the largest wildlife enclosure in Colombia, home to a pair of jaguars, shot and abandoned by poachers. Accustomed to humans, yet still dangerous, neither would ever again know the wild, a cruel irony not lost on the Cabildo Verde team that had saved them. Denied their destiny as predators, the cats live on a diet of water buffalo, great slabs of meat fed to them each morning by their keeper.

Coming down from a series of high perches and platforms, drawn by the scent, the beautiful creatures crept slowly toward us, their long and exaggerated tails gently sweeping the ground cover and foliage in their wake. Alerted by a sound, they hesitated, becoming perfectly still, fading away from sight, their fur a cryptic camouflage the very color and tone and shadow of the soil beneath their massive paws. One of them, a male, with muscles taut as iron, came close to the fence. His yellow eyes looked right through us, as if focused on another dimension. Only once have I met a great cat in the wild, a black jaguar at close quarters in the jungles of Panama, an encounter that, in the moment, left me feeling as transparent as an X-ray. A mixture of uncertainty and fear gave way to wonder and awe as the magnificent animal leapt from the trail, disappearing in an instant, a shadow of memory, the faint echo of the shape-shifter, the shaman's spiritual muse.

With their background in both environmental science and the law, James and his colleagues focus on finding a true and just balance between the needs of the rural poor, the economic ambitions of the state, and the well-being and survival of the plants, animals, and natural habitats that are the foundation of the nation's true natural wealth, the symbol and embodiment of all that makes Colombia unique in the world. The numbers are truly dazzling. Canada, to cite but one example, has some 3,000 native species of flowering plants. Colombia, one-tenth the size, is home to 26,000, including more orchids and more endemics than are found in any other country. In diversity of amphibians, freshwater fish, and butterflies, Colombia ranks second, just behind Brazil, a country eight times its size. With birds, Colombia stands alone, with 1,932 species, twice the number found in all the United States and Canada. Among these are no fewer than 165 distinct hummingbirds, delicate creatures known in the tropical lowlands not for the sound of their wings beating—in some species as much as eighty times per second—but for the promise of their desires, the passions they evoke as *beija-flores*—in Portuguese, "kissers of flowers." If Eden was God's first garden, as James remarked, it surely was located at this crossroads of continents: in the mountains, wetlands, coastal deserts, and lowland forests of a land that remains to this day the repository of fully 10 percent of the terrestrial biological wealth of the entire planet. Indeed, if the Earth's biodiversity were to be a nation, its name would be Colombia.

Of all the rare and endangered species of the Magdalena, perhaps the most important, the symbol of the space and the focus of Cabildo Verde's conservation efforts, is the Antillean manatee. A subspecies of the West Indian manatee once commonly found in shallow seas and brackish estuaries, in freshwater sloughs and rivers, along Caribbean shores from Mexico to Guyana, Trinidad south to Brazil, and on all the greater and lesser islands of the Antilles, this magnificent creature, long mistaken for sirens, the torment of ancient mariners, today struggles to survive. Across the entire range of the subspecies, there remain no more than twenty-five hundred individuals. They live in small clusters, isolated populations hidden away in biological refugia scattered along the northern flank of the continent. Among the largest and most vital of these natural sanctuaries is coastal Colombia and the entire length of the Bajo Magdalena, and it is here that the fate of the animal may well be decided.

From the small town of Puerto Wilches, our base as we visited James and the Cabildo Verde team, the Magdalena is flanked by *ciénagas* that become ever more numerous and expansive as the river flows north past Simití and Morales, Gamarra and La Gloria. A hundred miles downstream at El Banco, the Río Cesar, flowing south all the way from the Caribbean coastal plain and the flanks of the Sierra Nevada, joins the Magdalena; this confluence marks the traditional divide between the Medio and the Bajo Magdalena. Below the great bend in the river at El Banco, said by many to be the single most beautiful sight in all the Magdalena Valley, the entire landscape becomes one vast wetland reaching in every direction to the horizon. In this sea of fresh water, the two great arteries of the nation, the Ríos Cauca and Magdalena, come together almost as an afterthought, their confluence lost in a landscape dominated not by the joining of their waters but by scores of freshwater lakes and marshes linked one to the other by channels and streams and a complex hydrological cycle that is the foundation of life in a habitat as biologically rich and bountiful as any to be found in the world.

In this entire region, a land so limitless that Colombians could hide England and the English would never find it, the manatee serves as the benchmark, a keystone species whose well-being is a direct and immediate indicator of the overall health of an ecosystem it both creates and defines. The manatee is the only non-marine mammal that lives beneath the water, remaining for as long as fifteen minutes between breaths, feeding exclusively on vegetation, grazing for eight hours or more at a stretch. Reaching up to thirteen feet in length and weighing as much as thirteen hundred pounds, it consumes nearly 10 percent of its body weight each day. In doing so, the creatures play a vital role in keeping channels and wetlands open and clear. And though often compared to cows, they are not ruminants. The enormous quantity of plant life they eat returns as waste, rich in nutrients, directly into the ecosystem, providing food for scores of fish species that depend on manatee feces for their survival.

If sailors mistook manatees for mermaids, as indeed they did, they were not fooled by the animal's appearance; they were seduced by its character and gentle nature. Having evolved in the absence of natural predators, manatees are neither territorial nor aggressive, and they rarely fight. They have no fangs or claws. Their teeth lack incisors. In wetlands dense with dangerous creatures—caimans and jaguars, venomous snakes and toads, poisonous insects and bloodsucking bats—manatees are incapable of hurting anyone. In behavior and life cycle, manatees actually do resemble people far more than their plump and pink bodies would suggest. Like humans, manatees give birth to fully formed infants that nevertheless remain dependent for as long as five years, nursing all that time from a nipple behind the forelimb of the mother, a breast that in shape and form is not dissimilar to that of a woman. Manatees live as long as eighty years, roughly the length of a full human life. Though imposing in size, they are, unlike humans, incapable of accumulating fat, no matter what or how much they consume. When manatees swim, pushing forward by moving their tails up and down like a paddle, steering with their flexible flippers, achieving a steady speed of five miles an hour, perhaps three times that over short bursts, they exhibit a grace that is both mesmerizing and sensual, as gently seductive as one would expect from a mermaid.

Sensitive to the sun, manatees seek out the shade, their very presence a sign of the persistence of forest cover along the shores. Often they find protection in deep pockets, natural wells in the marsh where families gather, skin touching skin. Living in waters murky with silt, algae, and organic debris, they find their way not by sight but by sensation; they communicate by touch, using a complex code, or with vocalizations, squeaks and squeals that link mother to calf. There is some evidence that they respond to pheromones, in a manner much like elephants, their distant relatives. But the essence of the creature is its ability to interpret physical stimuli. Tactile hairs, as responsive and finely tuned as any found in nature, cover their entire bodies. If eyesight distills the glory of an eagle, an acute sense of smell the precision and genius of the wolf, the manatee, the most gentle and playful of all creatures, is unique in its ability to feel.

Not surprisingly, those who study manatees become smitten, as we discovered the following day when we joined James and two of his colleagues on a survey of the Ciénaga de Paredes, a great wetland on the eastern bank of the Magdalena several miles downriver from Puerto Wilches. It was a purely accidental adventure. Only the night before, our plan to head downriver to Simití had been foiled by an incident across the river at San Pablo, the sinking of a passenger launch that had temporarily curtailed commercial traffic. Stranded on the far shore of the Magdalena, with the sun softening and magic hour coming on, we had hired a launch to explore the Ciénaga Tabacurú, just upriver from San Pablo, a waterway that had for years served as the main supply corridor for the ELN guerrillas who had long dominated the heights of the Serranía de San Lucas, just to the west. In the golden light, with egrets and herons rising over the reeds, and raptors scraping the sky, it was difficult to imagine a time when such still and peaceful waters served as an essential conduit of war.

Our failure to secure passage downstream was a blessing, resulting as it did in both a beautiful night on the river, as we made our way back to Puerto Wilches, and the unexpected opportunity to join James and his colleagues on the Ciénaga de Paredes. On first impression, his two companions could not have been more different. Katherine Arévalo, a biologist in her late twenties raised in Bogotá, had spent five years at one of Colombia's finest universities, graduating with high honors and securing all the appropriate academic degrees. José Manuel Zapata, known to all as Morita, was born in La Gloria on the Magdalena in 1948. At twenty, he took to the open road, abandoning his home and his mother with no higher goal than to wander, embarking on a pilgrimage of sorts that lasted nearly twenty years and took him to every town and crossroads of the Medio Magdalena and beyond.

As a naturalist and scientist, Katherine knew everything there was to know about manatees. She had studied them in the field, surveying their populations, employing the latest scientific technologies, including sonar, to document their numbers. She had tracked their migrations as they responded to what she called hydroclimatic pulses, and measured the multiple ways they effectively manage the wetlands, from controlling the growth of aquatic plants to mitigating the impact of sedimentation just by the way they swim.

Morita, by contrast, had been working in the rice fields for fifty cents a day at El Cerrito, a small town on the edge of the Ciénaga de Paredes, when he first saw people shooting manatees for food. Capable of dreaming even in the light of midday, he had a vision, a revelation that convinced him that all of these beautiful creatures had to be loved. He told everyone who would listen, and some who wouldn't, that no harm was ever to come to what he now called the manatees of God. In 1981, when drought caused much of the ciénaga to dry up, he called on the entire community to help. He and one other man packed wild grass into hundred-pound loads, which they carried back and distributed throughout what remained of the wetland, the scores of small pools where stranded manatees faced starvation. The following day he did it again, only this time accompanied by the entire town. From that moment, he became the community leader, formally anointed by proclamation. It was his first taste of authority, his first experience of activism. In that instant, he saw the well-being of the manatee as inextricably linked to the health of his community. Manatee meat is delicious; however, as Morita knew, men hunt the animals not as gourmands or connoisseurs but because they are hungry and have to feed their families. Thus, to save the manatees, one had to save the people. In becoming, as he put it, the "doctor of his community, both its sorcerer and protector," he became, in effect, the avatar of the manatees.

The creatures, he maintained, were the source of his personal strength, the power that had allowed him to face down the armed groups that had on multiple occasions invaded El Cerrito. When paramilitaries once seized four innocent men, accusing them of collaboration with the guerrillas, Morita offered his own life in exchange for their freedom. Asked if he was armed, he replied, "Only with the courage to confront you." The paramilitary leader laughed, then let the men go. Another time, when FARC cadres arrived with gifts for the young and cows for the families, Morita turned them away, saying that if the children needed presents, he and the other fathers would provide them. He and his friends had no desire to be in debt to anyone. Told that such a response placed a target on his chest, Morita replied, "All we ask is that you respect us, as you expect us to respect you."

The most dramatic confrontation came when a band of guerrillas had the audacity to interrupt Morita when he was glued to a broadcast of the World Cup.

"When I am watching football," he told us, "nobody bothers me."

He had gotten up at five in the morning for the game, sitting happily in front of the television, his door bolted and barred, not out of fear of the guerrillas but just for the sake of quiet and privacy. Brazil was playing. There was a knock, which he ignored. Then another, even harder. Morita swung open the door to find the entire community assembled in front of his house, surrounded by twenty or more heavily armed guerrillas. Without hesitation, Morita turned to the one who seemed to be in charge, chastising him in no uncertain terms for having the nerve to intrude during one of the most important of all the matches in the tournament. Not only did the cadres release their hostages, they earnestly asked Morita if by chance they could watch the game with him. He invited them to do so, on the condition that they set their weapons down outside. The guerrillas agreed, and when the game ended, they slipped out of El Cerrito, leaving the town and the people in peace. Asked how he had the courage to repeatedly face down known and experienced killers, Morita replied, very simply, "I have a father who is called God who walks with me everywhere."

Katherine, in her own way, identified with manatees in a manner that went far beyond the conventions of science. Though trained in Bogotá, she was born in San Gil, a small town in the Magdalena Valley, east of Puerto Berrío. Her love of the animals initially grew not out of her academic studies but from the novels of Gabriel García Márquez. As a girl she became infected with Gabo's love of the river, enchanted by stories of *bogas* who slept buried in the sand to escape the heat, enchanted men who beneath the mantle of the heavens took the soft and placid creatures as lovers. She describes the Magdalena as the aorta of Colombia, its artery of life, the highway of the nation.

"For five years in college," she told us, "I studied math, physics, chemistry, but what I learned is not what my country needs. What it needs are people who will look at what we are doing to the water and ask what it will mean for our children. Men like Morita who will remind politicians that you can't drink oil, any more than you can eat gold. The river is not part of our culture; it is the essence of our culture. We are an amphibious people. We live in the middle of water. Every lake, wetland, and river, and all the animals, most especially the manatees, are here to remind us of just who we are and what we can be. My husband says I'm obsessed, but he sees it as passion, the same love that I bring to our family, and he completely understands. I am here to defend a creature that cannot speak, yet has so much to say."

Both Katherine and Morita shared these thoughts at Casablanca, in an abandoned farmhouse on the far side of the Ciénaga de Paredes, directly across from the landing at Campoduro where we'd launched our skiff that morning. Casablanca had been a ranch, then later, according to rumors, one of Pablo Escobar's many hideouts and processing labs. It was now an oil palm plantation, part of an agro-industrial push that in just fifteen years has seen more than seventy-four thousand acres converted to such production in the immediate environs of Sabana de Torres alone. As we made our way back to the boats, Morita mentioned as a point of pride that on the waters and along the shoreline of the Ciénaga de Paredes, he and the schoolchildren of El Cerrito had documented no fewer than seventy-two distinct species of butterflies. When we returned to Campoduro, and then to Puerto Wilches, I jumped online and was able to confirm, as I told Morita before we parted, that his count represented fully a quarter of the number of butterflies reported for all of Canada.

"In Colombia," he replied, "a butterfly is just a flower that has learned how to fly. That's why we have so many."

BAJO MAGDALENA

We are amphibious beings; we cannot live without the river.

—MARTÍN ESPAÑA

BAJO
MAGDALENA

Caribbean Sea

*Ciénaga Grande
de Santa Marta*

Bocas de Ceniza

Santa
Marta

Ciénaga

LA GUAJIRA

Barranquilla

*SIERRA NEVADA
DE SANTA MARTA*

Nueva
Venecia

Río Frío

Río Tucurina

ATLÁNTICO

Río Aracataca

CESAR

Río Fundación

Cartagena

Canal del Dique

Calamar

Río Cesar

*Bahía de
Cartagena*

BOLÍVAR

Tenerife

Río Magdalena

MAGDALENA

Magangué

Mompox

Chimichagua

*Ciénaga
de Zapatosa*

VENEZUELA

Botón de Leiva

Juana
Sánchez

El Banco

Hatillo de Loba

La Mojana

Barranca
de Loba

Tamalameque

(Mompisina Depression)

SUCRE

La Gloria

CÓRDOBA

Río Cauca

Arenal

Río Magdalena

BOLÍVAR

N

W   E

S

ANTIOQUIA

*SERRANÍA
DE SAN LUCAS*

SANTANDER

0	MILES	100

0	KM	100

The River of Cumbia

One hundred fifty miles inland from the Caribbean shore, the Río Magdalena falls beneath the level of the sea and ceases to flow. As the last of the Cordillera Central slips away to the south, and the valley meets the vast alluvial coastal plain, the river stills and spreads, its banks reduced to faint traces that leave little separation between an artery that for a thousand miles has dominated a nation and the shimmering wetlands and *ciénagas* of an amphibious realm that has defined it. El Banco is the linchpin. Upstream, the Magdalena in all its pride tumbles downhill. At El Banco it meets the Río Cesar, a significant affluent that originates two hundred miles to the north, draining both the Sierra Nevada de Santa Marta and the Serranía de Perijá, the far reaches of the Cordillera Oriental. Flush with the Río Cesar, the Magdalena surges around the great bend, past the high bank where the city sits, and then, like a satiated lover, simply rolls over in rest. Between El Banco and the Caribbean, the land falls away just one hundred feet. Below the city, the Magdalena does not flow; it is pushed to the sea by runoff from the mountains of the Cordilleras and the force of its own inertia and momentum, latent and growing since the river's origins in the *páramos* of the Macizo Colombiano far to the south.

La Mojana, this place of land and water, is a country within a country, a great depression two thousand square miles in extent where wind, gravity, and the moon generate subtle pulses that shift the still surface of the wetlands. Ebbs and flows mere millimeters in depth are just enough to reconfigure, on a regular basis, an entire world of water. Annual floods lasting for months replenish the marshes, bringing fertility to the soils. Seasonal rains cleanse the forests. Fish migrate in the river, sensing what remains of a current, only to spawn in the quiet waters of the *ciénagas*. Throughout the year, iguanas and lizards seek out the sun in the naked branches of blackwood and *macondo* trees, while below them, manatees find shelter in the shadows of dense thickets of *achira* and *platanillo*, cattails and cane. Stranded in the shallows, sun-bleached roots and trunks torn from the riverbanks protrude from the water like the submerged ribs of mythical beings, as if clues to a mysterious aquatic realm far beneath the surface where men mate with caimans, and spirits disguised as women conceal captive children in dazzling webs of golden hair.

If there is a hummock or a hill in the Momposina Depression, as this wide lowland basin is also known, a slight rise, a promontory, it may well be a natural feature, an accumulation of alluvial silt and sand, a rare outcrop of stone or slate. But many anomalies encountered on the land in fact conceal evidence of an ancient network of canals, dikes, and channels that comprised the most complex and sophisticated hydraulic engineering works ever constructed in the Americas. Though established two centuries before Christ, and abandoned more than a thousand years ago, the network can still be seen from the air: faint traces of irrigation ditches and artificial ridges, with broad platforms and terraces for villages and burial grounds. These were all part of an integrated and self-regulating system of flood control that liberated land for agriculture and intensive aquaculture, fish farms and fields that allowed the Zenú people, a million strong, to thrive as a civilization for twelve hundred years.

The Zenú did not exploit the wetlands; they wove their spirit into the landscape, creating a sacred geometry that integrated three major rivers, the San Jorge, Nechí, and lower Cauca, and over two hundred *ciénagas* into a topography of the imagination that allowed them to tame and domesticate more than a million acres of fecund but fiercely inhospitable land. Fertilizing their terraces and fields with nutrient-rich soils dredged by hand from the bottom of the marshes, they cultivated *plátano, piña, yuca, coca,* and *maíz.* Fruit trees covered the levees: *caimitos, guanábanos, nísperos, guayabos, mamones,* and *pitahayas.* Beneath the spreading branches of *guamos* and acacias, they kept turtles, anteaters, and caimans in great cages shaded from the sun, along with birds of a dozen species domesticated purely for the joy of hearing their songs at the break of day.

Just how they did it, the art and science of their engineering, remains unknown. By the time the Spaniards arrived from Cartagena in the first half of the sixteenth century, the Zenú were long gone, victims of a catastrophic drought that had afflicted their lands some five hundred years before. In their place were the Malibú, migrants from the north who occupied the ancient levees and village sites but had no knowledge of how or when the colossal works had come into being. By that time, the descendants of the Zenú had settled in the mountains of San Jacinto, with other populations scattered across the lowlands, in the valley of the Río Sinú, the Betancí wetlands, and along the banks of the Magdalena. They, too, had little to say about the achievements of their mysterious forefathers. Memories were faint after five centuries.

The Zenú as a people survive to this day, living for the most part in northern Córdoba in and around the municipality of San Andrés de Sotavento. Although their language disappeared more than two hundred years ago, the legacy of their ancestral civilization remains very much alive in stunning works of art celebrated in all the great museums of Colombia: Breastplates worn by both men and women as symbols of virility and fertility. Female figurines found in funerary chambers, perhaps to facilitate conception and rebirth in the underworld. Burial mounds shaped in the form of women in the final months of pregnancy, all planted with flowering trees having branches festooned with dangling objects of gold. Icons and effigies, decorative nose rings and necklaces, filigree threads of gold woven into braids and spirals. Gold that was valued not as coinage but as a numinous source of power, a symbol of eternity, the conduit for the energy of the sun.

Like the curious shadows in the fields, the strange ripples in the grass—all the clues still cloaked beneath the earth—each of these ritual treasures evokes the wonder and mystery of a lost world. For the Zenú, the land was the weft of the imagination. The designs woven into fishing nets and textiles or etched into ceramics echo the patterns inscribed on the landscape by the web of irrigation ditches and canals. Art aligned nature, politics, and religion. Women adorned in heron and egret feathers served as chiefs and fought alongside men, enjoying complete political and military authority. Religious leaders, their faces painted red and white, their bodies decorated with achiote, controlled the fate of the dead.

We will never know what these priests saw as they beheld golden figurines in glittering sunlight: Idols illuminated by the glow of torches. Animal effigies in the firelight. But whatever the ancestral Zenú believed, however they thought, their constellation of ideas, insights, devotions, and adaptations allowed them to achieve something that has defied us to this day. Though equipped with the latest industrial machinery, contemporary engineers in all their brilliance have yet to determine a way to live in a truly sustainable manner in the wetlands of La Mojana, a challenge that the Zenú civilization confronted and overcame more than a thousand years ago.

The Zenú, of course, were but one of many pre-Columbian peoples who lived out their destinies in this magical land of blue turtles and still water, red monkeys, cormorants, vultures, and toucans. As the early Spaniards made their way across the broad Caribbean coastal plain, they reported no fewer than fifty distinct indigenous languages. This rare and remarkable concentration of linguistic diversity included representatives of all three of the major language families of northern South America—Chibchan, Carib, and Arawakan—an astonishing testament to Colombia's role as a crossroads of culture from the earliest years of human settlement. The Chibchan family of languages originated in Central America. Arawakan began in the Guyanas, spread north into the islands of the Antilles, and later followed the Amazon from its mouth to the eastern foothills of the Andes. Carib came out of the savannahs of Brazil. Heading down the great rivers that drain into the Amazon from the south, the Xingu and Tapajós, it made its way north, ultimately establishing itself on the islands in the great sea that today carries its name. Eventually speakers from all three great linguistic lineages, families of languages as different one from the other as Mandarin and English, Russian and Yoruba, found their way to the shores of Colombia.

Then, as now, the Río Magdalena served as the conduit, an artery of life that in the wake of the Spanish conquest became a vector of death. European diseases, carried upriver, did not decimate native populations, for that would imply a mortality rate of just 10 percent. Throughout the Americas, smallpox and measles killed nine out of ten, leaving the survivors scarred for life, both physically and psychologically. To this day, oral traditions claim that pestilence took the form of blue clouds, a miasma of deadly mist that enveloped every man, woman, and child in its shadow. Such notions defy science but distill perfectly the horror that still resides in tribal lore and memory.

As the people died, so too did their stories. Of the fourteen hundred languages spoken in South America before the arrival of Columbus, more than a thousand would be lost, many within decades of European contact. Those living in the direct path of the conquest, along the trade routes of the Bajo Magdalena, beyond the banks of the river that drew the Spaniards into the heart of the continent, suffered the most. As entire nations fell silent, their tribal names alone endured; indigenous cultures from the depths of La Mojana such as the Pemeo, Pocabuy, Panzenú, and Chimila. Or closer to the sea, and along the islands running west to the mouth of the Atrato and the shores of Panama, the Urabá and the Calamarí. Dominating the coastal plain east of the Magdalena were the Tairona, broken and ravaged by the Spaniards in the last years of the sixteenth century, a once great civilization formally declared dead by a Catholic priest, Antonio Julián, in 1679.

What these cultures believed, and how they lived, we can only surmise through the study of what they left behind: ghostlike memories brought forward in the guise of myths, material remains dug from the ground—burial urns, ceramic chards, fragments of nets, hammocks, and woven cloth, textiles fine beyond imagining. Seeds and pollen, along with implements made of stone, shell, or quartz—mortars, pestles, grinders, and *budares*—reveal what they ate: iguana and maize, fish, beans, avocados, pineapples, and cassava. From oral traditions and early Spanish accounts emerge the faint outlines of their economies, systems of local and long-distance commerce made possible by the Río Magdalena that had flamingo feathers, butterflies, and jaguar teeth exchanged for salt, lime, and coca, children traded for parrots, fish hooks for arrow poisons, snake rattles for conch shells, dried meat and fish for a host of ritual sacraments, *flor de quinde, wilca, huachuma, chacruna,* and *yagé.* Trade items ranged from the quotidian to the precious: Feathered coronas that shone like the sun. Fringes of delicate gold, all that was deemed necessary to dress and secure the modesty of women.

Along the middle reaches of the Cauca, the principle tributary of the Magdalena, the Quimbaya for more than a thousand years worked with gold as wizards work with the wind. Masters of the art of lost wax casting, they fused copper and gold with a precision and elegance that defies scientific understanding to this day, producing, among countless other treasures, highly coveted lime containers of solid gold, *poporos* in the shape of fruits, animals, demons, and human beings. Their craftsmen hammered the soft metal into a myriad of forms, including paper-thin sheets, sacred shrouds that in death enveloped the faces of great lords and priests. The leitmotif of all their ritual and artistic expression was transformation: werejaguars, bats, harpy eagles, and frogs, shamans captured in ecstatic flight, anthropomorphic figures as mediators between realms of the spirit and the world of men.

The collapse of the Quimbaya in the tenth century, a fate shared by the Zenú not a hundred years later, appears today as just a point of inflexion in a long march of history, serving as a reminder that great chieftains and empires rose and fell in the Americas for two thousand years before the arrival of Columbus. No civilization long endures, even if few anticipate their demise. Every kingdom is born to die.

But the arrival of Europeans in the early years of the sixteenth century implied something altogether different. It was not just a clash of cultures, religions, and military power but, rather, the unleashing upon an entire hemisphere of the concentrated essence of death itself: biological pathogens, virulent, invisible, unknown. As the shadow of the Spanish conquest passed over the Americas, deadly microbes seeped into the land. They were carried by water and wind, transmitted by touch, an intimate embrace, a kiss. Entire nations succumbed long before ever encountering a Spanish soldier or a priest, the black robes who, in their evangelical zeal, exhaled pestilence even as they declared smallpox to be the will of God. One early account, describing just a short stretch of the Bajo Magdalena, reported that by 1579, a combination of abuse, fever, and slavery had reduced the local population of *los naturales*, as chroniclers described the natives, from 70,000 to a mere 800. In the islands of the Caribbean, some 3 million Arawakans died between 1494 and 1508. Within 150 years of Columbus, the original native population of 70 million in all the Americas would be reduced to 3.5 million. In the southern Andes of Bolivia, on a mountain of silver once sacred to the Inca, an average of 75 indigenous men and women were to die every day for 350 years.

In Colombia, in what can only be described as a small miracle, the voices of the first people of the land were muted but never fully silenced. The Spaniards did indeed vanquish the Tairona, laying waste to their temples, violating their women, feeding their children to dogs. But the spirit of that ancient civilization survives today to an astonishing degree in the Sierra Nevada de Santa Marta, distilled in the beliefs and ritual practices of the Elder Brothers. The Kogi, Wiwa, and Arhuaco believe, as did their ancestors, that gold absorbs the power of the sun. On auspicious days, when the celestial spheres align, they place in the sunlight sacred objects of crystal and gold, small treasures retained and hidden since the time of the conquest. Gold serves as the conduit of the divine, drawing the sun's energy to the object, from which it radiates to all dimensions and through the hearts of all people, for the benefit of the entire community. For the Elder Brothers, gold is equivalent to light, color, semen, and power. They call it *nyúi*, the same name as that of the sun.

That the *mamos* of the Kogi, Wiwa, and Arhuaco—in spirit and convictions the direct descendants of the sun priests of the Tairona—are alive and well, at work each morning praying for the well-being of the Earth and all of humanity, is a testament to the strength and enduring resonance of indigenous voices in Colombia. That such ritual devotions, such a universe of faith, may be found today not two hours by commercial jet from Miami, on the slopes of a volcanic massif that is home to every major ecosystem on the planet, in hamlets looking west to the Magdalena, beyond the very shores where Columbus's men landed in 1499, suggests a continuity of knowledge, wisdom, and tradition that can only inspire wonder and hope.

Five hundred years after the conquest, Colombia remains home to more than eighty distinct and vibrant indigenous nations. Though a small percentage of the country's total population, they are collectively nearly two million strong, roughly equivalent to the number of native people believed to have been living in Colombia at the time of European contact. They and all the generations before them have lived through a glass darkly. They are all the survivors of El Dorado. Today they no more resemble or mimic precisely the ways of their ancestors than any of us echo the exact behaviors and beliefs of our grandparents, let alone their parents and grandparents. Culture is never static. People in all traditions lean on the past, but they must live with the challenges of today, seeking always new possibilities for life. Change is the only constant.

Forty years ago, when I first set out to visit the Arhuaco, the parents of one of my university friends in Bogotá asked why I wanted to spend time with *la gente sucia*, the dirty people. Not two generations later, five Colombian presidents have on the eve of their inaugurations traveled to the Sierra Nevada to seek the blessing of the *mamos*, who have emerged as symbols of continuity and patrimony in a country long haunted by uncertainty and convulsed in violence. In his last days in office, in August 2018, President Juan Manuel Santos signed a decree recognizing and expanding the ancestral territory of the Elder Brothers as defined by *la Línea Negra*, the Black Line, a ring of sacred sites encircling the base of their homeland, lands long claimed by settlers, staked by miners, and exploited by drug lords. To those who opposed his decision, Santos declared simply that the protection of the environment and the rights of indigenous peoples were, on balance, more important than individual commercial interests, especially those secured by dubious means. For a Colombian president, the head of state, to acknowledge such a stolen legacy, and to seek meaningful restitution in such a way, would have been inconceivable just those few short years ago when I first fell under the spell of the Sierra, enchanted and inspired by the *mamos*.

By the end of the 1970s, missionary zeal and a legacy of brutality and exploitation dating to the terrible years of the rubber boom had brought the peoples of the northwest Amazon to the brink of cultural exhaustion. Then, in 1986, President Virgilio Barco decided, as he later wrote, "to do something for the Indians." In five extraordinary years, he did more than something. Working with Martín von Hildebrand, a young anthropologist appointed as head of the Office of Indigenous Affairs, Barco set aside no fewer than 162 *resguardos*, establishing a system of indigenous reserves collectively the size of the United Kingdom, with legal title and land rights that were formally encoded into law in the 1991 Constitution of the country. Nothing like it, on such a scale, had ever been done by a nation-state. In the years that followed, as Colombia endured the ravages of war, the federal government, preoccupied with the national crisis, largely turned its back on the Amazon. A veil of isolation fell upon the entire region, behind which, over the course of a decade, a cultural renaissance unfolded unlike anything that had ever occurred in the Americas. An old dream of the earth was reborn.

In securing the future for the native peoples of the Colombian Amazon, President Barco acted on intuition and humanitarian impulse, with little knowledge at the time that he was rescuing from oblivion a complex of cultures that we only now recognize and celebrate as the actual descendants of the great chieftains of the Amazon: contemporary societies that, in their beliefs and adaptations, provide a rare cultural lens onto a distant time when the great river was an artery of civilization, home to hundreds of thousands, indeed millions of human beings. With their lands protected, their homes and families secure, the Makuna and Barasana, in particular, began to share their stories, the tales and insights of their ancestors, in books, monographs, and films researched, written, and produced by their own scholars. Young men schooled in the finest universities of Bogotá returned to study at the feet of shamans, while their sisters, trained in agronomy and environmental sciences, came home to survey with their mothers the caloric output of forest gardens, the amount of fish protein to be found in a river, the ecological significance of shallows and side channels long protected by myth. Throughout the Colombian Amazon, traditional communities long the focus of anthropological inquiry became at last the ethnographers of their own lives.

As their revelatory accounts become more widely known, with the message of the Elder Brothers reaching each year an ever larger national and international audience, the voices of all indigenous people are being amplified. Whatever contempt a small minority of Colombians may once have had, and perhaps still have, for native people has increasingly given way, especially among the young, to pride and respect: a recognition that every indigenous tradition in Colombia represents a unique vision of life itself, and that each has something to say that the world needs to hear. Those who remain dismissive, as if shamed by the faces of their own nation, are often among the unfortunate few who, perhaps driven by insecurity, seek approbation by mimicking always what lies outside of Colombia, rather than finding identity, strength, and inspiration in the incomparable riches of their own homeland.

The 1991 Constitution, a touchstone in the history of modern Colombia, formally encoded pluralism and multiculturalism as foundational principles, fundamental to the very definition of the nation. *Resguardos*, autonomous indigenous reserves, today number over seven hundred, encompassing fully 30 percent of Colombia's territory, a record unmatched by any other country. Indigenous communities are not only key elements of Colombia's historical legacy, their survival and very existence is a celebration of the country's essential vitality as a place of unequaled cultural and biological diversity. To be sure, their ancestors endured a holocaust. But this should not suggest that any of the traditional cultures still with us today are somehow vestigial, as if archaic voices stranded in time, having at best a vague advisory role to play in contemporary life. To the contrary, the indigenous peoples of Colombia, the Barasana and Makuna, the Kogi, Wiwa, and Arhuaco, the Páez, Kamsá, Wayú, Tanimuka, and all the many others, are very much alive and fighting not only for their cultural survival but also to take part in a national and global dialogue that will define the future of Colombia and, quite possibly, the fate of life on earth.

. . .

No such outcome could possibly have been foreseen in the final years of the sixteenth century, as the Spaniards consolidated their conquest and set out to exploit the lands they had seized and the peoples they had vanquished. As mystified as were the victims by the virulence in the New World of diseases long endured in Spain, they bore witness to a demographic collapse that within two generations reduced the native peoples of the Bajo Magdalena to mere shadows in the sand, their voices but whispered messages in the forest. Desperate for men to work the gold mines, to pound stone and carry cargo, to serve as *bogas* on the river and menservants in their parlors, the Spanish colony turned to Africa. Of the more than ten million men and women dragged in bondage to the Americas over three centuries, some four hundred thousand came to Colombia, nearly twice the number of immigrants that arrived from Spain over those same years.

The slave trade touched every African shore, with tentacles that reached deep into the very recesses of the continent. Merchants, mercenaries, local predators, and kings came together in unholy alliances intent on draining the lifeblood of nations. The old kingdoms of Fula and Mandinka, north of Sierra Leone, rounded up Senegalese, Yoloffe, Foule, Bambara, Mandingu, Quiambasa, and Soso. Taken in shackles from the Gold Coast were the Bouriqui, Mesurade, and Canga, while farther east, toward the mouth of the Volta River, the Ashanti and Fanti Kingdoms provided Arada, Caplaou, Mines, Agoua, Soco, and Fantin. Still farther east, along the Slave Coast and the far reaches of Dahomey were found the Cotocoli, Popo, Fida, and Arada. From Nigeria came the Fon, Mahi, Aoussa, Igbo, Nago, and Moko. Many destined for the slave auctions of Nueva Granada originated in the Congo and present-day Angola, including the Mayombe, Mousombe, and Mondongue. Small but significant numbers were captured as far from the Atlantic ports as the grasslands of Mozambique and the far reaches of Madagascar.

Among the many tens of thousands dragged against their will to Colombia were artisans and musicians, herbalists, carvers, metal-workers, boat builders, farmers, drum makers, sorcerers, and warriors. There were men of royal blood and others who had been born into slavery in Africa. They had in common their experience with a heinous economic system that had ripped them away from their homes, families, and villages. But critically, they also shared an oral tradition that was unassailable—a rich repository of religious beliefs, music, dance, folk medicine, agriculture, and patterns of social organization that they carried with them into exile. Above all, they were children of Guinée, of Africa, the ancient homeland, a place that slowly drifted from history into the realm of myth. In time, what had been the collective memory of an entire disenfranchised people became the ethos of new generations and the foundation in the Bajo Magdalena of a distinct and persistent folk culture, a fusion of what was left behind and what was found in the forests of a new land.

From the earliest years, those caught in the net of the slave trade, sold as livestock from the docks of Santa Marta or locked away in the warehouses of Cartagena, refused to resign themselves to their misfortune. Knowing that in death awaited only a spiritual return to Guinée, many risked all to slip away from the plantations and mines, escaping into a torrid hinterland that intimidated the Spaniards but to equatorial Africans seemed like home. In their numbers, these runaways, or *cimarrones*, came together, forming small villages hidden in the recesses of the forests, well away from the rivers. Founded by men and women who had actually been born in Africa, these communities, known as *palenques*, became both repositories of rich and abiding traditions and refugia that, over time, experienced a fusion of cultures that would ultimately define the demographics of much of coastal Colombia.

With freedom as their creed, the *cimarrones* forged easy alliances with the Chimila and Pocabuy, scattered bands of survivors who would court death for generations rather than submit to the Spaniards. Though the natives and the fugitive slaves came from different worlds, in daily life they had much in common. Both dwelled in small marginal settlements, protected by palisades and rings of sentinels always watchful for bounty hunters and raiders. They lived on fish, wild fruits, and root crops grown as in Africa, in small garden plots slashed from the forest. Their hunters pursued the same game—monkeys, iguanas, and tapirs—using the same weapons, blowguns and arrows, with traditional preparations of curare augmented with new formulations from toxic plants and frogs, discoveries made in the forests of the Magdalena by those born in Africa, where the manipulation of folk poisons remains, to this day, perhaps the most ubiquitous trait of material culture across a broad swath of the continent.

Each tradition had warrior kings and chiefs, as well as powerful and respected roles for women, and religious specialists who served as both physician and priest. Their spiritual convictions had an uncanny symmetry. Both considered death not an end but a beginning, a passage to be embraced with joy, a moment for the living to bid farewell to loved ones who had simply moved on to another world. The funeral rites of the Pocabuy always featured a pregnant woman, around whom the living would dance in celebration of the new life embarked upon by the deceased. In Africa, death was seen as but a transition, as the soul of the individual left the body to become part of the vast ancestral pool of energy, out of which emerged the spirits of the pantheon. Music was essential, for it was upon the rhythm of the drums, the cadence of the chants, the assonance of songs that the deities rode as they returned to this earthly realm to momentarily inhabit the bodies of believers, such that for a brief shining instant, human being and god became one and the same. Spirit possession was the goal of religious practice, the moment of spiritual epiphany, the hand of divine grace.

The Chimila and Pocabuy also sought transformation, slipping toward the edge of trance as they made offerings to their principal deity, Marayajna. Each of their musical instruments was conceived and designed to echo the voices of nature. Wooden drums, open-ended trunks carved from ceiba trees and played with sticks wrapped in rubber, imitated the thunderous sound of trees falling in the forest. The *caña de millo* communicated directly with birds. Flutes captured the sound of running water, the slow surge of the Río Magdalena. Every melody carried a message. Each note was associated with an animal, allowing the shaman to bring to ceremony a universal score, songs that could shift perceptions and transform consciousness.

Africans, too, danced in circles, counterclockwise so as to ease the transition to the afterlife. To light the way, their dancers held aloft lamps or candles, even as they twirled. They also used wooden drums, which they covered with goat or crocodile skin, an innovation readily adopted by the Chimila and Pocabuy, impressed as they were by the seemingly infinite array of rhythms that fired the heart and soul of every *cimarrón*. Music was in their blood, a source of spiritual and psychological strength that did not go unnoticed by the Spaniards. As early as 1546, and again in 1573, by royal decree in Cartagena, Africans were forbidden to sing, dance, or play drums in public. Fifty years later, when they persisted in doing so, at funerals in particular, the Jesuits ordered that all drums be seized and destroyed. One hundred and fifty years later, the Crown was still at it, in 1768 ordering authorities in Cartagena to inform on all gatherings and fandangos that had circles of men and women dancing, an act by then defined as sinful by the church. Not twenty years later, in 1781, the authorities finally gave up, with the bishop of Cartagena concluding that nothing could be done, no sanction invoked, that would stop the "Indians, mulattos, mestizos, blacks, zambos, and other inferior castes" of both sexes from dancing, playing drums, singing erotic and lascivious songs, and drinking copious amounts of *aguardiente*, *guarapo*, and *chicha*, distilled and fermented potions all.

The Spaniards could no more silence the drums than quell the passions of those who danced. In Africa, there is no separation between the sacred and the secular, between the holy and the profane, between the material and the spiritual. Every dance, every song, every action is but a particle of the whole, each gesture a prayer for the survival of the entire community. The drummer is both musician and servant of the divine. Music is entertainment, but also the catalyst of transformation. Every drum has its own rhythm, its own pitch, and yet in ceremony, there is a stunning unity to the sound that sweeps over the senses. As invocations and chants slice through the night, the drummers beat a continuous battery, a powerful resonance that can have the very forest trees overhead swaying in sympathy.

By the end of the eighteenth century, throughout the Bajo Magdalena, love, nature, and desire had fused the worlds of Africa and the Americas into one. Intermarriage brought together bloodlines, along with beliefs, rituals, and customs. African men stripped of their wives came together with native women whose husbands had been lost to war, broken in torture, or worked to death in the fields or on the water. Miscegenation became the norm, the leitmotif of the land. If the mestizo was the product of a coupling of Spaniard and Indian, the *zambo* was the child of Indian and African. When Alexander von Humboldt made his way across Nueva Granada in 1801, the great naturalist reported with some confidence that Colombia was home to the largest population of *zambos* in all of the Americas.

Zambos certainly dominated the forests and wetlands of the Bajo Magdalena, serving above all as *bogas*, the independent boatmen upon whom all transport on the Río Magdalena at the time depended. Struggling against the currents, hauling all manner of impossible loads, these river rogues endured conditions that in but a generation had broken the spirit and shattered the bodies of every native pressed into service, work that no mestizo would even dare undertake. Fortified by freedom and blessed by their gods, *zambos* not only thrived as *bogas*, they triumphed as free men who, in their physical trials, made a muse of the river, offering up rhythms, melodies, and eventually songs that, in time, became the musical score of a new land. This was, in part, the genesis of *cumbia*, the heartbeat of Colombia and its singular gift to the world.

Cumbia is a rhythm, a beat, a dance—a choreography of seduction that ignites the spirit and shakes the soul, infusing one's entire physical being with a sensual promise as innocent and perfect as a prayer. The dance movements of the male recall the desires of the lone *cimarrón*: passionate, powerful, yearning. Those of the woman, the coy resistance of the native maiden, bright candles in hand, spinning in a whirlwind of indifference. The music builds through the night, an alchemy of spirit and sensation that with every performance enhances its authority and power, laying claim to its rightful place as the progenitor of all musical forms in a nation nursed on rhythm, inspired from birth by song.

A scholar who truly understands the essence and roots of *cumbia* is Carlos Vives, Colombia's beloved musical icon, an international star who arguably has done more to popularize the traditional genre than any living artist. Carlos is a child of Santa Marta, a product of the sun and the sea. The city lies in the shadow of the Sierra Nevada de Santa Marta, homeland of the Arhuaco, Wiwa, and Kogi, whose children Carlos played with as a boy. He grew up in the presence of multiple cultural realities, at ease in a town that never rests. Music was the backdrop of his youth, a cacophony of sound that greeted every dawn and heralded each night the growing radiance of the stars. Along the waterfront and in the neighborhoods, in hidden doorways and brightly lit bars, he absorbed the rhythms of an ever-changing and expanding repertoire of musical forms, each the outcome of a new passion—a fusion of unexpected and unanticipated possibilities, envisioned by men and women who were themselves the products of a melding of blood and culture so complete that to this day fully 85 percent of Colombians in a recent national census describe themselves as having no particular ethnic origins.

Carlos began his career as an actor, playing the lead in a series based on the life of Rafael Escalona, the father of *vallenato*, a musical genre that, as the word implies, was "born in the valley," along the dry riverbeds and dusty draws reaching north and south of Valledupar and the headwaters of the Río Cesar on the far side of the Sierra Nevada. As a boy, Carlos became enchanted by the sound: the plaintive notes of the accordion, the beat laid down by the *caja* drum of Africa, the rhythm of the *guacharaca*, an instrument clearly of indigenous origins. He was equally moved by the spirit of the songs, each a story of nature, freedom, and love; the birth of a child, a wedding gone wrong, the mysterious flight of a magical bird, the delicate movements of deer in the evening as the sun softens on the horizon.

As an actor, Carlos covered Escalona's songs much as the composer intended them to be sung. But as a musician with a passion for his country and a heart as expansive and all-embracing as the land he so clearly loves, Carlos in time completely reinterpreted the genre, fusing traditional *vallenato* with rock and pop and other Caribbean sounds in a manner that scandalized purists but electri-

fied the world. Beginning in 1993 with *Clásicos de la Provincia,* Carlos
and his band produced a string of massive international hit albums
recognized today as timeless classics, with songs that in Colombia's
darkest days served as antidotes to despair, even as they distilled all
that was decent and good in the country. Songs that told the truth.
Anthems of joy and redemption. Melodies of loss. A musical repertoire of love and belonging rooted in a spirit of place that perhaps
only a Colombian can fully understand, one who has suffered, which
today implies nearly everyone in the country.

Xandra and I caught up with Carlos in Barranquilla, even as
Carnaval spun the city into a fever pitch of joy. We knew him to
be a good man. Only the night before he had invited my daughter Tara and her Colombian band, L'Équipe Tambora, to play with
him onstage in front of an audience of many thousands. Sharing
the spotlight as he so often does, bringing little-known acts into his
circle and allowing them to shine in public as never before, is a sign
of both his immense generosity and his profound belief that music
is a universal muse that, like a spirit being, reaches out to all, as the
ultimate weapon of love. It is not the artist that sings the song, he
would say, it is the spirit of the song that sings the artist. The stage
is a temple. Music serves as prayer. Dancers spin into trance. The
audience as congregation rocks to the rhythms of devotion, not for
the artist but for his art; songs that touch the far reaches of the soul,
the most passionate depths of emotions, even while grounding the
spirit in the soil of a nation, leaving everyone not damp with sweat
but moistened by the purity of the rains, the promise of the rivers,
drenched in all the possibilities of a new day.

The morning after the concert, Carlos and his lovely wife and
partner, Claudia Elena Vásquez, along with their two young children, joined us as we crossed the Río Magdalena on a flat-decked
ferry to reach an island in the stream, a nature reserve and modest lodge owned by good friends. With industrial Barranquilla as a
backdrop, we stood together on the stern in the sun as Xandra and I
asked him about music and the river.

"*Cumbia* is the mother," he began very simply, "the mother of
all our rhythms. Its essence and power are so strong. It gave birth to
all others, every musical pulse born on the Caribbean coast: *porro,*

gaita, *bullerengue*, *chandé*, *paseo*, *puya*, and, of course, *vallenato*. And
if *cumbia* is the mother of our rhythms, the mother of *cumbia* is the
Magdalena. The river is our storyteller. It's what defines us as a people, what defines the nation. The Magdalena tells our story, and it
does so all the time. It was only by knowing the river that I was able
to discover the real origins of *cumbia* and, of course, *vallenato* and
every other expression of our hearts and desires and dreams."

Carlos traces the history of musical genres and rhythms much as
an anthropologist tracks descent through kinship, with each lineage
going back to a common ancestor, which in the case of Colombian
music is always the Río Magdalena. Like a siren rising from the
depths of the river, *bambucos* appeared, ballads that evoked the pure
poetry of romance, laments of lost love named for a tribal people
who had long before slipped away into the mists of time. *Porro* is
a rhythm commonly associated with the Llanos, the great eastern
plains. But if you listen carefully, Carlos explained, you can clearly
hear the influence of jazz, a fusion that could only have come about
during the glory days on the Magdalena when the *David Arango*, in
all of its luxury, carried internationally renowned musicians from
Barranquilla upriver to the notorious jazz clubs of La Dorada.
Merecumbé is a synthesis of *cumbia* and the traditional merengue of
the coastal department of Magdalena, invented in a flash by Pacho
Galán back in 1950 as he performed on stage in Soledad, just outside of Barranquilla. *Vallenatos* are also the offspring of *cumbia* and,
thus, of the river, perhaps less the Magdalena than the Río Cesar,
the entire history of which is recounted in their melodies and verse.
Cumbia, Carlos believes, goes back not just to the *bogas* but to the
sounds and rhythms of the Chimila and Pocabuy, the very word
being derived from two syllables in their language, a reference to
the sacred art of making music for the gods.

"The Chimila called the river Kariguaña," Carlos said, "Agua
Grande, the big water, the Río Grande. Maybe it's time to once
again make it great. For too long we've turned our backs to the
sea, to the mountains, to the river, hiding away in cities, always in
conflict with nature, in conflict with our land. Music makes us pay
attention, to look at the forests, the mountains, and especially the
Magdalena, because the origins and essence of everything we work

with musically comes from there—rhythms, phrases, melodies. The river is music, and music is the river. What the Magdalena needs is what Colombia needs. After all the violence, we need to cleanse our souls, and only then will we heal. And to heal ourselves, we must heal the river."

Land of a Thousand Rhythms

If *cumbia* is the pulse of Colombia, then the heart of the heartbeat, the place of all musical origins, lies on a high bank of the Río Magdalena, where the river takes a great turn and young lovers watch the sun set from stone steps that reach down to the river from the old colonial settlement of El Banco. When the Spaniards first arrived, it was the land of the Chimila, whose dominant *cacique* Loba is today remembered for the gold mines that bore his name, where so many of his people died, and from where escaped the solitary fugitive slave who in 1680 first called the town El Banco. Acknowledging the deep religious devotion of the people, not to mention the strategic significance of the setting, the government of Santa Marta in 1747 embellished the name to Nuestra Señora de la Candelaria de El Banco. At the highest point of a broad promontory overlooking the river, a church was dedicated to the Holy Virgin, the one spiritual force capable of protecting local women from the devouring passions of El Mohán, a mythical being that dwells to this day in the depths of the river, *amo y señor de las aguas*, master and lord of the waters.

Favored by geography, comfortable with contradictions, El Banco grew as a place of remarkable tolerance, a prosperous crossroads of commerce where Liberal women defended the tombs of Conservative generals and where ordinary people put up with the pecadilloes of priests, including those of one notorious cleric, father of twelve, who was embraced by his congregation on the one condition that he never marry. A priest with children could be indulged, but one bound in wedlock would surely be incapable of celebrating Mass and offering prayers and Holy Communion.

Alonso Restrepo, our old friend from Cali who went to work for the Naviera Colombiana in 1942, recalls the anticipation felt by all as a riverboat approached the docks of El Banco. On board might be an orchestra from Bogotá, a band of *costeños* playing *vallenato*, or jazz musicians riffing off the rhythms of Lucho Bermúdez, whose songs were the sound of romance on every journey along "our mother river," the Magdalena. On the jetty, there always stood a lone *zambo*, playing a drum or a flute. In the ravine running away from the shore would be dozens of men and women from the *palenques*, all dancing and singing. As long as a vessel was in port, there was a permanent party, with people gathering at all hours beneath the thatch of a great shelter mounted over the concrete slab at portside. There were no rules. The only constants were the rhythms of *vallenato*, *cumbia*, and *tambora*. Sleep was optional. "Even the *bogotanos* danced," Alonso recalled, "*cachacos* who had no rhythm at all, who eyed the locals with envy as they stumbled about looking like frogs jumping around." Those from the coast questioned whether anyone so clumsy could possibly be Colombian, but no one said a word. On the jetty, everyone was welcome.

"It was overflowing joy," Alonso remembered with a smile. "People had an amazingly good time. There were many nights when nobody went to bed."

Nothing quite so exciting awaited our small team as we crossed over the Río Cesar and reached the outskirts of the city. The sun had set over the river, and we were in a somewhat somber mood, knowing that Juan would be leaving us in the morning to return to his teaching duties at his university in Medellín. In just a fortnight we had become good friends, more than that, and both Xandra and I were truly sad to see him go. Naturally, in keeping with his passion for the story of the Magdalena, Juan had made plans to hand us off in El Banco to an equally inspired character, a good friend of his, a young ethnomusicologist named Martín España. Juan described Martín as the bridge, an independent scholar who, like the river, connects all the musicians throughout the entire Momposina Depression, a place that for him is less a geographical region than a great and precious incubator of rhythms, movements, and sounds, a cultural treasure of national and global significance. A talented musician in his own right, Martín performs not in a studio or a theater but on a stage spread across an entire landscape, for his ultimate mission is the preservation and promotion of all the musical genres that distill the spirit and identity of the Colombian people.

Martín's personal passion, according to Juan, is *tambora*, the rhythm of the *palenques*. He stumbled upon this raw and elemental sound while still a university student, even as the tradition, rooted in the forests and wetlands surrounding El Banco, faced an uncertain future. Upon graduation, Martín became a promoter, reaching out to every *tambora* group in every backwater and riverside settlement, forging, through music, bonds of trust and friendship that perhaps only a fellow player can establish. He created a foundation, Cantos del Río, and set out to document an oral tradition that lingered precariously in the memories and movements of men and women entering the final years of their lives.

None of the maestros of *tambora* had the means to travel. No folkloric group had access to a recording studio. Nor was it clear that music inspired by the spirits, conceived alongside the river, would translate if performed out of context, by players breathless in the grey light and cold of Bogotá. Instead, Martín found a way to bring technicians and sound equipment to the villages. Using social media, he attracted world-class producers and engineers from Europe and throughout Latin America; they arrived by the score, drawn to Colombia not for money or fame but merely to participate in the process, for the honor of being present as true musical genius was recorded for posterity, and artists of great integrity and authenticity had, at last, their moment in the sun.

We found Martín on the steps of the church, just across the square from the promenade where lovers strolled and boys and girls not yet fifteen exchanged innocent kisses in the glare and shadows of the streetlamps. A road ran down to the fish market and the docks, where dozens of water taxis, or *chalupas*, secured one to another, bobbed in the current. Crossing to the waterfront, we huddled for a time on a bench, watching as fishermen, moving along the lowest step, gently swept the river with great silver nets stiffened by narrow rims of wood. Only the astonishing grace of their movements kept the force of the river from tearing the nets to tatters.

Martín was short, plump, and cherubic, with a wild tangle of hair tied aloft in a knot, a lion's mane clearly impossible to tame. He wore a fresh white shirt, shorts, and flip-flops. He had an earnest air, without a hint of shyness. Music was his mission.

"Colombia is said to be the land of a thousand rhythms," he noted with a wry smile. "Ethnomusicologists have in fact identified one thousand and twenty-five."

After the briefest of such banter, Martín laid out his plans for the week: a musical journey that would expose us to the masters of *tambora*, including a legendary figure, Maestro Villafañe, whose energy and charisma he could only compare to that of Mick Jagger. "Imagine having Jagger right in front of you," Martín told us. "That's Villafañe's energy onstage."

Before entering the world of *tambora*, Martín suggested, it would be best to dispense with *cumbia*. This was a first sign that Martín's passion for *tambora* went hand in hand with an almost whimsical resentment of *cumbia*'s position as the iconic musical genre of the country. Martín, of course, loves all music, but he could not help but point out that whereas *cumbia* is just one rhythm, *tambora* has four. And each of these has its own subdivisions. The main percussive instruments are a cylindrical drum struck with two sticks and a conical drum played with the palms of the hands. The lyrics of *tambora* are raw and elemental, the poetic words of the unschooled, composed by mostly illiterate men and women singing about the simple moments in life: a bird in flight, a girl in love, the beauty of the river. Every *tambora* group has a leading voice, with all the others serving as a chorus. Each ensemble features among its players children, adults, and the elderly, ensuring that, like a heavenly choir, it represents every phase of life and each member of the community.

"To listen to *tambora*," Martín declared, "is to listen to the earth speaking. It's like listening to the river."

By this point we had moved from our bench, with Martín leading the way across the square, where we paused at the base of a small memorial. It was a bust of José Barros, a native son of El Banco, who, along with Lucho Bermúdez, elevated *cumbia* from a rhythm of the streets to the soundtrack of a nation. Barros, Martín explained, wrote more than eight hundred songs, each a portrait of the simple life: the daily struggle of a fisherman, the dusty solitude of a cowboy, the frustrations and follies of an artisanal miner, a life he knew well from his time in the gold fields of Segovia. Not unlike Gabriel García Márquez, he discerned the heroic in the mundane, employing lyrics as a lens that alone could magnify, making all things seem more colorful and grand, revealing in the most basic of daily tasks all the qualities of an epic saga. Like Gabo, Barros wrote of what he saw, perceptions and experiences that in his imagination became bigger than life. He had a way of making the ordinary seem extraordinary, the local appear universal, even transcendent.

"Though a child of a small town," Martín said, "Barros, through poetry and passion, inspired by what he experienced in his own travels, in time developed a vision that embraced the entire world."

Xandra glanced my way, delighted that we had found a musical guide of such knowledge and insight. I smiled and turned to Martín just as he casually asked whether we would like to drop in on José Barros's daughter Veruschka. "She lives just down the street."

Veruschka Barros was sitting in a folding chair just outside her door, chatting with family and friends and enjoying the night air. She greeted Martín warmly, and after a round of introductions, we all filed into her parlor. A young girl appeared with a tray of lemonade. Veruschka was slight and elegant, with beautiful eyes and long, dark hair with just a tinge of grey. She was both spry and surprisingly youthful. I scrambled to do the math, knowing that Barros had passed away in 2007 at the age of ninety-two.

Veruschka spoke with the pride and authority of a daughter who had clearly embraced her role as curator of her father's legacy. She seemed to know every story, each anecdote, the details of every encounter he had ever had. In her telling, his characters came alive in all their color and passion. In her devotion, she had become intimate with the inspiration that had resulted in every one of his hundreds of compositions. Veruschka, as Xandra later remarked, is herself a living treasure, her memory a repository of precious jewels, all facets of the life of one of Colombia's most revered artists and songwriters.

To understand her father, Veruschka explained, you had to begin with his humble upbringing. His mother was a native; his father, a Portuguese immigrant. José grew up on the streets of El Banco, working as a shoeshine boy, earning five cents a customer. When not sneaking into the movie theater with friends, or frolicking in canoes as the floodwaters swept clean the back alleys of the city, or spinning, as his daughter recalled, "a thousand pirouettes of joy," José spent most of his youth on the river with his uncle, a merchant who rented canoes and nets to fishermen in exchange for a portion of their catch. The Río Magdalena, Veruschka stressed, was the very source of her father's identity. Like blood, it ran through his veins, just as it coursed through the hearts of everyone who lived along its shores. All the stories he told her as a child revolved around his adventures on the Magdalena. His songs were odes not just to the river but to the life made possible by its bounty.

Known as Benito to his boyhood friends, José had no interest in school, never learned to write with any proficiency, and found real purpose only in the juke joints and bars where local musicians played *chandé* and *tambora* deep into the night. He formed his own band at ten, wrote his first song at twelve, and played parties up and down the river, earning the princely sum of twenty cents a gig. An older brother set him up in business, but when José blew his first earnings on a girlfriend, it was time to skip town, which he did, never looking back, leaving his grieving mother in tears, even as his family declared him dead.

Heading down the Magdalena, Barros ended up in Santa Marta, where for no particular reason he enlisted in the army. He learned guitar in the barracks, sketching out lyrics for boleros, which were all the rage at the time. Having avoided combat in the war with Peru, a spasm of violence that flared for nine months in 1932 and 1933, he left the army at eighteen, taking with him only the guitar of his closest friend, a soldier killed at the front, and made his way back up the river to Barrancabermeja. Swept up in the Segovia gold rush, he spent months pursuing his fortune, only to be spat back onto the streets of Medellín, where he survived on raw potatoes, pinched from market stalls. Finally, in 1942, he returned as if a ghost to El Banco, where his mother had long forbidden the family from mentioning his name, even as she secretly kept all of his clothes laundered and pressed, awaiting his return.

In the end, music would transform Barros's destiny, taking him away once again, this time to the far reaches of the continent: Argentina, Chile, Brazil, and Peru, where he recorded his first album. He lived in Mexico just long enough to get deported back to Colombia. Landing in Bogotá, he worked for a time with Lucho Bermúdez and Pacho Galán before abandoning the dreary capital for the coast and Cartagena, where he pulled together a band and headed east to Barranquilla. There, at the mouth of the river that had defined his life, along which he had traveled abroad and found his way home, José Barros wrote the song that would secure his fame and legacy, if not his fortune, "La Piragua," a hymn of universal love, longing, and fate, all inspired by a canoe. The deceptively simple narrative, in fact, distills the entire story of a nation.

As we bade Veruschka good night, she kindly gave us copies of a new CD, a collection of her father's most famous songs sung by Colombia's greatest contemporary artists, including Carlos Vives, who covers "La Piragua." It was a generous gesture, which left Xandra taken aback by Martín's shift in mood as we walked back to our hotel, a small pension by the church near the waterfront. Veruschka's conviction that *cumbia* had been born from the river, that it was the mother of all rhythms, seemed completely consistent with what Carlos had told us. What irked Martín, as he quietly explained, was her insistence that its roots could be traced exclusively to the indigenous people. Such an assertion, he maintained, is less a scholarly conclusion than a reflection of race and class, as if a conscious attempt to expunge from history the contributions of those of African descent. Indisputably, there are strong indigenous elements in *cumbia*, musical instruments, for example, like the *caña de millo* or the *gaita*, which clearly originated with the Chimila and Pocabuy. But the glory of the genre, as Martín saw it, was its inclusivity, the way it distills multitudes, including most assuredly the rhythms and voices of the *palenques*.

"Even José Barros had no idea how *cumbia* came into being," Martín said. "And for him, it really didn't matter. He said words were pointless, that whatever *cumbia* was, it could not be explained in words. It was something that you feel, that you live through. He's quoted as saying that *cumbia* gave him strength when he felt defeated, that it allowed him, when he had nothing, to forget that he was hungry. *Cumbia* is the body, the river, the totality of the Colombian experience—today, yesterday, and tomorrow. It's what brings us together, which is why it's so important that we never speak of it in ways that might pull us apart."

In the morning, we left town early, heading by road northeast to the Ciénaga de Zapatosa, Colombia's greatest expanse of fresh water, a vast natural reservoir of more than 1,000 million cubic yards of water spread across 115 square miles. In times of drought, and through the long season of the rains, this wetland determines the mood of the entire basin, regulating the ebb and flow of all the myriad of affluents that flow into the Magdalena and the lower reaches of the Río Cesar.

Though wondrous, hydrology was clearly the last thing on Martín's mind as we roared down the dusty track, with Xandra at the wheel and the speakers pounding with the music of José Barros. Carlos's classic cover of "La Piragua." The poetry of "El Pescador," which tells of a simple fisherman who speaks with the moon and finds love in the sand, along beaches that echo in their discretion the innumerable silences of the stars. Songs of joy and heartbreak. The plaintive cries of yearning in "Violencia," which is less a song than a curse, a rabid condemnation of all those who would steal from children their most precious birthright, the chance to live in a world at peace.

As a scholar, Martín makes his case for the importance of *tambora*, clearly a genre that historically has been underappreciated. But as a lover of words, an avatar of all musical sounds, he can't help but herald the beauty of every one of Barros's songs, each a message of truth, passion, and hope unleashed upon the world through the heartbeat of *cumbia*. By the time we reached the outskirts of Chimichagua, a small port, the gateway to the great *ciénaga*, Martín had completely lost track of his vehemence. He gently conceded that while the rhythm and tempo of *tambora* are faster, and *cumbia* features a wider range of instruments, and dancers of *cumbia* rival butterflies in their flamboyance, the essence of the two musical forms is, in fact, quite similar. As we stepped onto the pier that reaches out over the shimmering surface of the Zapatosa, Martín acknowledged that, at the end of the day, *"Bailar cumbia es bailar tambora más lento y con velas."* To dance *cumbia* is to dance *tambora*, only slower and with candles.

Inspired by the life of the *ribereños*, José Barros simply wrote of what he saw, using syllables as notes, making it almost impossible to translate his lyrics because each of his words is itself a musical score. "La Piragua," perhaps his most famous song, is on the surface a simple narrative, a tale of a canoe owned by a merchant, Guillermo Cubillos, that sails down the Río Cesar in the face of a violent storm, its cargo guarded by a notorious man, Pedro Albundia, who leads crew and vessel to salvation on what Barros celebrates as the "beaches of love at Chimichagua." Most Colombians—including, quite understandably, his daughter Veruschka—have been content to leave it at that. A song celebrated as an anthem, sanitized by selective memory, with its genesis being the innocent misadventures of a young Benito and his friends as they rode the canoe and pinched from its cargo whatever food could be had: bananas, pineapples, mangoes, and cane.

But there is a deeper story, one that the poetry and precision of José Barros's lyrics anticipate:

> *Capoteando el vendaval se estremecía,*
> *e impasible desafiaba la tormenta*
> *y un ejército de estrellas la seguía*
> *tachonándola de luz y de leyenda*

The canoe does not just endure the storm, it confronts the wind, much as a *torero* greets, for the first time, a fearsome yet glorious bull, with grace, honor, and respect. Overhead an army of stars, imbued with "light and legend," bear witness to what surely will be a dance of death.

Doce bogas con la piel color majagua
y con ellas el temible Pedro Albundia
en las noches a los remos le arrancaban
un melódico rugir de hermosa cumbia

Twelve *bogas* the color of copper make music with their paddles, slapping and pounding the water in rhythm with the most beautiful of *cumbias*. With them sits Pedro Albundia, a man with as dark and murderous a past as any of those who have stained the legacy of Colombia through all the terrible years of violence. "La Piragua," according to our old friend Alonso Restrepo, a veteran of so many years with the Naviera Colombiana, was inspired by actual events; Restrepo first heard about them during a radio interview with Lucho Bermúdez, one of José Barros's closest friends.

Guillermo Cubillos was a historical figure, a merchant from Boyacá with a transportation business that featured an enormous canoe capable of carrying all manner of goods, from bushels of rice to stand-up pianos. Harassed by thieves on the Zapatosa, with no relief or protection to be had from the police or army, he set out to hire private guards, fighters known as *peinilleros*, masters of the thirty-three recognized techniques of machete combat, a traditional martial art featuring a specialized blade, thin, long, and lethal. Traveling first to Barranquilla, then upriver to the Cauca, Cubillos finally found his man in Santa Fe de Antioquia, Pedro Albundia, the best of five brothers, all experts with a blade. They returned together to El Banco, and Cubillos posted Albundia as guard on his *piragua*. On their fifth trip to Chimichagua, they were assaulted by two smaller canoes. In the darkness, nothing could be seen. Then the *bogas* heard several loud splashes as Pedro dispatched the robbers one by one, leaving their shredded bodies to the caimans. The incident secured his reputation, even as it ultimately inspired a song about a beach of love where today sleeps a canoe, and all memories of violence lie buried in the sand. What endures is the river, and the courage of the men and women who survived and know it best.

. . .

On the pier at Chimichagua, Martín introduced us to a friend, Héctor Rapalino, a young man of perhaps thirty. In 2012, just as the conflict began to wane, Héctor founded Hijos del Folclor, Sons of Folclor, a nonprofit that to this day serves as a bridge between children and elders, with the goal of celebrating the maestros and ensuring that the musical traditions of *tambora* are sown in the hearts of the young. Héctor, as we learned, thinks of music as a seed, a universal language with a range of dialects. His father, a schoolteacher, played *cumbia*. An older brother became a master of bagpipes. Héctor and his three other brothers, by contrast, were drawn to *tambora*. Like so many of his generation in Colombia, Héctor yearns to move on, which for him means using music as a vehicle for peace.

"We should not blame anyone," he said, "for we are all guilty of something. We can't arm ourselves with guns; we must arm ourselves with our voices, our drums, and our dances. That's how we will make a new country."

At the moment, Héctor explained proudly, Hijos del Folclor is working with forty children, aged five to sixteen, many of them orphans, victims of the conflict. We passed from the waterfront to the gym of a local school where Héctor had arranged a small performance: three beautiful singers, all sisters, with the boys on the drums. The music was vibrant, hypnotic, and powerfully alive. Their voices soared as if laying claim to a rightful spot at the top of the pop charts in any market in the world. Equally moving was the way these teenagers spoke of their music, describing it as the rhythm of the land, the vital link between people, culture, and the Río Magdalena, which they described as the fountain of life, the inspiration of every song, the soul of every dream.

Yuliet Patricia Villarreal Ramos, just sixteen, goes to the river whenever she is sad, for the water is always quiet, and in its silence she finds clarity, even as it carries away all of her fears. Estefanía Villarreal, even younger at fifteen, says that the river is perfect, though a time may come when it simply disappears, taking away all that is alive and well along its shores. She can let go of her fears only when she is playing, for the drum is life and when she sings *tambora* she feels as if being lifted up by an angel into another world. José Carlos García Torres, fourteen, says very simply that the drum is joy and the river is joy, which is why so many songs name the Magdalena. At nineteen, José Enrique Pineda Cantillo is the oldest of the players. If the river is indeed the source of life, he suggests, surely it is time to rescue it from oblivion. Music is the way, with each song sending a message that the contamination and pollution must stop, if the people, the nation, and the river are to have any real chance of being reborn.

The following day, Martín cranked up his musical tour. We set out before dawn, catching one of the first *chalupas* to leave the docks. Getting aboard was a comical series of contortions as even Xandra struggled to squeeze past three market women who had taken possession of the front seats, sealing off all access to the rear. Happily, they were as jolly as they were corpulent; each roared with laughter as I went in through a side window only to end up splayed across their laps. The ice was broken, and from that moment on the passengers seemed as family, all delighted to be sharing the promise of a new day. With the canopy low and open to the wind, and the gunwales riding just inches above the waterline, the water taxi roared downstream, the driver completely unfazed by all the driftwood in the stream, deadheads that, if hit, could readily sever the motor at the shaft, as had occurred to that *chalupa* at San Pedro on the night Juan, Xandra, and I had tried to run the river from Puerto Wilches to Simití.

Martín sat alone, content as a cat. Along the shore, wading in the shallows and darting in and out of the tall grass were sandpipers and snipes, herons, egrets, and jacanas—all the birds, he later noted, that fly through the imagination of Maestro Ángel María Villafañe, inspiring his art, lending their sounds to his music.

We reached Barranco de Loba in midmorning, disembarked to a chorus of goodwill, and even before the *chalupa* was out of sight, three underpowered scooters, or *mototaxis*, appeared to whisk us through a warren of dusty tracks to the home and personal museum of Maestro Villafañe. The great man met us at a doorway flanked by wooden carvings of the saints. An umbrella hung suspended over the Virgen de la Candelaria, guardian of the Magdalena. Bright red lettering on the whitewash welcomed everyone to a place of *"Paz y Cultura,"* peace and culture.

Thin and fit, dressed in a red T-shirt and neatly creased white trousers, with a straw hat tilted at a rakish angle, Maestro Villafañe, at eighty-five, is the kind of man who pays little notice to attire yet appears handsome in whatever he wears. He greeted us warmly.

"The river has a magic that leads always to love."

These were his first words. I glanced at Xandra, knowing that we were in for a magical day.

Maestro Villafañe brought us into the cool recesses of his sanctuary, a series of small windowless rooms that led to a patio at the back of the house. As our eyes adjusted to the dim light, the floor, ceiling, and every wall came alive with a fantastic assembly of figures fully worthy of Hieronymus Bosch. Crafted from *totumo* wood, rock, bone, and mud, and inspired by the maestro's love of the river, every sculpture had a story to tell. A drunk fisherman holding two *bocachicos* and a bottle of rum. An enchanted forest full of riparian life—*caimanes, tigrillos*, and birds. *Bogas* working their canoes. Dangling from the ceiling was a school of *bagre*, an iconic Magdalena fish today facing extinction. Every work of art served as a living metaphor; each played a role in the pageant play that was the story of Villafañe's life. One piece showed a man leaving his home, only to be followed on the river by a hungry caiman. He heads for land, only to be met by a jaguar. He climbs a tree, only to come face-to-face with a deadly poisonous snake.

"What can this poor fellow do?" asked Maestro Villafañe. The answer to the riddle, he explained, is the trajectory that all men must follow to survive, as he put it, "this adventure we call life." A path of salvation that leads always to the eternal savior. The Virgen de la Candelaria, patron and protector, was the answer to all prayers. She appears in some manifestation, he acknowledged, in his every work of art, the inspiration for his every creative endeavor.

Music and dance came to him as a child. A restless lad, he was finished with school by the second grade, drawn instead to the rhythms, songs, and movements of the river. He learned to play guitar, violin, accordion, and just about any object or instrument that could produce sound. At five, he could sing with an authority and depth of emotion that belied his age. At eight, he became a professional dancer and was soon performing *faros* and *coyongos* at Carnaval and all the many festivals that brought the year alive in small towns up and down the Magdalena. He especially loved *rancheras*, the cowboy music of Mexico, and was a fanatical fan of Antonio Aguilar, "El Charro de México," whose 150 albums and 167 films influenced a generation of Latin artists. As his musical repertoire expanded, a young Villafañe became a voice for hire, dispatched into the streets of Barranco de Loba as a proxy by tone-deaf suitors keen to impress young girls with a serenade.

Living within reach of El Banco and the Río Cesar, Villafañe naturally embraced *vallenato*, and at twenty, he formed his first professional group, Los Nativos del Sur, "The Natives of the South." Before long, he was traveling the world, performing in France, Hungary, Switzerland, and Czechoslovakia. His visits to Brazil inspired his love of African masks, an aesthetic that to this day informs the elaborate costumes he creates for the local children to wear during the great processions of Holy Week. As his national and international reputation grew, Barranco de Loba enveloped him with love, celebrating his birthday as if a civic holiday, with a High Mass of gratitude and a public chorus of songs and serenades. In time, Colombia would recognize him as being a *patrimonio vivo*, a living national treasure. This singular honor includes a monthly salary for life, a stipend that allows him to devote all of his time and energy to his life's mission: keeping alive the musical traditions and passing along the heritage to new generations of players.

When Maestro Villafañe speaks of the four "airs" of *tambora*, he is referring not just to four rhythms but, as he puts it, to four distinct gifts of God. According to Martín, Villafañe truly believes that the cadence of the drums expresses the actual voices of the divine. God's eternal presence informs every musical note and renders every song sacred. As for proof of God's existence, one need look no farther than the river itself. Everyone knows that the Magdalena used to flow from El Banco past the old colonial town of Mompox, and beyond to Barranquilla and the sea. Barranco de Loba and all the many ports along the Brazo de Loba were for generations isolated in the shallows of side channels and sloughs, with no means of transporting goods and no easy access to the coast. But then God decided that the river should abandon Mompox and all its sinful history of gold, greed, and intrigue and flow instead through the thirsty and innocent settlements of the Brazo de Loba, before returning to its original path to the ocean. As Mompox withered, Magangué, not thirty miles to the west, became the new commercial and transportation hub. This was a mixed blessing to be sure, for the port would always be remembered as the place where the *David Arango* went up in flames, in a fire sparked by a hot iron improperly stowed by an impatient passenger keen to reach the captain's dinner. An era of river travel, infused to this day with romance and nostalgia, came to an end, and all for the sake of a neatly pressed blouse.

It was obvious to Maestro Villafañe that none of this had been the work of men. Not the loss of the *David Arango*, and most assuredly not the reconfiguration of the Río Magdalena. Only God could have done such deeds, bringing such sorrow to a nation, and yet such blessings to Barranco de Loba. And surely, if God had chosen to infuse the Magdalena with his light and power, calming the waters, redirecting the flow, then every drop of the river was no less sacred than the holy waters of the church, blessed by the hands of mere mortals, earthly surrogates of the divine. The Río Magdalena, by contrast, had demonstrably been sanctified by God himself.

"This is why," Maestro Villafañe said, "we have a duty to protect the Madre Magdalena. Bring it back to life. We are all of the river, dependent on its bounty, living as amphibian creatures, just like the birds and fish, the caimans and manatees. To poison the river is to poison ourselves. We cannot survive without her. She is the source and fountain of our culture, the origin of all our songs, the inspiration of every rhythm. The drum is the river's voice. The songs of the *guacharacas* and *gallinetas* are her melodies. Like the birds, I sing for the fishermen, but also for the fish. Without the river, we would all be nothing."

As we moved out onto the patio and into the hot sun, everything Maestro Villafañe had told us came alive through music. The sound of the drums drew men and women, children of all ages, seemingly from every corner of the town. The maestro wrapped his shoulders in a small Colombian flag; a *mochila* decorated with the same national colors hung from his left shoulder. Women from the neighborhood appeared, each more lovely than the last, with beautiful dark hair pulled back and adorned with flowers, all wearing long, flowing dresses as colorful and luminous as the sun. Boys and girls scarcely old enough to walk moved boldly to the beat. Teenagers hung on the maestro's every phrase, ready to echo his passion and cadence in the call and response that is the essence of *tambora*. Our new friend Martín knew every song; without a word being said, he slipped into the role of a drummer, taking his place beside the others, revealing himself to be, among his many gifts, a true master of rhythm. All around us, men and women spun in a whirlwind of joy.

At the center of everything was Maestro Villafañe. He began and carried each song. His energy infused every movement with passion. His eyes sparkled with life and love. As more and more people arrived, and the number of players and instruments multiplied, the strength of his voice only grew. He became the sound of thunder. He sang with the grace of the wind. His body shook and shuddered as if quivering in the wake of the very landslides, earthquakes, and volcanic eruptions that had forged the topography of his homeland. With sweat staining his shirt, causing the flag around his neck to cling to his skin, he seemed in the moment, as Xandra would later remark, to be not only the cultural heart of his community but the very personification of his nation, a living symbol of all that makes Colombia great.

When time came for us to leave, reluctantly to be sure, driven only by the demands of Martín's carefully planned agenda, one of the young dancers, Alexis Judith Arroyo, a lovely girl of seventeen, approached Xandra. She expressed an immense gratitude for what this remarkable teacher and mentor, this living legend, had done for the children of a town and community that a lesser man, touched by similar fame, might well have abandoned. Her words seemed to speak for all.

"I came to him when I was eight," she explained. "I didn't know how to dance. I could grab my skirt and move it but nothing more. Now I owe my life to *tambora*. He taught me, and thanks to him

I'm going to university, the first of my family to do so, and I'm studying folklore and culture. Maestro Villafañe is more than everything to me."

The elation we felt as we left Barranco de Loba lasted only as long as it took to tumble down to the river, catch a *chalupa*, cross the Magdalena, and, clinging to the waists of a new set of teenage drivers, find our way by *mototaxi* to Hatillo de Loba, the home of another of Martín's mentors and good friends, Gumercindo Palencia. A widely heralded singer, songwriter, and *tambora* master, Gumercindo, like Maestro Villafañe, has achieved considerable fame. This was clearly evident in the dozens of colorful posters decorating the walls of his modest house, all promoting his appearances at the scores of regional and national festivals that have burst forth in the wake of the resurgence of *tambora*.

Yet despite his popular success, Gumercindo, like many artists, survives on the edge, struggling to make ends meet. Kind and generous, warm and open to his many musician friends, he nevertheless lives alone, and there are times, he readily admits, when he lacks the will to carry on. Perhaps, as Martín later suggested, we simply caught him on a bad day, but rarely have I known a Colombian to indulge in such despair, openly and in front of strangers, as if cast adrift in a miasma of existential misery and helplessness so powerful as to overwhelm pride. His music, perhaps not surprisingly, echoes his dark moods, suggesting that his depression, so evident as we spoke, was less ephemeral than a real affliction. His lyrics speak of rivers of grief, forgotten and abandoned, with corpses kept afloat by vultures, mountains that burn as the sun scores the sky and looks down on the homeless as they walk alone in sorrow, seeking shelter in settlements shattered by war.

Even Martín felt relieved as we left Gumercindo to his misfortune and made our way back along the river to the next stop, Juana Sánchez, a settlement once famous as the source of the very finest *tinajas*, the great ceramic vessels in which all Colombians stored their drinking water before the advent of refrigeration. Today it is a sleepy town, and only the elderly can recall a time when the riverfront was dense with transports, the many boats and rafts that carried the production of dozens of small factories and family-owned workshops to markets all along the Magdalena.

Martín introduced us to another of his friends, Alonso Poveda, whose family had been among the pioneers of the *tinaja* trade. Alonso's grandfather, having learned the business in Barranquilla, trained by craftsmen from Mompox, arrived in Juana Sánchez with little more than ambition and hope. But in time, he took over a barren parcel of land that nobody wanted and slowly built up a business, a cottage industry of hand-built kilns and furnaces all serviced by an ingenious network of cooling pipes and vents, the remnants of which we admired as Alonso led us through what remained of his grandfather's dream, a few broken-down structures on the outskirts of town.

When we returned to Alonso's home in the center of Juana Sánchez, the conversation turned, as it often does in Colombia, to the challenges of peace. Alonso, like many small businessmen, remains skeptical, firmly opposed to any concessions being offered to those responsible for the very violence that had torn the nation apart. As he made his argument, I noticed for the first time that an older woman had been standing alone in the far corner of the room, still as a stone. When Alonso fell silent, she began to speak, with a voice that was both gentle and firm.

"Peace is possible," she declared, as if redefining history. "My name is Elizabeth Pérez. I am sixty-five, the mother of eleven, grandmother to twenty-two. One of my children died. Another was cruelly taken from me. Gualberto disappeared sixteen years ago. He was last seen at a checkpoint in Maicao. I've not heard from him in all this time. But I know he still lives. Now with the peace talks, he will be coming home, God willing."

In truth, as everyone in that room realized, her son almost certainly had been lost, one of the many tens of thousands to have vanished in the violence. Still, in standing for peace, this brave mother laid claim to hope, even while affirming both her dignity and her faith.

"Peace is the only solution," she continued, "the only solution to this whole mess. One has to forgive. Forgiveness is the only way out. Someday I will know about my son, and that's why I say that peace is beautiful. Peace alone is beautiful."

Night was coming on, and we still faced a long run by motorcycle back along the waterfront trails to El Banco. Martín was keen to get going before the sun was completely lost. As he paid for our drinks, Xandra and I slipped out Alonso's door with Elizabeth, and together we posed in the golden light for one of the very few selfies I will ever cherish.

With El Banco as our base, we fell into a lovely rhythm, heading out each morning on yet another musical adventure and returning at night as a waning moon softened the shadows on the waterfront. From the steps overlooking the river, one had only to spin the compass to find yet another community devoted to *tambora*, another group, another iteration of a creative legacy that has nurtured the ambitions and inspired the dreams of young musicians in towns and settlements throughout the entire Momposina Depression. Martín knew all of them, and thanks to his reputation and generosity, Xandra and I floated on a wave of goodwill, even as our new friend curated each day with that ineffable Colombian flair that turns work into play, and play, more often than not, into something unexpectedly revelatory, meaningful, and true.

From the small port of La Gloria, just upriver from El Banco, we hired a boat, which in an hour reached a small affluent that led to a landing and a narrow track that traveled overland some distance to Arenal. An old *palenque*, this settlement was originally established by slaves who had fled the mines of San Martín de Loba. Nestled at the base of hills, flanked by ravines and wetlands, surrounded by forests with only limited road access, the town to this day is defined by its isolation; a protective cloak has preserved *tambora* in what Martín maintains is its purest and most essential form. There are only three rhythms, he noted—*guacherna*, *tuna*, and *tambora*. And, as in Africa, the drums are loose and the vocals raw, coarse, and loud.

Awaiting us was Alegría de Arenal, a group that had been around for thirty years. Its lead singer, the *cantaora* Águeda Pacheco, had a truly sublime voice, with a range that ran through the octaves, allowing her to touch notes that, according to Martín, no one in the entire region could even dream of caressing. From the moment she heard Águeda sing, Xandra referred to her as simply "La Voz del Río," the voice of the river, much to the delight of all. Joy—*alegría*—was the name of their band and the title of their most popular tune, but it was also the way they lived, inspired by their music, with every song performed as if an ode to bliss. *Cariño* was their fuel. The members were all family, neighbors, or friends. Among the drummers were an accountant, a psychologist, two teachers, a plumber, a business administrator, and a communications expert. Sons, daughters, nephews, and nieces made up the dancers and filled the chorus.

As Alegría de Arenal had prospered, so too had Arenal. A settlement that within memory had been a warren of thatched huts with mud walls smeared and secured by dung is today a small but thriving town with a full range of modern services: paved streets and electricity, a sewage system, sanitation, water, and gas. In the schools, cultural traditions are proudly celebrated. Even as families look to the future, Águeda explained, they honor the past. When a person dies, for example, they sing, and when a child is born, they cry. Many people, she acknowledged, find this strange, but it's their way of always remembering what their ancestors endured as slaves in a haunted era when life implied suffering, and death but a gentle rest in the peace of God.

From Arenal, we returned to La Gloria, chasing, as always, the fading light even as a red sun infused the western sky. The next morning, the road from El Banco to Mompox took us to Tierra Firme, where we were warmly received by another family-based group, Los Hijos de Chandé, the Sons of Chandé, a musical school founded by Gilberto Márquez. As a teacher, he brings together elderly maestros with children as young as two and three, all with the certain knowledge that the rhythms of *tambora* will fire even a toddler's heart. The school promotes and celebrates, as Gilberto told us, a unique modality, with each of the four main rhythms having further divisions, as in *Chandé Pasiao*, *Chandé Jalao*, and *Chandé Brincao*. When I looked to Martín for a deeper explanation, or at least one that I had a hope of understanding, he turned to an eight-year-old boy, one of

Gilberto's prize students, and asked him to demonstrate. Without hesitation, the lad straddled a small drum and effortlessly progressed through every musical rhythm and beat, his hands and fingers just a blur as they tapped and pounded the instrument.

Before we left, Gilberto's wife, Edilma, brought out a large book in which she had faithfully transcribed the lyrics of all his songs. She sat down on a log, surrounded on all sides by her children, a boy of three, his older sister, a girl of seven holding in her arms their infant brother, another daughter, perhaps ten, clasping a pair of maracas, her two older sisters, both teenagers, moving still to the rhythm of the beat even as they leaned into the scrum to see what their mother was doing. The drummers fell silent. Flipping through the pages, pausing from time to time to relish a verse, Edilma finally settled on one of her favorite songs, a simple yet endearing tale of a market girl on her own in Mompox, selling *bollos de mazorca*, corn tamales made from an ancient recipe known only in Tierra Firme. As she read aloud, the story came alive. The plight of the girl in the song could well have been the fate of her own daughters or any young woman cast adrift, alone and hungry, scratching the streets of an unknown city, just trying to stay alive.

Each of Gilberto's songs had a cinematic quality. "Voices of Pity and Hope," which Edilma read next, recalls a time when fishermen worked together, corralling their canoes to trap *bocachicos* before casting their *atarrayas*—a tradition lost and forgotten in a world where men now work alone, using gill nets that indiscriminately sweep the river of all life. "Cumbia Ribereña" recounts Gilberto's dialogue with the Magdalena during all the years of violence, when the river, though stained with blood, refused to die. In "Canto al Río," Gilberto invokes the Magdalena more hopefully as the "fountain of life, his reason for being."

Every song told a story of the Magdalena; each spoke of the riparian life that had long served as a muse for Gilberto and all of his family. *Palo prieto* and *totumo* trees growing along the banks, branches aflutter with birds, *caracolís* and *chabarrís*, while on the shore *morrocoy* turtles and grey herons as still as driftwood in the sand.

"The river is in the music," Edilma said as she carefully passed the book of lyrics to Xandra, "and the music is in the river."

Later that same day, just outside Mompox, Martín introduced us to yet another *tambora* maestro, Samuel Mármol, known to all as Abundio. If Gilberto Márquez and his young players had an infectious lightness of being, Abundio, by contrast, carried the burden of a lifetime of small disappointments, nearly all related to what he described as the slow death of the Río Magdalena. His grandmother had died at 106, a singer who pounded a cooking pot for percussion and performed for anyone who could spare a bottle of rum. His father was a comedian, a "dancing devil in a time when everything was beautiful." Abundio's weakness is nostalgia. He dwells in a state of longing for a world that never was, or at least never again will be, when the river was alive, and the birds—*coyongos, pisingos,* and *pato yuyos*—hovered over the water waiting to snatch fish as they leapt and flashed in the sun. Today, as he sees it, the glory of the Magdalena survives only in music, in the songs and the dances that he and his group perform each year on the streets of Barranquilla during Carnaval. They are the custodians of tradition, Abundio declared proudly, and with every movement and note they remember the river of his youth, and a time when forests blanketed the valley, great flocks darkened the sky, and children in every settlement drank from the Magdalena without worry or fear.

As we left Abundio to his memories, Xandra expressed how much she admired his band of players, men and women who each year manage to find the resources—food, money, and transport—to bring their creative passions to El Carnaval de Barranquilla, Colombia's greatest stage, as if personally responsible for preserving a nation's deepest cultural memories. I recalled something Carlos Vives had told us that day on the river: All the music of the Magdalena eventually floats downstream to Barranquilla, where it is judged, celebrated, filtered, and perfected before being sent out into the world.

"The river has always been the inspiration," Martín remarked. "The music of Carnaval is the music of the Magdalena. The city is like a vortex, a whirlpool spinning with all the rhythms, melodies, colors, creeds, passions, and desires of the entire country, all of it made possible by the river. This is what makes Carnaval and Barranquilla so important. You really can't think of one without the other.

Just as a river, any river, replenishes its floodplain with nutrients, the Río Magdalena refreshes Colombian culture, El Carnaval de Barranquilla in particular, with new musical forms, as new generations of *ribereños* reinvent sound and reimagine choreography in towns running the entire length of the drainage. And the river doesn't just introduce or facilitate the diffusion of new styles and genres; it serves as the actual geographical corridor that carries both musicians and their music to the coast and, from there, to the world. José Barros. Lucho Bermúdez. Maestro Villafañe, for that matter."

Among the many characters carried to fame by the river was a particular favorite of Martin's, an old man of uncertain age who claimed to have traveled the entire world, equipped with nothing but a magical toothpick. We met him one morning en route to Mompox, when Martín, quite in defiance of his musical loyalties, insisted on a stop in Botón de Leiva, a small town that, along with Gamal, is one of just two islands of *cumbia* in the sea of *tambora* that surrounds El Banco. Xandra teased him about entering enemy territory. Martín smiled and promised that it would be worth the sacrifice, for the man waiting for us was none other than Aurelio "Yeyo" Fernández, acknowledged by all as the absolute master of the *caña de millo*, perhaps the finest player, or *cañamillero*, in all of Colombia. Crafted from carrizo cane or the stalks of millet and wild grasses, the *caña de millo* is a small flute, open at both ends, with four finger holes and a vibrating reed or tongue cut from the same material as the tube itself. Though simple in appearance, it is the very voice of *cumbia*, the sound that reaches back to the Chimila and Pocabuy, the one instrument that can mimic the wind and speak the language of birds.

"I am the warrior who never once had to go to war," Yeyo declared, even as we gathered around him in a circle of chairs on the dirt patio behind his modest home. An arbor of tree branches provided shade. Chickens darted in and out of his house, which was no more than a wall of wooden poles bound together with lashings of bark and hemp. The roof was thatch. The only furniture was a wooden bench and the chairs we sat in. Yeyo wore a loose cotton shirt, unbuttoned to the chest, and a straw hat too small for his head; it perched birdlike atop a head of hair that would have been the envy of men half his age. His lovely wife, Dominga, sat at his side, snapping open *tamarindo* pods she had just gathered from a tree in their garden. The fruit was delicious, tart, tangy, and sweet. Dominga smiled with delight as Xandra, with her permission, scavenged the seeds so that she could take them back to her farm in Antioquia to plant alongside her beans.

"With this little stick, I traveled the world," Yeyo said, holding aloft his flute. *"Con este palito yo he recorrido el mundo."*

Yeyo and his band had played with Totó la Momposina in El Carnaval de Barranquilla for more than two decades, twenty-two gigs altogether, performances that had, in fact, led to any number of national and international tours, including a seven-month European jaunt that had brought them to Russia, Holland, Poland, Germany, and Switzerland. But, as was the case with Maestro Villafañe, fame meant nothing to him, and all the time he couldn't wait to return home to his garden in Botón de Leiva. Without the sound of birds, there was a risk that his *caña de millo* might fall silent. And not just any bird. He had a special fondness for the *toche de agua*, a soulful creature that sang every dawn in the high branches of the mango tree that hovered over his house. Just thinking of the bird brought tears to his eyes as he recalled the day, many years ago, when he had decided to try to imitate its sound with his flute. Before long, they could communicate, strange as that may seem. The result was one of his most beautiful songs, "Mañanita de Diciembre," a simple story about the gifts of nature brought to a man through the grace of a bird.

A Great Republic of Nature

As much as Martín feels at home in El Banco, with its clapboard façades and chaotic charm, he looks upon Mompox as a place for tourists, a remnant of the past, a colonial settlement heralded by UNESCO for having preserved its architectural core as if in open defiance of history, when, as every Colombian knows, the city remained untouched precisely because it was bypassed and largely forgotten by history. Martín likens it to a theatrical stage set, dramatic and beautiful but so disconnected from the pulse of the region that its preferred form of music, aside from what's played in the barrios, is modern jazz. He loves jazz, as he loves all music, but not when performed by a host of international stars flown in at great expense for a festival that attracts only the wealthy elite, men and women with the scent of gardenias who drop in from Bogotá, New York, and Miami and stay just long enough to hear the ringing of the church bells, endure a torrid afternoon on the Albarrada promenade, and relax for an evening over drinks at the upscale bars that line the famous plazas of the city. Needless to say, as Xandra and I made plans for Mompox, Martín was content to stay behind in El Banco, which was probably a good thing, though it was once again heart-wrenching to say good-bye to someone who had given us so much, and for whom we had, in such a short time, developed such affection.

Truth be told, Mompox is one of Latin America's great treasures, less a colonial settlement captured in time, as Martín implied, than a living city still dressed in the elegance of the past. Spread out along the waterfront, on an island surrounded by a sea of wetlands, it has a beguiling majesty that seems, on first impression, almost otherworldly. García Márquez captured this mysterious allure when he described Mompox as "a place to dream about, a place that might not exist at all."

Xandra and I first came upon the city from the water, much as Alexander von Humboldt did in 1801. He described a river of jewel-like islands, some floating forests, others covered by thickets of delicate willows, and still others open meadows, with reeds and wild grasses swaying in the breeze. The shores at the time were thick with *chingalé* palms, calliandras, and wild figs, ficus trees with broad, spreading branches draped in lianas and festooned with epiphytic bromeliads, aroids, and orchids. High above the riverbank, the branches of massive ceiba, *cantagallo*, and *caracolí* trees met and intertwined to form a dense canopy that the great naturalist described as a "carpet floating in the air," a layer of botanical life that all but blocked out the sun, leaving the forest floor a shaded garden of luscious herbs and heliconias, *platanillos*, and prayer plants, an impenetrable darkness that, as Humboldt wrote, "brings a sense of doom and dread to the soul."

The life of the river soon washed away this hint of despair. Along the shores, Humboldt reported families collecting turtle eggs by the thousands. He came upon fishermen with canoes weighted down to the point of danger with great hauls of *bagre, barbudo, nicuro, sardina, garlopa, bufeo, raya, temblone, machote*, and *doncella*. These local names meant little to him, but the morphology of the fish surely did. Each specimen was strange to his eye and thus, in all likelihood, a species new to science. Among the many novelties was the *mayupa*, a fish that defecates through its head, and the *mariapalito*, a spider that consumes its mate. The male embraces the female from behind. Once satiated, the female turns back to him with her massive eyes, clamps her teeth onto his body, and slowly devours the flesh, all the time perched as if in prayer, with her forelegs folded neatly before her. As for the birds and monkeys, snakes and insects, the giant snails and miniature frogs, poisonous to the touch and marked by all the colors of the rainbow, there was little for Humboldt to do but collect and preserve, document and draw, all with the hope that his scientific supplies, so seemingly ample when he set out, and now so limited in the face of such biological abundance, might last long enough for him to reach Bogotá, where he might lean on Mutis for help.

To be sure, the Mompox that greeted us was not the city that had welcomed Humboldt. The forests are long gone—the result of an ecological transformation that began in the early years of the colony when haciendas supporting as many as sixteen thousand head of cattle provided much of the wealth of the settlement. Wildlife sightings today are limited to the odd bewildered caiman that stumbles ashore, sending children into a panic of glee as they tumble and dive into the river from the height of the promenade that runs the length of the waterfront. To support their families, fishermen increasingly turn to the construction business, using their canoes to reach low points in the river, where by hand they dredge sand, and then return to shore, where in a series of relays they manage to shovel their loads up the escarpment to be loaded into trucks and taken to building sites throughout the city. There are pigeons and parrots in the plazas, and ravens and vultures in the steeples of every church. But many of the birds that enchanted Humboldt—*iguazas, guacharacas, chavarríes,* and *agamíes*—are as rare as jaguars and manatees, anacondas and angels.

Even in Humboldt's day, Mompox, long a symbol of wealth and prosperity, was in the throes of a commercial decline from which it would never recover. It had been established in 1537, in the wake of Pedro de Heredia's victory over Mampó, chief of the Simbay, a Carib-speaking people who controlled the land where the modern city sits today. Like many of the settlements that came into being at that time—a wave of exploration that saw the founding of Barrancabermeja and Cali in 1536, Popayán in 1537, Tunja in 1539, and Santa Fe de Antioquia in 1541—Mompox in its early years struggled to survive. For those accustomed to the pleasures of Spain— the olive groves and the wheat fields of Andalucía, the orchards of Lérida, the gentle sea breezes flowing over the land at Valencia—the jungle location of the new settlement, said to be the hottest place in all the Indies, was not auspicious. The humidity and heat were difficult to bear. The immediate surroundings, both wetlands and woodland, were ominous and threatening. Decomposition, key to the health of tropical forests, was believed at the time to be the very source of pestilence, creating miasmas that rose out of vegetative rot to infect the unworthy and punish the sinful.

Mompox was sited mere feet above a river that was infested with crocodiles, creatures that in great numbers crawled ashore each night, coming so close to waterfront homes that, as Humboldt reported, "their unbearable musk-like scent penetrates all the rooms. There are times when one is sure the crocodile is in the next room, so strong is the stench." The local mosquitoes, which rose like clockwork from the water to darken the night sky, were capable, he noted, of penetrating the thickness of three layers of cotton trousers. The only sources of relief from the plague of insects and flies were cattle dung and turtle oil. Field hands slept as close to their heifers as they could manage. "Everyone on the Magdalena gets sick," Humboldt wrote, "but no matter the circumstances, one always feels sicker in Mompox."

Knowing death and disease as lifelong companions, enduring unimaginable trials and hardships, those who ransomed their lives to build Mompox ultimately sired a city that by 1770 was one of the richest in the Americas, with a population of seventy-one hundred at a time when Bogotá was home to just seventeen thousand. The key to its prosperity, at least initially, was less civic or commercial virtue than the vulnerability of a sister city destined to become the most coveted jewel of the Spanish Indies.

Cartagena had been founded in 1533, four years before Mompox, by the same Pedro de Heredia, a rogue and misfit who had escaped a triple-murder rap in Spain only to find refuge in a colony where killing, at least of natives, was a solemn duty. A villainous man with a good eye for geography, Heredia located the settlement along the shore of a wide, deep, and protected coastal bay. The site was ideally positioned, with close access to the mouth and lower reaches of the Río Magdalena, all the nearby islands of the Caribbean, and the sea-lanes that led west to the isthmus of Panama, the route over which moved, by mule, all the riches of Peru. Cartagena, from its inception, was to be the repository and transhipment point for the wealth of a continent, all the gold, silver, and precious stones looted from the Kingdoms of the Sun and the Moon destined for the royal coffers of Spain.

As stories of plunder spread, rumors of warehouses bulging with bullion, treasure chests brimming with jewels, Cartagena became the target of every brigand and buccaneer sailing in search of pillage along the length of the Spanish Main. An even greater threat, looming offshore, beyond the visible horizon, were the mercenary fleets of England, Holland, and France, envious European rivals whose own possessions in the New World produced little more than salt cod and tobacco, beaver pelts, timber, molasses, and rum. The first serious attack occurred within a decade, even before the city was fortified, as a French Huguenot, Roberto Baal, waltzed into town and only left once burdened with a hefty ransom. French raiders returned in 1551, the same year that a fire destroyed much of the settlement.

Undaunted, the Spaniards rebuilt the city in stone, even as their thoughts turned to battlements and bastions, fortress walls with racks of cannons capable of commanding the approaches to the harbor. The wave of construction was still underway when the French came again in 1559, pirates led by Martin Cote, who again escaped with a great treasure. The most notorious assault occurred in 1586 when Sir Francis Drake—a hero and a gentleman to his queen, a murderous pirate in the eyes of the world—sent ashore a thousand men, who stormed and sacked the city, leaving in their wake only ruins as they carried off gold and silver and virtually anything that could be lifted and moved, right down to the church bells and cannons.

Drake's raid, both devastating and humiliating, forced the Spaniards to get serious about security and defense. As they reimagined the city for a second time in less than forty years, the military engineers and architects incorporated into their plans sketches and designs for the massive fortifications and imposing perimeter walls that remain to this day emblematic of the city: bastions and bulwarks built by slaves and blessed by bishops with the names of the saints.

At a cost that challenged faith in avarice, the Spaniards, over time, transformed Cartagena into the most heavily defended redoubt in the Americas. This supreme effort and financial sacrifice only confirmed for their enemies the extent of the wealth in treasure moving through the city. Inevitably, the attacks continued. The infamous Henry Morgan was repulsed in 1668. Laurens de Graaf successfully blockaded the city in 1683, a cordon that was broken only when the Dutch pirates, having ransomed scores of hostages, set sail for the French colony of Saint-Domingue (now Haiti), all a great deal richer for their efforts. The worst came in 1697, when the French under the command of Barón de Pointis managed to overrun the battlements and seize control of all fortifications. Once again, the city endured the indignity of occupation and plunder.

Scarcely a decade later, during the War of the Spanish Succession, a naval battle off the coast at Cartagena left among its many casualties a sunken wreck, discovered only in 2015, with a cargo that reveals just what was at stake in these furious struggles for the city. At rest in the sand some two thousand feet below the surface lies the *San José*, a three-masted, sixty-four-gun galleon that was the flagship of the Spanish fleet until sunk by the British in 1708. Even as the ship engaged a mortal enemy on the open seas, it was weighted down with treasure: gold, silver, and emeralds that today remain buried on the ocean floor, as nations dispute claims and stakeholders squabble over ownership of a bounty said to be worth upwards of $17 billion. The *San José* was just one of hundreds of ships that set sail from Cartagena every year, each swollen with the loot of a stolen continent.

The allure of such wealth stirred many a mercenary heart, even as it moved nations to war. In 1741, Admiral Edward Vernon, with the full support of the British government, attacked Cartagena with some thirty thousand men and a fleet of 186 ships, fully a quarter of the English navy. In the last major assault on the city, the British were repulsed by a much smaller force, a mere six thousand defending the ramparts. They emerged with a rare victory in what had been for the Spanish Crown two centuries of costly conflict, and for the people, generations of torment and anxiety, with each day haunted by the possibility of yet another surprise attack, a threat that hovered over Cartagena like a shroud.

With war between England and Spain as constant as the seasons, and British tactics just piracy dressed up in a flag, many citizens of Cartagena looked to escape. For the poor, the indentured servants and slaves, options were few. But families of means and influence sought refuge in the hinterland, away from the coast and beyond the reach of the terror. Some who could endure the journey went to Bogotá. Most brought their wealth—and, better yet, their titles and lineages—to Mompox, a settlement that was ideally situated. It was sufficiently distant from the sea, yet close enough that merchants and traders, smugglers and speculators could maintain their networks, with the Río Magdalena serving as their conduit to the coast. In the early decades of the seventeenth century, the settlement flourished, becoming a sanctuary of trade and contraband, with ambitious men free to impose their own taxes and tariffs on anything that made its way up or down the river. Warehouses packed with goods—candles and wine destined for the growing settlements to the south, iron tools and fabrics heading to the mines, vast stores of cotton, tobacco, and cinchona bark awaiting export—became emblematic of the city.

The axis of trade connecting the upper Magdalena to Mompox and Mompox to the coast, so vital to the well-being of the colony and so lucrative to those in power, led one man to envision the impossible: an engineering challenge of truly pharaonic scale that promised to transform transportation on the lower reaches of the Magdalena and further enrich both Mompox and Cartagena. Don Pedro Zapata de Mendoza, then governor of the province of Cartagena, viewed the conquest of nature, the domestication of landscape, as a simple matter of will—strength and enterprise tempered by faith. In many ways, he was not unlike the modern engineers who seek constantly to improve the river, buoyed by the same unbridled confidence that leaves children befuddled when holes dug at a beach invariably fill with water and sand. The one key difference being that Zapata de Mendoza's plan, ambitious as it was, at least had a chance of success.

Cartagena at the time had no direct link to the Río Magdalena. All goods destined for the interior had to move over land by horse or mule, along a forty-mile track that ran east from the coast, passing between two great wetlands before turning southeast to Barranca del Rey, a small port on the Magdalena, known today as Calamar. Since the late sixteenth century, efforts had been made to exploit waterways linking the Ciénaga de Matuna with the Bahía de Barbacoas, on the coast, but only in 1650 did the Spaniards, led by Zapata de Mendoza, set out to survey a route for a practical canal that would allow transports, bypassing the river mouth, to proceed directly from the Bahía de Cartagena to navigable stretches of the lower Magdalena, located well above the estuary. Those supervising the survey work and, ultimately, the construction were the same military engineers and architects responsible for the battlements and fortifications of the city. Those who did the actual work, living and dying by the scores in wetlands infested with serpents and caimans, were some two thousand slaves and indentured laborers, *zambos* forcibly conscripted from every coastal settlement and plantation as far south and west as Tolú. Equipped only with machetes, axes, picks, hand shovels, and hoes, half-starved and driven by the whip, these cursed and tormented men in only four months excavated by hand an artificial channel that ran through forested swamps and formidable wetlands for well over a hundred miles.

The original dimensions of what became the Canal del Dique remain uncertain, for over the years the waterway underwent any number of modifications as governments well into the twentieth century worked to maintain and expand its capacity. That any transport corridor would warrant such attention nearly four hundred years after its construction is impressive, though, as always, its upkeep proved to be a daunting task. In times of drought, as the river falls, the Canal del Dique often runs dry. When the rains return to the headwaters, the inevitable seasonal floods can leave the channel so clogged with silt as to be impassable.

At Calamar, as the canal reaches the Río Magdalena, and even more so at its outlet on the Bahía de Cartagena, where freighters in the harbor and skyscrapers along the shore distort the scale, the Canal del Dique appears today, on first impression, a fairly modest channel, scarcely worthy of its storied history and reputation. Caramel in color, thick with sediments, in places as still and stagnant as a pond, it cuts a narrow swath across the coastal plain like a long-forgotten country road. Still, after nearly four centuries, the canal has indeed become a thing of beauty, a ribbon of slow curves and long straightaways fully integrated into its landscape, with the charm shared by all great engineering works that over time become embraced by the very vistas they set out to violate.

Not that the land is beautiful. For most of the distance between Cartagena and Calamar, the countryside is almost treasonous in its monotony: worn and dusty fields, low-lying and tortured by the sun, with cattle clustered along both banks, all seeking shelter beneath the few shade trees to have been spared the woodsman's ax. Aside from canoes and a few small skiffs, there's hardly a sign of commercial activity the entire length of the canal. The local fishermen and their families, the *vaqueros* and the priests are as threadbare as the land, spare with their thoughts, parsimonious with their words, having little to say about an ancient and moribund waterway along which they just happen to live.

Only once on the water, moving at high speed in a motorboat past one *municipio* after another—Arjona, Arroyohondo, Mahates, María la Baja, San Cristóbal, San Estanislao, Soplaviento, and Turbaná in Bolívar and, on the other side of the canal, Santa Lucía, Suan, Manatí, Repelón, and Luruaco, all in Atlántico—can one grasp what these two thousand men, laboring against their will, achieved *a pico y pala*, by pick and shovel. Distance alone reveals the magnitude of their task. Every stretch of the canal, each day of work, required the excavation by hand of tons upon tons of rock and dirt. The banks had to be reinforced with cut stones sourced from far beyond the wetlands and carried to the site by the same men who lined the bed of the canal with clay moistened by their own sweat and blood. Their agonies and sacrifice opened a window in Colombia's destiny, allowing Cartagena to flourish as the port city of the nation for well over two hundred years. The canal was their gift to a country still waiting to be born. Freedom was their legacy. The glory of the Canal del Dique is not to be found on the ground, among the physical remnants of a colonial canal. It lingers in the eternal spirits of those who built it. Like whispered messages reaching forward in time, they hover, awakening our memories to the truth, even as they imbue their creation, the entire length of the waterway, with an unexpected, even sublime, beauty.

Mompox has a way of slowing down the world, reducing the day to its most casual core, gestures and interludes choreographed only by the heat of the sun. At first light, with mist still hovering over the river, there is a flurry of activity as schoolchildren and shopkeepers, porters, boatmen, and builders take advantage of the cool and pleasant air. Along the waterfront, splintered shutters creak open to reveal shaded courtyards and private fountains, hidden gardens of fruit trees and orchids, calatheas and aroids. At every turn, one encounters echoes of Córdoba in the spring. Elderly couples sip their coffee, already at ease in the wicker rockers where they will spend most of the morning and, quite possibly, much of the day. Their postures suggest lifetimes of commitment, with no certainty that a meaningful word has been exchanged in years. Not that it matters. In Mompox, life is not grounded in time. Cars and trucks are banned from the roadway by the river. The odor on the waterfront is not of diesel and exhaust fumes, as in so many settlements along the Magdalena, but of citrus and plumeria blossoms, the fragrance of climbing roses and the intoxicating scent of *borracheros*, the ultimate tool of the shaman, but also the most enchanting of all ornamental plants, admired and respected by all Colombians.

Doorways along the façade of the promenade open to reveal a people at ease with their neighbors, families insulated from uncertainty by the sheer weight of their history. This, more than anything, distinguishes Mompox today from Cartagena. Both cities suffered in the nineteenth century. In 1849, a cholera epidemic killed two thousand *momposinos* in a season. The population of Cartagena, once the jewel of the Spanish realm, dropped from twenty-five thousand in 1810 to less than eight thousand in 1881. As Barranquilla grew to become the port city of the Río Magdalena, Cartagena's decline only continued. As those of wealth and influence abandoned the heart of the city, moving to new and trendy neighborhoods in Bocagrande, the colonial core entered a period of decay that was reversed only when affluent *bogotanos* discovered its considerable charms. Seeking holiday retreats on the coast, the *cachacos* picked up properties for a song, thus setting in motion the long process of renovation and revitalization that has made Cartagena internationally known as a tourism destination, the one city that foreigners still flocked to even at the height of Colombia's troubles. In Mompox, by contrast, the great families never left, and it is their fidelity to place that lends authenticity to the city.

Among those with deep roots were good friends of Xandra's family, Enrique and Isabel Cabrales, an elegant and generous couple living in retirement on the waterfront in one the most beautiful private homes in Mompox. Isabel, in particular, welcomed our morning visit as a rare opportunity to reminisce, going as far as to shatter protocol by launching into one delightful story after another before the maid even had a chance to bring us *tintos* and cake.

Isabel's memories were vivid and enchanting, and almost all of them recalled the river: the beautiful landscapes she knew as a child, the abundance of wildlife, the size of the enormous paddle wheels on the *vapores*, the distant nights on board the vessels when her nanny would tuck her into bed as her parents slipped away to dance under the moonlight, sometimes not returning until dawn.

"We were scheduled to take the *David Arango* on the very day of the fire," she said with a sigh, still wistful after so many years.

Keen to enliven the conversation before his wife slipped too deeply into nostalgia, Enrique shared a tale of two Germans, Adolfo Held and August Tichen, who arrived shortly after the Great War and purchased some fifty thousand acres of land along both sides of the Magdalena. Their dream was to drown all their memories of the war and create new lives as dairy farmers. In 1927, Tichen traveled to Hamburg to buy a Holstein cow. By chance, he ran into a zoo owner who persuaded him to try instead an Indian zebu, the ideal breed for a tropical climate. Tichen gambled on the man's word and returned with Palomo, the first zebu bull ever to graze on the grasses of Colombia. From modest beginnings, Enrique remarked, great things arise. Tichen had wisely named his bull after Simón Bolívar's favorite horse, surely an auspicious move. Today, the country ranks seventh in the world in beef production, with no fewer than twenty-four million head of cattle, the progeny of an immigrant's dream.

Enrique led us away from the courtyard and down a corridor that reached a sitting area, clearly the inner sanctum of their home. Disappearing for a moment, he soon returned, his hands carefully cradling an oil painting. The veneer and patina suggested an age comparable to that of the house, but the subject itself confirmed a much more recent date. Enrique's prized possession was an actual portrait of Palomo, from the side, with the bull's massive body filling the entire picture frame. The painting had pride of place in the Cabrales home. It hung in their most formal room, prominently displayed over the mantel as if the portrait of a revered ancestor.

"Here he is," Enrique beamed.

As Enrique turned the painting into the light, the expression on his face left little doubt that, at least for him, Palomo trumped ancestry. The iconic creature was the embodiment of civilization. Though, in fact, a relatively recent arrival, the bull had been embraced by the Cabrales family as a symbol of all that had been achieved by the many generations that had occupied this house and found a way to stay. As Enrique continued to extoll the virtues of a bull, we all posed for a selfie, huddled around Palomo's portrait like movie fans lucky enough to have stumbled upon a favorite star.

Once the painting was back on the wall, hung with care and reverence, the three of us joined Isabel on the open patio for a proper *momposino* breakfast: *bocachico* and *arepas de huevo*, a basket of fresh bread, bowls of passion fruit, mangoes, and watermelon, coffee strong enough to be dispensed by syringe. The conversation was mostly about family, the Uribes and Cabrales, and all the unexpected connections that seem to link every Colombian of a certain class in a single web of marriage, business, and blood. When Xandra and Isabel finally paused to catch their breath, Enrique suggested we move to a more comfortable sitting area by the fountain. As a storyteller, he was in his element, and we were all ears.

As Xandra had promised, Enrique had an encyclopedic knowledge of local history, with a particular passion for Simón Bolívar, the man who liberated not a country, as our new friend was quick to point out, but an entire continent. Out of Bolívar's revolution would emerge Venezuela, Colombia, Panama, Ecuador, Peru, and Bolivia, encompassing altogether close to two million square miles of land, dwarfing the size of the one nation George Washington bequeathed to posterity. Enrique clearly relished the comparison. Each revolution, he noted, had been inspired by the ideals of the Enlightenment. Both were offspring of the same spasm of intellectual insight, the same philosophical and political whirlwind that left Louis XVI still pondering the divine right of kings, even as the guillotine rose over his neck in Paris at the Place de la Révolution on that fateful day in January 1793. The revolutionary leaders, north and south, shared the same passion for freedom and justice, rule of law, the rights of men. Victory in both struggles came only after bloody and prolonged wars of independence, as local militias, hastily assembled and ill equipped, confronted and ultimately defeated two of Europe's most illustrious professional armies. Washington's fight went on for eight years; that of Bolívar, sixteen.

Despite these obvious similarities, Enrique continued, the actual circumstances leading to each revolution, the settings and scale of the warfare, and the ultimate consequences of victory were, in fact, very different, and in ways beyond the obvious. A key distinction lay in the character and relative importance of the colonies to the European powers. When the French, for example, were obliged to hand over New France to the British following their defeat in 1763, they abandoned their largest colonial possession with scarcely a whisper of regret. The colony had long been a drain on the royal treasury. Its only useful product was a humble rodent, the pelt of which would, in time, inspire a fashion statement, the beaver hat. Hardly the stuff of empire, even for the sartorially obsessed citizens of the ancien régime.

The British possessions along the Atlantic seaboard offered even more modest returns. Their value, in the end, would be not what they produced but what they absorbed, all the disaffected religious cults that emerged out of England's centuries of bitter sectarian violence and war. The Thirteen Colonies were settled by those seeking religious freedom but also, and in greater numbers, by those seeking a place to practice their unique brands of religious intolerance.

"Spain was another story," Enrique said.

Having landed on gold and silver, it remained true to form for three centuries, promulgating without compromise an extractive model dedicated only to raw and brutal exploitation. Oblivious to the winds of change, deaf to the voices of a criollo plutocracy its colonies were intended to spawn, dismissive of their every political and economic aspiration, the Spaniards grew only more ruthless, punitive, venal, and corrupt with each passing year. Divide and subjugate was their only agenda, an uncompromising dogma that, in a decade of tumult and transformation, all but invited revolution. Indeed, had any imperial power deliberately set out to design and impose policies certain to foment an uprising in its colonies, it could do no better than to mimic the folly of Spain in the last years of the eighteenth century.

Spanish oppression implied torment for the poor, degradation and dishonor for the rich. Among those burdened by the colonial regime, exposed to such indignities, was one of the wealthiest families in the Americas, an extended clan from Caracas with roots going back to the early days of the conquest.

"That family had a son," Enrique continued, "a boy destined for greatness."

Our friend paused for a moment. Taking the last of his coffee, he leaned forward, thumping the top of the table with his hand, forefinger pointed to the ground.

"And it was here that everything came together. The story of Colombia. Mompox, Bolívar, and the blessed Magdalena."

Enrique fell back in the cushions as the maid brought a fresh round of *tintos*. Isabel had taken up her knitting and was settled deeply in her corner of the sofa. She had the slightly distracted air of a wife who has heard a family tale more than once but is still pleased to indulge the storyteller, knowing that nothing brings a husband greater joy. With a sympathetic glance her way, Enrique continued with the history of the Bolivarian Revolution. Coming from him, a *momposino de pura cepa*, a true son of the city, it felt like a gift.

. . .

Born in 1783 in Caracas to an aristocratic criollo family of American origins, Simón Bolívar came of age in a culture of tyranny conceived to quell the ambitions and opportunities of all but those of
Spanish birth. In 1767, the Spanish king, Carlos IV, expelled five
thousand clerics, allowing the Crown to take complete control over
education, with the explicit goal of keeping the colonies mired in
ignorance, that they might be easier to control. Books and newspapers of anything but Spanish origins were banned. No colonial
subject could own a printing press. No foreigner could visit a colony
without permission of the king; no local was permitted free passage,
even within the colonies. All movement was monitored. Possession
of contraband was punishable by death, even as those born in the
colony were denied the right to participate in legitimate business
activities. By law, only those of Spanish birth could own mines,
shops, or vineyards, grow tobacco or olive trees, plant grapes, or
sell goods on the streets. Only true Spaniards were allowed to trade
in gold, silver, copper, indigo, sugar, pearls, emeralds, cotton, wool,
tomatoes, potatoes, and leather. Economically crippled, the criollo
families were nevertheless subjected to punishing taxes that each
year generated $60 million for the royal coffers, not a penny of
which was reinvested to improve conditions in the colonies. Simón
Bolívar distilled the Spanish legacy in a single line: "We are a region
plagued by vices learned from Spain, which, through history, has
been a mistress of cruelty, ambition, meanness, and greed."

Authoritarian rule, with all its small humiliations, instilled in
Bolívar from the earliest age a festering hatred for Spaniards, an
anger as deeply felt as the sorrow that swept over his life as first his
father, and then, six years later, his mother succumbed to tuberculosis, leaving him an orphan at the age of nine. Happily, he was raised
by a kind uncle, who placed him in the care of an extraordinary
teacher, Simón Rodríguez, who awakened in the lad an insatiable
appetite for learning. They studied together in the wild, often on
horseback, with all the forests, mountains, and beaches of Venezuela
as their classroom. Rodríguez believed, as he wrote, that "a child
learns more in one second, carving a little stick, than in one whole

day, listening to a teacher." Receptive to all that was unexpected and new, Rodríguez, in time, introduced his young charge to the writings of Voltaire, Locke, and Montesquieu, instilling in him a love of ideas that, along with a deep appreciation of nature, became two of the foundational pillars of Bolívar's life. The third came more slowly, as Rodríguez, like a wizard, gave flight to the boy's spirit, allowing fury, bitterness, and resentment to spin into a passion for justice and a burning desire to liberate the New World.

But first came love. Bolívar's family was among the most illustrious in Caracas, with a powerful presence that reached back to the early years on the conquest. For fully two centuries before Spain tried to salvage a fading empire by quelling the ambitions of its finest and most loyal subjects, generations of Bolívars had prospered. As early as 1569 the family had endowed one of the few side chapels of the Cathedral, the glorious symbol of the city. Their extensive holdings—sugar plantations and *encomiendas*; silver, gold, and copper mines; vast estates throughout the colony worked by native and African slaves—generated astonishing wealth, allowing the family, in time, to buy its way into nobility, selecting favorite titles with the casual ease of gentlemen sampling the scent of blossoms before choosing a bouquet for a mistress.

Such wealth and lineage insulated the Bolívar family from the most vulgar impositions of Spanish rule, but position and privilege did little to help a young student whose hunger for knowledge would never be satisfied under a colonial regime that, as a matter of policy, promoted ignorance. Fortunately when Simón turned fifteen, another uncle, living in Madrid, invited him to continue his education in Europe. A year later, Bolívar reached Spain, where he immediately came under the care and guidance of a close friend of the family, the Marqués de Ustáriz, a scholar as generous, wise, and inspiring as his first mentor, Simón Rodríguez. Mobilizing a small army of tutors, the *marqués* introduced Bolívar to French and Italian, Spanish literature, world history, and all the luminaries of the Enlightenment. Ustáriz didn't just expose the lad to new horizons; he actively worked to identify gaps in his knowledge and experience that needed to be addressed. Noting Bolívar's passion for books, he flung open the doors to his personal library, among the finest in

Spain, casting the boy into trance. The *marqués* exposed his charge to music, introducing him to Beethoven and the finest composers of France and Spain. Bolívar took up fencing. He learned to dance, an art of movement Bolívar would embrace with all his passion, becoming not only highly skilled but so fluid as to transcend time and space. In the many dark passages of a life of triumph and tragedy, he would always find peace and forgetfulness in the stillness of a pirouette. His finest speeches would be composed on the dance floor.

Of all the wonders brought his way by the Marqués de Ustáriz, none could compare to the gift of love that swept over him the moment he was introduced to María Teresa Rodríguez del Toro in 1802, three years after his arrival in Madrid. With the blessing of their families, they married, and immediately set sail for Venezuela, where Bolívar looked forward to a long and comfortable life as one of the wealthiest young men in the colony.

Fate had other plans. His beloved María died of yellow fever within six months of arriving in South America. Alone and bereft at twenty, Bolívar slipped into the depths of despair, a dark meditation out of which emerged a man transformed: hardened by loss, oblivious to pain, and fully dedicated to a revolutionary struggle destined to leave every river, field, and forest stained with Spanish blood. "Had I not become a widower," he later wrote, acknowledging the impact of María's death on his life, "I would never have become 'El Libertador.' When I was with my wife, my head was filled only with ardent love. The death of my wife placed me early in the road of politics, and caused me to follow the chariot of Mars."

In 1804, Simón Bolívar traveled to France, drawn as if by a lodestone to Paris. In a city still damp with the afterbirth of revolution, he came under the spell of the two most famous men in Europe, a naturalist and a soldier. Alexander von Humboldt and Napoleon Bonaparte would long inhabit Bolívar's dreams, one for the better, the other very much for the worse. Humboldt had only just returned from the Spanish Indies, having unveiled over six years the natural wonders of a continent. En route to Europe, he sailed first to Virginia to meet Thomas Jefferson, author of the Declaration of Independence, and discuss with America's third president the challenges of his fledging nation, advising him, among other issues, as to the merits of the Louisiana Purchase and the hazards and scientific promise of the Lewis and Clark expedition. Such was Humboldt's influence and reputation on both sides of the Atlantic.

As a scholar and a naturalist, Humboldt embodied the intellectual and philosophical promise of the Enlightenment. It was evident in what he knew and how he thought, as well as, most essentially, in his devotion to the democratization of knowledge, science in particular. As a storyteller, he shone on stage, his charisma mesmerizing as he addressed audiences that included aristocrats and royals but also students and servants, soldiers and bricklayers. At a time when women had no access to university education, Humboldt welcomed them as having every right, as he put it, "to listen to a clever word." Invariably, half of those who flocked to his lectures, often scrambling to secure seats hours in advance, 'were mothers, wives, and maidens. In his many books and essays, he presented scientific ideas in a literary style that was accessible, even intuitive, infusing his prose with poetic flourishes certain to fire the hearts of his readers.

In a slow-moving world of horse and sail, quill, paper, and ink, Humboldt was the first international celebrity, with a notoriety in the capitals of Europe matching that of Napoleon, his only equal in the firmament of Simón Bolívar's imagination. In Parisian salons, purveyors of gossip relished how the great naturalist left the self-proclaimed emperor pink with envy and jealousy. Napoleon more than once complained to his wife, Empress Josephine, that he just did not understand how a student of birds, an observer of stars, a plant collector and chronicler of obscure and seemingly useless information could possibly challenge, in the public imagination, the glory of a conqueror. But Alexander von Humboldt most assuredly did.

That a scholar and scientist achieved such fame speaks to the power of ideas at the dawn of modernity. Humboldt's acclaim, however, did not diminish so much as complement the brilliance of Napoleon, an upstart soldier, a general by the age of twenty-four, a military genius whose meteoric rise offered such promise to Simón Bolívar, his young admirer. Napoleon, as much as Humboldt, was a product of the torrent that had swept away the dynastic residues of feudalism, erasing borders and frontiers, leaving all Europe fallow and fertile, ready to be sown with new dreams of *liberté, égalité,* and *fraternité.* Victors in war write the first draft of history, and sometimes the last. In the wake of Waterloo, it served British interests to portray Napoleon as a tyrant and rogue, an existential threat to all that was decent and democratic in the hearts and minds of men. This persistent caricature masked an inconvenient truth. Wherever he ruled, Napoleon set in place structures of governance and redress woefully lacking in Britain at the time: true equality before the law, religious tolerance, freedom of the press, property rights for all, meritocracy as a civic ideal, support for science and the arts, and the greatest codification of laws since the fall of the Roman Empire.

As Simón Bolívar reached Paris, Napoleon was approaching the height of his power, the embodiment of revolutionary passions that in a short generation had descended into terror and dictatorship, only to erupt once again in a spasm of imperial conquest. Bolívar in body or spirit was with Parisians as they poured into the streets to celebrate the defeat of Russia and Austria at the Battle of Austerlitz, the annihilation of Russian forces at Friedland, the humiliation of Prussia at Jena. In all his finery, the future Libertador was present at the Cathédrale Notre-Dame as Napoleon orchestrated his own coronation in December 1804.

Dazzled by the specter of French armies marching from one victory to another, crushing the forces of reaction, Bolívar initially paid little heed to the cult of personality and all the many contradictions that would, in time, precipitate Napoleon's fall—a rare lapse of judgment that foreshadowed his failure, a generation later, to anticipate the tangled circumstances and political betrayals that led inexorably to his own exile and doom. In the ruthless audacity of a little known Corsican rising out of nowhere to seize the reins of history, Bolívar saw only the single-minded zeal that the liberation of a continent demanded. In Napoleon's seemingly invincible armies, he envisioned the forces that would drive his enemies into the sea, leaving not a Spaniard alive to taint the soil of a new land. "Either Americans allow themselves to be exterminated gradually," Bolívar declared, "or they undertake to destroy an evil race that, while it breathes, works tirelessly toward annihilation." With iron confidence, he anticipated victory, and found in the political and judicial structures of Napoleonic rule a model for the administration and governance of the great nation that would arise out of the shadows of Spanish humiliation and defeat.

Alexander von Humboldt initially dismissed Simón as a dreamer, but he took the young man under his wing, grateful for the many kindnesses that had come his way from the Bolívar family during the weeks he and his companion Aimé Bonpland had spent in Caracas. The baron had particularly enjoyed his time with Padre Andújar, the priest who had taught mathematics to all the Bolívar children, including Simón. As a frequent guest at Humboldt's elegant Paris apartment in the Faubourg Saint-Germain, Bolívar was exposed to every pulse, inspiration, and idea whirling through the imagination of the greatest mind of the age. He had access not only to Humboldt's publications but also to his private notes and diaries, altogether some four thousand pages from his American expeditions alone.

As Bolívar savored accounts of lands he had never known, whose people he had promised to free, he sensed a symmetry to their thoughts that only tightened the bond between protégé and mentor. Humboldt's scientific eye embraced the entire universe of nature. He wrote of plants, birds, insects, and strange mammals. As an astronomer, he traced the trajectories of planets and stars; as a cartographer, he mapped rivers, most notably the Magdalena; as a surveyor, he measured the height of mountains, including Chimborazo, Ecuador's crown jewel, an ice-clad volcano that soars farther from the center of the earth than any summit on the planet. Humboldt was among the first to appreciate the biological complexity of wetlands, cloud forests, and *páramos*; to study the dynamics of climate and ocean currents; and to record the effects of elevation and topography on the dispersal of flora and fauna, observations that marked the beginning of the academic discipline of biogeography. Before the advent of photography, every landscape had to be captured in a sketch, an artistic portfolio of watercolors and oils that grew with every mile covered, each new horizon embraced by the expedition. Humboldt was simply, as Charles Darwin would write, the "greatest scientific traveler who ever lived."

Humboldt reveled in the radiance of the equatorial sun. Nothing escaped his notice, and the breadth of his vision reached far beyond science. In language that must surely have ignited Bolívar's fury, he wrote of the "barbarism of civilized man," the "insatiable avarice" of Spaniards, which had resulted in the annihilation of ancient civilizations, each, by definition, a fountain of knowledge, culture, and genius. He professed great admiration for native people, including the complexity of their languages, the sophistication of their religious beliefs, and their ability to find their way through the densest of jungles. They were, as he wrote, "excellent geographers," true natural philosophers who knew every tree in the forest, distinguishing species simply by the taste of the bark, a skill that completely eluded him, though he did his best to learn.

Such sentiments grew from Humboldt's profound belief that no race was superior to another and that all humans shared a common origin. Just as plants adapt to various habitats, he wrote, people in different parts of the world take on certain traits of appearance, but they all belong to one great family of man. And no matter where or how men and women determine to live out their destinies, whatever the constraints of culture, as individuals, they "all are alike designed for freedom."

With his quill deployed as rapier, his ink as bitter as bile, Humboldt exposed the ecological consequences of Spanish rule, the inhumane treatment of natives and slaves, the systemic corruption of a colonial government informed only by "immorality." He despised the tyranny and disgrace of slavery, "the greatest evil," which he identified as the very essence of colonialism. Only through slavery could merchants profit from sugar, cotton, indigo, and coffee, crops that filled not the mouths of the poor but the pockets of the rich. The spread of plantation economies infused the land with misery and shame, even as they celebrated and precipitated a relentless and ruthless assault on the natural world. With a prescience almost inconceivable for his era, Humboldt connected colonialism to environmental devastation; slavery to power, economics, and politics; the exploitation of natural resources to the violation of tribal peoples; and climate, soils, and agriculture to demographics, monoculture, and the distorted distribution of land. "Slavery arrived in the wake of what the Europeans call their civilization," Humboldt wrote. "But it was European barbarity . . . and their thirst for wealth" that created an unjust world, the very colonies Simón Bolívar knew as the land of his birth.

From Humboldt's journals, Bolívar saw ever more clearly how the Spaniards had promoted hatred between the races, violence between communities, envy and greed among the privileged classes. With the eye of a spy, Humboldt recorded the condition of roads and ports, agricultural yields and production figures of mines, tax revenues and the status of military installations—figures that only confirmed the extent to which Spain gave little and took much as it siphoned off the wealth of a continent. Humboldt taught him, as Bolívar would later write, that even the most fertile of fields and the richest bodies of ore would never satisfy the lust of a colonial power motivated exclusively by greed.

If such an unsparing critique only deepened a hatred for Spain that was already, as Bolívar remarked, "vaster than the sea between us," Humboldt's uplifting, even transcendent, accounts of the rare beauty of his native land turned the young patriot away from gloom and toward distant horizons of hope. The great scholar heralded the unequaled abundance and diversity of biological life as the essence of South America's identity, revealing a continent that was glorious, powerful, and strong, wealthy in ways no covetous Spaniard could understand or imagine. Simón Bolívar declared Humboldt "the true discoverer of the New World," an apostle of freedom who, through his travels and explorations, scientific gifts and revelations, had done for America "more good than all the conquerors." His words had "uprooted him and his fellow revolutionaries from ignorance," leaving them proud and profoundly grateful for having been born in a land of such natural wonders. "With his pen alone," Bolívar wrote, "Humboldt awakened South America."

Humboldt's vision infused Bolívar's imagination, leading ultimately to a politics of inclusion that called for an end to slavery and the creation of a people's army, a guerrilla force cobbled together with *zambos* and campesinos, natives and vaqueros, the poorest of the poor and any titled squire keen on spilling Spanish blood. In some magical and mysterious way, Bolívar internalized Humboldt's reverence for the land. When Humboldt wrote that "nature is the domain of liberty," he was surely speaking in metaphor. Every creature plays a role. Each contributes to the whole. Humans are but a single species, one form of life among the infinite multitudes. Everything is interconnected. Nature, as he proclaimed, is "one great republic of freedom."

Simón Bolívar took his mentor at his word, embracing nature as the literal antidote to tyranny, ecological harmony as a blueprint for political and moral truth. He was perhaps the only major revolutionary hero whose political ideology was fundamentally informed by natural history. He did not distinguish between the destiny of nations and the fate of nature. How could a continent, he demanded to know, "so abundantly endowed . . . be kept so desperately oppressed and passive?" This question would carry him back to the Americas as he set out on his great crusade.

In victory, he would declare before Congress, "Nature is the infallible teacher of men." Colombia's very freedom, won in battle two hundred years ago, grew in good measure out of Bolívar's transcendent faith in the messages of the wild, the threads of loyalty that bind a people to their mountains, forests, rivers, and wetlands. The natural bounty of the land, he believed, was the mystic endowment of the nation.

As Enrique brought this portion of his saga to a close, Xandra, in her inimitable way, perceived a possibility of immense promise. If only Colombians today would embrace this distant legacy, she remarked, they might come to see environmental protection not as a political issue or a mandate to be ignored but as the raw invocation of patrimony, with stewardship of nature being recognized as the purest expression of patriotism.

"And if we really did align our thinking with the vision of Bolívar and Humboldt," she continued, "people would surely see the senseless violation of nature, motivated by the same greed that drove the Spaniards, as an act of treason, not to mention an insult to the memory of the man who gave up his fortune and life to bring freedom to a continent."

Xandra had in mind a completely new way of thinking about conservation and the Río Magdalena. What if advocates presented the restoration of the river not as an environmental issue but as a symbol of national pride? Instead of calling for more government sanctions, rules and regulations impossible to enforce but certain to alienate potential supporters, what if we appealed instead to the emotional ties of memory and longing that bind every Colombian family, in one way or another, to the river that made possible the life of the nation? Only the people of the *cuenca*, rich and poor, urban and rural, fishermen, farmers, bankers, and priests, can give back what they have taken. And only the love that resides in the hearts of the Colombian people, patriots all, has the power to work such a miracle, the resurrection of the Río Magdalena.

The General in His Labyrinth

The sun was hot. Enrique had much more to share, but he insisted that we visit La Piedra, a small monument on the waterfront. He led us first to the Plaza de la Libertad, the birthplace of the revolution. In Enrique's telling you could almost hear the sound of the many hundreds of *momposinos* who gathered in the square on August 6, 1810, determined "to be free or to die," a slogan that immediately brought to mind Lexington and Concord, and the patriots of another American revolution. Mompox became that day the first town and province in El Nuevo Reino de Granada to proclaim its absolute independence from Spain. Enrique's eyes dampened at the thought. Xandra detected a tear on his cheek as he read the inscription on the base of the statue that is the centerpiece of the plaza, words attributed to Simón Bolívar: *Si a Caracas debo la vida, a Mompós debo la gloria.* "If I owe my life to Caracas, then to Mompox I owe my glory." Our next stop, Enrique assured us, would explain all.

The Piedra de Bolívar is a modest white slab protruding from the low wall on the river side of the promenade, not far from the Cabrales home. Undecorated, it merely records the dates of Bolívar's comings and goings, eight visits to Mompox altogether, from his first in 1812, when he arrived the day after Christmas, to his final departure on May 20, 1830. Enrique recalled that day as if he had been present, his voice breaking as he described how Simón

Bolívar, desperate and betrayed, slipped down the Río Magdalena in disgrace, traveling by choice in a modest *champán*, with the rhythm and chants of the *bogas* masking the agonies of a man broken in body and spirit, and destined soon for death.

"Before the revolution," Enrique said, "Bolívar was one of the richest men in the Americas. George Washington lived out his days in comfort, on vast estates, surrounded by his slaves, a wealthy man to the end. Bolívar freed his slaves, lost his land, and died in abject poverty, having committed his entire fortune to the struggle. He never wavered from his ideals, even if it meant the sacrifice of everything his family had acquired over three hundred years. The way Bolívar met his end will always be a shadow in our lives. The founder of six countries surely deserved better."

Xandra photographed the memorial from all sides, then pulled us out of the sun to the cool of a nearby café, where she ordered *jugos*, fruit juice for all: *maracuyá*, *piña*, and *mora*. Once settled in the shade, Enrique picked up his tale in Paris, at Alexander von Humboldt's lodgings in Saint-Germain. The great naturalist and his associate Aimé Bonpland, along with Simón Bolívar, had gathered to discuss colonial politics. As Bolívar made his case for revolution, he asked Humboldt whether the people of the Americas were ready to govern themselves. Refusing to take the bait, Humboldt agreed that the colonies were ready for freedom; what they lacked was a leader to show them the way.

"But they had one," Enrique protested, "and he was standing right in front of them. Humboldt still didn't see, which only made young Bolívar more hungry to succeed. In the end, Humboldt, of course, would herald him as 'El Libertador,' the father of freedom."

Simón Bolívar began his fateful march in 1808, even as Napoleon's armies assaulted Spain, providing an opening for an uprising in the Americas. After parting in Paris, he and Humboldt would not meet again. And yet, as Bolívar confessed, his mentor remained always by his side. Though separated by an ocean, they maintained an active correspondence. With a bevy of secretaries, Bolívar dictated at all hours, from saddle or hammock, posting thousands of letters each year, many of which found their way to Paris. Throughout all his campaigns, Bolívar's baggage brimmed with copies of

Humboldt's maps and journals, annotations about climate, geography, condition of roads and trails, navigable stretches of rivers, the character of the local people, locations of towns, villages, and hamlets—a veritable road map of a continent, all the lands that Bolívar did not know but was destined to liberate. Humboldt's notes and maps were crucial to his ultimate success.

As Bolívar reached the restless streets of Caracas, and ultimately made his way to Cartagena, the revolution was little more than a chaotic assembly of splintered and unruly factions, independent and still nominally free only because Spain and its armies were preoccupied in Europe. Some dismissed the fledging rebellion as *la patria boba*, the republic of fools. Bolívar moved quickly to establish his leadership. Recognizing words as weapons of war, he took control of the unfolding narrative, as both writer and speaker. He honed his oratory until his voice had the cadence of prophets. His use of language was said to challenge the poetry of stars. If the Spaniards shrouded the people in darkness, he would brighten their lives with the truth. He started a newspaper, envisioned to be the conscience of a new nation. A printing press would accompany his every military campaign. The written word, he said, was the infantry of his army of liberation.

His first strategic move was to focus the conflict through a barrage of pamphlets and speeches conceived to unite the rebellion in a cult of violence, a war to the death that alone might drive the Spanish from the Americas. Having awakened the street, securing the support of the common people, he then seduced the wealthy, the rich criollos long embittered by Spanish policies and in a position to aid his cause. With money in hand, he recruited an army, offering glory and advancement, not to mention food and clothing, to the forgotten and abandoned: runaway slaves, landless peasants, slum dwellers without work. George Washington's soldiers, by contrast, were mostly white farmers and militiamen, strong, self-sufficient, decently fed, and familiar with firearms since childhood; they brought their own muskets to the fight. Bolívar's recruits came to him shoeless, hungry, and unarmed, with tattered rags as clothing and perhaps a flea-ridden blanket for the cold. From the dregs of colonial society, Bolívar, himself an aspiring soldier with no formal military training, pulled together the beginnings of an army that, in time, would take on the world.

From the start, Bolívar recognized that control of the Río Magdalena was critical to the republican cause. He began his campaign in the last days of 1812, moving his men upriver in a small flotilla of ten *champanes*. On December 21, with a force of just two hundred, he stunned the Spaniards at Tenerife; the entire garrison, some five hundred royalists, scattered in panic and wild abandon. Having scavenged muskets, swords, powder, and shot, Bolívar assembled the local *ribereños*, chastised them for their fidelity to Spain, and then, through the power of his oratory alone, enlisted hundreds to his cause. The next day, reinforced and well equipped, the rebel force moved on Mompox, where they encountered not bloodshed but jubilation as the *momposinos* welcomed them with a festive ball. By all accounts, Simón Bolívar's charm and grace on the dance floor yielded another substantial infusion of volunteers by morning.

Leaving Mompox on December 29, his force having doubled, Bolívar set out to capture in short order every river town along some three hundred miles of the Magdalena: Guamal, El Banco, and Tamalameque. His greatest weapons were fear and surprise. His men came off the river silently, wading through waters infested with crocodiles, crossing wetlands and passing through thickets crawling with vipers, emerging from the shadows with ungodly cries that heralded a ferocity in battle that few Spaniards dared endure. Those royalists who stood their ground were dispatched by knives. Ears, heads, and severed limbs ended up in the river, food for reptiles and fish.

By January 8, 1813, after a lightning campaign lasting just fifteen days, Simón Bolívar had taken control of the entire length of the Bajo Magdalena. In doing so, he had forged the nucleus of a small but formidable fighting force, while securing his own reputation as a rare military leader comfortable with uncertainty and fully capable of improvising tactics and strategy on the run. On a small scale, and in one sweeping gesture, he had brilliantly executed two of Napoleon's fundamental maxims of war: destroy the enemy and conquer the country. His task now was to take his rebellion to scale. "A weak man," he declared, indicating his intentions, "requires a long fight in order to win. A strong one delivers a single blow and an empire vanishes."

Patience was not one of Bolívar's virtues, and no one would ever describe him as weak. With piercing black eyes and an unsettling gaze, he had a herculean capacity to endure adversity and a wizardly ability to energize the weak, inspire the valiant, and give comfort to the dying. Like Napoleon, he was a small man who refused to yield to the embarrassment of his stature; at five foot, six inches, Bolívar weighed just 130 pounds. Though but a skeleton wrapped in skin, his strength and stamina in the saddle would earn him the name "Iron Ass," a term of endearment from soldiers who would march with him seventeen hours a day for weeks on end, as together they liberated for all time lands far greater in extent than those encompassed by Napoleon's continental empire, which endured for but a decade.

Following his victory on the Magdalena, Bolívar strove to maintain the initiative, knowing full well that his forces were inferior to the Spaniards by every conventional measure: weaponry, training, and experience. His counter was stealth, ingenuity, and terror. On June 15, 1813, he issued a proclamation, "War to the Death," indicating to friend and foe alike what awaited on the fields of battle. In three months, he would capture Caracas. Massacres on both sides soiled the campaign. Republican firing squads targeted anyone loyal to the Crown. Royalist forces murdered any woman who refused to marry a Spaniard. Rivers became graveyards; hospitals, morgues. Fields and meadows stank of the dead. The landscape of every province touched by the war was a vista of devastation.

After months of stalemate, with no obvious path forward, Bolívar made plans to take his campaign to Venezuela. Disaster struck in May 1815 when a powerful royalist force, fighting on its own terms, decisively defeated the republican army, forcing its leader into exile. Seeking to rally foreign support, Bolívar went first to Jamaica, where his welcome was marred by an assassination attempt orchestrated by his nemesis, Pablo Morillo, Count of Cartagena, whose sole mission was the destruction of the rebel armies and the restoration of Spanish rule. Bolívar took it as a sign, for his sojourn in Jamaica did not go well. Having finally defeated Napoleon after twenty years of war, the British had little interest in new entanglements. The colonial government offered nothing.

Rebuffed and denied, his personal resources dwindling by the day, Bolívar hovered in exile for nearly seven months. It was a dark passage, with little to occupy his mind save the failures that had landed him in Jamaica and the precarious state of the revolution. There were moments when he questioned both the viability of the struggle and his own capacity to endure. In a note to a friend, he professed a preference for death over dishonor, leaving some associates fearful that he might take his own life. Boredom no doubt was a greater threat, for as he wallowed in limbo, his thoughts embittered, history took a fateful turn. In the throes of self-pity, Bolívar drew from his humiliation the worst possible lesson, an assessment tainted with indignation that foreshadowed his tragic fall.

While still in Kingston, Bolívar shared his thoughts in a letter addressed to a Jamaican colleague, Henry Cullen, but intended for the world, especially the British, whose aid he still coveted. Known as "The Jamaica Letter," it was less a missive than a manifesto in the guise of correspondence, a declaration of convictions almost certain to elicit condemnation. Bolívar must have known what he was doing. He was a master propagandist who understood the power of words. As a soldier, he would liberate a continent, but as a writer and orator, he set free a language. His stately and lyrical prose, so unlike the ornate and cumbersome Castilian of his era, invigorated Spanish with a new energy, infusing it with light, restoring an ancient tongue to the innocence of youth. His references to nature, the simplicity of his phrasing, and the wisdom of his metaphors quite literally transformed the language. Bolívar spoke as people feel. He wrote as if embedded in their dreams. His dazzling prose marked, in the eyes of many, "the dawn of a new literary age."

With one eye on posterity, the other on the British, Simón Bolívar selected his words with care as he placed quill to paper on September 6, 1815. Thanking his correspondent for the honor of his attention, he began with a historical review, citing Spanish deeds that had led inexorably to revolution, noting the promise and hazards of a war still underway. Having surveyed the social and political landscape of the struggle, Bolívar looked to the future, anticipating the challenges of victory: determining the structures of governance, codes of laws, and the geographic configurations of the sovereign states destined to rise out of the ashes of Spanish defeat. One nation or many.

Rarely does history hinge on a phrase, but as Bolívar made his case for a single nation, encompassing the breadth of a continent, he fatally turned his back on democracy. "As long as we don't have the political virtues that distinguish our brothers to the north," he wrote, "a democratic system, far from rescuing us, can only bring us ruin." What the new nation will need, he suggested, is a strong and benevolent leader, wise and just, with a firm but cautious hand, placed into office for life. No doubt, Bolívar's motives were sincere. He rejected democracy, monarchy, autocracy, and all European models of government as being inappropriate for the unique reality of the Americas; his goal was to devise something altogether new and original. Unfortunately, what he proposed sounded awfully like something very old, dictatorship, a rap he would never shed.

Leaving Jamaica at last in December 1815, Simón Bolívar traveled to Haiti, yet another nation to have emerged from the ashes of revolution. In Les Cayes he found asylum, as well as a friend and ally in Haiti's first president, Alexandre Pétion, a man with no love for the European powers. In the wake of the initial uprising in 1791, the only successful slave revolt in history, Haiti had fought off separate invasions by Spain, Britain, and France, each keen to seize control of an export economy that had made the French colony of Saint-Domingue the richest jewel of an imperial age. Exploiting some five hundred thousand African slaves, the plantations had produced 163 million pounds of sugar a year, two-thirds of the world's coffee crop, and vast stores of indigo and hides that filled the holds of the four thousand ships that sailed each year to France. In a brutal war that lasted thirteen years, as many as 350,000 Africans perished, with independence coming at last in 1804. For a century, Haiti would be the only black nation on earth. As a matter of pride and policy, the national government went after the slave trade, purchasing shipments of shackled cargo only to grant the victims freedom and the promise of a new life in Haiti.

It was in this spirit that Alexandre Pétion proposed a deal. Haiti would offer diplomatic recognition, as well as weapons, supplies, soldiers, and ships, on the condition that Bolívar free the slaves throughout the Spanish realm. Condemning slavery as "the daughter of darkness," Bolívar readily agreed. On his return to Venezuela in 1816, he immediately liberated his own slaves, promising freedom for all in exchange for military service; true emancipation would come only in 1826, when abolition was written into law. Still, at a time when African blood was destined to flow for another half century in Brazilian plantations and the cotton fields of the American South, it was a bold move that swelled the ranks of Bolívar's armies, even while sending a message to the world that there was no going back. His revolution would not be denied.

The first months of 1819 found Bolívar in Angostura (today Ciudad Bolívar), a rebel stronghold on the lower reaches of the Orinoco River. That the remote settlement was host to Venezuela's Second National Congress, which anointed Bolívar president on February 15, reveals more about the status of the republican cause than the power of a fictive presidency or the charms of a rather dismal city. As a soldier, Bolívar knew only that Angostura was a long way from Caracas, the metropolitan heart of a colony that, after years of war, was back in the hands of the Spaniards. Though enmeshed in political intrigue his entire adult life, Bolívar had little patience for frivolous men jockeying for position in a nation that would come into being only through victory in battle. His energy focused on a strategic vision and plan. Royalist forces clung stubbornly to coastal Venezuela and were about to be reinforced by a large expeditionary force being assembled in Spain. Republicans controlled the south, the open forests and grasslands that reached west a thousand miles to the foothills of the Andes. Simón Bolívar decided to do the impossible. He would march his army to the mountains, crest the summits of the Cordillera Oriental, and descend from the heights on Bogotá. While royalist troops newly arrived from Spain endured their first exposure to yellow fever, malaria, and plague, not to mention the tedium of garrison life in Caracas, he and his citizens' army would liberate Nueva Granada.

With such ambitions, Bolívar moved quickly to train and expand his forces. In need of a cavalry, he recruited more than a thousand *llaneros*, all veterans of a fight that had shattered a Spanish army of four thousand, leaving the grasslands darkened with the dead. To the Spaniards, they had appeared like demons, thundering into attack, riding bareback, dressed only in loincloths, their bodies greased with meat and fat, their only food. Their weapon of choice was a lance cut from alvarico palms, its point hardened by fire. Bolívar was especially keen to see what these horsemen might accomplish with modern weapons of war. Not that they would be easy to control. Living outside the law, loyal to everywhere and nowhere, free to administer their own justice, they had nothing but contempt for authority and the privileged classes. They were not *vaqueros*, mere cowboys. They were literally the people of the Llanos, the vast eastern plains, men best defined as being the land upon which they treaded. Undisciplined and wild, they reveled in hardship, finding comfort on the stony ground, sharing food with vultures, sleeping without shelter, enduring torrential rains with no cover save a mantle of hide. They lived with a stoic indifference to pain and hunger. Exhaustion had no meaning; danger was but a condition to be endured. As Bolívar had anticipated, their example would inspire the entire campaign.

By the spring of 1819, the republican forces could legitimately be called an army. In addition to the *llaneros*, the ranks had been further augmented by some five thousand British and Irish soldiers, veterans who in the wake of Waterloo had no interest in returning to the coal pits of Wales or the squalor of London and Liverpool. Hardened in battle, forged in war, the British Legions brought experience and discipline to a republican army that would need both as it set out, marching west into the light of the setting sun.

Over the course of his short life—he would die at forty-seven—Simón Bolívar would traverse on foot or by horse some seventy-five thousand miles of the most challenging terrain in the world. He would endure malaria and dysentery, torrid wetlands and the bitter cold of snow-swept mountains. In camp, he slept as did his soldiers: sometimes in a hammock, never in a bed, often on the hard ground or a bare floor, wrapped only in a cape, curled up like a dog. His one indulgence was personal hygiene. In an era when British laborers and lords took a bath once a month, if needed, Bolívar bathed every morning at dawn, and twice more during the day. Meticulous about cleanliness at the table, he carried his own silverware. Though a notorious womanizer, he rarely drank and never smoked; he was especially proud of his teeth, a complete set, perfectly aligned and brilliantly white, a rare achievement in a time of wooden dentures and toothless grins. He also had a passion for cologne, which his immediate entourage struggled to supply. His soldiers tolerated the cloying scent as the one flaw in their otherwise exemplary and truly exceptional commander.

Bolívar's men performed miracles, on the march and in battle, in good measure due to the trust and faith he inspired. He was, above all, a soldier's general. No detail escaped his concern. He never rested. After fifteen hours in the saddle, he would work deep into the night, gathering intelligence, seeing to the wounded and sick, orchestrating the flow of supplies: salt, flour, and cooking oil for the field kitchens, medicines and bandages for the surgeons, tobacco for the officers, ammunition and food for the men. Dawn would find him, lying in his hammock, still issuing directives to his staff: marching and battle orders but also instructions concerning logistics and supply—the number of cattle necessary to feed the army, the weight of corn required to keep those cattle alive. He worried about the well-being of the horses, the condition of the powder and shot, the thickness of a blanket, a soldier's only comfort in the cold. More than once, Bolívar would be seen on the march, personally carrying a soldier too weak to stand. General Francisco Santander, his companion in battle, a close friend and later a nemesis, described Bolívar as "the anchor of our hopes; the essence of our vitality." Daniel O'Leary, his aide-de-camp, wrote that Bolívar "could calm troubles by his very presence, [such was] the magic of his prestige." Santander, who by the end of his life had every reason to disdain and even despise Bolívar, confessed: "His force of personality is such that on countless occasions when I have been filled with hatred and revenge, the mere sight of him, the instant he speaks, I am disarmed, and I come away filled with nothing so much as admiration."

Simón Bolívar would need all of his charisma and genius to draw his army to the heights of the Andes. With soldiers as young

as thirteen, as ancient as forty, they crossed the grasslands of the
Llanos, only to climb into the foothills, following or cutting tracks
that rose gradually to the rain and mist of the cloud forests, until
finally, after a tortured ascent, they fell upon the limitless *páramos*.
As the army crested the final pass at thirteen thousand feet and
began the long traverse of the Páramo de Pisba, the men walked
blood-shod. What shoes had survived lacked soles. Their clothing
was tattered and shredded; many had no clothes at all. Local peasant
women, appalled by the condition of the soldiers, dressed them in
shirts and pants sewn on the spot from their own clothes. Hundreds
had endured hypothermia; a quarter of the men from the British
Legions were dead.

Bolívar not only held his army together through this horrific
trial, he managed in short order to sweep away memories of loss and
privation, restoring morale as readily as he quelled hunger, with supplies requisitioned from a thousand mountain farmers sympathetic
to the cause. Within days of descending from the *páramos*, the vanguard of Bolívar's army, under the command of General Santander,
engaged a royalist army at El Pantano de Vargas. Though the Spaniards enjoyed a complete tactical advantage—they controlled the
high ground, had more trained men, better arms—the bedraggled
forces of freedom, with little more than machetes, spears, and the
bloodlust of the *llaneros*, drove the enemy from the field. Santander
would later write that the battle had been won by the intensity of
the horsemen and the calm determination of the British soldiers, all
made possible thanks to Bolívar, who, like an apparition, a mythic
god of war, had been present everywhere at all times.

Only days later, the republican army swept down upon the
Spaniards at the Battle of Boyacá. In just two hours, killing scores
and taking sixteen hundred prisoners, Bolívar scattered the only
royalist force capable of defending the approaches to Bogotá. He
seized the moment. As one observer noted, "A lightning bolt doesn't
fall from the sky as swiftly as General Bolívar descended on the capital." A letter from a royalist general to Spain's Ministry of War
acknowledged, "The rebellious Bolívar has occupied the capital of
Bogotá. . . . In just one day, Bolívar has undone all we have accomplished in five years of this campaign, and in one single battle he has

reconquered all the territory that soldiers of the king have won in the course of so many past conflagrations." Simón Bolívar and his army's arrival in the streets of the capital of Nueva Granada took everyone by surprise. The viceroy, who had believed that Spanish forces had prevailed in both battles, abandoned the city in such haste that he left a bag of gold on his desk, half a million pesos in the vault, and enough arms and ammunition to replenish the entire republican army. Disguised as a campesino, the viceroy reached the Río Magdalena, made his way to the coast, and then ignobly fled to Spain. Among other items left behind in Bogotá were his makeup and rouge, as well as a fine collection of powdered wigs.

The liberation of Nueva Granada did not imply an end to the war; Spain retained control of Cartagena, Caracas, and the Caribbean shore, the southern mountains around Pasto, Quito, and Lima, and the far reaches of the Viceroyalty of Peru. But the façade of Spanish hegemony in the Americas had cracked, and would soon crumble. To the north, Mexico gained independence in 1821, as did the lands that would become Guatemala, El Salvador, Nicaragua, Costa Rica, and Honduras. That same year, Simón Bolívar's crushing defeat of the royalists on the savannah of Carabobo, near Valencia, brought freedom to Venezuela. A year later, almost to the day, a republican army under the command of Antonio José de Sucre, Bolívar's favorite general, liberated Ecuador, annihilating a Spanish army on the slopes of Pichincha. At the forefront of the fight was a contingent from the Macizo Colombiano and the Alto Magdalena, men who had no trouble killing Spaniards at twelve thousand feet. The next challenge would be Peru, where General José de San Martín, having freed Chile in 1818, had landed his forces at Paracas Bay in September 1820. By the summer of 1821, clearly a fateful year, republican forces were, for the moment, in control of Lima, the very symbol of the Spanish legacy.

The disintegration of the Spanish Empire presented Simón Bolívar with an extraordinary challenge. There was still fighting to be done in Peru; Lima, in particular, remained stubbornly loyal to the Crown. But the ultimate military outcome was no longer in doubt. Republican armies, led by Bolívar, Santander, and Sucre in the north and by San Martín in the south, had decisively defeated their foe on every field of battle. Success had come faster and more definitively than anyone had anticipated. Within just two years of the Battle of Boyacá and the liberation of Bogotá, the republican cause inherited responsibility for the stability, prosperity, and security of lands encompassing three million square miles. Virtually overnight, with a bitter war still raging, Bolívar and his colleagues had to establish a government that would serve the many millions in whose names they had fought: ordinary people, now citizens of a great republic of freedom, living in every crease and wrinkle of a wild and formidable land larger than the continental United States. Imagine for a moment George Washington's quandary had he inherited as president in 1789, responsibility for not just the Atlantic seaboard but lands it would take his new nation more than a century to settle and control.

In October 1821, a hastily convened Congress elected Santander as vice president of La Gran Colombia, Bolívar's singular vision of a nation encompassing all lands north of Peru. Leaving Santander in charge in Bogotá, Bolívar hastened to Angostura, where, as president of Venezuela, he persuaded his countrymen to accept union with Nueva Granada, a step clearly fundamental to his plan. Returning on a wave of success, he became president of the new nation, La Gran Colombia, just as had been anticipated by the authors of the Constitution of Cúcuta, the founding document of the new nation. Yielding to Bolívar's will, lawmakers in Congress codified the marriage of Venezuela and Nueva Granada, before the groom had even proposed. Within months, and by a similar sleight of hand, Bolívar orchestrated the addition of Ecuador to his growing realm.

For reasons difficult to understand, the Constitution of Cúcuta placed the vice president in charge of the executive branch of government, insisting that he remain at all times in Bogotá. The president, by contrast, was free to travel. This suited Bolívar, who intended to remain at the head of his armies until the last drop of Spanish blood was spilled. But it also meant that Santander would occupy the seat of power as the political, judicial, and economic structures of government were set in place. This only reinforced an emerging divide between the two men. Santander, a lawyer, embraced the tedious yet essential tasks of democratic rule, the mundane challenges of the nation-state; in his first months in office he dealt with economic crises, developed tax and trade policies, created guidelines for immigration, and resolved, to the extent possible, the tensions between federal authority and regional autonomy, a constant irritant in a mountainous land defined by topography.

Simón Bolívar, for his part, could not escape the shadow of Napoleon. He would never forget that day at the Cathédrale Notre-Dame in Paris, the spectacle of a simple soldier declaring himself emperor, the coronation of a commoner. It was less the pomp and pageantry than his own reaction that haunted Bolívar. At the time, both he and Humboldt had dismissed the ceremony as garish and vulgar, a betrayal of the ideals of the Enlightenment. Still, Bolívar could not help but admire the sheer audacity of the deed. Napoleon's naked and unapologetic claim to power had an irresistible allure. Such a triumph of personal will, Bolívar believed, marked every man destined for glory, the very few who actually moved the dial of history.

Bolívar saw in Napoleon the full measure of his own ambitions. Modesty and humility are hardly virtues to a man on a mission to liberate a continent. Dazzled by Napoleon's drive for conquest, Bolívar was equally drawn to what he achieved in lands that came under his control, all the political, economic, and judicial reforms that allowed the French in but a decade to reconfigure the face of Europe. Such a record surely offered a model for the challenges of La Gran Colombia. Fundamental to Napoleon's success, as Bolívar duly noted, was the central authority of a benevolent leader, an all-powerful emperor, a soldier born literally of the people.

Events continued to unfold at a breathless pace. From Bogotá, Bolívar returned south to take his place at the head of the army. Royalist forces remained active in Peru; within a year, Lima would be back in their hands. San Martín, whose armies had liberated Argentina, Chile, and much of Peru, came north to confer with Bolívar. They met privately on July 26, 1822, in Guayaquil, on the Pacific coast of Ecuador. What was said will never be known; no secretaries were present, and no record of their conversation has been found. What is known is what came of the meeting: a stunning reversal of fortunes that has baffled historians to this day. Even as Bolívar accepted command of all republican forces, San Martín, a revered general, who had marched his Army of the Andes the breadth of a continent, lifting it to the heights of glory as they crossed the cordillera to liberate Chile, resigned his commission and walked away from war. Having made public a personal vow to never again engage in politics or military affairs, San Martín, still young at forty-four, abandoned the Americas altogether, moving to France, where he would die in exile. On the eve of final victory, with independence at hand, San Martín slipped off the stage of history.

Perhaps he was pushed. Certainly this was the conclusion of a growing list of political enemies, among them rivals as well as former friends, shameless politicians but also men of integrity and honor, such as Santander. All were concerned about Bolívar's predilection for power and his conviction that power was best exercised by an authority of one. The mysterious meeting in Guayaquil, and the loss of San Martín to the cause, did not inspire confidence. Nor did the political moves that followed shortly upon Bolívar's stunning victories in Peru.

With the Spaniards in possession of Lima, Bolívar marched south at the head of an army of nine thousand. At his side was Sucre, the hero of Pichincha. At twenty-seven, he was already a veteran of ten years of war. Bolívar trusted him completely. "If God had given us the right to choose our families," he later wrote, "I would have chosen General Sucre as my son."

Having reorganized the army at Trujillo, on the northern coast of Peru, Bolívar led his force to the heights of the Andes, then followed the old Inca route south along the spine of the mountains toward Cusco. They first clashed with the royalists at Junín, in a cavalry skirmish elevated to the status of battle only in the wake of Peruvian independence. But then in December came Ayacucho, the battle that determined the final outcome of the war. It ranks with Yorktown, where Cornwallis surrendered to Lafayette and Washington, as a defining moment in the history of the Americas.

With Bolívar in Lima, negotiating loans and awaiting reinforcements from Colombia, Sucre was in command as some twenty thousand men met in battle on the Pampa de Ayacucho. The Spanish forces were led by the king's representative, Viceroy José de la Serna, whose very presence in the line of fire implied that the fate of Peru and the Spanish Indies would be decided before the sun slipped from the sky.

By early afternoon, it was over. Sucre had lost three hundred men. The Spaniards peered through the smoke and haze and wreckage of a field where eighteen hundred of their men lay dead. Among the seriously wounded was De la Serna, who had fallen into republican hands shortly after noon. With their commander evacuated from the field by the enemy, their ranks shattered, their medical tents overflowing with the wounded, the royalists yielded the field. Sucre's terms of capitulation, sent by runner under a flag of truce, addressed the fate of the viceroy's army and, more significantly, laid out the stages by which Spain, with honor, would be permitted to leave the Americas, surrendering not an army but an empire, one that had endured for far too long. Ayacucho was the final blow.

Simón Bolívar heralded Sucre for his victory, then moved quickly to consolidate his rule. Within weeks, the landlocked towns and settlements of the altiplano and southern Andes declared independence, severing their historic but impractical ties to Lima. Naturally, they offered the presidency to Bolívar, who politely declined, citing his presidential obligations in La Gran Colombia, three thousand miles to the north. Instead, in his place, he nominated his confidant and protégé, General Sucre. Though a son of Venezuela, with little knowledge of a distant land he had never visited, the young general was nevertheless delighted to become a president, especially of a new nation soon to be named Bolivia, in honor of his mentor; it was, at the very least, a good career move. Simón Bolívar, meanwhile, having refused to accept Bolivia's offer, and for good reasons, eagerly took on the presidential office in Peru. By the end of 1825, Bolívar had his man Sucre in control of Bolivia, while he served as head of state in both La Gran Colombia and Peru. None among his growing entourage dared to remind him of the obvious: no man can ride three horses at the same time. Bolívar alone, with his dreams and limitless ambitions, believed that by sheer force of will he would be able to hold together a continental nation that nobody, aside from him, seemed to want.

· · ·

Even as Bolívar contemplated the virtues of installing a dictator in Venezuela and a president for life in Bolivia, Santander, in Bogotá, was building a republic based on laws and institutions, the structures of governance of a democratic society. His challenge equaled that of the delegates who gathered in Philadelphia in 1787, with the fate of their young nation, also won in war, hanging in the balance. At the Constitutional Convention, it took the wisdom and authority of men such as James Madison, Alexander Hamilton, George Washington, and Benjamin Franklin—all legends in the American firmament—to craft an enduring document that would transcend the passions of the moment to provide generations as yet unborn the legal framework of liberty, the foundation of freedom.

Their quixotic and unexpected success inspired Santander, who had a messianic faith in constitutional government. Before becoming a soldier, he had been a student of the law, obsessed with its promise for open and democratic societies. In his view, laws did not restrict the life of a nation; they provided the structure of civilization, a moral and ethical matrix without which liberty and freedom would always remain elusive. He would be known to historians as, simply, "El Hombre de las Leyes." The Man of Laws. Santander's greatest legacy is Colombia's Constitutional Court, the highest legal authority in the country and to this day the institution most respected, trusted, and revered by the Colombian people. The court convenes in Bogotá at the Palacio de Justicia, itself a living monument to Santander. Colombia remains a nation of laws, and anyone coming before its highest court will notice the words adorning the building's façade, a phrase that perfectly distills Santander's vision for the nation:

"Colombianos, las armas os han dado la independencia, pero solo las leyes os darán la libertad." Arms have given you independence, but only laws will give you freedom.

At the core of the conflict between the two leaders was a contradiction. In Paris, Simón Bolívar had told anyone who would listen that the Spanish colonies were primed for independence, prompting Humboldt's oft-cited response that the people were indeed ready for representative government, if only a leader could be found. Bolívar eagerly took on the mantle of leadership, but once in power he rejected democracy as being unworkable in Latin America; what the undisciplined masses needed, he believed, was a strong executive, an omnipotent authority wielding power without bias or prejudice.

Santander had stood with Bolívar in war. In command of the republican vanguard, he had played a decisive role at both El Pantano de Vargas and the Battle of Boyacá. A soldier at eighteen, promoted by Bolívar to the rank of major general in the wake of Boyacá, he understood the importance of an inflexible and well-defined chain of command. Only a nation of fools would fill the highest ranks of its military by popular vote. But, as Santander argued, if a country was to be ruled not by generals and clerics but by laws, republican government implied and demanded the active participation of the people. What Bolívar proposed—an alliance of church and state with a central authority entrenched at the seat of power, untested by the ballot, unaccountable over time—challenged the very principles for which so many of their friends and comrades had sacrificed their lives. As even Humboldt confessed, Bolívar was moving in the shadow of Napoleon, flirting with dictatorship, while dreaming of becoming a king.

Dictatorship would come first. The tipping point came in August 1828, as Santander and his supporters blocked in Congress one of Bolívar's cherished proposals for reform. In response, this son of the Enlightenment, believed by all to be a supporter of republican ideals, seized control of the government, disenfranchising his rival by unilaterally abolishing the office of the vice president, Santander's locus of authority. Some objected, comparing Bolívar to Napoleon; others likened his behavior to that of Julius Caesar. Darker elements plotted his end. At his lowest ebb, Bolívar endured two attempts on his life, six weeks apart, both in Bogotá and both mercifully foiled by the one person he could still trust, Manuela Sáenz, his beloved mistress. Manuelita saved him on the first occasion by feigning hysteria, drawing him out of a private party where killers stalked. Bolívar escaped death a second time by scrambling out a bedroom window; he landed on the cobblestoned street half-dressed and fully humiliated. These trials and threats did nothing to quell Bolívar's ambitions; quite to the contrary, the assassination plots gave him what he needed to move on Santander.

Though not a shred of evidence connected Santander to the deed, he was arrested, tried by a military court, condemned, and sentenced to death, all in a day. Only at the last moment did Bolívar spare his life, issuing a presidential pardon that forced his nemesis into exile. Santander viewed the entire episode as farce: the false accusations and concocted evidence, a show trial followed by a fawning display of compassion. What kind of man imposes a death sentence before noon only to commute it by the end of the day? Only one, he believed, poisoned by hubris and touched by the cruelty of gods. This final reckoning left Santander more certain than ever that Bolívar, at whose side he had fought and for whom so many had died, was beyond redemption, irretrievably lost in a labyrinth of power and delusion.

Though his authority was now absolute, Bolívar felt increasingly under siege, burdened by disappointment, embittered by failure and loss. At night, he struggled to sleep, haunted by memories of the dead. Blood, it was said, flooded his dreams. By day, he was too often alone with his thoughts, which too readily indulged in despair. He was incapable of comprehending a world unfolding by its own volition, beyond his control. For a quarter century, since the loss of his young wife, he had served with absolute devotion a single cause: military victory over a foe that had ravaged his homeland and denied him the innocence of youth, drowning his childhood in rivers of bile and hatred. His fate and that of the revolutionary cause were as one, each incapable, in his mind, of surviving on its own. In the midst of the armed struggle, he failed to envision the complex challenges that awaited victory, just as he remained blind to the possibility of defeat.

In 1822, at the height of his glory, Bolívar had slipped away from his armies to follow the footsteps and memories of Humboldt on the slopes of Chimborazo, believed at the time to be the highest mountain in the world. In the one poem Bolívar wrote about the war, "Delirium on Chimborazo," he presented the mountain as a metaphor, equating his ascent, which reached well beyond that of Humboldt, with the revolutionary struggle that had landed him at the head of the army. Only from such mystic heights, he claimed, an altitude achieved only by him, could the future of the nation be perceived from the perspective it deserved. He admitted to being just a "plaything of the revolutionary hurricane." Still, as the last verse of the poem attests, destiny has chosen him alone for glory: "Here on the icy slopes of Chimborazo, the tremendous voice of Colombia cries out to me."

Such a grand sense of self, touching on the maniacal, was no doubt critical to Bolívar's success as a military commander, but as his world came apart, hubris left him only more isolated, embittered, and confused. As fissures cracked the façade of La Gran Colombia, and regional politics of identity and place eroded the foundations of the nation, his one country soon to become three, Bolívar simply could not comprehend what had gone wrong: *"He arado en el mar y he sembrado en el desierto."* How could history deny, he wrote in despair, a man who has plowed the oceans and seeded the deserts?

On April 27, 1830, Simón Bolívar resigned the presidency, driven from office by his peers. By then, his only goal was to leave the country. Venezuela, the land of his birth, had revoked his citizenship, confiscated his property, and denied him the right of return. His only asset, a remote copper mine, was buried in litigation. To survive, he sold the family silverware. He had no income or pension. The government initially offered nothing, refusing even to recognize the years he served without compensation in the army. Having committed his entire family fortune to the struggle, Simón Bolívar, "El Libertador de la Gran Colombia," emancipator of a continent, found himself alone on the streets of Bogotá, broke and impoverished, without sufficient means even to abandon the nation that so cruelly had abandoned him.

Some weeks later, he met with the French ambassador, Auguste Le Moyne, new to Bogotá after a two-month journey up the Río Magdalena. Bolívar's appearance shocked his visitor. An innocent question about his health provoked from Bolívar an acidic reply: "It isn't nature that has reduced me to this, but the pain gnawing at my heart. My fellow citizens couldn't kill me with daggers, so they are trying to kill me with ingratitude. When I cease to exist, those hotheads will devour each other like a pack of wolves, and what I erected with superhuman effort will drown in the muck of rebellion."

Broken and bitter, Simón Bolívar made his way to Honda in

May 1830. For his last journey on the Magdalena, six hundred miles downriver to the sea, he traveled not by steamboat, where luxury awaited, but in a simple *champán*, customized to meet his needs. There was room for his hammock, a small table and chairs, cushions and mats to soften the floor. His lone companion was his cook, Fernanda Barriga, who each day prepared *arepas* and *mazamorra*, the only food, aside from fruit, Bolívar could tolerate. Though just forty-seven, he was little more than a bundle of bones: gaunt and frail, unable to walk, and scarcely able to breathe, so corrupted were his lungs, corroded by tuberculosis. His face hung yellow with jaundice; his eyes were dark as coal. Only his mind remained untarnished and alert, ensuring that his final days on the river, the last passage of his life, would be a torrent of regrets and recriminations.

It was the height of the rainy season, and the Magdalena was in flood. Any land exposed to the sun was dark with serpents and crocodiles, even at midday. On the water, Bolívar shivered in the heat, slipping from time to time into delirium, only to bolt awake in his hammock, lucid and alive. He counted the ragged clearings along the shore, hacked from the forest. Steamboats, though new to the river, had already transformed the shores with their ravenous consumption of wood. As he drifted downstream, slipping in and out of awareness, Bolívar could not help but remember the man who had opened his eyes, allowing a revolutionary soldier to become, in the words of one of his generals, "a true lover of nature." Whatever the fortunes of war, Bolívar had always found peace in the wild. Rivers, forests, and mountains had long ignited his imagination. His soul, he wrote, was always "dazzled by the presence of primitive nature."

Once in power, Simón Bolívar had codified the protection of nature with decrees and laws the likes of which had never been written, regulations and sanctions on a national scale that would not be seen again until the rise of the modern environmental movement in the 1970s. Bolívar introduced sweeping reforms designed to protect waterways and forests across all of La Gran Colombia. In 1825, he obliged the Bolivian government to plant a million trees. Concerned about the uncontrolled harvesting of cinchona bark for quinine, he set in place legislation that criminalized the extraction of any timber from forests belonging to the state. The statute, like all decrees proclaimed by those with dictatorial powers, was a personal declaration, Simón Bolívar's way of saying that the tree must always trump the ax, and that nature in all its mysteries must be defended as the foundation of life and the cradle of the nation.

Such policies did not long endure. As the world closed in around Bolívar, his ideals fared as poorly as his health. Drifting past charred fields and tangles of slash, he saw in the future of the Magdalena only devastation. The entire drainage, he predicted, would be ravaged by settlers—some desperate with hunger, others blinded by greed, all foolish enough to believe that the destruction of tropical forests, surely among the most precious of God's creations, was a sign of the upward march of civilization. The scabrous openings and scarred earth along the Magdalena's shores represented not progress to Bolívar but, rather, the spreading shadows of Armageddon. Touched by fever, he shouted at his secretaries, spitting out words and phrases that were less bitter than apocalyptic. As his small party approached Mompox, they discovered that even the river had turned on him, shifting its flow from his beloved city to the Brazo de Loba near Magangué.

Every church bell in Mompox heralded Bolívar's arrival. But the warm welcome was mostly a measure of the town's isolation; Mompox knew little of the political intrigues and twisted betrayals that had determined his fate and that of La Gran Colombia. Many *momposinos*, Bolívar discovered, did not know that he'd been forced from office and no longer served as their president. Those who had betrayed him now held the reins of power in Bogotá. While he had been lost on the river, his enemies had destroyed his legacy. La Gran Colombia had broken into fragments, with Venezuela, Ecuador, and Colombia formally proclaiming independence. In the streets, they were burning his effigy and cursing the Bolívar name. Once revered as liberator, now reviled as oppressor, he understood that his betrayal was complete. They pushed on for the sea, leaving the sons of America, as Bolívar wrote, free to destroy each other. His words were prophetic. After fourteen days on the river, they disembarked at Barranca Nueva, where a dusty track carried them by mule to the coast and, ultimately, Cartagena. A letter awaited, and Bolívar learned that an assassin had killed his favorite general,

Sucre, the soldier he loved as a son. Now there was nothing left for him in life but death.

Betrayed and abandoned by his countrymen, Bolívar found refuge in the home of a former enemy, a wealthy Spaniard, Joaquín de Mier, whose estate, San Pedro Alejandrino, had miraculously survived the war. Nestled in the shadow of the Sierra Nevada de Santa Marta, to the east of the city, where the land rises gradually toward the foothills of the mountains, the plantation straddled sacred sites of the Arhuaco, with vast fields of sugarcane, all fed by the rivers of the Sierra. Everything it produced was sweet: rum, honey, *panela*.

Bolívar arrived in Santa Marta by sea from Cartagena. The brig that ferried him to his rest sailed across the mouth of the Río Magdalena, through seas the color of the river. To the south, the Caribbean fused with the shimmering surface of the Ciénaga Grande de Santa Marta. On the approach to the city, Bolívar gazed upon the highest summits of the Sierra and the icefields that shroud the abode of the Great Mother. It was six months since he had embarked on a *champán* in Honda, with exile his only goal, oblivion his only destination. Now he understood that he would die in Colombia. On December 9, he took his last sacraments and, from his deathbed, dictated his final testament:

> Colombians! You have witnessed my efforts to launch liberty where tyranny once reigned. I have labored selflessly, sacrificing my fortune and my peace of mind. When it came clear that you doubted my motives, I resigned my command. My enemies have toyed with your confidence, destroyed what I hold sacred—my reputation, my love of liberty. They have made me their victim and hounded me to my grave. I forgive them. As I depart your midst, my love for you impels me to make known my last wishes. I aspire to no other glory than the consolidation of Colombia. . . . My last vote is for the happiness of our native land. If my death can heal and fortify the nation, I go on to my tomb in peace.

He died eight days later, on the anniversary of the founding of La Gran Colombia. Tuberculosis was the cause, but history would see it as a symptom. His last words were a distillation of despair. Serving the revolution, he allegedly whispered, was as futile and pointless as trying to plow a furrow into the sea.

On December 20, 1830, a modest procession carried Simón Bolívar's body from the customhouse in Santa Marta to the cathedral. No one of note attended the service. Even the bishop stayed home, feigning illness. Not for a decade would Bolívar's bones be repatriated to his birthplace in Venezuela. His heart would remain in Colombia, protected and preserved in a small urn in Santa Marta.

Enrique was damp with tears and sweat as he came to the end of his story. Xandra passed him a glass of water. Our friend added a final coda.

"When Bolívar conquered Peru," he said, "the people of Lima offered him a reward of a million pesos, with another million for his army. He accepted on behalf of the troops, but refused his share. He turned down the money. As president, he decreed the death penalty for anyone stealing more than ten pesos from the public treasury. He took nothing. And he died with nothing, having given everything."

What haunts Enrique is how little is known about that final fortnight on the river. Over his life, Bolívar, a furious correspondent, wrote more than ten thousand letters. During fourteen days and nights on the Magdalena, he dictated only three, possibly four. No one with him chronicled the journey. The last and perhaps most fateful passage of Simón Bolívar's life remains a void, which over time has been filled by the passions of his admirers, all those touched by his tragedy and inspired by his life.

Enrique looked away to the river, and, as if speaking to no one, recited a strange line, at once both cynical and apocalyptic:

"Los peces tendrán que aprender a caminar sobre la tierra porque las aguas se acabarán." The fish will have to learn to walk, because all the water will be gone.

"Did Bolívar write that?" I asked.

"No," said Enrique, "Gabriel García Márquez. It's from *The General in His Labyrinth*, the best historical account we have of Bolívar's last journey."

"But that's a novel," I said, "a work of fiction."

"A work of the imagination," Enrique replied. "García Márquez saw what Bolívar saw, and he made sure that they both saw the same thing, a world and a river degraded beyond recognition. Two men across the ages sharing the same memories, both trapped in the gyre of passing time."

A Geography of Hope

What is life but a story we lose the power of comprehending as we grow old? In his last years, long after his Colombia had itself become but an illusion of memory, Gabriel García Márquez declared the Río Magdalena to be dead, its waters poisoned, its animals exterminated, its forests destroyed. In the first volume of his memoirs, *Vivir para contarla*, he scoffed at the idea that its scorched and barren riverbanks might ever again be lush with jungles saturated with the scent of blossoms and alive with the sounds of monkeys, jaguars, and macaws, as they had been in his youth. To replace what had been lost would require, he claimed with curious precision, the planting of "fifty-nine thousand, one hundred and ten million trees" on properties that were now privately owned, removing arable land from production and reducing income for landowners by 90 percent. The river itself was beyond redemption, with water unsafe to drink and fish too soiled to eat, all rendered toxic by raw sewage and industrial waste disgorged into its flow by every town and city in the drainage. García Márquez went on, sharing an anecdote of two guerrillas who, fleeing the army, flung themselves into the river only to die, infected by its waters. He recalls that the only person with a serious plan to rehabilitate the Magdalena, a young engineer from Antioquia by the name of Jairo Murillo, had himself died in the river, drowning along with his dreams. Coming from a national treasure, a Noble laureate who upon his death in April 2014 would be declared by then-president Juan Manuel Santos as "the greatest Colombian who ever lived," this was a powerful indictment, a statement of despair that fell somewhere between bitterness and the truth.

Few Colombians, and certainly no Colombian writer, have been as closely associated with the Río Magdalena as Gabriel García Márquez. The river was not just the setting but an actual character in two of his greatest novels, *Love in the Time of Cholera* and *The General in His Labyrinth*, books that are completely inspired by the author's passion for the Magdalena. All of the themes that informed his work—forgetfulness and love, violence and hope, progress and decadence, fertility and death—are to be found in the eddies and back channels and currents of a river that literally carried him, as a boy, to his destiny, allowing him to enter a world of language and literature where he would discover just what words can do.

There is scarcely an image or a phrase in *Love in the Time of Cholera* that does not correspond to an actual episode in García Márquez's life. When he portrays, for example, Florentino's journeys on the Magdalena, the first to heal a broken heart, the second in pursuit of pure love, he is writing of riverboats he knew so well as a youth, magnificent three-story *vapores* with soaring black chimneys, passing in the night like brightly lit carnival tents, trailing in their wake music and poetry and phosphorescent dreams. Along the shores, he recalls, sand beaches were dark with caimans lounging in the sun, their jaws wide open, filled with small clouds of butterflies. Flocks of herons in the sloughs, flights of egrets scraping the sky, and in the shallows along the shore, and in the *ciénagas*, manatees suckling their young, their skin pale and soft like that of a woman.

On board, the third-class passengers swung in hammocks hung from the rafters of the lower deck, while the *gente bien* paced the perimeter of the upper decks, watching life and the river flow by. Men wore cotton or linen, suits tailored for the tropics. Women dressed as they would for a transatlantic crossing, with sufficient outfits to allow them to change several times a day, along with extravagant hats adorned with flowers, silk gloves, fans, and umbrellas for the sun. Each man carried aboard a small leather case containing grooming essentials: hair tonic, cologne, and scented powders. Women brought their own feather pillows and linen sheets, along with several pairs of white shoes, all oversized, for a lady's feet were certain to swell in *tierra caliente*. The steamboat captains, as García Márquez wrote, were larger than life, firm and steady, impeccably dressed, with the strength of roots and a pronounced weakness for wildlife. They towered over the vessel, just as the giant ceibas rose above the riverbanks, the one forest tree, sacred to all the ancestors, that never fell to the woodsman's ax.

On the river, everything receded in time and space, with memory itself being forgotten. The slow, languid days seemed to last longer with each passing mile. The length of the journey was itself never certain, dependent always on the river, its depth and current, the shifting sands and sediments, the turning of the seasons. If a vessel ran aground and the journey was delayed, it caused no alarm, for no one expected punctuality, and with each day the passengers grew as a family, causing the music and dancing that followed every captain's dinner to reach ever deeper into the night.

From time to time, the vessel came to shore to purchase *burros de leña*, fuel for the boilers, or to offload cargo onto mules for the long ascent to the cities and towns of the cordilleras. There was always a sense on board that anything could happen, that life-changing encounters were to be expected, that all was possible. García Márquez writes of a medical student who at a random stop entered a wedding party uninvited, flirted with the most beautiful woman, and ended up being shot by her jealous husband. He also recalls another passenger who, after a wild night in Puerto Berrío, woke to discover that in his drunkenness he had gotten married. He and his wife would have nine children and live happily ever after. He tells, too, of a woman who carried her baby about the ship in a wooden birdcage, hanging it from the open deck, and of another great beauty who used fireflies as accessories, creating broaches and decorating her hair with the glowing creatures.

Altogether, García Márquez would embark on eleven round-trip journeys on the Magdalena, traveling back and forth from his home on the coast to school in the capital, always convinced that he learned more in his few days on the river than in his many months in the classroom. His very first trip in 1943, when he was but sixteen, was perhaps the most memorable for it was on the *David Arango*, the most elegant of all vessels ever to travel the river—the *Titanic*, many would say, of the Magdalena. As an orchestra welcomed the passengers and the ship made ready to sail, García Márquez rushed to the highest deck and watched as the lights of the town of Magangué slowly receded in the darkness. Tears filled his eyes, and he remained, as he later recalled, in a state of ecstasy throughout the entire night and, indeed, the entire journey. It took six days to reach Puerto Salgar, where he caught the train for Bogotá. A boy from the coast who had never stood higher than the hood of a truck found himself climbing into the Andes, whistling and wheezing like a struggling *arriero* gasping for air.

Bogotá came as a shock, with its cold and wet chill, the men all dressed in black trudging to their places of work and no sign of a woman in the streets, no laughter, no joy, no color. Nothing to dazzle his gypsy eyes. A grey city of solitude and despair. Within hours, he longed for heat and home. He counted the days and weeks as the calendar turned toward December. In his yearning, the Magdalena became the antidote to Bogotá, his lifeline to the coast, where everything was awash in color and passion, where flirtations with parrots and sunbirds were the norm and daily life, as he would later write, was but a pretense for poetry.

He had been raised by his grandparents in a world of multiple realities, not unlike the country itself, a nation that he would embody as a writer and a man. His grandfather, a veteran of the War of a Thousand Days, never escaped his memories of fire, obsessions that over time enveloped their home in a shroud of gloom, leaving García Márquez haunted by the specter of death for all of his life. His grandmother, by contrast, lived in a realm of the imagination where everything was possible, where common garden frogs were *brujas* by night, river stones the eggs of dinosaurs, and plants only people in another dimension of reality. Fantasy and the supernatural were but glimmers of liminal space where heaven and earth converged to reveal glimpses of the divine.

García Márquez had a way of being present at those moments when Colombia cleaved from its past. In 1928, when field hands went on strike and bananas rotted on the stem, agents of the United Fruit Company in the guise of soldiers slaughtered their families with machine guns, leaving the plaza of Ciénaga blanketed with the dead, corpses that were cast into the sea. The survivors fled south only to be murdered in the Aracataca graveyard before the eyes of a desperate priest. As an infant, García Márquez rested in his cradle within earshot of the massacre. Years later, he was living as a student in a Bogotá boardinghouse just blocks from the Black Cat Café, where Jorge Gaitán was murdered. García Márquez watched as workers poured into the streets and the capital burned. He was there as the army turned its tanks on the people and a terrible violence was born that would leave generations of Colombians looking over their shoulders in fear, waiting for the moment when death would find them. Like all of his generation, he came of age in a land where death was not a distant fate but a burden to be borne in every moment of life, a threat as constant as the night.

García Márquez grew to view death as a swindle, a cosmic trap, the ultimate betrayal. "Not dying," he declared, "is the only option I accept." And yet he would live to see too much of death, even as Florentino, on his last journey, comes upon three corpses floating in the river, green and bloated, with vultures perched on top. By then the forests were gone, along with the animals and birds. The Magdalena had become a cemetery, leaving the river, his Magdalena, as he wrote, but an illusion of memory. His deepest fears were confirmed not long after he abandoned Colombia for a life in Mexico, when a phone call from Bogotá confirmed that the *David Arango*, docked in Magangué, had been destroyed by fire, reduced to ash by a conflagration that marked for him not just the end of an era of travel but the final death of innocence. "That day," he later wrote, "ended my youth and what was barely left of our river of nostalgia was now a total mess."

What in fact had died was just one man's story, one thin chapter of a chronicle of a river that has flowed for three million years and touched the lives of countless people. García Márquez once said, "The only reason I would like to be young again would be the chance to travel again on a freighter going up the Magdalena." His life was bookended by his first journey on the river in 1943 and the news that the vessel that had carried him on that journey had been lost to fire in 1961, a span of less than two decades in which the Río Magdalena, according to García Márquez, had been transformed from paradise to wasteland, heaven to hell. To be sure, those years brought ecological devastation. But forests can grow back and animals be reclaimed, even from the abyss of extinction. All that has been irrevocably lost is one man's passionate identification with a moment in time, a trivial instant impossible even to record in the life of a river. The robber of memories is surely the one trapped in nostalgia who would deny to those coming in his wake the chance to celebrate a river that still lives, flowing to the sea and bringing the promise of life to the land as it always has. In truth, the Río Magdalena remains an open book, one with countless pages and chapters yet to be written. Like the families condemned to live one hundred years of solitude, it too deserves to have, at last and forever, a second chance on earth.

The Caribbean sky is the color of dreams, and the clouds appear as shadows on the still surface of the Ciénaga Grande de Santa Marta. Our skiff scudded over the water as we left the narrow neck of shoreline behind at Tasajeras. The wetland expanded in every direction. At full throttle, our small party was soon skating over a mirror of glass, with only a distant fringe of mangroves to suggest the presence of horizons and the mundane separation of earth from sky. The faint silhouette of the Sierra Nevada de Santa Marta hovered not thirty miles to the east. As the sun melts the ice on those frozen summits, glacial streams from those heights grow into seasonal rivers—the Fundación, Tucurinca, Aracataca, and Riofrío—that replenish the wetland with fresh water and, more essentially, according to the *mamos*, infuse it with *aluna*, the generative essence of the Madre Creadora, the Great Mother. Running away from the *ciénaga* to the south and west are natural canals that ultimately fuse with the floodwaters of the Río Magdalena. Like the arteries and veins in the human body, a network of waterways reaches across the ancient delta to connect the snowfields of the Sierra Nevada, the most sacred destination of the pilgrims, with the river that made possible the life of the Colombian nation.

The *mamos* still speak of a time when the Ciénaga Grande was wet with the innocence of birth, an aquatic Eden that was home to manatees, jaguars, caimans, and no fewer than 244 species of birds. Open to the Caribbean, recharged by the annual surge of the Magdalena, the wetland was a perfect balance of river and sea. Often described as the most beautiful body of water in Colombia, it was certainly the most productive. *Bocachico, bagre,* and more than a dozen species of edible fish thrived in the shallows, softening the mangrove roots with their spawn. The fishery was so bountiful that those who stumbled upon it decided to stay. Men from Soledad and Santo Tomás, Sitionuevo, Malambo, and all the exhausted fishing settlements of the coast settled first at the mouth of Aguas Negras. All they needed to prosper was at hand: salt, fish, and the sun. Their only challenge were the flocks that darkened the sky: cormorants, screaming gulls, and egrets that feasted on the catch as it dried. To escape the scavengers, families took to the water, building shelters on pilings that over time grew into floating villages serviced only by canoe and small skiffs. The oldest, Bocas de Aracataca, dates to 1786. The other two, Buena Vista and Nueva Venecia, first known as El Morro, go back at least a century, some say to 1847.

After an hour on the water, tracking the eastern shore of the *ciénaga,* we slipped through the narrows and came upon Buena Vista, a rather forlorn place that clearly has seen better days. From a near distance, it seems little more than a warren of tired shacks that paint alone keeps from tumbling into the water. Nueva Venecia was altogether different. Laid out in a neat grid, with waterways in place of roads, it's a lively and exuberant town of two thousand, fishing families for the most part, all living in neat, brightly painted wooden homes with elevated gardens and enclosed pools where they grow fingerlings, fish to replenish the wetlands. The community is serviced by an assortment of bars, *tiendas,* billiard halls, and soccer fields, all perched above the water, save the church, the anchor and sanctuary of the community. It alone occupies solid ground, land built up by hand, *a pico y pala,* by pick and shovel.

According to our pilot and host, Ahmed Gutiérrez, things began to go wrong in 1955, when the government authorized the construction of a highway along the Caribbean shore. The goal was to shorten the travel time between Santa Marta and Barranquilla by eliminating the long loop south and north around the Ciénaga Grande. With insufficient conduits beneath the roadway to allow for the ebb and flow of water essential to the health of the wetland, the causeway effectively served as a dam, shutting off the sea, to the detriment of all the creatures adapted to live in brackish water. Some sixty-four thousand acres of mangroves perished, all vital spawning habitat. As the shore took on the aspect of a desert, fish populations collapsed, even as birds fell dead from the sky.

To make matters worse, the natural infusion of fresh water, also essential to the equilibrium of the system, fell dramatically as rivers draining the flank of the Sierra Nevada were diverted to deliver water to the banana and oil palm plantations that, on an industrial scale, consume much of the fertile land surrounding the vast *ciénaga*. The Río Aracataca, originally a hundred feet across and thirty deep, was reduced to a heavily sedimented stream just twenty-six feet wide with a depth of a foot and a half. In place of glacial flows, cold and pure, the *ciénaga* increasingly absorbed agricultural runoff tainted with pesticides, nitrogenous fertilizers, and herbicides. In time, the salinity of the wetlands surpassed that of the sea. In June 1994, a much degraded Ciénaga Grande earned the terrible distinction as the site of the largest incident of fish mortality in Colombian history.

"It got so bad, you couldn't touch the water," Ahmed recalled. "The salt made your skin itch. Cats would swim but dogs became afraid. In some places the whole *ciénaga* turned red, almost like blood."

Ahmed had generously offered to put us up, and as his daughter pulled together a simple lunch, we hung our hammocks in a vacant storage area at the back of his home. Our new friend claimed to be fifty-five but looked forty, with thick black hair and a generous mustache showing not a speckle of grey. As a local merchant, boat owner, onetime mayor, and national park guardian with a passion for education and conservation, Ahmed naturally knew everyone in Nueva Venecia. But his style and charm suggested a cool confidence that would have registered in any setting. He acted more like a maître d' than a small-town politician, radiating a warmth and civic pride that was both sincere and infectious. When Ahmed said the government had done nothing, leaving the people to save both the *ciénaga* and their town, we took him at his word. He was a man easy to believe.

The good people of Nueva Venecia, Ahmed explained, whose grandparents had built an island by hand to erect a church, had no trouble opening an outlet to channel fresh water from the Magdalena into the wetland. To do so, they simply ignored the government authorities. Still, the main conduits remained obstructed at the *caños* of Torno, Clarinuevo, Aguas Negras, and Renegado.

"But God is wonderful," Ahmed said with a smile, "and he sent us a great winter!"

Divine intervention took the form of torrents of rain that overwhelmed the floodgates, eroding small gaps that grew into chasms, allowing water from the Magdalena to surge into the wetland. The salutary impact was, according to Ahmed, almost immediate. Within a season, the mangroves began to recover. Fishermen returned at dawn with food for their families. Fathers and mothers struggled to remember stories of manatees, creatures their children had never before seen.

"The *ciénaga* is so resilient," Ahmed said in wonder, "just like the people. Forty years ago, no one had power—no ice, radios, outboards, television. Just simple lamps, wick and oil. The entire town was lit with tufts of hair. It was pure poetry at night; rare was the man who was not a poet. Verse after verse in the same sequence, the same rhyme, all the verses carrying the rhyme. There was a chorus to accompany the black dances, and always palm fronds. Without palms, you can't have a black dance. And without the dance, the town couldn't survive, because the black dances never end. Poetry and black dancing, that's what kept the place alive."

Ahmed had in mind a time when the people of Nueva Venecia still sketched the stories of their lives, asking nothing of the state save to be left alone to feast on *bocachico*, *bagre*, and *corvina*, fish now lost to memory. An era impossibly distant, yet as near as yesterday, the childhood of his own grandfather.

Later that evening, Ahmed introduced us to Armando Martínez, a much admired elder. We found him in a rocker in the corner of his wooden room, flanked by doorways that opened directly to the water. Still spry at eighty-eight, Armando appeared to be working out, a sort of calisthenics of goodwill. A gentle wave of his right hand greeted boats and canoes passing one side of his house, while his left acknowledged those coming along the busier channel in front. The traffic at dusk kept him active and clearly content. The sun warmed his face. He had a wonderful profile: bold, proud, and distinguished. After a busy day in his herb garden, he was dressed for the evening, in a white shirt and dark trousers, both neatly pressed. His bare feet were the color of the floor. The patina made me wonder about the age of the house, and how long mangrove wood lasted as pilings, joists, roof beams, and boards. Maintenance was the key, Armando explained. He had been born in the very room where he now sat, as had his father before him. His dad had lived to be ninety.

"And we will continue to live," Armando proclaimed, as if speaking for his lineage. "I certainly intend to continue living. I still do not want to die."

"He's a very brave man," Ahmed interjected. "He was one of the few not to leave."

"I did not go out. I stayed here. My family urged me to flee, but if I was going to die, they would kill me here in my village."

Armando moved the conversation to safer ground, tracking the history of the town. Ice and electricity had been a mixed blessing. Young people abandoned the traditional ways. They began to fish with industrial nets that caught and destroyed everything. Metal roofing was another evil invention, displacing thatch and turning every house into an oven at noon.

"My grandfather used to sleep in the swales, on beds of mangrove poles. His sail was his blanket, bed, and shelter. If the candles went out at night, by morning they'd be sleeping with caimans. He had nothing modern and yet he lived to a hundred and ten. Why? Because he lived in a world that made sense."

Armando was not indulging sentiment, as Ahmed made clear. He knew what life had been for his grandparents: precarious and uncertain, fraught with all the difficulties encountered by pioneers on the raw frontier of the wild. Armando looked back to those years not in nostalgia but simply to affirm that there really had been a time when things were normal, when life had yet to be indelibly stained by the horror of that morning, the darkest hour in the history of Nueva Venecia.

Like so many rural communities in Colombia at the height of the conflict, the floating villages of the Ciénaga Grande had been caught in a vise, vulnerable and exposed to the wrath of all combatants. On the day of Carnaval, a Saturday, in 1998, ELN cadres from the Domingo Barrios Front slipped into Nueva Venecia to warn the community that the region was about to become a war zone. The guerrillas moved on, but not before purchasing food, fuel, and other supplies, transactions that no local dared deny. And that was all it took.

Ahmed remembers the night before the massacre as the most beautiful he had ever known: a clear sky, the surface of the *ciénaga* a blanket of stars, a cool and pleasant breeze blowing from the north. The town that night had been lively and gay, with families and children already looking ahead to Christmas. Ahmed and his brother, visiting from Barranquilla, set out around two a.m. and had just reached the fishing grounds when they heard the muffled roar of high-powered boats in the distance. Working the nets, Ahmed thought nothing of it until a loud explosion shattered the dawn. They then saw six boats coming their way—not police, as he had expected, but paramilitary, some sixty armed men, all outfitted in camouflage. If they fled, as his brother urged, the *paras* would take it as a sign of guilt. Instead, Ahmed knelt and prayed, asking God to protect them. One of the boats pulled alongside their canoe. Ahmed feared the worst as the *paras* hooded his brother. He could smell the guns, and knew that people had already died.

Ahmed recognized no one, but, mercifully, one among them knew him. Seeing that the fishermen were unarmed, the killers let them be, and sped south through the eye of the needle toward Remolinos and Pivijay, where they had a camp. Ahmed and his brother returned to their nets, filled their canoe with the catch, and were well on their way back to Nueva Venecia before either of them realized how miraculous their reprieve had been. The waters all around town were dark with canoes, families fleeing in panic and despair. Ahmed saw a close friend weeping like a child. Only then did he learn that his own father-in-law was among the dead, an innocent man of seventy-six.

Ahmed did what was necessary. He gathered the dead, thirty-nine victims altogether. Elsy Rodríguez, the town baker, lost two brothers and a nephew, all that she had. "Even my beauty left that day," she would later say. The entire family of Roque Parejo was killed, including an eighteen-year-old boy who had only just married. None of it made any sense. Among the dead were five men from Soledad and Sitionuevo who just happened to be working in Nueva Venecia. They were shot in the church, the first to be murdered. By the time Ahmed came upon their corpses, the sun had already bloated the bodies.

"When you tried to lift them, everything came out." Ahmed said very quietly. "I called out to God: What is this? Why am I living this hell?"

Ahmed and those recruited to his side used boards as stretchers to remove the dead from the church, laying them on a nearby rooftop to await the arrival of their relatives. Fear kept everyone away. In the end, by boat, Ahmed and a cousin delivered the bodies to the authorities in Sitionuevo.

"All day we lived in terror, but come the night, it was worse." Ahmed recalled. "Even the dogs howled in fear. If you had a heart, you could only weep, and then try to get away."

Overnight, Nueva Venecia became a ghost town, as families fled both the horror and the helplessness they felt as the full story of the massacre came to light. The raid had been led by Rodrigo Tovar Pupo, alias Jorge 40, operating under orders of the Autodefensas Unidas de Colombia, the AUC. That ELN guerrillas had entered the community, their armed presence beyond any civilian's control, was sufficient cause to target Nueva Venecia for retribution, all part of the AUC's scorched-earth policy of terror and intimidation. In the early hours of November 23, 2000, the paramilitaries began their rampage, with the first killings occurring between three and four a.m. As early as one a.m., phone calls were made, alerting police in Sitionuevo and army battalions in both Santa Marta and the nearby municipality of Malambo that a paramilitary assault was underway. Despite these warnings, nothing was done. Tovar's men remained in Nueva Venecia through the dawn, with no opposition. Journalists from Caracol Radio and TV, traveling by car and boat, reached Nueva Venecia long before the army; a single military helicopter finally arrived at three-thirty p.m., roughly nine hours after the paramilitaries had fled the scene.

Ahmed was among those who conferred with the authorities, urging them to go after the killers. The water levels were low, so their progress would be slow. The boats had been seen heading south on a trajectory known to all. They could be readily intercepted and caught. But the officer in charge had no more interest in a chase than sympathy for the survivors. The helicopter was on the ground for all of five minutes before it returned to base, leaving the bereaved families alone to deal with their dead. The army came in force only five days later, by which time Nueva Venecia was largely abandoned. There was no one to protect, save a few stubborn souls like Armando Martínez, a man who needed no help at all.

Some who fled found new lives in Barranquilla, and never returned. Others came back out of necessity, unable to survive away from the *ciénaga*. For them, the threat of violence proved less daunting than the certainty of starvation on the streets of strange towns. Most of the displaced found their way home on their own, with no help from the government. For many months, they lived in dread, haunted by the nights. According to Ahmed, it took fully two years before Nueva Venecia regained even a semblance of its former self.

"We shed so many tears," Ahmed said, "not only for the dead but for our community, which we feared might disappear. But thanks to the Lord, we are here."

Today, nearly twenty years on, Nueva Venecia remembers the victims of the massacre in a simple memorial: thirty-nine round stones, each darkened with a cross but unnamed, spread in a prominent row along the base of the church, visible to all who pass by or enter the temple. Ahmed prefers to speak of a living memorial: those born in Nueva Venecia since that terrible day, the scores of children and teens who now make up half the town's population. Working with the schools, he has made it his mission to free these kids from the weight of the town's trauma by connecting them to nature, the beauty of the *ciénaga*, the wonder of the river.

"We are encouraging the young to have a sense of belonging," he told me. "The Magdalena for us means life. We are an amphibious culture. Nature is a chain. The river was the most beautiful in Colombia. It gave life to the *ciénaga*. And then for years we treated it like a sewer. Just like we treated each other. But it's possible to renew the river. We endured a massacre, but now we are living in peace. We are a good, loving people. I say this to the whole world: Colombia is beautiful. Come and meet her."

Not a week after Ahmed and his boatman dropped our small team back on the docks at Tasajeras and the road to Santa Marta, Xandra and I, quite by chance, met an inspired young scholar, Gabriel Ruiz, who had spent time in Nueva Venecia during his dissertation research. Gabriel was interested in the dynamics and institutional challenges of post-conflict Colombia, essentially trying to figure out what works and what doesn't, as communities and government agencies cope with the legacy of violence. Nueva Venecia was one of his field sites, a significant case study, as he recalled. The community was isolated. Its experience of conflict had been singularly horrific. The initial response of the police and military was so flaccid as to suggest complicity if not outright collaboration with the paramilitary. Twenty years on, the massacre is not forgotten, but the people have found a way to endure. Prosperity remains elusive, and fish stocks are still in decline. But tourism is growing. Children are healthy, schools sound, families hopeful. Nueva Venecia, alone, has been responsible for its recovery and salvation.

Trying to understand the nature of such resilience, Gabriel interviewed, among others, a local fisherman, Jesús Suárez. He asked first what the community most needed, should the government offer reparations of any kind.

"Repair the houses," Jesús replied, before quickly changing his mind. "No, better yet, the environment, you have to repair the *ciénaga*. What's the point of repairing houses if there's nothing to eat and no decent place to live?"

Gabriel busily scribbled some notes, until noticing that Jesús was once again reconsidering.

"Actually, if you want the *ciénaga* to be healthy, you have to work on all the channels and sloughs and canals that carry the fresh water into the wetland."

Again Gabriel scratched a few lines, only to look up once more, sensing further hesitation.

"*¡Mierda!* It doesn't do much good to clean up the small streams if you do nothing for the main body of water that feeds all these waterways. No, what we need for Nueva Venecia, the only thing that could possibly compensate us for the suffering and injustice, would be for the government to clean and bring life back to the Río Magdalena. All of it. That's what we want. And that's what the country needs."

Epilogue

The sun was golden, and from the heights of Monserrate, perched a thousand feet above the savannah of Bogotá, we could see the distant silhouette of El Nevado del Tolima soaring above the snow-capped peaks of the Cordillera Central. Just to our south, toylike in the distance, was the statue of Our Lady of Guadalupe, an apparition of Mother Mary spreading her alabaster arms, as if blessing the city below. Both summits, venerated by the Muisca as fulcrums of the sun, had been sanctified by the Catholic Church in the first years of the conquest. Bogotá's cathedral, raised in 1539, was effectively positioned to align with Muisca notions of landscape and sacred geography. From the Plaza Bolívar, today the symbolic heart of the Colombian nation, the sun on the summer solstice rises directly over Monserrate. Over the same cobblestones where presidents, ambassadors, supreme court justices, generals, archbishops, shoe-shine boys, and thieves now tread, Muisca priests awaited, each year, the morning light of Sué, their solar god.

Shining over the city, the sanctuary of Monserrate is beautiful but modest, befitting a space originally created as a hermitage retreat. The charm lies in the views to the west and the glorious gardens that fall away toward the dark Andean valleys to the east. As one of Bogotá's main attractions, the shrine is generally crowded with tourists, but Xandra and I found it delightfully free of visitors.

We even managed to grab an open table in one of the elegant cafés perched on the side of the mountain. She ordered *chocolate con queso* for us both. The piped music catered to the traveler, and it wasn't long before we heard "El caimán," the classic *porro* tune with its catchy refrain *"se va el caimán, se va el caimán, se va para Barranquilla,"* the same earworm of a chorus that kept me up on a hundred all-night bus trips in the 1970s. Written by José María Peñaranda, it's a cartoon melody, a simple folkloric tale of a man from Plato, a small port on the Río Magdalena, who becomes part crocodile and, naturally, heads downriver to Barranquilla.

But, as in all things Colombian, there is a deeper and more complicated story. The song recounts a tale of a young fisherman who asks a *bruja* from the Guajira for a potion that will momentarily turn him into a caiman so he can watch women bathing naked in the Magdalena. The witch gives the lad two bottles, one with a preparation to transform him into a reptile, the second to bring him back as a man. Unfortunately, a witness to the magic becomes so frightened that he spills the potions, leaving his friend a creature in limbo, with the head of a man and the body of a crocodile, condemned for all time to travel the length of the Río Magdalena in search of a cure. What comes across on the radio as a simple ditty is actually an invocation of an ancient Chimila totemic symbol that speaks to the hybrid reality of an amphibious people living through seasons of rain and drought, with one foot on land, the other in the river.

Peel back the moments of any place, day, or time in Colombia, dig through the memories of any family, and you will always find the Río Magdalena. An old song heard in a mountainside café at ten thousand feet. A cloud forest where every drop of rain slips downhill to a river that falls over the Salto de Tequendama—a waterfall where Muisca flung themselves toward freedom, leaving this world to take the form of eagles—and cascades to meet the Magdalena at Girardot. The chocolate in our cups, the coffee, sugar, wheat, butter, milk, and virtually every delicious item being served in the café were all products of the fields of the *cuenca* of the Magdalena. Beneath the surface there is always the river.

Like a young girl, Xandra held her cup with both hands, her face aglow in the sun. She had clearly been moved by the beauty of the day: the sight of Our Lady of Guadalupe, luminous against the dark foliage of the cloud forest, the old nuns and pilgrims making their way up the steep paths of the mountain, in the church young children in prayer in the shadow of the saints. Still, what she said took me by surprise, though it perfectly distilled the message I hoped to convey to Colombia and the world. Her mind, in a wonderful way, was still on the river. She began by reminding me how Rodrigo de Bastidas, sailing across the mouth in 1501, had named the river El Río Grande de la Magdalena.

"If you think about it," she said, "that was an odd choice back then, though today it seems perfect, given what became of the river and, more importantly, what the river can become."

At the time of the conquest, Xandra continued, María Magdalena had a less than sterling reputation. In the sixth century, Saint Gregory the Great, in a notorious sermon, had branded the woman as a promiscuous sinner, remembered in the scriptures only because Jesus, in his infinite mercy, had allowed her to wash his feet with her tears and touch them with her hair. But, as it turned out, Pope Gregory was mistaken. Jesus had indeed forgiven a repentant prostitute, but her name was Mary of Bethany. For fourteen hundred years, the Roman Catholic Church had focused its contempt on the wrong woman.

The real María Magdalena was neither wife, mother, nor woman of the night. She was a pure and simple devotee of Christ, just as the Gospels reveal. She stood by Jesus during his crucifixion and burial and was the first to see him after the resurrection. He specifically asked her, among all others, to spread the joyful word of his rising and rebirth. She had always been the most faithful, traveling with him in life, anointing his body in death, sharing his message in the wake of his final passage and ascent to the side of God. As surely as any male apostle, she deserved recognition as one of the founders of the Christian church. Indeed, her very name spoke of strength: *magdala*, meaning, in Aramaic, tower or fortress. Through Christ's ministry on earth, and in the glory and eternal promise of his death, María Magdalena always stood tall, the spiritual watchtower of the world.

Not until 1969 did the Roman Catholic Church formally

remove the scarlet letter of sin from María Magdalena's name. And only in 2016 did Pope Francis finally sanctify her as *apostolorum apostola*, the apostle to the apostles, the one and only. Having been slandered for centuries, María Magdalena is today considered a saint by Roman Catholics and all those of Eastern Orthodox, Anglican, and Lutheran faith.

In other words, Xandra exclaimed, more than two billion people, all raised to think of María Magdalena as a whore, are a generation later eager to recognize and celebrate her as a saint.

"It's a story of redemption. And I see the same thing happening to our Magdalena. The river gave us everything—*cumbia* and coca, *bogas* and Bolívar, aviation, transport, commerce, music, our culture, and even our freedom. Yet in the same way the church slandered María Magdalena, we soiled the river, turning an artery of life into a conduit of death. We declared it beyond hope, its condition irredeemable, absolving ourselves of any responsibility for its fate and well-being. We turned our backs on the river that gave us life. But to deny the Río Magdalena is to betray all that we are as Colombians."

Xandra drained the last of her chocolate.

"María Magdalena was condemned until history took an unexpected turn. Now she's a symbol of love, loyalty, and grace. Can't we do the same for the river?"

At that very moment, a small yellow bird landed on our table, pecked at the crumbs, and darted off into the trees.

Acknowledgments

Magdalena is less a work of scholarship than a compendium of stories shared by Colombians encountered along the river and beyond, living narratives strung together with historical accounts deliberately selected to reveal and celebrate the true wonder of a country that has long been overlooked and misunderstood. The characters whose voices come together to tell this story represent but a few of the many inspired people met and engaged during several journeys covering much of the drainage. Each embodies and personifies a fundamental theme in the Colombian experience; each distills something of the essence of the country. And each, to recall Hemingway's adage about good storytelling, most assuredly has something to say that the world needs to hear.

For their insights and immense generosity, I would like to thank and acknowledge José Aguirre, Katherine Arévalo, Ximena Arosemena, Alexis Judith Arroyo, Veruschka Barros, Héctor Botero, Enrique and Isabel Cabrales, Jenny Castañeda, Juan Manuel Echavarría, Alejandro Echeverri, Sergio Fajardo, Aurelio "Yeyo" Fernández, Blanca Fernández, Dominga Fernández, Germán Ferro, Juan Guillermo Garcés, José Carlos García Torres, Ahmed Gutiérrez, Samuel "Abundio" Mármol, Gilberto and Edilma Márquez, Armando Martínez, Francisco "Pacho" Luis Mesa, Hugo Hernán Montoya, Diana Ocampo, James Murillo Osorio, Águeda Pacheco,

Gumercindo Palencia, Elizabeth Pérez, José Enrique Pineda Cantillo, Adelfa Pineda Ibáñez, Diógenes Armando Pino, Alonso Poveda, Héctor Rapalino, Alonso Restrepo, Antonio Restrepo, Gabriel Alberto Ruíz Romero, William Vargas, Ángel María Villafañe, Estefanía Villarreal, Yuliet Patricia Villarreal, and Jose "Morita" Manuel Zapata.

Among those who assisted me in many ways, I would like to thank Héctor Abad, Liliana Janeth Amaya, Ana Lía Anacona, Alessandro Angulo, Wendy Arenas, Guillermo Arias, Gustavo Arias, Jorge Arias de Greiff, Wilfrido de Ávila Barrios, Brigitte Baptiste, Tatiana Bensa, David Bojanini, Juan David Botero, Fernando Cano, José Iván Cano, Sergio Cervantes, Mamo Camilo and the Arhuaco community of Katanzama, Felipe Clavijo, Alvaro Cogollo, Gonzalo and Dorothea Córdoba, Marta Correa, Tara Davis, Carlos Debia, Nadia Diamond, Jules Domine and Expedition Colombia, Cristina Echavarría, Miguel Echavarría, L'Équipe Tambora, Germán García Durán, Maria Estela Gómez, Martha Isabel Gualdrón, Carlos Guerra, Gilberto Hernández, Maria Jimena Hernández, Martin von Hildebrand and the team at Fundación Gaia Amazonas, Paula Jaramillo, Robert Kennedy Jr., Luis Enrique La Rotta, Elsa Laverde, Arnulfo Males, Jimmy Marín, José Luis Marrugo, Miguel Marulanda, Alicia Mejía, Juan Luis Mejía, Pedro Mejía, Susana Mejía, Alfredo Molano, Tiberio Murcia, Andrés Ospina, Andrés de la Ossa, Gulbert Papamija, Parménides Papamija, Noel Prince, Antonio Restrepo, José María Reyes Santo Domingo, Diana Rico, Jaime Uribe, Margarita Uribe, Pablo Uribe, Tomás Uribe, Andrea Vargas, Jaison Pérez Villafaña, Danilo Villafaña, and Jorge Villamizar. Juan Luis Mejía, chancellor of the Universidad Eafit, most generously gave me a copy of *Hilea Magdalenesa*, an exceedingly rare book by Enrique Pérez Arbeláez that is both visionary memoir and a wondrous ode to the Río Magdalena. This gesture was typical of the extraordinary support I had from the Colombian people throughout this project.

A very special thanks is due the *Savia* team: Héctor Rincón and Ana María Cano, Federico Rincón, Luis Quintana, Mateo Rincón, Jose Iván Cano, Hilda Samudio, Patricia Nieto, Simón Ospina, Silvia García, and David Estrada, a photographer of rare sensitivity and vision. Héctor and Ana invited me to Colombia in 2014, setting in motion a magical series of events that culminated in my being honoured by President Juan Manuel Santos with the gift of citizenship in 2018. I will always be in their debt. Grupo Argos generously supported the project from the beginning. This support came without conditions, save perhaps for an unwavering insistence that we were to have at all times complete editorial and artistic independence and freedom to tell the story of the Magdalena in all of its complexities and drama. I am very pleased to note that all of my royalties for the Spanish-language edition of this book will go to the Fundación Grupo Argos, earmarked for environmental and cultural initiatives.

My thanks to Andrew Miller at Knopf, an insightful and most generous editor, and to our good friends at the Bodley Head in the United Kingdom, and Planeta in Bogotá: Stuart Williams, and Luis Fernando Páez. My sincere thanks to a wonderful production team at Knopf: Maria Massey, Soonyoung Kwon, and Bonnie Thompson. David Lindroth provided the beautiful maps. Maris Dyer, working with Andrew Miller, assisted at every phase of the editing process. I would especially like to single out my editor at Knopf, Canada, a dear friend, the inspired Louise Dennys, who was a constant source of advice and support.

Several friends and colleagues read drafts of the manuscript. My thanks to Wendy Arenas, Ross Beaty, Gonzalo Córdoba, Simon Davies, Karen Davis, Martin von Hildebrand, Tomás Uribe, and Corky and Scott McInytre. Peter Matson, friend more than literary agent, has been wonderful as always, and both of us sorely miss the late Michael Sissons. And, as always, my gratitude to my family, Gail, Tara, and Raina.

Finally, I offer thanks to some very special Colombians. The image on the cover of the book was generously provided by Camilo Echavarría, Colombia's renowned landscape photographer. The photograph, from Camilo's ongoing project, *Atlas of the Andes*, shows the Río Cauca, the main affluent of the Magdalena, passing through the Pipintá Canyon, just before reaching the town of La Pintada in the department of Antioquia. The snowcapped volcano is Nevado del Ruiz, also known as Kumanday. In the same way that the western landscape paintings of Thomas Moran and Albert Bierstadt anticipated and informed the work of Ansel Adams, so too did the paintings of Frederic Edwin Church inspire the art of Camilo Echavarría. Church, though associated with the Hudson River School of landscape painters, made two extensive trips to Colombia and was deeply influenced by Humboldt. Camilo's dissertation was a study of Church, and his photography portrays landscapes as if seen through the eyes of the American artist, and infused with the spirit of the great naturalist.

To travel with William Vargas was to recall with such fondness my time with Timothy Plowman so many years ago. William, like Tim, is a botanical explorer, but his primary mission is the rehabilitation of natural habitats—riparian forests, wetlands, and mangroves. In 2018, the Society for Ecological Restoration honored William with its highest award for "Excellence for Restoration," acknowledging him as the most effective practitioner in all of Latin America. His success is an inspiration to many and a constant reminder that, in a country long encumbered by class, education remains the key to social mobility, thanks in good measure to a system of public and private universities unrivaled in Latin America. Colombia needs professional men like William now more than ever. Throughout the country, forests long protected by the conflict are under assault. In 2018 alone, some 640,000 acres were lost. A nation with some of the strongest environmental regulations on paper nevertheless suffers on the ground rates of illegal deforestation that are among the highest in Latin America.

Clara Llano is perhaps best described as a Colombian bodhisattva, godmother to a nation. Clara hovered over the project, just waiting to make things happen, working with the *mamos*, facilitating the encounters with both President Santos and President Uribe, making any number of introductions that invariably led to deep and meaningful encounters. Clara's angelic nature is recognized by all. Some years ago, when my daughter Tara returned to Los Angeles from South America suffering from a serious but undiagnosed illness, Clara, having never met the girl, took her in for a month and nursed her back to health as if her own child.

Through Clara, we met Carlos Vives and Claudia Elena Vásquez, a dazzling couple whose love for each other and their family is matched only by their love for the Colombian people. Carlos was the key that unlocked in my imagination the true meaning of sound, the rhythms of the river, allowing a writer with little understanding of music to sense, hear, and feel, in the percussive pulse of *cumbia*, the story of the Magdalena, the very heartbeat of Colombia.

Juan Gonzalo Betancur laid his country before me like a gift. With no compensation, simply as a gesture of goodwill, he left his family for two weeks during the holidays, in order to share his love of a river that had long inspired his dreams. As the text reveals, he is a brilliant journalist, an inspired teacher, a scholar of deep intellect and soul who thrives on the frontiers of emotion and passion. Juan Gonzalo introduced me to many of the key figures in the book: Jenny Castañeda, Diana Ocampo, and, of course, his good friend Martín España, who in turn opened the entire world of *tambora* and *cumbia*, guiding us to the maestros, the living legends of La Mojana, and, through his knowledge and wisdom, illuminating the raw musical genius to be found in every settlement and hamlet along the length of the Magdalena.

Finally, there is Xandra Uribe. We met by chance at Río Claro, a fleeting encounter, and only intuition, whimsy, and some kind of faith could have led either of us to set off with Juan Gonzalo to explore the Medio Magdalena: three complete strangers, with vastly different experiences of Colombia, coming together to forge within hours a camaraderie that in retrospect was surely preordained. In the end, Xandra would work on every phase of the project. In the field, she served as videographer and journalist, recording and transcribing interviews, chasing down leads, and in my absence interviewing key figures such as Alonso Restrepo, whom she found living in retirement in Cali. Thanks to Xandra, I met Juan Gonzalo, but also such key personalities as Enrique and Isabel Cabrales in Mompox, Juan Manuel Echavarría in Bogotá, and Sergio Fajardo and Alejandro Echeverri in Medellín. Critically, it was Xandra who, from the start, identified the relationship between Humboldt and Bolívar as being key to the story of Colombia.

A brilliant researcher, Xandra combed the Biblioteca Pública Piloto and EAFIT library in Medellín, the archives of the Biblioteca Luis Ángel Arango in Bogotá, used bookstores such as the magnificent Merlin, also in Bogotá, and Medellín's Los Libros de Juan, sourcing books, monographs, diaries, letters, and reports that would have taken me months to find, let alone read in Spanish. With an uncanny appreciation of my sensibilities as a writer, Xandra distilled the essence of this mountain of material, providing written summaries, identifying points of wonder, and directing me to the original text of anything she deemed essential for me to read unfiltered in Spanish. During the writing phase of the project, Xandra served as my primary editor, displaying an understanding of the nuances of the English language, not to mention a formal knowledge of grammar and composition, that would put many a native speaker to shame, including, I dare say, many of my academic colleagues. Truth be told, Xandra Uribe's contributions to this book can scarcely be measured. Only the conventions of publishing, and the fact that I did the actual writing, can account for why her name does not grace the cover alongside my own.

Hemingway famously quipped that anyone who says that writing is easy is either a bad writer or a liar. Books are hard, and there were moments when both Xandra and I were uncertain whether this one would ever get finished. We were in touch on a daily basis, often several times a day. After one particularly grueling session, we signed off with a final e-mail exchange, utterly spent. Apparently I followed up five minutes later with a personal note, one that I completely forgot until, many months later, a journalist happened to ask me, in her presence, to explain my curious infatuation with Colombia. Before I could answer, Xandra read these lines from her phone, words I had written in a few moments, thinking they might lift our morale after a difficult day:

I do long for the air of Bogotá, that unmistakable scent that tells me I've landed on the savannah. It's hard to explain. When I talk about loving Colombia, it's something visceral, even sensual. To be away for too long is to be on life support. To step again onto the soil of the nation is to feel instantly that very sense of belonging that so long ago gave me the freedom to envision the man I've become. Whispered messages of a landscape unlike any other. The wild embrace of a people that allowed a vagabond boy to grow into a content and realized scholar. It is the very madness of Colombia that rescued me. Like a sweet coefficient of the soul. My fire was so bright, so all-consuming that I came very close to self-immolation. Only Colombia could match and give purpose to my passion. I was saved by that, and this is the key if anyone wants to understand my loyalty to the country.

Bibliographical Essay

Like many Colombians, I had always turned my back on the Río Magdalena. As a young traveler and botanical explorer in the 1970s, I crossed the river dozens of times, by road and rail, without ever really seeing it, focused as I was on the pristine frontiers of the country, Guaviare and Vaupés, Amazonas, Chocó and Putumayo. The book *One River* chronicles both my travels and the far more extensive explorations of Richard Evans Schultes over twelve uninterrupted years beginning in 1941. He, too, must have passed over the Magdalena many times, if only to reach the mountains of Nariño, San Agustín, and the valley of Sibundoy, a botanical paradise he returned to time and again. Schultes documented his travels with his camera, generating a vast archive of several hundred photographs, including scores of snapshots that proved invaluable as, during the writing of *One River*, I tried to reimagine his life in Colombia. I cannot recall a single image of the Magdalena in his collection. As for the book, which stretches to 639 pages in the Spanish edition, *El río*, the word "Magdalena" appears five times, incidentally and only in passing.

Imagine my delight when I finally escaped what many have described as Colombia's collective amnesia to discover, for the first time, the river that actually made possible the nation. Those who know and love the Río Magdalena won't be surprised to learn that what began as a modest seven-thousand-word assignment, an essay to introduce an illustrated portrait of the river, grew inexorably into a doorstop of a book rivaling in length and effort the obsession that became *One River*.

In a project that grew unexpectedly to have a life of its own, there was never a plan. In that inimitable Colombian way, things just happened. Perhaps the best way to convey a sense of how *Magdalena* came about would be to recall a story that did not find its way into the book, a surprising few days that began at Bocas de Ceniza when I first learned from the fishermen that the *mamos* periodically make ritual payments at the mouth of the river. I left immediately for Katanzama, an Arhuaco settlement east of Santa Marta on the Río Don Diego, where I ran into several old friends, including Jaison Pérez Villafaña, as well as Mamo Camilo, who confirmed that the Magdalena does, indeed, lie within spiritual purview of the Arhuaco. Offering to cover the costs of transport and lodging, I asked if it might be possible to organize a ritual payment, a small pilgrimage to the river. Within minutes, it was agreed, and the following day, along with two dozen Arhuaco men, women, and children, we were heading west, back along the Caribbean shore to Barranquilla. En route, Mamo Camilo casually mentioned that in four days, President Juan Manuel Santos would be making his first visit to the main Arhuaco settlement of Nabusímake. He asked if I could be there to take part in the welcome. I promised to try, knowing full well that the only option, given the timing and logistics, was to hitch a ride with the presidential party.

A phone call to a Colombian friend in Los Angeles, the irrepressible Clara Llano, was, as if by magic, redirected to the Palacio de Nariño in Bogotá. Within twenty-four hours word came back that President Santos would be pleased to have me along. The following morning, I caught an early flight from Barranquilla to Bogotá, where I was met by a young soldier who brought me to the presidential jet, soon to be joined by President Santos and several of his ministers. We then flew back the way I'd come, toward the coast, stopping at Valledupar, where our entire party transferred to military helicopters for the short flight into the Sierra Nevada to Nabusímake.

En route, several of the staff peppered the president with statistics as he prepared his formal remarks, a speech that would be covered by the national media. I rather sheepishly raised my hand and mentioned that for the *mamos*, statistics mean little. What matters to them is what lies within the human heart. I then repeated what Mamo Camilo had said: that peace would not matter if it was only an excuse for the various sides of the conflict to come together to maintain a war on nature. The president made this the theme of his speech, even as his aides tweeted out the message to the nation.

Before the formal presentation to the community, the presidential party gathered in the ceremonial temple to be welcomed by the *mamos* and gifted by the women with beautiful *mochilas*, each filled with Sierra Nevada coffee, among the finest grown in Colombia. President Santos then introduced his party. When he came to me, he could not have been more generous. But in the midst of his remarks, one of the *mamos*, another old friend, politely interrupted him, explaining that I needed no introduction as I served as their ambassador in the United States, which was true only to the extent that their delegations often stayed with us when they had occasion to be in Washington, which was more often than one might expect.

The visit to Nabusímake was a great success, and the entire Arhuaco nation was there to see us off, as we returned to Valleduar, and then by evening to Bogotá. I came away from the day deeply impressed by President Santos, convinced that his commitment to conservation was sincere, an intuition that was confirmed only months later when, before leaving office, he set in motion a massive expansion of a system of national parks and protected areas which was already the envy of the rest of Latin America. Among the many peace dividends was the doubling in size of Serranía de Chiribiquete, Colombia's biggest national park, an enormous expanse of wilderness now among the largest rainforest preserves in the world. In protecting the land, the Santos government also embraced and acknowledged the indigenous people, working not just in collaboration with tribal organizations but legally recognizing their political rights and authority in a manner that has no precedent in any other nation-state.

In Colombia, there is no limit to what can be squeezed out of a day, and this one had only just begun. From Bogotá, I jumped on a commercial flight back to the coast, arriving in time to see my daughter Tara and her Colombian band, L'Équipe Tambora, join Carlos Vives onstage as they performed "Río Yuma," her anthem to the Magdalena, before several thousand fans on the opening night of El Carnaval de Barranquilla. From the stage, Carlos announced our dream of cleaning up the Magdalena as a symbol of the rebirth of the nation. To hear his words, so hopeful and clear, and to watch my daughter swing to the rhythm, her body at ease in the sensual promise of *cumbia*, with her voice reaching notes heard only in the depths of forests, left a tired father in a perfect state of bliss.

The next day took me to Medellín, where word unexpectedly came from Clara that ex-president Álvaro Uribe was available and ready to welcome me at his finca in Rionegro. As my driver negotiated the curves climbing to the heights above the city, Clara rang to warn me to expect a large crowd, urging that I try to catch just a minute with the former president, that I might share our passion for the river.

The security at the finca was tight, but once cleared, the car seemed to float toward the main house, where a solitary figure stood at the entrance, ready to welcome me. It was Lina Moreno, the much admired wife of the ex-president. Lina could not have been kinder or more hospitable. As she escorted me into the house and through the living room, she asked if I had eaten lunch. No, I stuttered, still coming to terms with the realization that there was no fiesta and that I was the only visitor. It made for a lovely interlude, sitting together at a picnic table on the back porch, sharing a simple Sunday meal with the family.

Initially we exchanged stories of Colombia, with ex-president Uribe displaying an almost supernatural knowledge of the country. There was no crossroad or settlement unfamiliar to him. He not only knew the families and authorities in every town, he could name the local landmarks, recall the most trivial of historical events, cite statistics on health, employment, and income, distilling the past and anticipating the future as if holding the entire nation in his mind. For nearly an hour we toured the country. Then, having cataloged much of Colombia, he cut short our banter and invited me to join him for coffee apart from the family, so that we could have a serious conversation about the river.

He viewed the plight of the Magdalena through the eyes of a technician hardwired to solve problems and a politician who never confuses activity for results. Displaying formidable powers of recall, Uribe identified in every river port the men and women who would have to be swayed should any initiative have a chance of success. His knowledge was encyclopedic—a considerable resource, I thought, should he lend his influence to a campaign calling for the rehabilitation of the river. We spoke for nearly two hours, and I shared photographs from our travels—a presentation that ended, by chance, with a shot of President Santos at Nabusímake. I could sense former president Uribe's discomfort as the image appeared. When finally I took my leave, he thanked me for being a friend of Colombia. I thanked him and shared my conviction that history will indeed record that, in a country afflicted by war for half a century, it took two presidents to make possible the conditions for peace. It was a message I was able to deliver to both men, as just part of five perfect days in Colombia.

For an understanding of the worldview of the Elder Brothers, the publications of Gerardo Reichel-Dolmatoff remain a fundamental source. See: "Training for the Priesthood Among the Kogi of Colombia," in *Enculturation in Latin America: An Anthology*, ed. J. Wilbert (Los Angeles: Latin American Center, UCLA, 1976), 265–88; "The Loom of Life: A Kogi Principle of Integration," *Journal of Latin American Lore* 4, no. 1 (1978): 5–27; "The Great Mother and the Kogi Universe: A Concise Overview," *Journal of Latin American Lore* 13, no. 1 (1987): 73–113; and *Los Kogi*, 2 vols. (Bogotá: Nueva Biblioteca Colombiana de Cultura, Procultura, 1985). Additional sources include: Alan Ereira, *The Elder Brothers* (New York: Knopf, 1992); Antonio Julián, *La perla de América: Provincia de Santa Marta* (Bogotá: Academia Colombiana de Historia, 1980); and Éric Julien, *Kogis* (Paris: Albin Michel, 2004); Donald Tayler, *The Coming of the Sun*, Pitt Rivers Museum, Monograph No. 7 (Oxford: University of Oxford, 1997).

Reichel-Dolmatoff, along with his wife, archaeologist Alicia Dussán, also made seminal contributions to our understanding of San Agustín and, indeed, all pre-Columbian civilizations of Colombia. See: Gerardo Reichel-Dolmatoff, *San Agustín: A Culture of Colombia* (New York: Praeger, 1972); *The Art of Gold: The Legacy of Pre-Hispanic Colombia* (Bogotá: Banco de la República / Fondo de Cultura Económica, 2007); and *Goldwork and Shamanism: An Iconographic Study of the Gold Museum of the Banco de la República* (Bogotá: Villegas Editores, 2005). For more on San Agustín, see: Robert Drennan, *Las sociedades prehispánicas del Alto Magdalena* (Bogotá: Instituto Colombiano de Antropología e Historia, 2000); Konrad Theodor Preuss, *Arte monumental prehistórico* (Bogotá: Escuelas Salesianas de Tipografía y Fotograbado, 1931); and María Lucía Sotomayor and María Victoria Uribe, *Estatuaria del macizo colombiano* (Bogotá: Instituto Colombiano de Antropología, n.d.).

The general literature on the ethnography of Colombia at the time of the conquest is limited. See: Instituto Caro y Cuervo, *Atlas lingüístico-etnográfico de Colombia (ALEC)*, vol. 4 (Bogotá: 1983); Hermes Tovar Pinzón, *Relaciones y visitas a los Andes, Siglo XVI*, vol. 2: *Región del Caribe*, and vol. 4: *Alto Magdalena*, (Bogotá: Colcultura, 1993); Jorge Isaacs, *Las tribus indígenas del Magdalena* (Bogotá: Ediciones Sol y Luna, 1967); William Jaramillo, *Geografía humana de Colombia* (Bogotá: Instituto Colombiano de Cultura Hispánica, 1996); and Liborio Zerda, *El Dorado* 2 vols. (Bogotá: Biblioteca Banco Popular, 1972). For general accounts of the conquest in Colombia, see: J. Michael Francis, *Invading Colombia: Spanish Accounts of the Gonzalo Jiménez de Quesada Expedition of Conquest* (University Park: Pennsylvania State University Press, 2007); and Rafael Gómez Picón, *Timaná, de Belálcazar a la Gaitana: Parábola de violencia y libertad* (Bogotá: Editorial Sucre, 1959).

For surveys of the forests, wetlands, and basic geography of the country, see: *Mapa de bosques de Colombia* (Bogotá: Instituto Geográfico Agustín Codazzi, 1985); *Diccionario geográfico de Colombia* (Bogotá: Instituto Geográfico Agustín Codazzi, 1996); *Atlas histórico geográfico* (Bogotá: Archivo General de la Nación Colombia, Grupo Editorial Norma, 1992); *Estudio Nacional del Agua 2014* (Bogotá: IDEAM, 2015); and *Sistemas morfogénicos del territorio colombiano*

(Bogotá: Instituto de Hidrología, Meteorología y Estudios Ambientales, 2010).

There is a vast literature on Colombia's natural history. Sources that were especially helpful to this project include: Augusto Antonio Repizo and Carlos Alfonso Devia, *Árboles y arbustos del valle seco del río Magdalena y de la región Caribe Colombiana: Su ecología y uso* (Bogotá: Pontificia Universidad Javeriana, 2008); Andrés Barragán, *Guía ilustrada de la avifauna colombiana* (New York: Wildlife Conservation Society, 2018); *Flora del bosque seco* (Cartagena: Instituto Colombiano de Desarrollo Rural, 2014); Germán Márquez Calle, *El hábitat del hombre caimán y otros estudios sobre ecología y sociedad en el Caribe* (Barranquilla: Corporación Parque Cultural del Caribe, 2008); Alfredo Olaya, *Del Macizo Colombiano al Desierto de la Tatacoa* (Bogotá: Universidad Surcolombiana / Editora Guadalupe, 2005); Enrique Pérez Arbeláez, *Plantas útiles de Colombia* (Bogotá: Librería Colombiana, 1956); and Juan de Santa Gertrudis, *Maravillas de la naturaleza,* 4 vols. (Bogotá: Biblioteca Banco Popular Bogotá, 1970).

For Mutis, see: José Celestino Mutis, *Escritos científicos,* vols. 1 and 2 (Bogotá: Instituto Colombiano de Cultura Hispánica, 1983); Enrique Pérez Arbeláez, *José Celestino Mutis y la Real Expedición Botánica del Nuevo Reyno de Granada* (Bogotá: Fondo FEN Colombia, 1998); Real Jardín Botánico, Consejo Superior de Investigaciones Científicas, *Mutis y la Real Expedición Botánica del Nuevo Reyno de Granada,* vols. 1 and 2 (Bogotá: Villegas Editores, 1992); and Florentino Vezga, *La expedición botánica* (Cali: Carvajal & Compañía, 1971).

For Caldas, see: John Wilton Appel, *Francisco José de Caldas: A Scientist at Work in Nueva Granada,* Transactions of the American Philosophical Society, vol. 84, part 5 (Philadelphia: American Philosophical Society, 1994); Alfredo D. Bateman, *Francisco José de Caldas: El hombre y el sabio* (Bogotá: Planeta, 1988); and Santiago Díaz Piedrahita, *Francisco José de Caldas: Episodios de su vida y de su actividad científica* (Bogotá: Panamericana Editorial, 2012).

For Humboldt, see: Enrique Pérez Arbeláez, *Alejandro de Humboldt en Colombia* (Bogotá: Biblioteca Básica Colombiana, Instituto Colombiano de Cultura, 1981); Mariano Cuesta Domingo y Sandra Rebok, eds., *Alexander von Humboldt: Estancia en España y viaje americano* (Madrid: Real Sociedad Geográfica y Consejo Superior de Investigaciones Científicas, 2008); Stephen T. Jackson and Laura Dassow Walls, eds., *Views of Nature: Alexander von Humboldt* (Chicago: University of Chicago Press, 2014); *Alexander von Humboldt en Colombia: Extractos de sus diarios*, Academia Colombiana de Ciencias Exactas, Físicas y Naturales y la Academia de Ciencias de la República Democrática Alemana (Bogotá: Flota Mercante Grancolombiana, 1982); *La ruta de Humboldt: Colombia y Venezuela*, 2 vols. (Bogotá: Villegas Editores, 1994); and, especially, the wonderful book by Andrea Wulf, *The Invention of Nature: Alexander von Humboldt's New World* (New York: Knopf, 2015).

For additional travel accounts of the nineteenth century, see: Eduardo Acevedo Latorre, *Geografía pintoresca de Colombia: La Nueva Granada vista por dos viajeros franceses del siglo XIX; Charles Saffray y Edouard André* (Bogotá: Litografía Arco, 1968); Salvador Camacho Roldán, *Notas de Viaje*, 2 vols. (Bogotá: Banco de la República, 1973); Malcolm Deas, Efraín Sánchez, and Aída Martínez, *Tipos y costumbres de la Nueva Granada: Colección de pinturas y diario de Joseph Brown* (Bogotá: Fondo Cultural Cafetero, 1989); Alberto Gómez Gutiérrez, ed., *La Expedición Helvética: Viaje de exploración científica por Colombia en 1910 de los profesores Otto Fuhrmann y Eugene Mayor* (Bogotá: Pontificia Universidad Javeriana, 2011); Ernest Rothlisberger, *El Dorado: Estampas de viaje y cultura de la Colombia suramericana* (Bogotá: Banco de la República, 1963); and Charles Saffray, *Viaje a Nueva Granada* (n.p.: Biblioteca Popular de Cultura Colombiana, 1948). See also: Alberto Gómez Gutiérrez, *Al cabo de las velas: Expediciones científicas en Colombia siglos XVIII, XVIX y XX* (Bogotá: Instituto Colombiano de Cultura Hispánica, Giro Editores, 1998). A highly significant undertaking of the nineteenth century, mentioned only in passing in the book, was the Expedición Corográfica, a national initiative led by Agustín Codazzi that attempted to decipher, document, map, and catalog the geography, hydrology, topography, and natural history of Colombia. See: Manuel Ancízar, *Peregrinación de Alpha*, vols. 1 and 2 (Bogotá: Biblioteca Banco Popular Bogotá, 1984); Nancy L. Appelbaum, *Mapping the Country of Regions: The Chorographic Commission of Nineteenth Century Colom-*

bia (Chapel Hill: University of North Carolina Press, 2016); and Beatriz Caballero, *Las siete vidas de Agustín Codazzi* (Bogotá: Carlos Valencia Editores / Instituto Geográfico Agustín Codazzi, 1994).

There have been a number of illustrated books and general accounts of the Río Magdalena, including: *Atlas: Cuenca del Río Grande de la Magdalena* (Bogotá: Cormagdalena, 2007); Enrique Pérez Arbeláez, *Hilea Magdalenesa: Prospección económica del valle tropical del Río Magdalena* (Bogotá: Contraluría General de la Nación, 1949); Carlos Castaño Uribe, *Río Grande de la Magdalena* (Cali: Banco de Occidente Credencial, 2003); Manuel Rodríguez Becerra, ed., *¿Para dónde va el Río Magdalena? Riesgos sociales, ambientales y económicos del proyecto de navegabilidad* (Bogotá: Friedrich Ebert Stiftung en Colombia and Foro Nacional Ambiental, 2015); Rafael Gómez Picón, *Magdalena, río de Colombia*, 6th ed. (Bogotá: Biblioteca Colombiana de Cultura, Instituto Colombiano de Cultura, 1973); Museo Nacional de Colombia, *Río Magdalena: Navegando por una nación*, 2nd ed. (Bogotá: Museo Nacional de Colombia, 2010); José Alvear Sanín, *Manual del Río Magdalena* (Bogotá: Cormagdalena, 2005); and María Soledad Reyna, *El Magdalena: Voces de un río mundo* (Bogotá: Letrarte Editores, 2015).

Without doubt, our single most useful and important source was: Aníbal Noguera Mendoza, *Crónica grande del Río de la Magdalena: Recopilación, notas y advertencias*, 2 vols. (Bogotá: Banco Cafetero / Fondo Cultural Cafetero, Ediciones Sol y Luna, 1980). Commissioned by the Banco Cafetero to celebrate its twenty-fifth anniversary (1954–79), this two-volume tour de force, compiled by the journalist Aníbal Noguera, contains book excerpts, newspaper articles, drawings, and illustrations and touches upon every theme associated with the river—stories of the early settlements, the lives of indigenous peoples, the *bogas*, *zambos*, and criollos, the challenge of navigation and the glory of the *vapores*, the saga of conquest and the trauma of endless wars, the redemption of poetry and song, and the wonder of awestruck European naturalists who lacked even the language to describe the natural abundance and biological wealth encountered in this new land. The botanist Enrique Pérez Arbeláez, author of *Hilea Magdalenesa*, cited by Noguera, writes very simply that the "Magdalena is an ocean, a sea of peoples, places, geographies, and traditions. An ocean of stories which I was thrilled to dive into and immerse myself in for three full years."

For the challenges of transportation in Colombia, see Germán Ferro's wonderful book on the *arrieros, A lomo de mula* (Bogotá: Fondo Cultural Cafetero, 1994). For the steamships, river commerce, and the creation of the network of trails that made possible the trade, see: Pedro Gómez Valderrama, *La otra raya del tigre* (Bogotá: Siglo Veintiuno Editores de Colombia, 1977); and Antonio Montaña, *A todo vapor* (Bogotá: Bancafé, Santa Fe de Bogotá, 1996). Excellent accounts of the early days of aviation include: Herbert Boy, *Una historia con alas* (Madrid: Ediciones Guadarrama, 1955); Héctor Mejía Restrepo, *Don Gonzalo Mejía: 50 años de Antioquia* (Bogotá: El Sello Editores, 1984); and Iván Obando, *Me llevarás en ti* (Bogotá: Editorial Planeta Colombiana, 2016).

For the history of Colombia, see: David Bushnell, *The Making of Modern Colombia: A Nation in Spite of Itself* (Berkeley: University of California Press, 1993); Antonio Caballero, *Historia de Colombia y sus oligarquías (1948–2017)* (Bogotá: Planeta, 2018); Ann Farnsworth-Alvear, Marco Palacios, and Ana María Gómez López, eds., *The Colombia Reader: History, Culture, Politics* (Durham, N.C.: Duke University Press, 2017); Robert A Karl, *Forgotten Peace: Reform, Violence, and the Making of Contemporary Colombia* (Oakland: University of California Press, 2017); Michael La Rosa and Germán Mejía, *Colombia: A Concise Contemporary History* (Lanham, Md.: Rowman & Littlefield, 2017); Jorge Orlando Melo, *Historia mínima de Colombia* (Mexico City: El Colegio de México; Madrid: Editorial Turner, 2017); Marco Palacios, *Between Legitimacy and Violence: A History of Colombia, 1875–2002* (Durham, N.C.: Duke University Press, 2006); Diógenes Armando Pino Avila, *Tamalameque: Historia y leyenda* (Bucaramanga: Fundación para la Promoción de la Cultura y la Educación Popular, 1991); Frank Safford and Marco Palacios, *Colombia: Fragmented Land, Divided Society* (New York: Oxford University Press, 2002); and Enrique Serrano, *Colombia: Historia de un olvido* (Bogotá: Planeta, 2018). For the history of the Canal del Dique, see: Manuel Castillo Ardila, *Canal del Dique* (Barranquilla: Grafitalia, 1981); and José Vicente Mogollón Vélez, *El Canal del*

Dique (Bogotá: El Áncora Editores, 2013). For the death of Gaitán, the Bogotazo, and La Violencia, see: Arturo Alape, *El Bogotazo: Memorias del olvido* (Bogotá: Planeta, 1987); Daniel Pécaut, *Orden y violencia: Colombia, 1930–1954*, 2 vols. (Bogotá: Siglo Veintiuno Editores, 1987); and Mary Roldán, *Blood and Fire: La Violencia in Antioquia, 1946–1953* (Durham, N.C.: Duke University Press, 2002).

Some would say that in seeking a just and lasting peace, Colombia is sailing into the winds of its own history. The peace agreement signed in Cartagena on September 26, 2016, left many Colombians in a state of euphoria, but their hopes were dashed not a week later, on October 2, when the deal was narrowly rejected in a national referendum. (The vote was 50.2 percent against to 49.8 percent for—a difference of less than 54,000 votes out of the almost 13 million cast.) The no vote maintained that the terms of the agreement were excessively lenient, allowing former members of the FARC to go largely unpunished. Five days later, President Santos was awarded the Noble Peace Prize, a powerful endorsement from the international community. He subsequently sent a revised deal directly to Congress, thus avoiding a second national vote. Though legal, the maneuver infuriated the opposition. Indignation that the original referendum had been effectively bypassed ultimately fueled a conservative surge that allowed Iván Duque, a young protégé of Álvaro Uribe's, to split a divided field and win the presidency in 2018. His platform promised to modify, if not dismantle, a peace agreement that, though flawed, had within a year seen homicide rates drop to levels not known in Colombia since 1975.

Three years after the signing of the historic accords, peace in Colombia remains precarious. Key commitments from the government concerning the welfare of rural Colombians—promises of universal access to education, potable water, electricity and roads, economic investments and subsidies—have yet to be implemented in any number of regions previously controlled by the FARC.

In a country ravaged by war for fifty years, the obligations taken on by the state are daunting. Full implementation of the peace agreement—all 578 terms of the deal—will cost an estimated US$45 billion, at a time when Colombia's revenues from oil have plunged by a third and the nation has absorbed the brunt of a massive humanitarian crisis in Venezuela, providing basic services for more than a million refugees.

An even greater threat to peace may be the weight of history, as elements of the extreme right continue to target those who challenge the established order, as they have since the birth of the nation. The effective capitulation of the FARC inspired long-suppressed community and indigenous leaders to action even as it left a vacuum in much of the country that the government has failed to fill. Instead, into the void came opportunists, a corrosive mix of drug traffickers, resurgent paramilitary forces, and dissident factions of the FARC with little interest in peace—criminal groups for whom the voices of the people and the local town councils calling for government action only drew unwanted attention to their illegal activities. Since 2016, some 500 activists, community leaders, and journalists have been killed—252 in 2018 alone.

A fundamental pillar of the peace accord, a reconciliation process by which former combatants under a broad immunity would testify before public tribunals, confessing their crimes much as the paramilitaries were encouraged to do in 2006, has been undercut by a conservative government intent on exposing former guerrillas to more severe sanctions. Faced with uncertainty and the prospects of betrayal, an uncertain number of ex-FARC cadres have vowed to once again take up arms. Meanwhile, cocaine production has increased, with deforestation spreading even within the boundaries of national parks. Colombia, having come so far, will never revert to the madness of the last fifty years. A people exhausted by violence will not tolerate a return to war. But the path to peace will surely be as challenging as it has been throughout Colombian history.

For the years of conflict and the roots of war, see: Mauricio Aranguren, *Mi confesión: Carlos Castaño revela sus secretos* (Bogotá: Editorial La Oveja Negra, 2001); Charles Bergquist, Ricardo Peñaranda, and Gonzalo Sánchez, eds., *Violence in Colombia* (Wilmington, Del.: Scholarly Resources Books, 1992); Ana Carrigan, *The Palace of Justice: A Colombian Tragedy* (New York: Four Walls Eight Windows, 1993); Maria Dolores Morcillo-Méndez and Isla Yolima Campos, "Dismemberment: Cause of Death in the Colombian Armed Conflict," *Torture* 22, supplement 1 (2012): 5–13; Steven Dudley,

Walking Ghost: Murder and Guerrilla Politics in Colombia (New York: Routledge, 2004); Robin Kirk, *More Terrible Than Death: Massacres, Drugs, and America's War in Colombia* (New York: Public Affairs, 2004); Mario Murillo, *Colombia and the United States: War, Unrest, and Destabilization* (New York: Seven Stories Press, 2004); Gonzalo Sánchez and Ricardo Peñaranda, eds., *Pasado y presente de la violencia en Colombia* (Bogotá: Fondo Editorial CEREC, 1986); and Maria Victoria, *Uribe: Matar, rematar y contramatar* (Bogotá: Cinep, 1996). For the conflict in the Medio Magdalena and the NNs of Puerto Berrío, see: Juan Manuel Echavarría, *Works* (Bogotá: Editions Toluca, 2018); Juan Gonzalo Betancur and Kim Manresa, *Los olvidados: Resistencia cultural en Colombia* (Medellín: Editorial UNAB, 2004); Alfredo Molano, *En medio del Magdalena Medio* (Bogotá: Centro de Investigación y Educación Popular, 2009); Amparo Murillo, *Historia regional del Magdalena Medio: Un mundo que se mueve como el río* (Bogotá: Instituto Colombiano de Antropología, 1984); and Patricia Nieto, *Los escogidos* (Medellín: Editorial Universidad de Antioquia, 2012).

The authority on the botany and ethnobotany of coca has long been the late Timothy Plowman, whose seminal studies between 1973 and his death in 1989 transformed our understanding of both domesticated and wild species of the genus *Erythroxylum*. With Jim Duke of the USDA, Tim conducted the first nutritional assay of the leaves. See: J. A. Duke, D. Aulik, and T. Plowman, "Nutritional Value of Coca," *Botanical Museum Leaflets* 24, no. 6 (1975):113–19.

Tim recognized two cultivated species, *E. coca* and *E. novogranatense*, each of which he suggested had two varieties. *Erythroxylum coca* var. *coca* was the classic leaf of the southern Andes. *E. coca* var. *ipadu* was the coca of the northwest Amazon, propagated vegetatively and originally derived from Peruvian and Bolivian cuttings or seeds carried down the Amazon River in pre-Columbian times. The coca of highland Colombia was not related to Amazonian coca but, rather, was a unique species, *Erythroxylum novogranatense*. This was the sacred plant of the Sierra Nevada de Santa Marta, the *hayo* of the Elder Brothers, but also the coca of Cauca and the flanks of the Macizo Colombiano. What became of coca in Ecuador in the wake of the conquest remains a mystery; today the use of the plant is virtually unknown in that country, save for the odd bush grown for purely medicinal purposes. Yet Colombian coca, Tim surmised, was at one time most assuredly found south of the Ecuadorian frontier; indeed, the preferred leaf of the Inca was a variety of Colombian coca, grown to this day in the desert valleys of Trujillo, Peru. Tim named this variety *Erythroxylum novogranatense* var. *truxillense.*

A key morphological distinction between the two cultivated species is the absence of heterostyly in *Erythroxylum novogranatense*, allowing Colombian coca to self-pollinate, a trait that is universally recognized in botany as being derivative. Based on this and other lines of evidence, Tim concluded that the domesticated Colombian coca was of more recent origins than that of Bolivia and southern Peru. For a summation of his proposed solution to the puzzle, see: B. F. Bohm, F. Ganders, and T. Plowman, "Biosystematics and Evolution of Cultivated Coca (Erythoxylaceae)," *Systematic Botany* 7, no. 2 (1982):121–33.

Critically, all of this research was based on field observations, chemical analysis, breeding experiments, and morphology, the external aspect and structure of the plants. What was not available to Tim were techniques based on DNA that today allow botanists to examine the genetic essence of a plant. Using such methods, Dawson White, an inspired young researcher at the Field Museum of Natural History in Chicago, has respectfully challenged Tim's conclusions. See: Dawson M. White, Melissa B. Islam, and Roberta J. Mason-Gamer, "Phylogenetic Inference in Section *Archerythroxylum* Informs Taxonomy, Biogeography, and the Domestication of Coca (*Erythroxylum* species)," *American Journal of Botany* 106, no. 1 (2019):154–65.

White suggests that the two cultivated species of *Erythroxylum* may, in fact, have had completely distinct origins, parallel tracks of domestication by which ancient peoples separated by the length of the Andes independently recognized the unique properties of *Erythroxylum*, a genus that includes at least twenty-nine wild species known to contain trace amounts of cocaine. The progenitor of the cultivated species appears to be *E. gracilipes*, a plant found throughout much of the western Amazon. Genetic analysis suggests that *E. coca* may have been derived from wild populations of *E. gracilipes* growing in the forests on the eastern flanks of the Andes in southern Peru and Bolivia; whereas *Erythroxylum novogranatense*, the coca of Colombia, may have had its origins from other populations of *E. gracilipes*, thriving in the lowland forests of the Colombian Amazon. There remains much to be learned, but one thing is clear: When I suggest that coca was born in Colombia, it's because it really was.

For more on the botany and ethnobotany of coca, see: Catherine Allen, *The Hold Life Has: Coca and Cultural Identity in an Andean Community* (Washington, D.C.: Smithsonian Institution Press, 1988); George Andrews and David Solomon, eds., *The Coca Leaf and Cocaine Papers* (New York: Harcourt Brace Jovanovich, 1975); Anthony Henman, *Mama Coca* (Cali: Edición Cristóbal Gnecco y Dora Troyano, Biblioteca del Gran Cauca, 2009); W. Golden Mortimer, *History of Coca: The Divine Plant of the Incas* (San Francisco: And/Or Press, 1974); and Laurent Rivier, *Coca and Cocaine* (Lausanne, Switzerland: Elsevier Sequoia, 1981). For two travelogues that capture the early years of the cocaine trade in Colombia, see: Charles Nicholl, *The Fruit Palace* (London: Heinemann, 1985); and Robert Sabbag, *Snowblind: A Brief Career in the Cocaine Trade* (New York: Vintage Books, 1976). To witness what the trade became, see the astonishing memoirs of two Colombian journalists, both exceedingly brave women, María Jimena Duzán, *Death Beat: A Colombian Journalist's Life Inside the Cocaine Wars* (New York: HarperCollins, 1994); and Silvana Paternostro, *My Colombian War: A Journey Through the Country I Left Behind* (New York: Henry Holt, 2007).

For the dark world of cocaine, see: María Clemencia Ramírez, *Between the Guerrillas and the State: The Cocalero Movement, Citizenship, and Identity in the Colombian Amazon* (Durham, N.C.: Duke University Press, 2011); Patrick Clawson and Rensselaer Lee, *The Andean Cocaine Industry* (London: Macmillan, 1996); Paul Gootenberg, *Andean Cocaine: The Making of a Global Drug* (Chapel Hill: University of North Carolina Press, 2008); Clare Hargreaves, *Snowfields: The War on Cocaine in the Andes* (New York: Holmes & Meier, 1992); Scott MacDonald, *Mountain High, White Avalanche: Cocaine and Power in the Andean States and Panama* (New York: Praeger, 1989); Felipe E. MacGregor, ed., *Coca and Cocaine: An Andean Perspective* (Westport, Conn.: Greenwood Press, 1993); William Marcy,

The Politics of Cocaine: How U.S. Foreign Policy Has Created a Thriving Drug Industry in Central and South America (Chicago: Lawrence Hill Books, 2010); and Alfredo Molano, *Loyal Soldiers in the Cocaine Kingdom: Tales of Drugs, Mules, and Gunmen* (New York: Columbia University Press, 2004).

For Simón Bolívar, there is no better source than the excellent biography by Marie Arana, *Bolívar: American Liberator* (New York: Simon & Schuster, 2013). For Mompox, see: Giovanni di Filippo Echeverri, *La independencia absoluta: Santa Cruz de Mompox; Algo del pasado, para el presente y por el futuro* (Santa Cruz de Mompox: Gdife, 2010); Virgilio A. Di Filippo Rodríguez, *Manual de historia y geografía local I: Municipio de Mompox* (Santa Cruz de Mompox: Vidir Editores, 2011); Orlando Fals Borda, *Mompox y Loba: Historia doble de la costa* (Bogotá: Carlos Valencia Editores, 1980); and Sylvia Vera Patiño, ed., *Candelario Obeso, Santa Cruz de Mompox: Poetry and Architecture* (Cali: Editores Spatiño, 2009). For the music of *tambora*, see: Diógenes Armando Pino, *La tambora: Universo mágico* (Tamalmeque: Casa de la Cultura y Turismo, 1989).

The works of Gabriel García Márquez that take the Magdalena as a central theme include: *El amor en los tiempos del cólera* (1985; repr., Colombia: Vintage Español, 2014), *El general en su laberinto* (1989; repr., Colombia: Grupo Editorial España, 2014); and his memoir *Vivir para contarla* (Bogotá: Grupo Editorial Norma, 2002). For a portrait of the literary and artistic scene of Barranquilla in his time, see: Heriberto Fiorillo, *La Cueva: Crónica del grupo de Barranquilla* (Barranquilla: Ediciones La Cueva, 2006). The late Michael Jacob took the theme of memory and García Márquez and wove a touching narrative that carries the author the entire length of the Magdalena. See: *The Robber of Memories: A River Journey Through Colombia* (London: Granta Books, 2012). For biographical portraits of Gabo, see: Gerald Martin, *Gabriel García Márquez: A Life* (New York: Vintage, 2010; Silvana Paternostro, *Solitude & Company: The Life of Gabriel García Márquez Told with Help from His Friends, Family, Fans, Arguers, Fellow Pranksters, Drunks, and a Few Respectable Souls*, trans. Edith Grossman (New York: Seven Stories Press, 2019).

For the promise of peace and reconciliation, see: Linsu Fonseca, *Una Colombia que nos queda* (Bucaramanga: Fundación Mujer y

Futuro, 2007); and Leonel Narváez, ed., *Political Culture of Forgiveness and Reconciliation* (Bogotá: Fundación para la Reconciliación, 2010). For a traveler's portrait of Colombia today, Tom Feiling has written a lovely account, *Short Walks from Bogotá: Journeys in the New Colombia* (London: Penguin Books, 2013). Anyone interested in the visual glory of Colombia and its people should be sure to pick up any illustrated book by the wonderful Colombian photographer Fernando Cano, especially *Colombia: Carnavales y fiestas populares* (Bogotá: Ediciones Gamma, 2007) and, more recently, *País* (Bogotá: Fernando Cano Busquets Photography, 2018).

Index

of, 100–101; violence in,
101–5, 106; volcanoes
in, 100, 107–12. *See also*
Puracé National Natural
Park
Cordillera Occidental, 103
Cordillera Oriental, 35, 47, 52,
84, 86, 103, 237; Bolívar's
march across, 311–14;
geographic divides and, 35
Cormagdalena, 72
Cortés, Hernán, 48
Cote, Martin, 284
Cotocoli, 247
cotton, 120
criollos, 294, 306
crocodiles, 250, 283, 307, 324,
345
Cruz Usma, Jacinto (known
as Sangrenegra, or "Black
Blood"), 102–3
Cuba, 102, 104, 170, 171, 173,
174; Havana peace talks
and, 99, 177, 178, 183, 184
Cubillos, Guillermo, 265
Cúcuta, 120, 121; Constitution
of, 316
Cullen, Henry, 309
cumbia (musical genre), 6,
251–52, 253–54, 256, 257,
260–65, 278, 347; Barros's
legacy and, 260–65; *caña
de millo* (small flute) in,
262–63; origins of, 254,
262–63; "La Piragua,"

262, 263, 264–65; *tambora*
compared to, 259, 263–64
Cundinamarca, 37, 86–87, 91,
103, 119–21

Dahomey, 76, 247
dams, 70, 72–73
Darwin, Charles, 20, 127–28,
299
daturas, 22–23, 26, 41
David Arango, 127, 163,
222, 254, 270, 290, 332;
destroyed by fire, 206, 270,
290, 333–34
Davis, Tara, 253
deforestation, xix, 135, 352;
along shores of Magdalena,
122–23, 124–26
De la Serna, José, 318–19
deslizador (engine-propelled
river barge), 87–88, 90
Día de la No Violencia ("Day of
No Violence"), 196–97
the disappeared, 85, 179, 188,
218, 273–74; memorialized
by Echavarría, 219;
number of, 169; Puerto
Berrío's concern for dead
and, 208–19, 221
Dominican Republic, 173
Don Quixote (Cervantes), 38
Drake, Sir Francis, 284
Drug Enforcement Agency,
U.S. (DEA), 143, 181

Wade Davis is a writer and photographer whose work has taken him from the Amazon to Tibet, Africa to Australia, Polynesia to the Arctic. Explorer-in-Residence at the National Geographic Society from 1999 to 2013, he is currently professor of anthropology and the BC Leadership Chair in Cultures and Ecosystems at Risk at the University of British Columbia. The author of twenty books, including *One River, The Wayfinders,* and *Into the Silence,* he holds degrees in anthropology and biology and received his Ph.D. in ethnobotany, all from Harvard University. In 2016, he was made a Member of the Order of Canada. In 2018, he became an Honorary Citizen of Colombia.

A NOTE ON THE TYPE

This book was set in Janson, a typeface long thought to have been made by the Dutchman Anton Janson, who was a practicing typefounder in Leipzig during the years 1668–1687. However, it has been conclusively demonstrated that these types are actually the work of Nicholas Kis (1650–1702), a Hungarian, who most probably learned his trade from the master Dutch typefounder Dirk Voskens. The type is an excellent example of the influential and strudy Dutch types that prevailed in England up to the time William Caslon (1692–1766) developed his own incomparable designs from them.

Composed by North Market Street Graphics,
Lancaster, Pennsylvania

Printed and bound by Berryville Graphics,
Berryville, Virginia